S0-BDL-894

FOOD STORAGE FOR THE CLUELESS

FOOD STORAGE FOR THE CLUELESS

Clark L. and Kathryn H. Kidd

Bookcraft
Salt Lake City, Utah

Copyright © 1999 by Clark L. and Kathryn H. Kidd

All rights reserved. No part of this book may be reproduced in any form or by any means without permission in writing from the publisher, Bookcraft, Inc., 2405 W. Orton Circle, West Valley City, Utah 84119.

Bookcraft is a registered trademark of Bookcraft, Inc.

Library of Congress Catalog Card Number: 99-73568

ISBN 1-57008-680-X

First Printing, 1999

Printed in the United States of America

For Dale and Lynne Van Atta,
who can laugh with us about
the days when we were
young and stupid,
now that we're
no longer young

Contents

Acknowledgments

We extend grateful acknowledgments to: Jane Brady and Steve Walker, for asking questions, questions, and more questions, many of which made it to the question and answer sections at the end of the chapters.

Judy Willis, who loaned us thousands of reference books, and who bravely tested the recipe for "Over My Dead Body" survival bars on her own loving family, after the evil Jane Brady convinced us they were fit for human consumption.

Marsha Zimsky, who knows everything about food storage and who cheerfully shared her knowledge when called upon to do so, and who provided up-to-date medical information concerning the deadly side-effects of the traditional wheat and honey storage.

Jeanne Jankus, one of the few successful siegers, who told us of the existence of diastatic malt, and convinced us that breadmakers would benefit by this unusual information.

Marla Jolley Jensen and Carla Child, for recipes that came from such diverse places as Utah and Kenya. Some of the best substitutions in the book came from one or the other of them or from Missy Hooper, who supplied recipes that had been posted on the Internet by Eileen deMars, a benevolent stranger (some of these were created by Louwanna Young, a talented stranger).

John Hansen, for telling us how Hurricane Mitch jeopardized his son's access to Dilantin.

Michele Henderson, Donna Kneeland, Nancy Clark, and others who passed along food storage information that came to their attention.

Brian Dixon, an Oregonian who has been baking with sourdough for nearly twenty-four years, for the sourdough information that became Appendix B, (thanks to Darryl Greenwood of Vancouver, B.C., for posting it on the Internet!).

Leland Phipps, whose excellent talk on the spiritual side of food storage gave us information we needed for the epilogue (and who provided us a second copy of that talk after some nameless incompetent author lost the first copy).

The Utah State University Extension Service, for providing tons of useful material (visit their web site and get even *more* valuable information!).

Scott Card, for cheerful food storage-related editorial comments throughout the writing of this book—some of which resulted in additional helpful sections in assorted chapters.

Janna DeVore, whose gentle editing made the proofreading less odious than it otherwise would have been, and Jana Erickson, whose art design made the book as visually appealing as we hoped it would be.

And to Cory Maxwell of Bookcraft, whose enthusiasm for the project kept us writing during those sixteen-hour days.

Introduction

Where Do You Fit?

There are a lot of food storage books on the shelves. If this is the book you've chosen, you probably fit into one of two groups of people.

The first group is a big one. It consists of people who aren't interested in food storage but who have a nagging feeling that maybe they should be interested.

Maybe you've heard counsel from your church leaders that you should be storing food in case of a national catastrophe. Members of The Church of Jesus Christ of Latter-day Saints (LDS) are counseled to keep a year's supply of food and other essentials on hand (that's *one* year's supply, people!), just in case. There are more than 10 million members of the LDS Church, and a hefty percentage of them are either working on their food storage, or are feeling guilty that they aren't.

If you're not a member of the LDS Church, you may think you should be interested in food storage anyway. Anyone who follows the stock market or reads the newspapers could be nervous enough to believe that a food storage program might be a good idea. And if you've ever visited the grocery store before a snowstorm, you know how quickly those supermarket shelves can be stripped of all the essentials of life.

In fact, it has been theorized that there is only enough food on the shelves of your city's supermarkets to feed your city for three days. This alone may inspire you to wonder if you should be interested in food storage, even if you aren't.

Years ago, the authors of this book read the personals section of a San Francisco newspaper. The "Women Seeking Men" column was full of notes from a lonely woman who advertised herself in nearly a dozen brief ads, each of which showcased a different facet of her personality in the desperate hope of attracting a mate. One of the ads that has always stuck with us was the comment, "I would like to be interested in macramé." She didn't say she wanted to be *proficient* in macramé; she said she wanted to be *interested* in it. All we could assume was that at the time she wrote the ad, she had no interest whatsoever in macramé. The very thought of macramé was so boring to her that it put her to sleep. Indeed, people who were fascinated by such a tedious subject were pathetic human beings who were only worthy of her disdain. Nevertheless, for some reason only she could explain, she wanted to cultivate that fascination despite her distaste for the art. One can only hope that over the years she overcame her aversion to macramé, and has finally developed an interest in it.

If you feel the same way about food storage, this is the book for you.

The other group of people who may buy this book are at least marginally interested in food storage, but they haven't been motivated enough to do any work on it. This, too, is a big group. As we move into the new millennium, we find that life is becoming increasingly complex. There are more things to do than there are hours in the day. Being a "soccer mom" alone is a full-time occupation. With such compelling things as soccer to consider, other things that may interest us—and even things we may consider to be important for our well-being—are all too often lost in the hustle of day-to-day living.

Maybe you're too busy living your life to devote a whole lot of energy to food storage. Maybe you don't think you have enough money to devote to something you will probably never need anyway. Perhaps you have the time and the money to do something, but you've been hesitant to do anything because you don't know what's the best solution for you.

Whether you're uninterested or merely uninformed, this book can be a lifesaver. This is the book that tells you everything you always wanted to know about food storage, but were afraid to ask. And it's written in such an easy-to-understand way that even the most food storage impaired among you will understand exactly what you need to do to customize a food storage plan for your own family.

 Here's a brief list of things you'll learn from the pages of this book:

- Why you absolutely should have food storage even if you don't want it, and how you can afford it even if you don't think you can;

- All the major ways you can store food (and there are zillions of them), with the advantages and drawbacks of each option;

- Foolproof instructions that will help you create your own food storage plan—complete with charts to help you determine what to buy, and recipes to help you use that food storage in a way to ensure that your family will eat what you've socked away;

- A primer for do-it-yourselfers, teaching you how to bottle, freeze, dry, or culture your own food—as well as instructions on how to buy food if you'd rather be a "power shopper;"

- Instructions on where you can put your food to give you access to it in emergencies, how to rotate it so that it stays fresh and nutritious, and how to store food if you've no place to store it;

- Resources where you can go to supplement your food storage knowledge once the "food storage bug" has bitten you;

- Suggestions for nonfood essentials that your family may want to store in case of emergency.

Finally, each chapter will end with some questions you may have had about each topic, but were afraid to ask. All this knowledge, and easy to assimilate, for just a few dollars of your hard-earned money. Such a deal!

About the Authors

You may not be aware of it, but here's the news: You are holding a book that was written by the self-appointed Food Storage King and Queen of North America. Pause here for a moment of silent contemplation.

Clark and Kathy Kidd are the best people on the planet to have written this book, because between them they have made every mistake that is humanly possible to be made by people who do food storage. Have you ever heard of bottled cantaloupe? Do pickled green tomatoes sound appealing? Are you interested in Eggplant Cubes with Human Hair? Yes—these things are disgusting to contemplate. But because the Kidds have already experimented with these and other delightfully tasty items for you, you can embark on your food storage career secure in the knowledge that you will not have to make any mistakes on your own.

Clark is the scientist in the group, as well as the keeper of the checkbook. Always willing to save a few cents, he was the inspiration behind the Kidds' custom of buying thirty pounds of mushrooms whenever they went on sale and bottling them in half-pint containers. He discovered a means for slicing mushrooms with egg-slicers many years before the egg-slicer people discovered the same use and created mushroom-slicers that are exactly the same as egg-slicers except that they come in a cute mushroom shape.

Not all of Clark's brainstorms have had happy endings. A rabid fan of artichokes, he bought a whole raft of them when they were on sale and bottled them to take to work every day for his lunch. As he was to discover, bottled artichokes are artichokes in shape only. They taste like solid green water, and they're messy enough that only the foolhardy would dare eat them at work except on "casual day."

Kathy is the artist in the group. It was her idea to substitute jalapeños for some of the green peppers in bottled baked beans—a wild success in the Kidd family food storage plan. She was also the one who learned that adding a sprig of parsley to mushrooms when they are bottled alters the taste so that no human being would want to eat them.

Kathy is lazy enough that she's constantly searching for ways to do things that are quicker and easier. She's the one who thought that if grated, dried Parmesan cheese was quick and convenient, grated, dried cheddar cheese would be equally so. Thanks to her, you don't even have to waste an ounce of precious cheddar on that miserable experiment.

Clark and Kathy have dabbled in three of the four basic food storage programs. They started off with "siege" food storage, as so many people do—amassing wheat and other foodstuffs that most people would only eat to survive during Armageddon. (Don't despair: If that's the kind of food storage you absolutely insist on having, this book will show you how to succeed at it.)

After realizing that no matter what they did to make wheat palatable Clark's system was never going to be able to tolerate it, the two of them progressed to "practical" food storage. From there it was natural that they'd supplement their supplies with "investment" food storage, which is an extension of the practical variety. All these plans will be discussed in this book, along with the fourth plan, "provident" food storage, which is the one the Kidds are working on today.

Unless you're determined to practice the buy-it-and-forget-it variety of siege food storage, storing food is an ongoing process. Clark and Kathy have also been miserable failures at keeping their food storage current, so you as a reader will be able to benefit from their mistakes.

In fact, by reading this book you'll become so aware of what you shouldn't be doing that you'll do the right things simply by osmosis. And doing your food storage instinctively is the best way you can possibly do it. Every time you use those instincts you'll be able to thank Clark and Kathy for allowing you to be perfect at food storage on your first try. They made the mistakes so you can be a rousing food storage success.

Why Store Food?

The fact that you are reading this indicates you have some interest in the storage of food, and that something has motivated you to at least think about storing it, even if you have not yet bought that first can of beans. We have found that people who store food fall within four different camps, based upon their motivation. As you read about the four groups, try to determine which ones apply to you. It is possible to belong to more than one group at the same time. Similarly, over time you may move from one group to another, based on your experiences, family status, and financial situation. During the twenty-plus years of our married life, we have visited all these camps at one time or another.

Siege Mentality

Those of us who grew up in the 1950s and 1960s were never very far from the Cold War. The United States and the Soviet Union were the two major superpowers of the world, and the planet always seemed to be teetering on the brink of global extinction. Both nations had invested billions of dollars in nuclear weapons, and possessed the ability to destroy the world many times over. Each side tended to paint the other side as a nation of unstable fanatics who were looking for any excuse to launch a nuclear strike and then dominate what was left of the world.

As children growing up in that era, the authors of this book were never far from thoughts of this nuclear Armageddon. Clark regularly practiced drills in school where he was taught to "duck and cover," which meant he would practice diving under his desk and shielding his eyes from the nuclear flash and the flying glass. This, he was told by his naive teachers, would offer some level of protection when the nuclear missiles arrived. Even the teachers admitted that such precautions would be useless if the school suffered a direct hit, but they held out the hope that "duck and cover" might help some students survive if the bomb hit several miles away.

The government established a group of fallout shelters in schools, libraries, and other public buildings. These would offer some protection from the deadly fallout that would blanket the Earth for several weeks after the initial blasts. Those who were lucky enough to survive the initial destruction could gather in these shelters and then hopefully avoid death from radiation sickness.

Each fallout shelter was properly labeled with signs, and was stocked with food, water, medicines, bandages, and other supplies that would be needed in such circumstances. For those who didn't want to mingle with the unwashed masses, several companies manufactured personal fallout shelters that could be installed on private property, such as in a backyard. These could be stocked with supplies and then locked up until the day that they would be needed to protect Mom, Dad, and the kids from the end of the world. Many nervous parents invested the money that might otherwise have been spent on a family swimming pool to install a bomb shelter somewhere near the house.

The filmmakers of the day were not immune from thoughts of life after a nuclear strike, and responded by making many movies that sought to portray life in such circumstances. These were generally disturbing portrayals of life in a world ruled by violence and disease, where all authority was gone, and people survived through cunning, barter, and ruthlessness. These filmmakers certainly did not paint a picture of life going on pretty much as usual after a few slightly uncomfortable weeks in the local fallout shelter. Perhaps we should thank these filmmakers for convincing us that nuclear confrontation should be avoided at all costs, because it would bring about the end of life as we know it.

Given this background, it is not surprising that many of us who grew up during the Cold War have a siege mentality when it comes to food storage. You buy some basic foods that store well, throw them down in a corner of the basement, and then forget about them until the disaster occurs. Every ten years you throw out the food, replace it with fresher supplies, and then forget about it again. Food storage is not something you use every day. You only use it in times of disaster. Even though it costs you money to throw it out and replace it every decade, you consider this to be insurance money well spent, and you hope that you never have to use it.

Political and economic changes over the past decade have thawed the Cold War a bit, giving the world some hope that nuclear disaster may not be just around the corner. But those who possess a siege mentality can always find new fuel to fan the flames of their fear. The news is still filled with stories of terrorist groups and radical nations that are experimenting with nuclear, chemical, and biological weapons. As if these man-made disasters are not fearful  enough, Hollywood regularly reminds us of the possibility of destruction by asteroids, earthquakes, and alien invasions.

As we were writing this chapter, many people were convinced that the next thing to destroy the world was going to be the millennium bug, also known as the Y2K problem. This problem with older computers and software would cause them to malfunction at the turn of the century unless every program was adapted to handle the date change. According to the Y2K prophets, every computer and device containing a computer chip would stop working, leaving us without telephones, electricity, automobiles, and other modern conveniences, and causing a collapse of governments and the world economy. Disciples of the Y2K crisis even developed an acronym to describe the chaos that would occur—TEOTWAWKI (The End Of The World As We Know It).

If the year is 2000 or later, and you are reading this by candlelight or propane lantern, then perhaps the doomsayers were right. But as this book was being written in the twilight of the twentieth century, we surmised that the year 2000 would roll by with a few minor computer problems, and then life would go on pretty much as it always had.

Although food storage plans based on a siege mentality are marginally better than no food storage at all, they are definitely the least effective.

They are expensive, because siege shoppers spend money outside of their normal food budget for commodities that will, hopefully, never be used. They are also ineffective, because foods that are stored under the siege mentality will be difficult if not impossible to use should the need ever arise. Assuming all that forgotten food in the basement has not spoiled,

> *Foods that are stored under the siege mentality will be difficult if not impossible to use should the need ever arise.*

or lost its nutritive value, how easy do you think it will be to switch from your current diet of fast food and processed meals to a menu based on raw wheat and powdered milk? Those who have experimented with such a transition report a host of medical problems caused by such a radical change in diet. Even those with no medical problems often experience periods of depression caused by the loss of favorite "comfort foods."

If you have a supply of food stored because of a siege mentality, you are to be congratulated. At least you have started on a food storage program. Perhaps as you read through the remainder of this chapter, we can convince you to move to a higher level on the food storage evolutionary scale. And if you haven't yet started your food storage, read Chapter 2 before you buy your siege food. You may have second thoughts after you read about siege storage in more detail.

Practical Mentality

How many times has this happened to you? At the end of a long day, you are finally at home for the night. The car is in the garage, the doors are locked, and you may have even changed into your pajamas for the evening. All of a sudden, you get an urge. It may be for a tuna fish sandwich, or a handful of potato chips, or a chocolate bar, or a bag of microwave popcorn, or a bean burrito. You run to the refrigerator, or the freezer, or the kitchen cabinet. You know you have seen the object of your desire recently. Where was it? Was it upstairs? In the basement? In an unexpected place, such as the trunk of the car? After fifteen minutes of frantic searching, you decide that the object of your craving is not to be found. Now you have a choice. Do you suppress your urge, substitute something else, or get dressed and drive to the store?

We have probably all had experiences like these, and they usually make us resolve to implement some type of practical food storage program. We may not even recognize this as food storage, because it may be done on a small scale. Perhaps when we finally drive to the store for that coveted can of tuna we will buy three extra cans and store them in the kitchen cabinet. Maybe those three cans will turn into six, and then into twelve. Maybe our favorite brand of tuna will go on sale, and we will double that twelve to make twenty-four. Maybe we will expand our cache to include not only tuna, but soups, jams, baking supplies, and other things that we use on a regular basis that have a reasonable shelf life.

From the simple example above, you should immediately see two differences between the siege mentality and the practical mentality. First, those possessed of a practical mentality actually eat the foods that they store. Rather than buying a pile of food that will eventually rot in the basement, practical storers actually buy food that they plan to eat. If they use some care and caution in buying and rotating these foods, they will never lose a calorie of it to spoilage. This leads us right into the second difference. Those who store food under a siege mentality are spending money above and beyond what they normally would spend on food, while those motivated by a practical mentality are financing their storage through their regular food budget. Granted, their weekly grocery

> *Those possessed of a practical mentality actually eat the foods that they store.*

budget might have to be a bit higher at first, because they are buying in bulk. But once an adequate supply is achieved, their weekly grocery bill will drop because they will then be living partially on their storage, and only replacing items when the supply runs low. Even then they will have an advantage, because they can wait to buy until the price is good, and not always have to pay the going rate for the goods they need.

You can see that those who are motivated by a practical mentality really do have cause to celebrate. Not only are their practical habits saving them money, but they have the security of knowing they can survive without going to the grocery store for weeks or even months. This does not mean that they are waiting for a TEOTWAWKI event, although their storage would help them cope with such a thing. It is more likely they would use their storage to get them through smaller-scale disasters that befall all of us from time to time.

We live in a part of the country that gets very little snow, although we do get our share of ice storms in winter. Rain falls upon the cold ground, and it turns into a sheet of ice that covers roads, cars, and sidewalks. Schools and businesses close, and people are urged to stay home unless they have an emergency that requires them to go out and spin around on the ice. Our neighbors respond to such occasions by storming the local grocery stores, cleaning the shelves of milk, bread, toilet paper, and canned goods. We experience no such feelings of panic, because we can stay home, enjoy our unexpected days off, and eat a delightful variety of foods prepared from our food storage.

In contrast to our own situation, we met a tired woman when we passed through Williamsburg, Virginia, after the ice storms of Christmas, 1998. Eighteen people had converged on her house for Christmas, ranging from babes-in-arms to the eighty-year-old matriarch of the family. The house was full of food, but all of it had to be cooked. (The hostess assumed the family would be eating leftovers from that turkey dinner.) Then the power went out and stayed out—for five days. The only warmth in the house came from a kerosene heater. Eighteen people relied on that small kerosene heater to stay alive. Their only food during that five-day period, including Christmas day, consisted of cans of soup that had been warmed atop the kerosene heater. The woman considered herself lucky to have found some kerosene to fuel that lifesaving heater. We felt so sorry for her that we didn't even point out to her that if she'd been faced with a *real* crisis, rather than one that would end as soon as the ice melted, the man who sold her the kerosene would have either kept the kerosene for his own use or have charged more money for kerosene than most families could afford to spend.

When was the last time the world experienced a TEOTWAWKI event? You could argue that the Great Depression of the 1930s was such a catastrophe, but that would be a real stretch. So how much sense does it make to store food that would only be used in such a situation? In contrast, how many people per year are involved in much smaller disasters, such as hurricanes, snowstorms, ice storms, floods, and mud slides? Doesn't it make much more sense to store foods that would be helpful in those situations as well as in a catastrophic world event? So, perhaps we have uncovered a third difference between the siege mentality and the practical mentality. The latter has a more optimistic view of the world, and envisions using his food storage to get him through the minor problems of life, rather than the big catastrophe that will propel mankind back to the Stone Age.

A few years ago a good friend of ours went without a job for quite a long period. Fortunately, this friend believed in food storage and had a pretty good supply of food to carry his family along while he found new work. Although this experience was quite traumatic for him, he would have been in worse shape with the pressures of having to stretch a limited budget to cover large grocery bills. He confided to us one day that if he didn't believe in food storage before, he certainly would after experiencing that time of unemployment. Not all disasters are rooted in nature. The loss of a job or the inability to work because of health problems can be even more of a disaster than being snowed in or being without power. Those who have built a food supply based upon a practical mentality will be protected from many kinds of disasters.

People who are locked into a siege mentality should be encouraged to adopt a more practical outlook. It will save them money, it will protect them from more types of troubles, and it will improve their outlook on life. Why would anyone not want to have those things?

Provident Mentality

If those who are possessed of a siege mentality fall at one end of the food storage spectrum, then the other end is populated by those with a provident mentality. Those who have this mentality want to fully integrate their food storage with their daily diet. There is no longer a category of "emergency food," because all edibles are candidates for the family dinner table. In addition, the provident person tries to become less dependent upon outside sources of food, so that trips to the grocery store are less frequent, and result in fewer bags of groceries. This is accomplished by producing more of one's own food, using things such as gardens and animals (where permitted), and then freezing, canning, or drying that food. The ultimate provident living environment was represented by the family farms of the late 1800s. Other than an occasional trip to the hardware store, our ancestors who lived on such farms were pretty much self-sufficient. They produced and preserved their own food, and made their own clothing and tools as well.

Well, put your boots away, because we're not advocating a return to the farming lifestyle, although some have pursued this approach in an attempt to return to a simpler life. Although we can't turn back the clock, many of us could benefit by adopting a few more of the provident ways practiced by our ancestors. We can be provident by choice; they had to be provident to survive.

Going back to the practical mentality, people who take the practical approach to food storage can put their food supplies into three categories. First, they may have a portion of "emergency only" food, left over from

What's the Difference?

Siege Storers

- Use money outside of their regular food budget to buy in bulk those foods that they hope they'll never have to use.

- Barrels of wheat, jugs of water, and cartons of powdered milk fill their shelves, but they really don't know how to use them.

- They are waiting for the end of the world to use their food storage.

Practical Storers

- Eat what they store, and therefore don't spend extra money to buy food that will never get used.

- Their shelves are full of foods they like, because they buy a few extra cans or cartons or boxes of those things each time they go to the store.

- Eventually, they will have a cache of tuna or peanut butter or frozen corn on hand that could readily be used in case of a winter storm or a break in employment.

Provident Storers

- Spend less money on food and less time in the grocery store because they produce and preserve many of the foods they eat.

- There is no "emergency food" for these storers—their regular diet includes their food storage.

- They can, garden, dry, dehydrate, freeze, and culture their foods—therefore they've learned to not rely so much on others for their food.

their siege days. Second, they have the food storage that is regularly purchased, stored, rotated, and incorporated into the family menus. Third, they have the perishable foods, such as produce, meats, and dairy products that are purchased regularly at the grocery store. The only difference between the practicals and the providents is that providents strive to increase the amount of food in the second category (stored, rotated, and consumed), while decreasing or eliminating the amount of food in the other two categories (emergency and purchased weekly).

You can reduce the amount of "emergency only" foods by incorporating them as part of your daily diet. If you have wheat, you can modify your recipes to include it in cooking and baking. Staples such as powdered milk and honey may also be included as ingredients in many recipes. If you made the mistake of buying siege food that you would never eat except to avoid starvation, either learn to cook with that food or give it to someone else who will consume it before it rots. You can use the room that was formerly set aside for that old siege food to store foods your family will eat.

As you increase the number of items contained in your stored-rotated-consumed foods category, that should also reduce the amount of food you need to purchase weekly at the grocery store. This may also require a modification to your diet to incorporate more preserved foods and fewer fresh foods. That may be a real challenge to those of us who eat few processed foods now. If all your fruits and vegetables are fresh, it may be hard to incorporate canned items into the mix. However, you can make sure that you at least know what ingredients you're eating by processing your own food. Dehydrators help. Home canning is another option.

The most difficult part of adopting a provident mentality is making the mental and behavioral changes that it requires.

And if you haven't tasted fruits and vegetables off the grocer's shelves for many years, you may have a pleasant surprise in store. There have been changes in the canned food front. Today canned fruits and vegetables don't have to be mushy and tasteless. You can find the good stuff if you keep your eyes open.

Although frozen corn is never quite as good as fresh corn on the cob, having a case of frozen corn in the freezer will allow you to eat corn for months, and will reduce by one item the food that you have to purchase weekly. If you have the space to grow vegetables and fruit, they can also reduce your dependence upon fresh foods that must be purchased weekly. Those weekly trips for meat can also be reduced by substituting frozen or canned meats, and many people would probably benefit from reducing the amount of meat in their diets. And if you're a health food person already, you may have a built-in tolerance for the whole wheat that so many others are unable to cook or consume. Yes, you can be a provident person even if you now subsist on fresh foods. All it takes is a little education.

The most difficult part of adopting a provident mentality is making the mental and behavioral changes that it requires. Society seems to be moving in the opposite direction, as grocery stores are stocked with more convenience foods and snacks designed to be bought on impulse and then consumed immediately. Many stores now feature delicatessens that specialize in single-portion gourmet foods that may be purchased, taken home and microwaved, and then consumed for dinner. The message here is simple. You've had a long, hard day at work, and the last thing you need is to spend more mental energy on planning a meal. Just drop by our store every night, search until you find something that looks good, take it home, heat it up, and you're ready to eat. One less problem to solve, and one less decision to be made.

The siren song of convenience foods and fast foods is strong, and we all indulge ourselves occasionally. But doing it on a regular basis takes us about as far away from provident living as you can get. Living a provident lifestyle will definitely take more mental energy, particularly at first, while you are building up your supply of stored foods and designing various menus that will draw upon those foods. Those who have the most success seem to have adopted the outlook that being provident is a desirable attribute, and anything that makes them more independent from the rest of the world just makes them happier. They take it as a point of personal pride whenever they can save a dollar, or repair something, or reuse something, or do without something. This has created a rash of books and newsletters where people share ideas for becoming more provident. One enterprising soul even suggested that people could avoid the cost of Halloween costumes by making masks for their children out of dryer lint! Frankly, people who get on the fringes of the provident mentality can be just as scary as those with extreme siege mentalities. Perhaps a more moderate approach would protect you in case of a catastrophe, but still allow you to live a relatively sane life in the interim.

The advantages of living a provident mentality are the same as for a practical mentality, only more so. First, you are more independent from the rest of the world, and better able to withstand both large and small disasters. Second, there are financial advantages associated with bulk buying and home production and storage.

Our goal should be to develop a provident mentality when planning and using our food storage. After all, it's only practical to eat what we store—to say nothing of cheaper! But only you can decide how far along the provident road you wish to travel. Some readers may feel comfortable only if they can become totally independent from the rest of the world, and they will achieve that independence only by buying a farm or making radical lifestyle changes. There are plenty of books available that teach the types of homesteading skills that will be needed by these folks. But most people are more comfortable with a less radical approach, and would rather just have some general guidance about being more provident without making major lifestyle changes. This is the kind of information we will try to provide in the rest of this book.

Investment Mentality

Perhaps none of the previous arguments have convinced you of the wisdom of food storage. Or, perhaps you are convinced, but you don't believe you have the financial resources to store food at this point in your life. If this is the case, you need to understand that food storage can be used as an investment that will make your scarce budget dollars stretch even farther. Thus, those who believe they can't afford to store food should really be saying that they can't afford *not* to store food. Do you find this hard to believe? If so, here's something that might change your mind.

A few years ago we read a book about financial planning by Andrew Tobias. His books are excellent for people who want to invest their money but don't know how to go about it, because he can make such topics understandable and even interesting to the average reader. Although a certain portion of this particular volume did explain common investment vehicles such as stocks and mutual funds, Mr. Tobias made one statement that was surprising to find in such a book. He said that people who don't have the time or interest to learn about investing can often make the same return on their money simply by investing in food storage.

The idea of using food storage as a financial investment may seem dubious or even outlandish when you first hear it, but a little investigation and common sense will prove that Tobias is 100 percent correct. This hypothetical example should show you why.

Harry Hotshot considers himself to be quite an investor. In January of last year, Harry bought $50 worth of stock in a hot new technology company. The stock did so well that Harry sold it in November for $75—a 50 percent return on his investment.

When he isn't dabbling in the stock market, Harry has a weakness for a particular brand of tuna fish. Just about every week his wife buys two cans for $.75 each when she shops. She bought one hundred cans of it last year, so every penny of Harry's $75 return from the stock sale was used to finance his tuna fish habit.

Peter Prudent doesn't know the difference between the stock market and a fish market, but he does know how to shop for food storage.

Peter's family also likes the same brand of tuna fish, but he knows that each autumn a local discount drugstore will often have a sale on the tuna for $.50 a can. Peter watches for the sale and spends $50 for one hundred cans of tuna when it goes on sale in September.

What's the difference between Harry and Peter? Both started the year with $50 in their pockets, and both ended the year with one hundred cans of tuna fish sitting in the pantry. But look how much harder Harry had to work, and how much risk he had to take in order to finance his tuna addiction.

First, he had to find an investment that would return 50 percent in less than a year—no easy feat even for professional investors. Second, he put that money at risk. Rather than climb to a value of $75, Harry's original investment could have just as easily declined to be worth $40, $20, or nothing at all.

Peter, on the other hand, took virtually no risk. The worst that could have happened to him was that the tuna would not have gone on sale, and he would have had to pay full price for it, or substitute something else. But it did go on sale, so Peter also received a 50 percent return on his investment last year, but with far less research and risk on his part.

Looking below the surface of this simple example will reveal even more advantages to investing in food storage rather than in other financial schemes. Harry will have to pay federal and possibly state tax on the $25 profit he made on his investment, reducing the total return he'll be able to put in his pocket. Also, stockbrokers usually charge a fee for buying or selling stocks, so the $25 profit could be further reduced by up to two trading fees. If Harry lives in a state that levies sales tax on food, he will have to pay sales tax on $75 worth of purchases, while Peter only pays sales tax on $50. Once these additional factors are considered, it would not surprise us to learn that Harry's risky stock investment actually did not perform as well as Peter's safe investment in food storage.

Buying cans of food may lack the excitement of playing the stock market, but the average person will consistently do better by investing in food storage than by pursuing other more traditional investments. This does not mean that regular financial investments should be avoided, because they have their place when planning for long-term goals such as retirement, college, or the purchase of a home. But before you spend that first dollar on a speculative, short-term investment, consider investing in food storage if you still have deficiencies in that area.

About the only risk associated with food storage investing is buying something that you never finish eating. This could be because you bought too much of an item and it lost its freshness, or possibly just because you got tired of eating tuna fish sandwiches somewhere around the seventeenth can. After a little experience buying large quantities of food, you should rapidly develop a sense for the kinds and quantities of foods you should be buying.

There are only three talents that need to be developed for those that invest in food storage. First, you need to identify the foods that lend themselves to bulk purchasing. These should be foods that are used regularly, can be kept for long periods of time, and can regularly be found on sale in your area. Second, you need to become familiar with the prices of those foods, so that you can recognize a price that really is a good deal. You also need to be aware of when your current supply is running low, so that you can start looking for a sale to replace it. Third, you have to have a small cash reserve available to make bulk purchases.

Food Storing Talents

- The ability to identify foods that lend themselves to bulk purchasing.

- A good understanding of prices and the ability to recognize a good deal.

- The ability to save so that a small cash reserve is available to make bulk purchases.

Ironically, those who would benefit the most by investing in food storage are the ones who are least likely to be able to afford it. Students, those who are newly married, and those just starting their careers are least likely to have the spare cash needed to start investing in food storage. Yet even these folks can probably find sources of funding if they look hard enough. Most of us get unexpected cash on occasion because of presents or tax returns. Couples might consider giving food storage to each other in place of birthday, anniversary, and Christmas gifts. Expenses for items such as vacations and entertainment could be reduced or eliminated until some food storage program is in place. None of these are easy choices, but they all will provide a feeling of thrift and security, and the eventual cost savings that will result from an investment made in food storage.

Okay, Any Questions?

?   *So, wise grocery buying being such a great deal, should I take my money out of the stock market and invest in food? How about out of the bank?*

If you've already got money tied up in investments, you know that the key to successful investing is to diversify. If you've got ten thousand dollars tied up in mutual funds, you certainly wouldn't want to take it all out and put it into food storage. A year's supply of food isn't going to cost your family ten thousand dollars, for one thing. Also, the investment is helping you right where it is—at least as long as the stock market continues to climb.

No, food storage is an item that is part of an investment portfolio. It's like an insurance policy. Just as you may never have a house fire that will justify your homeowner's insurance policy, you've got that policy anyway—just in case. It's the same way with food storage. You may one day learn that because of some personal or general calamity your food storage is the most important part of your investment portfolio—or you may never really need it. But you'll sleep better just knowing the insurance is there.

If you have money sitting around in the bank, food storage is a great investment. In fact, if you don't have money sitting around in the bank, food storage is a good enough insurance policy that you may want to forego that trip to Bermuda and lay aside your food storage first.

?   *If one year's supply of food is good, isn't two years' supply twice as good?*

Another similarity between homeowner's insurance and food storage is that you can have too much of a good thing. There's no reason you'd want to get a ten million dollar insurance policy on a $150,000 house, because even if your house were carried away by a tornado, the insurance company wouldn't give you more than the house was worth.

It's the same thing with food storage. Why would you want more than a year's supply of food in your house? It takes a whole lot of space, and a lot of the food won't last longer than a year anyway. Unless you're planning on selling food on the black market after a natural catastrophe, you'd have no need to stockpile food. (And we hope you're the kind of person who would give away excess food rather than sell it—but we'll get to that in the epilogue.)

Here's one more comparison with homeowner's insurance. (We promise it will be the last!) Even though it's possible to buy too much homeowner's insurance, homeowners are penalized for purchasing too little. If you've only insured that $150,000 house for $100,000, the insurance company isn't going to cough up a penny more even if there's nothing left of your house but the "Home Sweet Home" sign. The same is true for food storage. If your breadwinner is out of work for a year and your family needs a year's supply of food, having a three-month supply of food is better than nothing—but it's just not good enough.

? *Which of the mentalities actually gets the most people to the store?*

We haven't tallied the statistics, but we can tell you there are a whole lot of companies making a whole lot of money catering to people who have the siege mentality. Siegers can find everything from natural gas-powered freezers to a wide assortment of chemical toilets. In the waning days of the twentieth century, the survivalist mentality was so strong that doom-and-gloom prophets appeared on television talk shows, and companies dealing in survivalist products flourished. If there's a human need, there's a product that will fill it—and somebody has it stockpiled in his basement, waiting to sell it for a big markup after whatever worldwide calamity befalls us.

But when you define food storage as any food you possess that will be eaten sometime in the future, it's easy to see that most people go to the store under the practical mentality. These people may not have more than three days' supply of food in their homes at any one time; nevertheless, there is enough food in the pantries of American households right this minute to relieve a famine in almost any third-world nation.

CHAPTER 2

What to Store

★ **IN THIS CHAPTER**
  ✔ Storing just emergency foods
  ✔ Making storage part of your regular diet
  ✔ Buying food when strapped for cash
  ✔ Basing your storage on the meals you eat
  ✔ Answering common questions

In order to know what to put in your food storage, the first thing you'll need to determine is who will be eating the food. There are three choices: bugs, the sewer system and/or landfill, or your family. You decide.

If you don't store your food properly, moths and weevils will get it . . . unless something worse gets it first. You don't want mice in your house, do you? If you don't store your food properly, cockroaches, mice, and even rats are a distinct possibility.

No matter how well you store your foods, if you don't choose the right foods to store—or rotate your supply before it goes bad—nobody will eat the food, and you'll end up putting it out with the trash or grinding it up in the garbage disposal.

But if you choose the right foods, store them correctly, and use them before they rot, your family will eat the foods.

Let's assume this is the option you've picked. The bugs and rodentia can fend for themselves, and other people can feed the landfill and sewer systems. You have chosen to feed your family. Congratulations! You have just made a prudent decision.

Now there's another choice you'll need to make. You must decide what kind of food storage you want in your family—"siege," "practical," or "provident." ("Investment" is a subset of practical and provident and won't be mentioned here.) People who store food under the siege mentality are survivalists. They envision a time in the not-so-distant future when every family will be sequestered in its own concrete bunker, complete with heavy artillery to fend off scavengers who may try to steal their lifesaving commodities. Practical and Provident storers can be lumped together as "SOPs." SOP stands for "standard operating procedure," and SOPs are people who assume that when food storage is going to be used, it will more than likely be consumed during periods when the breadwinner is ill or unemployed. They store food in case a bad storm makes the roads impassable and nobody can get to a grocery store, or if a crop failure or other crisis temporarily drives up the price of food. SOPs don't build bunkers, and they don't assemble the heavy artillery. They assume—and hope—that during this crisis, life will go on pretty much the way it always has, with the exception that for one reason or another they're eating food from food storage rather than from the supermarket.

Siege Storage

A surprising number of people who store food do so under the siege rules. There are reasons for this. On the surface, siege food storage is the easy way to go. There are only a few foods that need to be stored, and it's easy to determine the exact amounts you'll need for every family member. Thus siege food storage is cheaper to buy, it takes up less space, and it's easier for families to assemble. It's so easy to store siege food that most people put it in the basement and forget about it, which is exactly what they want to do. After all, nobody wants to be reminded that hard times may be just around the corner.

But despite these apparent advantages, there are huge drawbacks to siege food storage. These drawbacks are so great that almost all siege food will never be eaten by human beings. The mice will get the wheat. The weevils and moths will get the flour. Oil or shortening will go rancid. Families will refuse to eat the food—even if they're in the direst of circumstances. Siege food storage is worse than no food storage at all for some families because it gives them the illusion that they have food storage, but without the actual means to keep the family alive.

Unfortunately, there are some people who can only store siege food. Families who have extremely limited storage space, for example, may have room to store only the basic items that siege storage requires. Or new families may opt to start off with siege food and then supplement it with SOP supplies. There are numerous reasons why people use siege storage, so this book is going to teach you how to do it. We'll also tell you what pitfalls you can expect, so you can go into the adventure with your eyes open. If you absolutely have to store food under the siege program, you can succeed. It's going to take a whole lot of work on the part of the people who prepare the meals, and a whole lot of adjustment on the part of every member of your family, but success is possible.

What Do I Need to Store?

Figuring out what to store is a huge advantage of storing under the siege mentality. That's because there's no thinking involved when the list is only six items long. Here's what you'll need for one adult for one year, if you're storing food under the siege system:

Grains (wheat)	300 pounds
Nonfat dry milk	75 pounds
Honey	60 pounds
Salt	5 pounds
Shortening or oil	20 pounds
Dried legumes (beans)	60 pounds

Sounds easy, doesn't it? You put 520 pounds of assorted foods away somewhere in your house for every human being, and that human being will be able to survive for a year under siege conditions. You can complicate the table by varying the amounts of food needed for different members of the family, but the equation isn't what you'd expect. Teenagers need slightly more than adult women, for example, and very young children need less. You might as well go with the above list, and it'll average out that you'll have enough food for everyone for a year.

But don't run down to your friendly wheat vendor and stock up on all these items until you've read the rest of this section on siege storage. This information is going to be extremely discouraging, especially if you're in a situation where you have to store siege food or no food at all. But it's information that could save your life, so read every word before you blindly buy that wheat and powdered milk and throw it in the basement against times of famine.

Where's the Yeast?

If you really studied the list of foods you're supposed to store under the siege plan, a lot of questions have probably popped into your mind.

That's because although siege food storage is the easiest food storage if all you plan to do is put it in the basement and forget about it, siege food is the hardest of all the food storage plans to actually use. Keeping a supply of siege food that is actually usable is an extremely difficult proposition. Here's a list of problems that must be solved if you plan on storing food via the siege method.

▶ Leavening Agents

Many years ago, a national advertising campaign focused on the comparative sizes of two popular fast-food hamburgers. In a scene whose punchline became a national slogan, a little old lady looked at a competitor's hamburger and said, "Where's the beef?"

After looking at the above ingredients, which are allegedly the only ingredients a person is supposed to need to sustain life for one year, one can only echo that long-deceased little old lady. This time the question is, "Where's the yeast?"

Just about everything you can do with wheat requires yeast or baking powder or something else that will make a little amount of dough turn into a big amount of product. Unless you're an expert in the art of sourdough cooking (and we'll give you enough information later in this book that you can start a sourdough hobby if you care to do so), you're going to have to find some way to leaven all that wheat you've stored.

➡ **Here's a rule of thumb: If you're going to be storing food under the siege method, buy half a pound of dry yeast, one pound of baking powder, and one pound of baking soda per person to last out your year.**

Yeast is a living thing, and it's going to die on you. So watch that expiration date! Store your yeast in the freezer, and scrupulously rotate it when it passes the expiration date. Dead yeast is like unsalty salt—it's good for nothing. So use those leavening agents, or toss them out and replace them on a regular basis. It's your choice.

▶ Water

The assumption we're going to have to make is that if you're relying on wheat and beans and shortening and powdered milk and honey and salt to keep your family alive, the situation outside your home bunker is pretty bleak indeed. That being the case, nobody should assume the drinking water in your neighborhood is going to be safe to drink.

Without safe drinking water, siege food storage is virtually useless. Beans are inedible unless they've been soaked in water first. Lots of water. And if you're using all that wheat for anything besides wheat flour, you're going to have to soak the wheat as well. (Plan on three cups of water for a cup of wheat, and an equivalent amount for beans.) All of a sudden, you're dealing with a whole lot of water. Water that's used to soak all that wheat and all those beans is going to be water you'll need to store over and above the drinking water you'll need. Suddenly the concept of siege food storage is not nearly as easy as you thought it would be.

Storing drinking water can be done—and indeed, a certain amount of it *should* be done. Elsewhere in this chapter, we'll give you a guideline of how much drinking water should be stored per person, along with possible ways the storage can be done. But even storing the recommended two weeks' worth of drinking water in your home is going to take some effort. If you want to store a whole year's worth of water, the task will be considerably harder.

There are water purification kits on the market. If you store food under the siege mentality, investigating these kits and buying a supply of tablets or other water purification devices should be a high priority for your family.

▶ Power

Not to sound alarmist, but if the world has deteriorated to the point that you're relying on siege food storage to survive, there's a strong likelihood that you're going to be doing it without those wonderful gas and electric appliances you take for granted.

With the other means of food storage, you can eat food without having to cook it first, even though you'd rather not. A cold can of beef stew isn't exactly palatable, but it does sustain life. Bottled cherries are meant to be eaten just as they come out of the bottle—no cooking required. MREs are just what the letters stand for: Meals Ready to Eat. They don't need cooking, either. But there's not a heck of a lot you can do with wheat and dried beans if you don't cook them. This means that siege food storage is more susceptible to siege conditions than are any of the other methods of food storage, with the possible exception of freezing.

See Chapter 9 for more resources.

If you're storing your food under the siege mentality, you need to think of caching away enough fuel to cook all that food. Even if it means you'll be cooking off a kerosene heater, you need to have that fuel accessible somewhere. The very thought of storing a year's worth of flammable liquid near your home is daunting all by itself, so you may want to think about learning to cook on campfires. Cooking bread products over campfires for a year is a miserable thing to contemplate, but it can be done.

If you plan on storing food under the siege mentality, there are two books you have to buy—*Roughing It Easy* and *Backyard Roughing It Easy*, both by Dian Thomas. *This is not negotiable. These books are your siege storage Bibles.* In fact, you'd be even better off if you'd find some way to lure the author into your house and keep her there for a year during the lean times. (We don't know the author, but chocolate is always a good bait.) These books tell normal human beings how to use ordinary items in camping situations—and the siege condition is the ultimate camping situation. If you store food under the siege plan, these books may literally save your life.

▶ You Have to Baby the Babies

There's no one area of siege storage that shows you how outdated the program is more than the counsel to store honey for every man, woman, and child in your family.

Doctors have known for more than a decade that honey should not be consumed under any circumstances by children under the age of one, and many doctors recommend that no child consume honey until he's passed his third birthday. There's a good reason for this: Honey causes botulism in young children. Botulism is fatal. If you like your infants, don't feed them honey no matter what the food storage instructions tell you to do.

Some doctors say that if honey is cooked into bread, it's acceptable for young children. Other doctors disagree. Botulism is a hard organism to kill. You may consider the risk to be acceptable if you've baked your honey into bread, or you may not. The decision is yours.

For reasons that the authors of this book fail to understand, virtually every siege food storage plan recommends buying honey for your infants and toddlers despite the facts about infant botulism. *Do not do this.* Use sugar or some other natural sweetener instead. This may mean preparing two sets of meals for your family members, but if you're using the siege method you're used to a little inconvenience. (Pardon the siege humor, but we couldn't resist it.)

But that's not the only problem of siege storage as far as children are concerned. Children should not—*should not*—drink nonfat or even lowfat milk until they're about three years of age. Even though fat is a four-letter word in these days of nutritional correctness, fat is a vital building block of children's bodies. That means powdered milk is out of the question for young children unless it has been supplemented with some other form of fat.

If you're a sieger with young children, make sure you make allowances for your children's specific needs when you store your food. You've spent a lot of time on your children, so you might as well keep them.

▶ Wheat and Lactose Intolerance

In a fair world, your family would be able to eat siege food just because you went to the trouble of storing it for them. But the world doesn't always work like that. Siege food may be easier to purchase than food on the other food storage plans, but two of the mainstays of the program also happen to be two of the items that human beings have the least ability to digest—wheat and milk. There are so many people who are allergic to one or the other of these staples that it's a rare family who will be able to survive for a year on a diet of these foods with every family member intact.

In our own family of two, we spent a year of our early marriage as food fanatics. Out went the sugar. Out went the white flour. Out went anything that had been processed by any human hands but Kathy's or Clark's. We even gave up meat for a trial month. We were so determined to make our new food program work that Kathy was stupid enough to throw out all her recipes that contained forbidden ingredients—even her treasured recipe for Kool-Aid pie.

We'd done an exhaustive study of the subject, and we knew we had to ease into healthy eating on little cat feet. We did everything right— we started by incorporating tiny bits of whole wheat flour into bread recipes with the white flour, and added more as time progressed. Finally we got to the point that we were cooking exclusively with our own stone-ground flour, feeling extremely virtuous as we did so.

One would think Clark's system would be grateful for all this healthy food, but it wasn't. Not only did his body not like anything with whole wheat in it, but the situation got progressively worse. The more whole wheat flour he ate, the more his intolerance grew. Finally we had to give up and return to our pre-fanatic lifestyle. Now that he isn't eating whole wheat flour exclusively, Clark can tolerate small amounts of it—but if we went back to a whole wheat diet, his inability to digest wheat products would quickly escalate to its previous dimensions.

Since then, Kathy has developed such a strong intolerance to one of the components in baked bread that if she walks into a grocery store when bread is at just the wrong stage of the baking process, she has to spend the rest of the day in bed. This hasn't always been the case—it's a new feature in the Kathy personage. Thus 100 percent of our two-person family would not survive on siege food.

In both cases in our family, we didn't begin with an allergy for these foods. We were both cheerful about our new eating habits, and we spent a lot of time making tasty recipes that would continue to fuel our enthusiasm. But despite our efforts, the intolerance grew. That's the danger of food allergies—you don't know ahead of time what you're going to be unable to eat a year from now. If you embark on a diet where you'll be subsisting exclusively on six ingredients, the chances are huge that you're soon going to develop allergies that are similar to ours.

Until now we've been talking about adults. But here's something else to consider: Wheat is too harsh for young children. They don't need to develop an intolerance for it—there's one built right into their systems. If you have a family that contains young children, they will probably not be able to thrive on a diet that consists primarily of whole wheat.

Are you African-American? African-Americans have a strong racial tendency toward lactose intolerance. Even adults who are not of African-American descent are often unable to tolerate milk. Increasingly, we're seeing infants who are also unable to digest lactose, or milk sugar. Take this into account if you're tempted to store siege food. It would be sad to be killed by the very thing that's supposed to save your life.

And speaking of being killed by what's supposed to save you, siege food isn't a great idea for diabetics. You can imagine that the honey and powdered milk aren't great for diabetics, but even wheat is a problem. Wheat is a carbohydrate, and carbohydrates are converted into sugars in the human body. If diabetes runs in your family, take that into account before you store food under the siege method.

▶ Human Tastes

During World War II, some anonymous "they" did a study of the psychological effects of food during times of stress. What they learned was a real shocker. *People who are under stress will often die rather than eat foods they aren't accustomed to eating.* Unfamiliar food can be the last straw in a human system that is already overburdened with trauma. If people have to endure horrible situations, some of them can survive only if they can continue to derive comfort from eating. If even this comfort is deprived them, they're likely to curl up into a ball and just give up.

We've already established that you're storing food under the siege philosophy in order to use it under some terrible calamity. That being the case, storing siege food almost guarantees you that you're storing exactly the kind of "last straw" food that may cause your family members to give up. You don't want this to happen, but it's a real possibility.

> *People who are under stress will often die rather than eat foods they aren't accustomed to eating.*

Your family members may prefer to eat nothing at all rather than to eat the siege food that you've so carefully stored for them.

Another problem with human taste is a factor called "appetite fatigue." Human beings aren't like dogs, who can eat the same flavor dog food every day from the time they're weaned until they keel over from old age. Human beings need variety, and siege food is sorely lacking in the variety they need. Even if your family is initially excited about the siege food you have socked away in the basement, they're going to be considerably less excited once appetite fatigue sets in. Eventually, unless you've developed an extremely versatile repertoire of recipes from your siege food, your family members may draw the line and refuse to eat another bean or another grain of wheat.

If you must store under the siege plan, do everything you can to mitigate appetite fatigue. There are other grains you can store to supplement the wheat. Read up on these grains, decide which ones will be best for your family, and learn to cook appetizing dishes using these grains as a base.

▶ Oil Rancidity and Other Facts of Siege Shelf Life

One of the big selling points of the siege method of food storage is that you can buy the ingredients you need, throw them in the basement, and forget about them until needed. Unfortunately, this isn't true. Anything that has a nutritive value to it also has the potential to rot. The healthier something is, the more likely it is to go bad on you. (This should make you think twice before you buy that next package of Twinkies, but that's a different soapbox.)

Although it is true that grain that was frozen into a glacier during the last Ice Age has been germinated even after zillions of years, grains do lose enough of their nutritional value over time that people who specialize in these things have recommended that even grains be rotated. "Rotation" is something you're going to read a lot about in this book, but people who store under the siege mentality have long believed they don't need to eat their oldest supplies first. However, if you want to get the most nutrition out of your food storage buck, even wheat and beans should be rotated every ten years or so. Indeed, as you'll learn later, beans use more water in cooking and take more time to cook if they're more than a year or two old.

Wheat and beans are the least of your problems, however. If you have shortening or oil in your food storage (and you should be storing twenty pounds per person per year), these items have only a one-year shelf-life. Powdered shortening will probably last longer (check with the manufacturer), but even so you're talking about an ingredient that is only going to last so long before it goes rancid. Powdered milk also has a limited shelf life. Check with your particular supplier or manufacturer so you'll know how long you can keep it before you have to toss it out.

Yeast lasts only for a year, but that can be extended by freezing. Even so, there's a finite shelf life on yeast and other leavening products. Honey lasts for a long time, but it should be thrown away if it develops mold. Elsewhere in this book we'll give you instructions on how to take care of your honey, because honey has a nasty habit of crystallizing if you leave it to its own devices.

As far as we can determine, salt isn't going to go bad unless it's contaminated by humidity. But here's a big word for you as far as storing siege food storage is concerned—"contamination." A lot of people buy their grain and beans and powdered milk in big paper sacks. If they leave those things in the paper sacks, the food is at risk for being destroyed by excess humidity. Even worse, it's likely to be discovered by an assortment of creeping and crawling things. Once grain has been ground into flour, it's an immediate attraction for moths and weevils.

Moths are attracted to anything that has sugar in it. As we've already mentioned, powdered milk is heavy on milk sugar. Moths will love it even more than they love whole wheat flour, and they're crazy about whole wheat flour. They leave nasty weblike things in whatever they discover, in addition to laying their eggs there and dying there and doing all sorts of other unappetizing mothy things.

Moths prefer a flourlike consistency to their food, although they'll wreak havoc on your noodles if you give them half a chance. Weevils don't need the grain to be ground into flour, though. Weevil infestation in wheat is so common that if a weevil ever walks into your home (or is carried in through contaminated groceries), she will find your flour or wheat and breed there. Weevils are an annoyance at best, because they can be sifted out of flour or picked out of grain. In fact, considering the danger of appetite fatigue, you may not want to think of weevils as contaminants at all: Think of them as protein! (Sorry—we've succumbed to yet another bit of siege humor.)

Although weevils are relatively harmless, grain attracts vermin that aren't so harmless. Mice and rats are a definite possibility if you've stored siege food without taking the proper precautions. See Chapter 8 for advice on how to store your siege food to keep it away from crawling things.

▶ The Learning Curve

If you've really got your family's welfare at heart, you're going to do more than just buy your siege food and throw it in the basement. You're going to learn to use it so that if the time comes you'll be able to cook with it and your family will be able to eat it. This is not easy. You'll need to invest in a wheat grinder so you can grind that wheat into flour. (And make sure you get one that can be used without electricity!) You'll also need to learn the tricks of kneading and gluten.

There are many books on the market that can help you learn how to cook with your new siege food, and we'll give you a whole list of resources in Chapter 9. If you're going to be one of the few human beings who can succeed in the siege method of food storage, it will take a lot of research. Indeed, instead of just throwing that stuff in the basement, you'll have to make a family hobby out of food storage cooking and consumption. Perhaps you'll want to set aside one day a week as Food Storage Day, where you'll eat a dinner that was made exclusively from your siege food.

But you'll be able to use your siege food before you set down another penny on food storage research. Appendix D will give you a whole bunch of siege recipes. (And yes, people who are storing food under plans other than the siege mentality are allowed to use these recipes!) Despite all the cautions in this and the previous chapter, siege storage can be successful. *We know people who have succeeded at it, so it can be done if you're determined to do it.*

Perhaps the best way to succeed at siege food storage is to go beyond those Big Six ingredients that were outlined at the beginning of this chapter. (In case you haven't committed them to heart already, they're **S**hortening, **S**alt, **H**oney, **P**owdered **M**ilk, **L**egumes, and **W**heat. You can remember these ingredients with the sad statement that "**S**iege **S**torage **H**as **P**roduced **M**uch **L**oud **W**eeping.")

Despite the proliferation of plans for those Big Six ingredients, we've already pointed out you're going to have to add yeast and water. It's just a short step beyond that to add a dozen or so other ingredients, and make a plan that is considerably more workable for your situation.

Here is a chart that is circulating on the Internet under the name, "The LDS Food Storage Plan." These ideas aren't ours, but they are worthwhile. If you absolutely have to be a siege person, forget the Big Six ingredients—along with all the associated weeping. Each ingredient you add to your food storage will add more flexibility—and thus more survivability—to your program. This is a chart that you as a sieger can live with.

The One-Year
LDS Food Storage Plan
(Original Author Unknown)

Grains Group

Item	Females Ages 1–6	Females Ages 7–11	Females Ages 12–18	Females Over 18	Males Ages 1–6	Males Ages 7–18	Males Over 18
Wheat* (lbs.)	107	139	151	132	107	176	189
Flour, White Enriched (lbs.)	10	12	14	12	10	16	17
Corn Meal* (lbs.)	24	31	34	29	24	39	42

Item	Females Ages 1–6	Females Ages 7–11	Females Ages 12–18	Females Over 18	Males Ages 1–6	Males Ages 7–18	Males Over 18
Oats, Rolled* (lbs.)	24	31	34	29	24	39	42
Rice, White Enriched (lbs.)	48	62	67	59	48	78	84
Pearled Barley (lbs.)	2	3	3	3	2	4	4
Spaghetti & Pasta (lbs.)	24	31	34	29	24	39	42
Total (lbs.)	**239**	**309**	**337**	**294**	**239**	**391**	**420**

Whole grains should supply about 65% of the grain group.

Legumes Group

Item	Females Ages 1–6	Females Ages 7–11	Females Ages 12–18	Females Over 18	Males Ages 1–6	Males Ages 7–18	Males Over 18
Beans, Dry (lbs.)	25	25	25	25	25	25	25
Beans, Lima, Dry (lbs.)	1	1	1	1	1	1	1
Beans, Soy, Dry (lbs.)	1	1	1	1	1	1	1
Peas, Split, Dry (lbs.)	1	1	1	1	1	1	1
Lentils, Dry (lbs.)	1	1	1	1	1	1	1
Dry Soup Mix (lbs.)	5	5	5	5	5	5	5
Total (lbs.)	**34**	**34**	**34**	**34**	**34**	**34**	**34**

Fats/Oils Group

Item	Females Ages 1–6	Females Ages 7–11	Females Ages 12–18	Females Over 18	Males Ages 1–6	Males Ages 7–18	Males Over 18
Vegetable Oil (gal.)	2	2	2	2	2	2	2
Shortening (lbs.)	4	4	4	4	4	4	4
Mayonnaise (qts.)	2	2	2	2	2	2	2
Salad Dressing [Miracle Whip] (qts.)	1	1	1	1	1	1	1
Peanut Butter (lbs.)	4	4	4	4	4	4	4
Total (equivalent lbs. of oil)*	**26**	**26**	**26**	**26**	**26**	**26**	**26**

One gallon of vegetable oil weighs 8 lbs. One quart of mayonnaise equals 1.5 lbs. of vegetable oil. One quart of salad dressing equals 1 lb. of vegetable oil. One pound of peanut butter equals one-half lb. of vegetable oil.

Milk Group

Item	Females Ages 1–6	Females Ages 7–11	Females Ages 12–18	Females Over 18	Males Ages 1–6	Males Ages 7–18	Males Over 18
Milk, Nonfat, Dry (lbs.)	14	14	14	14	14	14	14
Evaporated Milk (12 oz. cans)	12	12	12	12	12	12	12
Total* (Equivalent in lbs. of dry milk)	**16**	**16**	**16**	**16**	**16**	**16**	**16**

6 cans of evaporated milk are equivalent to 1 lb. of dry milk.

Sugars Group

Item	Females Ages 1–6	Females Ages 7–11	Females Ages 12–18	Females Over 18	Males Ages 1–6	Males Ages 7–18	Males Over 18
Sugar, (lbs.)	40	40	40	40	40	40	40
Sugar, Brown (lbs.)	3	3	3	3	3	3	3
Molasses (lbs.)	1	1	1	1	1	1	1
Honey (lbs.)	3	3	3	3	3	3	3
Corn Syrup (lbs.)	3	3	3	3	3	3	3
Jams & Preserves (pints)	3	3	3	3	3	3	3
Orange Drink Crystals (lbs.)	6	6	6	6	6	6	6
Flavored Gelatin (lbs.)	1	1	1	1	1	1	1
Total	60	60	60	60	60	60	60

Miscellaneous

Item	Females Ages 1–6	Females Ages 7–11	Females Ages 12–18	Females Over 18	Males Ages 1–6	Males Ages 7–18	Males Over 18
Dry Yeast (lbs.)	½	½	½	½	½	½	½
Soda (lbs.)	1	1	1	1	1	1	1
Baking Powder (lbs.)	1	1	1	1	1	1	1

Item	Females Ages 1–6	Females Ages 7–11	Females Ages 12–18	Females Over 18	Males Ages 1–6	Males Ages 7–18	Males Over 18
Vinegar (gal.)	½	½	½	½	½	½	½
Salt, Iodized (lbs.)	8	8	8	8	8	8	8
Drinking Water (gal.)	14	14	14	14	14	14	14

As you can probably see, this list is a lot more complete than the basic siege fare. Nevertheless, it is not without faults. For one thing, the list cheerfully recommends purchasing three pounds of honey per person—even for babies. For another, it includes some foods without ever revealing what should be done with them. Have you ever eaten a soybean in soybean form? We haven't. We'd have no idea what to do with your basic soybean, other than looking for a recipe for soy sauce.

Another major drawback of this list is that it's just a tad deficient on such minor garnishes as fruits and vegetables and meats. As a matter of fact, the closest thing to a fruit or vegetable or meat in the whole list is the orange drink crystals that are listed in the Sugars section.

One can only assume that the orange drink crystals are a Tang-like substance, and that they have thus been fortified with vitamin C. But anyone eating this expanded siege food would do well to invest in vitamin and mineral supplements.

The Old SOP Story

Just as the siege people have survival as their ultimate goal, the SOPs have a goal of getting through a crisis in as normal a fashion as possible. SOPs go beyond surviving: They intend to *thrive*. And they can do it almost as cheaply, and with a whole lot less trouble, than their siege brothers and sisters.

Here's what you need to store if you want to do your food storage in a practical/provident/investment sense: Everything you eat on a regular basis. You don't need any specialized knowledge or any unusual gizmos to fix the foods you normally eat—you just need to buy more of it. (And people think siege storage is the easy stuff!)

What Is an SOP?

SOP stands for "standard operating procedure," and SOPs are people who assume that when food storage is going to be used, it will more than likely be consumed during periods when the breadwinner is ill or unemployed. They store food in case a bad storm makes the roads impassable and nobody can get to a grocery store, or if a crop failure or other crisis temporarily drives up the price of food. SOPs don't build bunkers, and they don't assemble the heavy artillery. They assume—and hope—that during this crisis, life will go on pretty much the way it always has, with the exception that for one reason or another they're eating food from food storage rather than from the supermarket.

You probably have no idea what your family eats on a regular basis. If not, it's easy enough to find out. Make a list of everything your family eats in the course of a month, and multiply it by twelve. That may seem simplistic, but sometimes the simple things are the most effective. Find a notebook and write down everything your family consumes during the course of that thirty-one-day period. (Don't choose a holiday month; you don't want to base your year's consumption on what you eat during the Christmas season!) Choose a regular month—a winter month if possible, because unless you're a gardener you won't be relying on fresh produce during that time of crisis—and scrupulously write down everything your family consumes.

Needless to say, you won't just be recording the groceries that are brought into the house—even though that will be a big part of it. You're also going to have food in the house that you'll be using because it's already there. Baking powder comes to mind. You don't want to buy new things just for the sake of the inventory, but if your family uses cinnamon during the course of the month, or dips into an open jar of peanut butter, write that down. That way you'll know you need cinnamon or peanut butter on hand sometime during the course of a year if you're storing food in either of the SOP methods.

Once you've written down everything your family eats during the course of a month, go through the list and figure out what you may not be able to buy in the event of a crisis. Fresh eggs may not be available, for example. Lettuce may be impossible to get. Highlight all those items and find ways to substitute them with things that can be stored. (See Appendix A for recipes for common kitchen staples that may help you as you make your decisions, and Chapter 9 for sources of such irreplaceable items as powdered eggs.)

You'll also need to think about meals you usually eat away from home. If your three kids will be eating a total of sixty school lunches during the course of the month, you should supplement your food storage plan either by setting aside that amount of cash so they can continue to eat school lunches, or by allowing for enough extra food in your food storage to make sack lunches. If your family has a tradition of home-delivered pizza on Monday nights, either put that money

aside to continue the tradition or compensate by allowing for extra food.

Remember, whether you're a practical or a provident food storer, your goal as an SOP is to get through any crisis with the illusion of normalcy. Your kids don't physically need that Monday night pizza, but they may have a strong emotional need to continue that tradition. When you're planning your year's supply, take emotional considerations into account. Plan for birthdays and holidays and family celebrations. Even if your breadwinner is lying flat on his back, your six-year-old is still going to expect fanfare on his birthday. Planning for that fanfare is part of the SOP agenda.

One more thing to take into account is really a two-pronged goal. You'll need comfort foods, and you'll need sick foods. Comfort foods are exactly what the name implies—they're foods you eat to make you feel better about life, when everything else has fallen apart.

When we talked with the woman who spent five days over Christmas in a house with eighteen people and no food or power, she said to us, "I know this sounds stupid, but if I'd only had Spaghettios, I could have borne it. It wouldn't have mattered if I'd had to eat them cold. If I'd just had Spaghettios, everything would have been okay."

Comfort food doesn't have to be good for you. In fact, it usually isn't. Nutrition isn't the issue here. It doesn't matter whether your comfort food is chocolate or pickled okra or even Spaghettios—if there's a food you eat to give yourself the illusion that everything is all right, that food should be in your food storage. After all, food storage is designed to sustain us during times when the rest of the world has fallen apart. If there's any time that humans need comfort food, it's during those times that they're surviving on food storage.

This means that if you normally bake chocolate chip cookies once a month, you may want to store enough ingredients to allow you to bake chocolate chip cookies on a weekly basis. If Jell-O is your comfort food of choice, buy enough for three Jell-O meals a week, instead of just one. Needless to say, you can't indulge your craving for comfort food if the food you crave is something extremely perishable. Fresh kiwifruits are not on anybody's food storage agenda, unless you live in New Zealand. But if your family's comfort food is something that can be stored, make that a fairly high priority in your food storage program.

The same thing is true of "sick foods." When you're sick, nothing but your chosen sick food will do. If lemon sherbet is your sick food of choice, you may be out of luck. But if your sick food is a particular soft drink or a particular flavor of soup, be sure to keep plenty of it on hand to tide you over during periods of cold and flu. (By the way, don't even think of storing soft drinks in the cans, unless you want to end up with empty cans and sticky food storage shelves. In the case of food storage, those plastic bottles are the only way to go.)

Plan 5-5 for the Cash-Challenged

Just after we were married, Clark was given the assignment to try to encourage food storage among the members of our church group. Part of his research for this assignment involved determining the primary reasons people used for not starting a food storage program. His research revealed two primary excuses used by those who had no food storage:

1. They just didn't have the money set aside quite yet to start a program.
2. They just didn't have the time to plan such a program, and determine the foods they wanted to store.

Clark responded to these excuses by developing something he called Plan 5-5. It draws its name from the fact that following it will cost you about five dollars and five minutes a week. Such a plan should not tax the budget or time schedule of anyone, no matter how impoverished or pressured for time you may be.

Even though Plan 5-5 was developed more than twenty years ago, a recent trip to the grocery store proved that it still works, and that you can still start and maintain a decent food storage program with a minimal investment of both time and money.

Plan 5-5

$5 a week
+
5 minutes a week =

A good start on your year's supply of food at minimal cost and minimal effort

Perhaps you are at a point in your life where you want to be storing food, but your funds are extremely limited. Or perhaps money is not a problem, but you just don't have the time to get heavily involved in the process of food storage. If you fall into either of these camps, then Plan 5-5 might be the answer to your prayers. It will get you started down the food storage road, and will make you feel better that you are storing food, but it will not cause a major strain on your time or money. Then later, when time and money are no longer an issue, you can expand what you have already started into the type of food storage program that you really want.

The first step of Plan 5-5 involves you developing a list of foods that you would like to store over the next year. These should generally be foods that you use on a regular basis, and not siege-type foods. The second criterion is that each item should be inexpensive, typically less than $5, and readily available at the store where you do your weekly grocery shopping. Granted, this will require some preliminary work before you can implement Plan 5-5, but it shouldn't take you more than an hour of your time. When combined with a few extra minutes at the grocery store each week, it should still allow you to come in with an average of less than five minutes per week over the next year.

We can get you started by presenting a list of items that we found at the grocery store the day this segment was written, along with their sizes and prices:

Potential Items for Plan 5-5 Storage

Canned Vegetables/Meats

Food Item	Size	Price
Stewed Tomatoes	14-oz. can	0.79
Tomato Paste	6-oz. can	0.35
Tomato Sauce	8-oz. can	0.25
Pork and Beans	15-oz. can	0.50
Refried Beans	16-oz. can	0.79
Baked Beans	27-oz. can	0.79
Mixed Vegetables	14-oz. can	0.65
Sweet Peas	15-oz. can	0.65
Kernel Corn	15-oz. can	0.65
Green Beans	15-oz. can	0.45
Yams	29-oz. can	0.89
Condensed Soups	11-oz. can	0.99
Chunk Tuna	6-oz. can	0.69
Assorted Stews	24-oz. can	1.39
Assorted Chilis	15-oz. can	1.29
Spaghetti	15-oz. can	0.69

Canned Fruits

Food Item	Size	Price
Pineapple Chunks	20-oz. can	1.19
Fruit Cocktail	15-oz. can	0.99
Sliced Peaches	15-oz. can	0.99
Applesauce	48-oz. bottle	1.89

Dried Foods/Mixes

Food Item	Size	Price
Red Kidney Beans	16-oz. bag	0.69
Navy Beans	16-oz. bag	0.50
Lima Beans	16-oz. bag	0.99
Green Split Peas	16-oz. bag	0.50
Macaroni & Cheese	7-oz. box	0.69
Spaghetti	16-oz. box	0.69
White Rice	5-lb. bag	1.79
Gelatin Dessert	3-oz. box	0.55
Corn Muffin Mix	8-oz. box	0.33
Oatmeal	42-oz. carton	2.79

Cooking/Baking Supplies

Food Item	Size	Price
All-Purpose Flour	5-lb. bag	1.29
Granulated Sugar	5-lb. bag	1.89
Powdered Sugar	2-lb. bag	0.95
Brown Sugar	2-lb. bag	0.95
Corn Meal	5-lb. bag	1.55
Cornstarch	1-lb. box	0.90
Baking Soda	1-lb. box	0.50
Baking Powder	7-oz. can	1.39
Dry Yeast	4-oz. bottle	4.29
Salt	26-oz. carton	0.40
Cooking Oil	48-oz. bottle	1.99
Shortening	48-oz. can	2.25
Evaporated Milk	12-oz. can	0.79

Liquids

Food Item	Size	Price
Bottled Water	1.5-liter bottle	0.69
Flavored Drink Mix	1 packet	0.25
Soft Drinks	2-liter bottle	0.79

Miscellaneous

Food Item	Size	Price
Peanut Butter	28-oz. jar	3.00
Jams and Jellies	32-oz. jar	1.99
Pasta Sauce	28-oz. jar	1.79
Mayonnaise	1-qt. jar	1.69
Ketchup	40-oz. bottle	1.99
Vinegar	1-gal. bottle	2.99

We tried to include some items of prepared foods, such as canned spaghetti, as well as basic food items such as flour and dried beans. We also tried to select items that would store well, perhaps not for ten years, but for the one to two years it will take to consume the food while you rotate it through your daily menu. If we have not included your favorites, feel free to add them. If you would not eat canned vegetables on a bet, feel free to drop them, or substitute something else such as frozen vegetables. (That only works if you have a freezer!) This table is not sacred. It is just a starting point for you to generate ideas of the foods that you wish to store. It would also be helpful if you can start to estimate the amount of each item you wish to purchase during the next year, although that can be done along the way.

Also, it's not realistic to put every item you want on the list. If you've got a hundred items on your list, you're going to spend an hour agonizing over your list every week in the grocery store. Just for the purposes of simplification, start off with a list of ten to twenty items you're looking for. Once you get stocked up on those items, you can add new items to your master list.

Once you have a basic list of the foods you wish to store, you need to rearrange that list so that it is ordered based on the price of each item. We have done that for you, using the items in our list:

Plan 5-5 Storage Items by Cost

Food Item	Size	Price
Dry Yeast	4-oz. bottle	4.29
Peanut Butter	28-oz. jar	3.00
Vinegar	1-gal. bottle	2.99
Oatmeal	42-oz. carton	2.79
Shortening	48-oz. can	2.25
Cooking Oil	48-oz. bottle	1.99
Jams and Jellies	32-oz. jar	1.99
Ketchup	40-oz. bottle	1.99
Applesauce	48-oz. bottle	1.89
Granulated Sugar	5-lb. bag	1.89
White Rice	5-lb. bag	1.79
Pasta Sauce	28-oz. jar	1.79
Mayonnaise	1-qt. jar	1.69
Corn Meal	5-lb. bag	1.55
Assorted Stews	24-oz. can	1.39
Baking Powder	7-oz. can	1.39
Assorted Chilis	15-oz. can	1.29
All-Purpose Flour	5-lb. bag	1.29
Pineapple Chunks	20-oz. can	1.19
Condensed Soups	11-oz. can	0.99
Fruit Cocktail	15-oz. can	0.99

Food Item	Size	Price
Sliced Peaches	15-oz. can	0.99
Lima Beans	16-oz. bag	0.99
Powdered Sugar	2-lb. bag	0.95
Brown Sugar	2-lb. bag	0.95
Cornstarch	1-lb. box	0.90
Yams	29-oz. can	0.89
Stewed Tomatoes	14-oz. can	0.79
Refried Beans	16-oz. can	0.79
Baked Beans	27-oz. can	0.79
Evaporated Milk	12-oz. can	0.79
Soft Drinks	2-liter bottle	0.79
Tuna Fish	6-oz. can	0.69
Spaghetti	15-oz. can	0.69
Red Kidney Beans	16-oz. bag	0.69
Macaroni & Cheese	7-oz. box	0.69
Spaghetti	16-oz. box	0.69
Bottled Water	1.5-liter bottle	0.69
Mixed Vegetables	14-oz. can	0.65
Sweet Peas	15-oz. can	0.65
Kernel Corn	15-oz. can	0.65
Gelatin Dessert	3-oz. box	0.55
Pork and Beans	15-oz. can	0.50
Navy Beans	16-oz. bag	0.50
Green Split Peas	16-oz. bag	0.50
Baking Soda	1-lb. box	0.50

Food Item	Size	Price
Green Beans	15-oz. can	0.45
Salt	26-oz. carton	0.40
Tomato Paste	6-oz. can	0.35
Corn Muffin Mix	8-oz. box	0.33
Tomato Sauce	8-oz. can	0.25
Flavored Drink Mix	1 packet	0.25

These are the same items that were shown in the first table, but the categories have been eliminated, and the order was changed so that the most expensive items are listed first, and the price decreases as you read down through the list.

If you use the list above, go through and highlight each of the ten to twenty items that you have decided to focus on at the beginning. If you have your own list, then select those first target items. Now comes the easy part. As you do your grocery shopping each week, take this second list with you. Buy a different combination of items each week that will total approximately five dollars. You should be able to come pretty close to that by purchasing one or two expensive items, and then adding in some of the more inexpensive items from the bottom of the list.

The only remaining thing to do is to check on your accumulated purchases periodically to make sure your purchasing program is on track. Failure to do this might result in a food storage cache consisting of fifty-two jars of peanut butter and fifty-two bottles of ketchup, so it is important that you do this.

If you are the organized, methodical type of person, you might want to do this up front, before you've purchased your first item on the Plan 5-5 program. If you have a personal computer and know how to use a spreadsheet program, that can be very useful. This is the method we used to prepare the three examples that are shown below. You will be able to experiment with different quantities of different items, until you have just the right mix of products at just the right price. Try to shoot for a total price of $260, which would be your annual expense if you spent $5 per week.

Here are three examples of the amount of food you can accumulate over a one-year time period by spending approximately five dollars per week.

Plan 5-5—Example 1

36 assorted condensed soups
24 cans of pork and beans
24 cans of chunk tuna
24 cans of stew
24 cans of chili
24 cans of spaghetti
24 cans of sliced peaches
12 cans of fruit cocktail
12 bottles of applesauce
12 bottles of bottled water
12 bottles of soft drinks
12 jars of jams and jellies
4 jars of peanut butter

The above plan is for those who regularly think of making dinner as opening a can and turning on the microwave. All of the items are already prepared and ready to serve with just a minimum of effort. The cost for the items listed above would be $4.94 per week, based on prices these items were for sale the week we did our survey.

Plan 5-5—Example 2

100 lbs. of all-purpose flour
25 lbs. of granulated sugar
24 bottles of cooking oil
24 bottles of bottled water
12 cans of shortening
10 lbs. of powdered sugar
10 lbs. of brown sugar
10 lbs. of corn meal
10 cartons of salt
5 lbs. of cornstarch
5 lbs. of baking soda
5 cans of baking powder
5 bottles of dry yeast
48 boxes of gelatin dessert
10 boxes of spaghetti

10 jars of pasta sauce
10 boxes of corn muffin mix
10 cartons of oatmeal

This second plan is designed for those with a little more free time, as it consists of basic items used in home baking and cooking, plus a few items that can be prepared without too much effort. The cost for the items listed above would be $5.02 per week. And no, we don't expect that any family in its right mind would need twelve cans of shortening in a year's time span. If your family uses that much shortening, and you're not siegers, it's time to think of changing your eating habits.

Plan 5-5—Example 3

50 lbs. of all-purpose flour
15 lbs. of granulated sugar
3 boxes of baking soda
3 cans of baking powder
3 bottles of dry yeast
3 cartons of salt
48 cans of assorted condensed soups
48 cans of chunk tuna
48 cans of fruit cocktail
24 boxes of macaroni & cheese
24 cans of pork and beans
24 cans of mixed vegetables
24 packages of gelatin dessert
8 jars of jams and jellies
5 bags of white rice
4 jars of peanut butter

This final example is a composite of the first two examples, as it includes both basic cooking ingredients plus some prepared items. The cost of the items listed above would be $5.01 per week.

If you look at these lists, you can see that just a minor expenditure of $5 per week can build up and maintain a pretty impressive food storage program. No, your family won't have a year's supply of food after following this plan for a year. But if you follow the Plan 5-5 program, you'll have a lot more food on hand than if you didn't do anything. At least you'll be going in the right direction.

Here are a few more comments about the Plan 5-5 program:

- The program will work if you do just a little planning up front and then throughout the year. It is important that you buy something from the list each week. If you forget, then double up and spend $10 the next week.

- In the tables above, we tried to use average prices for each of the items. For example, if there were three brands of canned beans and they sold for 40 cents, 60 cents, and 80 cents, we chose the middle price of 60 cents. We found that such variations are quite common, and you can get much more for your dollar if the cheaper brands are acceptable.

- We also did not attempt to include any sale prices, or benefit from the economy of buying larger sizes. However, you *will* be taking sale items into account and buying larger sizes to accommodate the size of your family. If you're a wise shopper, you'll have considerably more to show at the end of the year than any of the above tables would indicate.

- You need to decide if the foods purchased through this program are to be consumed, or whether they should remain in "hands off" status until you have completed the first year and started your cache of food. In general, we recommend you start using the food, because it will get you into the habit of rotating and using your storage. But take caution that you don't consume the food as fast as you buy it, and then wonder at the end of the year how we cheated you out of $5 per week! One way to avoid this is to replace any item as you use it. If you use three cans of soup from your Plan 5-5 food, then put that on the list of things to buy next week. Obviously, when you replace it, purchase it as part of your regular groceries, and not using your Plan 5-5 funds.

Needless to say, Plan 5-5 will not give you a pantry of gourmet food, but at least it is a start. If you have stalled your food storage plans by giving one or both of the excuses listed at the first of this section, then maybe this plan is the incentive you need to get you started in the right direction.

The Meal-Based Storage Approach

For many of us, the concept of storing food is easy. The tricky part comes in learning to incorporate that storage into our daily diets. We tend to think of the "real" food that we use every day, versus the "storage" food that we keep in the basement. We're not quite sure how to magically turn storage food into real food, so that we can place it on the dinner table in a form that would be eaten by family members. If we could only find that magic wand that would turn wheat into pepperoni pizza!

Part of this problem has been our traditional approach to food storage. We store foods that are easy to store and then forget about. Instead of storing the foods we want to eat, we store unfamiliar foods and then try to adapt our eating habits to make ourselves like these foods. When we do this, we're setting ourselves up for failure.

One alternate approach that seems to work well is to design your food storage around the meals that you eat. This turns the whole concept of traditional food storage on its head. Instead of adapting your diet to include the foods you store, you adapt your storage to include the foods that your family already enjoys.

Using a meal-based approach to food storage takes more planning up front. It will take you awhile to decide what meals you want, determine which of those meals can be adapted for long-term storage, compile ingredient lists, and obtain the items you will need. But it saves you work later on, because you will be cooking with recipes you know, so you will not have to be as creative in presenting the food so that it will be appetizing.

Here are the steps you need to take to build your food storage using a meals-based approach:

❏ 1. Build a list of at least thirty recipes for main courses that your family enjoys. These should be the dishes that are commonly served around your house as the main course for dinner. Involve all family members in this project, and take at least a couple of weeks to build the list. Put it in a common place, and allow any family member to add a recipe to the list as it comes to mind.

❏ 2. Evaluate each recipe to determine whether it is a good candidate for storage. Your children may have added many items that are tasty family treats, but that would be difficult to produce from stored food. Eliminate recipes that are too elaborate, or have too many ingredients, or that contain foods that don't store well. Also make sure you have a wide variety of food groups represented, and that you are not including too many similar recipes. When eliminating recipes from the list, try to humor family members whenever possible. Even items such as pizza might be practical if you have enough freezer space for a stack of frozen pizzas, or if your family doesn't mind pizza made from a boxed mix. If you don't have at least ten recipes, come up with more. The greater the number of recipes, the greater the variety of foods you will have during the year. Keep track of the final number of recipes on your list, as this will be used in step 6.

❏ 3. Now that you have the main dishes, determine the side dishes that will be served with each main dish. Select foods that store well, and that also produce meals that are nutritionally well-balanced. For example, if your main dish is a bowl of beef chili, you can add a serving of frozen green vegetables, and a serving of fruit cocktail.

❏ 4. Go through all the recipes left at the end of step 2, plus the recipes for all the side dishes, and compile a list of all the ingredients you will need to make all of the recipes. For example, if you have three recipes that each call for a pound of ground beef, your total will be three pounds of ground beef. You can simplify this part of the project by keeping a notebook with dif-

DON'T TELL THE KIDS, BUT I SNUCK SOME CANS OF BEANS INTO THE DINNER!

ferent pages labeled with such headings as "Meats," "Baking Goods," "Vegetables," and "Pastas." As you go through each recipe, list each ingredient on the proper page. After all recipes are entered, summarize and add together the items on each page. When you get this list complete, you will have the master shopping list that can be used to buy the ingredients to make each main dish once, along with its accompanying side dishes.

❏ 5. Examine the master shopping list to see if it may be simplified or reduced to a fewer number of items. For example, you may have five hot dishes that are served over egg noodles, and one that is served over macaroni. Since one noodle tastes the same as another, could the latter recipe be modified to use egg noodles instead? It might pay to experiment before you do anything too drastic. Try the modified recipe on the family, and make sure they all approve. Then modify your master grocery list as needed.

❏ 6. The next step is to determine how many times the meals you have defined will be served over a one-year period. Get out the calculators, because the next couple of steps will involve math. For your first calculation, divide the number 300 by the number of recipes determined in step 2. The number 300 is used, rather than 365, because you want to plan your storage so that you can cook 80 percent to 90 percent of your dinners using food storage. The other 10 percent to 20 percent of the dinners are times when you may be eating away from home, or buying fresh seasonal foods, or cooking special family meals that will not involve your food storage. Dividing 300 by the number of recipes in step 2 will give you the number of times each meal will be repeated during the year. If your list from step 2 contains 25 recipes, dividing 300 by 25 gives you a value of 12. Thus, each recipe will be repeated 12 times during the 300 days of the year that dinner is being provided courtesy of your food storage.

❏ 7. The final step is to multiply all the food quantities on the master grocery list built in step 5 by the number of meal cycles calculated in step 6. This will result in your final shopping list for all the items you need to buy for the next year. As explained above, however, this does not account for the 10 percent to 20 percent of the time your dinner comes from places other than your food storage.

Once you have completed the steps outlined above, buy the items on the final grocery list. You may not wish to buy them all at once, but buy them throughout the year as you need the ingredients. You will sleep better at night knowing that you are actually eating from your food storage, and that most of the meals you eat for the next year are already planned, paid for, and sitting in your storage area.

If the plan works well for you, then consider expanding it to include other meals such as lunch and breakfast.

Make sure you revisit your plan at least once a year to account for changing tastes and different family needs. Drop recipes that weren't the most popular, and include new recipes that will add variety.

Okay, Any Questions?

?   *Do you recommend trying out the food storage to anticipate the kind of problems you found when trying to live off your storage?*

Absolutely—if, that is, you're storing food under the siege or modified siege program. (If you're an SOP, your food storage menus will be pretty close to the same as your regular menus, and adaptation won't be an issue.) If your daughter can't eat powdered milk or your son is allergic to wheat, you'll be much better off finding that out now than you would be if you waited until you were depending on your food storage rations to survive.

If you want to have the best chance at success under the siege plan, don't just change your family's diet overnight. Sneak a little whole wheat or powdered milk into your recipes, perhaps by using some of the recipes in Appendix D. If you're learning how to bake bread, for example, don't present your family with a loaf of whole-grain bread if they're accustomed to eating Wonder. Start off by baking a loaf of white bread, and sneak ever-increasing amounts of whole wheat flour into the recipe. And if you're trying to accustom your family to drinking powdered milk, first check around to find the best-tasting powdered milk available. Then add powdered milk to your regular milk a little bit at a time.

In most areas of life, deception is not a good thing. But when you're acclimating your family to siege food, you'll probably succeed only if your children don't know they're being acclimated until the deed is done. This is especially true for younger children.

?   *My family has been eating whole wheat bread for a month now, and loving it. They even adapted to powdered milk. Does this mean I can be a sieger?*

For the time being, it looks as though you can. Don't get too cocky, though. Both wheat allergies and lactose intolerance are notorious for building up over time. You may be able to digest wheat without any problem today: Tomorrow may be a different story. If you must store a strict siege inventory, try to supplement it with as many of the modified siege foods as possible. Then keep your fingers crossed. Your family may well continue to thrive on siege foods, or they may develop vicious allergies somewhere down the line. Unfortunately, that's something you can't predict.

?   *Given the complications you discovered in food storage, is it worth the hassle?*

Some of the things that yield the most rewarding results are a pain in the neck to accomplish. Having children, for instance. It's a rare woman who enjoys pregnancy, and an even rarer woman who looks back fondly on labor pains. But in the end, the child is usually worth all the pain and suffering.

Collecting your food storage isn't *nearly* as painful as childbirth, thank goodness, but the rewards are great. If you think getting your food storage is a "hassle," think of the poor woman who endured five days without electricity over Christmas—surrounded by eighteen unhappy relatives. If you don't have your food storage, unexpected crises such as this can be a disaster. If you've planned ahead, an unexpected crisis can be an adventure.

You should no more think about going without food storage than you should consider going without health insurance. Yes, it may be a pain in the neck to learn to cook whole wheat bread—but that miserable loaf of whole wheat bread could save your family. In addition, the knowledge you'll gain by learning to bake that whole wheat bread can sustain your family for the rest of your life.

Finally, food storage doesn't have to be a chore. If you read this book you can learn by our mistakes so that your experience will be considerably better than ours was.

? *Okay—I admit it. I'm a sieger. I have the wheat and the honey and the powdered milk and all that other stuff, and I'm trying to learn how to incorporate it into my diet. But now that you tell me the dangers of honey, I don't want to use it. I have a household of toddlers, and I'm not going to risk their health even if some experts say cooked honey is all right. I try not to serve my family a lot of sugar, so I don't want to substitute one for the other. Besides sugar, is there any other way to make bread taste sweet?*

You're in luck, because you can do what the Europeans have been doing for years. Sweeten your bread with diastatic malt—a malt you can make yourself in the privacy of your own home. One of the few people we know who has been successful with siege food, Jeanne Jankus, tells us diastatic malt adds a little extra flavor that is really appealing. It also increases the nutrition because it has extra enzymes and vitamins, and it helps bread stay fresher longer. With all those advantages, it's worth a try. Jeanne assures us it's so easy a child could do it.

In order to make the malt, place one cup of wheat grains (these are called "wheat berries") in a wide-mouth glass jar with a netting cover. (If your wide-mouth jar is a canning jar, you can use the canning jar ring to hold the netting in place.) Rinse the berries twice a day to keep them damp. Leave the jar on your counter or windowsill until the wheat has sprouted to the length of the dry berry, or a little longer. It should take about two days. At this point, drain the sprouts well and spread them out evenly in thin layers on two large baking sheets. You can dry the sprouts in the oven in about eight hours at a maximum temperature of 150°F. You also can dry them by placing the baking sheets in the sun. It will take several days if you use this method.

Using a blender or an electric grinder, grind the dried sprouts into a fine meal, one cup at a time. This will make enough diastatic malt for about 150 loaves of bread. (Use about one teaspoon per loaf.) Store the malt indefinitely in a tightly closed glass jar in the refrigerator or freezer. It isn't necessary to warm the malt to room temperature before adding to the recipe, as you would yeast.

Our friend Jeanne uses a breadmaker, and she substitutes the sugar or honey with equal amounts water and one-half teaspoon of malt per loaf. She highly recommends the results, and the process is easy enough that you may want to try it.

CHAPTER 3

Home Canning: An Addictive Option

★ **IN THIS CHAPTER**
- ✔ Knowing when canning is the best option
- ✔ Using a boiling water bath
- ✔ Learning the lingo of a canning pro
- ✔ Preserving tricky foods with a pressure canner
- ✔ Storing dry foods with the dry-pack method
- ✔ Answering common questions

The term "home canning" is probably misleading, because most food preserved this way is placed in bottles. But whether you think of it as canning or bottling, home canning is one of the oldest and most popular methods of food preservation, and many families use it regularly to preserve vegetables, fruits, and even more exotic items such as stews and sausage.

Learning to do home canning is one of the first things that many people do after they look at their barrels of wheat in dismay. Wheat storage is for survival—but who can deny the visual appeal of those rows of beautiful bottles?

You don't have to process your own food in order to have a good food storage program. In fact, home canning may not even be the most economical way of accumulating your food storage. It's time-consuming, and it's messy. Anyone who has bottled peaches, only to find peach fuzz in every crevice of the kitchen afterwards, will attest to that. But home canning is addictive. There's a huge satisfaction that comes from processing your own food. This is one area where you can see and appreciate the results of your work. Even more important, being able to process your own food gives you a sense of self-sufficiency. If the siegers are right, and we eventually wind up in a pre-Industrial Age, you'll be really glad if you know how to do it—and really nervous if you don't. We haven't bottled a single thing in more than a decade, but we could do it tomorrow if we had to. We've never regretted the time we spent in home canning, even though we may regret spending some of that time to bottle green tomatoes and other delicacies we wouldn't eat if they were the last foods on earth.

Many years ago we attended the Utah State Fair and entered an item in the canning competition. The Ball Corporation sponsored a contest for people to create their own recipes, with the winners possibly being included in the next version of the Ball canning book. Ours was a bottle of fruit bread, much like a pumpkin bread or a zucchini bread you may be making now, but cooked and then sealed in a wide-mouthed canning jar when it was fresh from the oven. It was a pretty good recipe, and it was nice to have a tasty dessert on our food storage shelves. The judges must have liked it too, because they awarded us second prize. The first prize winner received a check for $50, and the second prize winners got a check for a whopping $1. We never cashed the check, because it was more valuable as a conversation piece.

The recipe for that fruit bread is not included in this book—partly because we've lost it, but mostly because the people at the Utah State University Extension Service recently sent us a horrified note telling us that if we ate those quickbreads, we'd keel over dead. In fact, it's their position that any recipe that's designed or even slightly altered by anyone who doesn't have a degree in food science will kill you. Apparently the Ball Corporation people disagreed, or they wouldn't have sponsored the contest. Even so, we don't want any readers to die from one of our recipes. **In fact, we're so determined to keep you, the book-buying public, alive that we're going to strictly toe the line in this chapter, and we strongly recommend that you toe the line when and if you decide to do your own home canning.** The only information that you'll find here comes from approved sources, and most of the recipes you'll see here have come right from the USU extension service food scientists themselves. See Chapter 9 for the address of their web site, which is replete with zillions of recipes and tons of information that will help you in every phase of your food storage program. These people have spent their careers working with food storage, so they're an excellent source for anyone who is interested in the preservation of food.

In any event, in this chapter we will teach you the things you need to know to become an expert at home canning. Don't blame us if you get addicted to it. Filling your basement full of wheat and powdered milk is an exercise in meager subsistence, but when you can treat yourself with your own bottled mushrooms or clam chowder or watermelon rind preserves—that's living.

Advantages of Canning

Anyone who has ever used a refrigerator knows a sad fact of life: Food rots. The beautiful chicken breast you bring home from the market today will be slimy and green a week from now if you forget to cook it. The most beautiful apple on the tree will develop soft spots and will then go mushy inside. Even the egg, so perfectly protected in its shell, will soon be inedible unless it is promptly refrigerated—and even then its shelf life is not infinite.

Chapter 8 will give you all the specifics of why food goes bad, but for this chapter it's sufficient to say that bacteria cause the lion's share of the damage. If you can keep bacteria away from food, you can keep the food from decaying. Canning does an excellent job of that. Food that is put in a canning jar is heated to kill the germs. Then, when all the germs inside the jar are dead, the lid forms a vacuum that prevents any new bacteria from entering. Food that is properly treated can last for many years, and although some of the nutrients will fade over time, the food will still be safe to eat as long as the seal remains unbroken.

It is possible to can a huge variety of food items for your home use. Many people think home canning is limited to such products as jams and jellies, but the *Ball Blue Book* that is available wherever canning supplies are sold offers recipes for such diverse items as head cheese, hot tamales, carrot-orange marmalade, pumpkin bread, peach butter, English plum pudding, pear honey, Spanish rice, and Swiss steak with mushroom sauce. You can bottle meat loaf or fried chicken to go with your cucumber pickles, and you can spice your food with home-canned jalapeño peppers. Best of all, canning is easy once you get the hang of it. As long as you're scrupulous about following the processing directions, you can produce a host of mouthwatering delicacies that will delight every family member.

Clark once took a cooking class from a professional chef who told the class that cooking is an art, but baking is a science. By this he meant that cooks can change recipes in whatever way pleases them, but bakers have to follow the recipe. Successful baked goods depend on chemical changes that are made in the product as leavening agents react with other ingredients. If a baker adjusts the amount of any essential ingredient used in his recipe, the results will be completely different—and usually different in a bad way.

By this definition, canning is also a science. Canning is perfectly safe as long as you follow the rules, but if you break the rules you're playing Russian roulette with your family. We personally know someone who lost three family members after they sat down to a dinner that included homemade pickled beets that had been given to the family as a gift. If you're somebody who's tempted to cut corners and adapt the rules, canning is not a hobby you should pursue. Buy your canned goods from the grocery store and skip the rest of this chapter.

Canning's big advantage is also its potentially fatal weakness. By creating an airless environment inside the canning jar, canning kills the bacteria that would cause food to deteriorate—but at the same time, this "anaerobic" environment is exactly the environment that one bacterium needs in order to grow. This is the botulism spore. The botulism spore is common and harmless. It probably settles on most of the food you eat, and you swallow countless numbers of these spores every day without ever getting sick. But when a spore finds a low-acid environment without air, it sprouts and grows, and the vegetation can kill you. You can't look at a contaminated bottle of food and see if it's infected with botulism, and you can't taste botulism either. The only thing you can do to make sure that botulism doesn't grow in the food you can is to process that food long enough to kill the spore before it grows. That means following the canning instructions to the letter—no variations allowed.

We don't want to scare you away from canning; we just want to remind you that canning is a science. If you're willing to follow the rules, you'll never have a bad canning experience. But always remember that carelessness can have fatal consequences. If it's 4 A.M. and you're tempted to cut just two or three minutes off the processing time of that last batch of chili because you're dead on your feet—*don't do it.*

Boiling Water Bath

Beginners to canning usually start with the boiling water process. In fact, many home canners never go beyond the boiling water bath because it is so safe and easy, and because a pressure canner costs more money. The boiling water process is the preferred method for foods that are high in acid. High-acid foods are naturally resistant to the botulism spore, and can be processed for shorter periods of time and at lower temperatures than low-acid foods.

High-acid foods include fruits and vegetables that have an acidity of 4.6 or lower on the pH scale. Sauerkraut is a high-acid food—not because of the cabbage, but because of the brine. Pickles become high-acid foods because of the vinegar content. Other high-acid foods include jams and jellies, marmalades, relishes, and other fruit mixtures.

For many years, the chemical content of fruits and vegetables was a constant. Canning recipes were passed down from mother to daughter for generations. However, in recent years so many crops have been altered to produce different characteristics that the old recipes are no longer reliable.

Tomatoes are a good example. You may remember the days when you couldn't eat too many tomatoes because they caused canker sores. But in recent years, tomatoes have been specifically bred to be less acidic than they used to be. Today our tomato is more sweet and less tangy. For the most part, canker sores are a thing of the past. Due to this change, however, tomatoes can no longer be automatically classified as high-acid foods. As a little added precaution, today's canning rules call for tomato products to be acidified by adding lemon juice, vinegar, or citric acid to each bottle as an extra bit of insurance that the acid level will be high enough that the tomato can be safely canned with the boiling water bath method.

Experts now call for two tablespoons bottled lemon juice, half a teaspoon citric acid, or four tablespoons of a 5 percent acidity vinegar to be used per quart of tomato product that is being canned. This is a whole lot of vinegar, and as you can imagine it changes the taste of the product so that extra sugar or salt or other ingredients may need to be added to make the tomatoes taste like tomatoes rather than pickles. Thus the old recipes have to be altered to allow for the added acidity and then altered again to offset the taste. You can see why Grandma's recipe for spicy tomato juice just doesn't work with modern produce.

But tomatoes are not the only culprits. Many vegetables have been hybridized so that the acid content today is different from that of a generation ago. Because of that, canning recipes have changed. **If you've been using the same recipes since you started canning in the 1970s, it's time to throw away your old books and get new ones. In fact, food scientists recommend that any canning recipes that were designed before 1988 be discarded and replaced with recipes that were designed for today's hybrid crops.**

In addition to those new canning recipes, here's a list of the equipment you'll need when you process foods with a boiling water bath:

▶ Boiling water canner

The boiling water canner is a large pot that is made of steel or aluminum that has usually been covered with blue porcelain, just like the old turkey roasting pans that Mom used to use. The pot must come with a lid, because lids are essential to keep the temperature of the water steady during cooking.

If you have an electric stovetop, make sure that the bottom of your boiling water canner is flat. Canners come with flat or ridged bottoms, but only the flat ones are designed to work with electric heating elements. Gas burners can accommodate either the flat or the ridged canners, which makes you wonder why ridged canners are made. Nevertheless, the ridged canners are more common than the flat ones. Keep that in mind when you're shopping for a canner.

The inside of the canner should have removable racks or wire baskets. These are very important because they keep the bottles separated from one another. Without those baskets, the boiling water would jostle the glass jars together and breakage would be a big possibility. The baskets also keep the jars off the floor of the canner so water can circulate underneath the bottles.

▶ Canning bottles

Canning bottles come in several sizes, from half-pint jelly jars to half-gallon jars that are designed for pickles or juice. The most common sizes are half-pints, pints, and quarts. Wide-mouthed jars are also available, which come in handy for items such as meat loaf or tamales that should come out of the bottle in one piece.

Traditionally, canning books have recommended that home canners only use canning jars that have been specifically designed for home canning. In the past few years, however, these rules have been relaxed. Some mayonnaise jars are being made these days that accommodate the two-piece canning lids, and that are sturdy enough to be used for some canning purposes. Even though these bottles may start out sturdy and may look perfect after the mayonnaise has been used, repeated use of a metal spoon to dig out the mayonnaise may weaken the glass. Because of this, mayonnaise jars that are used for canning should be restricted to boiling water baths or to dry-pack canning. Make sure to use traditional jars in pressure canners, where the heat is higher and the contents are under pressure.

> ### Two Crucial Elements to Canning
>
> 1. Food must be heated to a high enough temperature for a long enough duration to kill the microbes inside.
>
> 2. The seal must remain tight enough to keep microbes from getting into the food after the canning procedure is finished.

If you decide to use a nontraditional canning jar, be sure to use one where the canning lid fits as well as it would on a traditional jar. There are two crucial elements to canning—first, that the food be heated to a high enough temperature and for a long enough duration to kill the microbes inside, and second, that the seal remains tight enough to keep microbes from getting into the food after the canning procedure is finished. The seal *must* be perfect; otherwise your food will go bad. In fact, if you insist on using mayonnaise jars you may want to save them for dry-pack canning, where the original mayonnaise lid can be used. That way you'll be absolutely certain that in cases where a perfect seal is essential, the canning lids are being placed on the jars for which they have been designed.

No matter what kind of jar you use, canning jars must be perfect. If there's a single nick in the rim of that jar, the lid won't seal. If there's a hairline crack, the bottle will probably not withstand the rigors of canning. Before you put food in a jar, make sure the jar is perfect. Otherwise you risk a jar that doesn't seal or—worse—one that breaks in your boiling water bath and causes a royal mess.

▶ Two-piece vacuum canning lids

Standard canning lids come in two pieces—a flat lid that goes on top of the jar and a screw band that goes over the flat lid. If you'll inspect the flat lid, you'll see that the place where the lid meets the jar is covered by a rubbery gasket. When this gasket is heated, the rubber softens. As air is forced outside the jar and a vacuum forms, the lid will be sucked onto the top of the jar and secured there by the rubber from the gasket. The seal that forms can hold for many years, and as long as the seal is intact the food should be safe to eat.

Jar lids and screw-tops are sold separately because the screw-tops should not be left on the jars after they have sealed. When the seal is made and the jar is cool, the screw-top lids should be removed from the jar, washed, and dried. Then they are free to be used for the next canning project. The jars may look prettier if you leave the shiny metal screw-top on the jar, but the metal will soon rust and corrode, making it hard to remove the screw-top when the time comes. Rusted and corroded screw-tops should not be reused, so it is to your advantage to remove those screw-tops when you're ready to put away those bottles of preserved food. When properly cared for, screw-tops should last for many years. The flat lids, however, are designed for one use only. If the jar doesn't seal and you have to reprocess the jar, throw away the original flat lid and use a fresh one.

screw top

flat lid
(top view)

flat lid
(underside view)

The same rules about perfect jars also apply to perfect lids. If the screw-top is bent, the jar may not seal. Nor will the jar seal if there's a gouge or scratch in the rubber gasket. If you have any defective screw-tops or lids, get rid of them or you may have to process that jar again with a fresh lid.

In addition to the standard two-piece canning lids, you may see two other types of canning jars with lids. There is a variety of jar that comes with a one-piece porcelain cap. A rubber ring is put under the cap to complete the seal. The second kind of jar is one that has a wire bail attached directly to the neck of the jar. A wet rubber ring is placed over the rim of the jar, and a glass cap is put on top of that. The glass cap is secured in place with the wire bail, and the ring forms the seal between the jar and the lid. Both types of lids are so rarely used that we won't even discuss them here, other than to say they exist. If you have some of these old-fashioned jars, you probably acquired them from someone who can show you how to use them. If not, they're always good for dry-pack canning.

▶ Jar lifter

A jar lifter is a metal and rubber contraption that looks like a large pair of tongs. It is designed for the one purpose of lifting hot jars from a pressure canner or a boiling water bath, but when a jar lifter is needed, nothing else will do. This is an expenditure that you shouldn't forego. If you try to get the jars out of boiling water without a jar lifter, you may misalign the lids in the process. Even worse, you may severely burn yourself. Invest in a jar lifter. You'll be glad you did.

▶ Canning funnel

A canning funnel is just like a regular funnel, except that it has a wider mouth. This is an optional piece of equipment, but it's worth the investment. Not only is it easier to fill jars with a canning funnel, but the funnel will also keep food or syrup off the jar rim. You can always wipe food off the jar rim, but it's easier not to get food there in the first place. In fact, you may want to buy a couple of these funnels so more than one person in your household can fill jars at a time. Big canning projects will go faster if you can get an assembly line going.

▶ Cooking thermometer

We have to admit it—we've never used a thermometer for canning. We always figured that if we followed the recipe (including those all-important instructions for altitude adjustment), the food we processed would reach the temperatures they were supposed to reach. But we haven't done any home canning since the magic 1988 cutoff date, and modern sources seem to unilaterally call for a cooking thermometer. What the heck. We'll take their word for it. Buy yourself a cooking thermometer. If you don't use it for home canning, you'll use it for something else.

▶ Plastic chopstick or rubber spatula

The last thing you should do before placing the flat lid on a jar of food should be to get the air bubbles out of the jar. There aren't any jar police who are going to come to your house and tell you how to do this. Some people recommend using a rubber spatula, but we've found a chopstick is a terrific tool for air-releasing purposes. Chopsticks are thin and nonintrusive. You can easily run the chopstick down the sides of the jar without damaging those seedless grapes or bruising those beautiful peaches. But be sure to use a plastic one rather than the bamboo variety, because there are a lot of crevices in those bamboo chopsticks where bacteria can hide.

▶ Assorted household tools that you probably already have on hand

All the other tools you'll need for water bath canning—other than the food itself—are already in your kitchen. If they aren't, you're probably looking for an excuse to get them. Huge metal mixing bowls are good for many uses besides canning, and canning is a great excuse to stock up on several of them. You'll also be using assorted utensils such as vegetable peelers, colanders, and measuring cups and spoons that you already have in your kitchen. Paper towels are handy for cleaning jar rims before the flat lids are added, and old bath towels are necessary to cushion hot jars after they're removed from the hot water bath. And you probably already have a working timer on your oven or microwave. If you have all these things already, you're ready to can. All you need is the food.

Glossary of Canning Terms

➲ Now that you've got your equipment, here are some additional canning terms you'll need before you begin your first canning project.

Cold pack—a technique where food is put into the canning jars without being heated first. A hot syrup or other liquid is poured over the food before the jars are sealed and the processing begins.

Headspace—the distance from the level where the jar is filled to the top of the jar. This is important because some foods expand during processing, and other foods need an extra amount of air in order to form a proper seal. Most recipes should tell you how much headspace to leave. The distance is usually one-half inch or one inch.

Hot pack—a technique where food is heated before being placed into canning jars and then covered with hot liquid. Generally, hot-pack canning gives better results than cold-pack canning. If your recipe offers both options, choose the hot pack.

Syrup, heavy—a concentration of 40 percent sugar and 60 percent water, used when canning tart or neutral fruit such as sour cherries, pears, tart apples, or plums.

Syrup, light—a concentration of 20 percent sugar and 80 percent water, used when canning very sweet fruit that needs little additional sweetening.

Syrup, medium—a concentration of 30 percent sugar and 70 percent water, used when canning fruits such as berries, sweet cherries, or sweet apples.

Syrup, very heavy—a concentration of 50 percent sugar and 50 percent water, used to process very sour fruit. Modern tastes are moving away from heavier syrups and toward the lighter ones, so don't can a whole lot of fruit in very heavy syrup until you see whether your family likes the sugary flavor.

Syrup, very light—a concentration of 10 percent sugar to 90 percent water, this syrup is most like the natural flavor of fruit. Naturally, it has fewer calories than the other canning syrups.

Your First Boiling Water Bath Experience

If you've never done your own home canning, the smartest way for you to do it is to start small. Pick an easy recipe and process a small amount of

it. That way you'll have the confidence to do something a little harder next time.

Just in case you want someone to hold your hand, we're going to pick a foolproof recipe for you and walk you through it. You don't have to use this canning recipe. There are no canning police who are going to come to your

house and make sure you have seven quarts of cherry pie filling on your shelf. But if cherry pie filling appeals to you, here's a no-fail recipe for it. You don't even have to pit your own cherries. We're going to recommend you use frozen cherries, right from your grocer's freezer case.

❑ 1. Go to the store and purchase whichever of these items you don't already have:

1 case of 12 quart-sized canning jars, with lids and rings
1 5-pound bag of granulated sugar
6 quarts frozen sour cherries (unsweetened)
1 ¾ cups Clear-Jel®, (it should be with the canning supplies in your
    supermarket)
1 bottle of lemon juice (the frozen stuff tastes a whole lot better
    than the stuff in jars, but it's your choice)
cinnamon
almond extract
red food coloring (optional)

❑ 2. Now that you're home, leave the cherries out of the refrigerator to thaw. They'll need to be thawed and drained before you add them to the recipe. Now put the jars (not the lids) in your dishwasher and run them through a normal cycle. If you don't have a dishwasher, wash them by hand, making sure to get out all the detergent when you're rinsing them.

❏ 3. Put the metal rack in your canner. Fill the canner about halfway up with water and heat over your largest burner. At the same time, fill a small saucepan with water and leave it on a smaller back burner, simmering and forgotten.

❏ 4. Before you do anything else, figure out how high you are above sea level. If you don't know, call the local library information desk, or the local weather station, or the county extension service. How long you process your food will depend on your altitude above sea level, so don't omit this step!

❏ 5. Next, put 7 cups of sugar in a large saucepan and add 1¾ cups of Clear-Jel®. Add 9⅓ cups of cold water to the sugar. Now add 1 teaspoon cinnamon, 2 teaspoons almond extract, and ¼ teaspoon of red food coloring. Stir and cook over medium heat until the mixture starts to thicken and begins to bubble. (Isn't this easy?) Then add ½ cup lemon juice and boil for one minute, stirring like crazy.

❏ 6. Turn off the heat. Quickly put seven flat canning lids in the small saucepan that has been quietly simmering on top of the stove. The water should cover the lids; if it doesn't, quickly add more water and raise the heat until the water is simmering again.

❏ 7. Add the drained cherries to the sugar mixture and stir until ingredients are blended. Then place your canning funnel in a clean quart jar and fill the jar to one inch from the top. Use a chopstick to dislodge air bubbles that may be hiding in the jar of cherry pie filling.

❏ 8. Take a damp paper towel and clean any cherry residue from the top rim of the bottle. When the rim is squeaky clean, take a jar lid from the simmering water and put it over the jar. (We don't need to tell you that the shiny side should be up and the side with the rubber gasket should be down, do we?) Then take a screw band and tighten it over the lid—not *too* tight. If you understand the term "loosely firm," you should have it about right. Continue adding pie filling to the jars, removing the air bubbles, and putting on the lids until all the bottles are filled.

❑ 9. When the jars are full and the lids are in place, pick up the jars one at a time with the jar lifter and place them in the rack of the canner. If the jars are properly in place, they will not be touching one another. There should be at least an inch of water covering the bottles. If there isn't, add enough boiling water to raise the water to the proper level.

❑ 10. Put the lid on the canner and bring the water to a vigorous boil. Then lower the heat and set the timer as follows:

- If you're 0–1,000 feet above sea level, set the timer for 30 minutes;
- If you're 1,001–3,000 feet above sea level, set the timer for 35 minutes;
- If you're 3,001–6,000 feet above sea level, set the timer for 40 minutes;
- If you're higher than 6,000 feet above sea level, set the timer for 45 minutes.

❑ 11. When the food is processing, your biggest assignment will be to make sure that the water continues to gently boil throughout the cooking time. Your only other task is to take an old bath towel and lay it on the counter or table where you'll want to put your hot bottles to cool.

❑ 12. When the timer goes off, turn off the heat. One by one, remove the jars from the canner with the jar lifter and place them on the towel, an inch or so apart from one another. Jars are fragile when they're hot, so be careful with them. One by one, your lids should seal—usually with a healthy popping sound. Within a few hours, your seven bottles of cherry pie filling should be sealed and ready for you to admire.

❑ 13. After the jars are completely cooled and sealed, your final task is to remove the screw bands, wash them, dry them, and put them away to be used on another project. If perchance one of the jars fails to seal by the time it is completely cool, you can either process that jar again with a fresh lid, or you can put the cherry pie filling in your refrigerator and make yourself a cherry pie within the next few days.

There you have it. The typical boiling water bath experience is *almost* as easy as the project we've outlined. The only step we skipped in this recipe was for you to get the fruit ready for processing. By using cherries that were already commercially packaged, we eliminated the task of having you inspect the cherries and then pit them yourself.

If you had used fresh fruit, an important part of the project would have been for you to inspect each cherry individually so that no bad cherries—or even bad pieces of cherries—entered your canning mix. In order to have a successful canning experience, you should always use only the best ingredients. Make sure that any bad spots are carefully removed; otherwise that one bad spot will weaken the quality of your final product.

Another thing you would have had to do was make sure the fruit wasn't exposed to the air long enough to lose its color and flavor. Cherries aren't the worst culprits; apples, peaches, nectarines, apricots, and pears are notorious in the fruit world for being quickly affected by oxygen—just as potatoes and mushrooms are vegetables that quickly deteriorate when exposed to the air. If you had been using one of these items, you would have had to soak the fruit in an ascorbic acid solution while it was waiting to be processed. This is easily done with powdered or prepared ascorbic acid, which is available in the canning section of your supermarket. A cheaper option may be as near as your medicine cabinet, though: Six 500-milligram tablets of vitamin C, dissolved in a gallon of water, are ideal for soaking sliced fruit until it's ready to be used.

If you bottled cherry pie filling along with us, you probably learned a few lessons along the way. These lessons can be summed up with one word: *more.* Canning always takes more room than you think it's going to take. Canners always use more utensils than they think they're going to use. And canning always takes more time than you think you're going to spend. Give yourself a lot of counter space, a bunch of clean measuring cups and spatulas and other utensils, and an extra couple of hours at the end of the project, and you should be fine. In fact, there's one more "more" of canning—once you've succeeded with your first project, you're immediately ready for more of them.

Step-by-Step Boiling Water Bath Checklist

No matter whether you're making quince jam or piccalilli, the steps you'll use to process your food in a boiling water bath are the same. Here are the procedures we used with the cherry pie filling project, organized into a handy checklist for you to use as you familiarize yourself with the boiling water bath process:

❑ 1. Fill up the canner about halfway with water and heat over large burner. At the same time, fill a small saucepan with a few inches of water and leave it on a smaller back burner. You'll turn the heat on under that small pan later.

❑ 2. Thoroughly wash your canning jars, making sure to rinse all the soap from the jars before filling them with food. If your jars are going to be processed for less than ten minutes, the jars must first be sterilized by boiling them for ten minutes in a pot of water that is filled at least an inch higher than the tops of the jars. (At altitudes of higher than 1,000 feet, add a minute of boiling time per thousand feet above sea level.) Washing your jars in the dishwasher is fine, but it doesn't take the place of sterilization.

❑ 3. Place the flat canning lids in the small saucepan of water. Turn on the water until it reaches a low boil, turn down the heat, and leave the lids in the simmering water until needed, checking occasionally to make sure they're still covered in water.

❑ 4. Place food into clean, hot jars, being careful to leave the proper amount of headspace. Pour hot liquid (syrup or water, as the recipe calls for) into the jar, again leaving the proper amount of headspace. Use a chopstick to dislodge air bubbles that may be hiding in the jar of food.

❑ 5. With a moistened paper towel, clean food and liquid from the rim of the jar. Be thorough, because even a single grain of sugar or salt may interfere with the seal of the lid. Then take a lid from the saucepan, put it on top of the jar, and secure it in place with the screw-top. Follow the manufacturer's directions for how tightly to secure the screw-top over the lid. Repeat until you have filled enough jars to load the canner.

❑ 6. Place the bottles into the canner by loading them directly onto the rack and then lowering the rack into the water, or by using the jar lifter. When the canner is fully loaded with jars, there should be at least an inch of water covering the jars. If the water level is too low, add more boiling water.

❑ 7. Put the lid on the canner and bring the water to a vigorous boil. Then lower the heat and set the timer for the number of minutes called for in the recipe, making sure to adjust the processing time according to your altitude above sea level. (See "Altitude Chart for Boiling Water Bath Canning.") The water should be kept at a gentle boil throughout the canning process.

❑ 8. Lay an old bath towel on a counter or table, ready to receive the jars when they are finished processing.

❑ 9. When the processing time ends, turn off the heat. Using the jar lifter, remove the jars from the boiling water and place them one by one on the towel. The jars should be close together but not touching, so that air can circulate between jars. Note: Jars that are hot from the processor are fragile. To avoid breakage, be careful not to hit them against any other jars or any hard surfaces.

❑ 10. As the jars cool, the flat lids will be drawn to the jar to form a vacuum. Jars that have been properly sealed will be tightly drawn toward the contents of the jar so that the lid seems to curve downward. Sometimes a jar doesn't seal for several hours, or even overnight. Give the lid time to do its work. If the jar doesn't seal after a reasonable length of time, either refrigerate the contents to be consumed over the next few days, or reprocess the contents with a fresh lid.

❑ 11. Before putting the jars away, use a grease pencil, magic marker, or gummed label to indicate the month and year the food was bottled. As you will find out later, this date is used to rotate your food properly, so that you will be eating the oldest food first.

Altitude Chart for Boiling Water Bath Canning

Altitude (feet above sea level)	Increase processing time
0–1,000	none; process according to recipe
1,001–3,000	5 minutes
3,001–6,000	10 minutes
6,001–8,000	15 minutes
8,001–10,000	20 minutes

Other Boiling Water Bath Foods

While you're still excited about the boiling water bath process, let's go into the three boiling water bath areas in more detail. There are three general categories of food that are best served by this canning method—fruit products, pickles, and a third category we'll call "tomato stuff." The fruit area is the least complicated, so that's a good place to start.

Fruits

Fruit products consist of just that—anything that's fruit-based, and that isn't "contaminated" by low-acid vegetables or meat. There are some exceptions to this, as you'll see when you read the recipe for cranberry chutney, below. Usually, anything that has a vegetable in it should be processed in a pressure canner. But chutneys (fruit relishes) generally have enough acid in them so they can be processed in a boiling water bath. Just don't try a boiling water bath with mincemeat!

Whole or sliced fruit, jams, jellies, pie fillings, and chutneys are fruit products that can be processed in a boiling water bath. There are two methods for preparing fruits to be placed into the bottles, cold pack and hot pack. Cold pack is a whole lot more convenient, because it involves preparing the fruit and then placing it into the bottle without heating it first. Thus the name "cold pack." The whole idea of gently layering peaches one atop the other in the cold-pack method seems infinitely more civilized than cooking them first and dumping them helter-skelter in the jar to be processed, so many old-time canners favor the cold-pack method. The hot-pack method is less convenient to use than the cold-pack method, because it involves boiling the food in a syrup for two to five minutes and then placing fruit and syrup in the bottle. Even contemplating all that hot fruit is discouraging, to say nothing about how painful it would be if a hot peach half accidentally slid into your lap.

Nevertheless, from a food preservation standpoint the hot-pack method is infinitely preferable to cold pack. Hot pack removes more air from the food before the jars are sealed, and this means the food keeps its color and flavor longer than if it had been cold packed. Hot packing makes for a stronger seal. It also shrinks the food, allowing more food to fit in the jars. From an aesthetic point of view, hot packing keeps the fruit from floating. This is less important than the long-range benefits of hot packing, however. If given a choice in your recipe, hot packing is the way to go. If your recipe only calls for cold pack, you may want to look for another recipe.

Many fruit recipes call for a syrup to be added to the jar. We've defined those syrups in the glossary that appears earlier in this chapter, but if you're interested in making your own syrups, here's a chart for you. In order to make a syrup, combine the water and sugar in a saucepan. Heat them together until the sugar dissolves and the mixture comes to a boil. Syrups are interchangeable in recipes, so feel free to experiment with lighter syrups that contain fewer calories.

Fruit Syrup Mixtures

Syrup Type	Nine-Pint Load		Seven-Quart Load	
	Cups Water	Cups Sugar	Cups Water	Cups Sugar
Very Light	6 ½	¾	10 ½	1 ¼
Light	5 ¾	1 ½	9	2 ¼
Medium	5 ¼	2 ¼	8 ¼	3 ¾
Heavy	5	3 ¼	7 ¾	5 ¼
Very Heavy	4 ¼	4 ¼	6 ½	6 ¾

If you prefer your food to be sugar free, you may choose a sugar-free method of canning any fruits except jams and jellies. Even though sugar is used to preserve the shape, color, and flavor of fruit, there is no danger in canning fruit without sugar. This can be done by substituting water, the fruit's own juice, or commercial fruit juice for the syrup called for in the recipe. Just be sure to heat the water or juice before adding it to the fruit, just as you would have done with the original syrup. Processing times are the same for fruit canned with or without sweeteners. (Artificial sweeteners should not be added to the fruit before processing, but can be added to bottled fruit when it's about to be consumed.)

Jams and jellies are products that are commonly processed by the home canner. Jams are pretty straightforward—you just follow the recipe in the cookbook. Jellies are a little more complicated, so we'll include some tips here.

Jams and jellies need an ingredient called pectin in order to make them harden. Some fruits naturally contain pectin; other fruits must have pectin added. Your recipe will tell you how much pectin to use. If no pectin is specified, you can assume that the product you're canning has a natural source of pectin in the fruit. Pectin can be purchased in the home canning section of your supermarket. It's available in powder or gel form. Adding pectin to jams and jellies doesn't just help it to gel—it also produces a larger yield and a better flavor than if pectin isn't used. But if you want to make jelly without adding pectin, we're going to tell you how to do it. That's the kind of authors we are.

If you want to make pectinless jelly, the first thing you need to do is to extract the juice from it. A handy chart appears below. If the fruit you're interested in doesn't appear on this chart, you can assume it doesn't have enough pectin in it for you to be able to make a successful batch of jelly without adding pectin. If that's the case, knuckle under and buy some pectin at the supermarket.

When you're choosing fruit for jelly making, you need to choose good fruit. There's a computer saying that also applies to home canning—*garbage in, garbage out.* The better your raw materials, the better your final product. Don't even think about processing fruit—for jelly or for anything else—that is past its prime. However, about one quarter of the fruit you use for jelly making should be just a little underripe. Don't ask us why—we have no earthly idea. If the USU Extension Service people tell us that's the way it should be done, we aren't going to argue with them. They're the pros.

The first thing you should do when extracting the juice from fruit is to wash that fruit thoroughly. Fruits may have pesticides sprayed on them to kill the bugs, or wax coatings added to make them shiny. Berries may have tiny insects or insect webs hiding in crevices and crannies. Anything that doesn't come out in the wash will end up in your jelly, so don't skip this step.

After you've washed your fruit, cut it into small pieces and put it in a large saucepan. Leave the skins on, the pits in, and the cores in place. (That's where the natural pectin lives.) If you're extracting juice from berries or soft fruits, squash the berries or soft fruits after you've put them in the large saucepan. The idea is to extract the juice, so don't be gentle. Add water to the fruit (see table in sidebar). Bring it to a boil, stirring so the fruit doesn't scorch. By the time the fruit has finished boiling (see that handy chart!), one pound of fruit should yield a cup of juice.

Juice Extraction Chart

Type of Fruit	Add This Much Water Per Pound of Fruit	Simmer Fruit This Many Minutes	Cups Sugar to Add to Juice After Straining	Half-pints Per 4 Cups Juice
Apples	1 cup	20–25	¾	4–5
Blackberries	¼ cup or less	5–10	¾–1	7–8
Crabapples	1 cup	20–25	1	4–5
Grapes	¼ cup or less	5–10	¾–1	8–9
Plums	½ cup	15–20	¾	8–9

After you've boiled the fruit until it is tender (according to the time on the chart), strain the mess through a colander. Then strain it through two layers of cheesecloth or a jelly bag (available in the canning section of your supermarket). Be careful how you strain the jelly through that cheesecloth or jelly bag, because if you manipulate it too much your jelly will be cloudy.

If you've survived to this point, the hard part is over. Now, using no more than 8 cups of juice at a time, put juice in a large saucepan. Add sugar according to the directions in the table. (If you're making apple jelly, you may want to add 1½ teaspoons of lemon juice per pound of fruit when you're adding the sugar. This is optional, but it may make for a better product.) Heat to boiling, stirring like crazy until the sugar is completely dissolved. Boil over high heat to the "jellying point," which you can determine in one of two ways. If you have a candy thermometer, use this chart:

209°F. / 6,000 feet
211°F. / 5,000 feet
212°F. / 4,000 feet
214°F. / 3,000 feet
216°F. / 2,000 feet
218°F. / 1,000 feet
220°F. / Sea level

If you don't have a handy thermometer, you'll have to eyeball it. Frankly, although the thermometer may be more accurate, eyeballing it is marginally more fun. Dip a cool metal spoon into the boiling liquid and then hold it up out of the steam (about a foot above the pot). Gradually turn the spoon to one side so the liquid runs off. The jelly is done when it forms a "sheet" of jelly as it runs off the spoon.

Another way to determine if your liquid has reached the jelly stage is to pour a small amount of the cooked product on a cold plate and put it in the freezer for a few minutes. In a few minutes you'll be able to tell if the mixture is gelling or not. This procedure causes a little trouble because you don't want your jelly to continue cooking while you're testing it. While you're waiting for the test results, remove the pot of jelly from the heat to prevent overcooking.

When your jelly has reached the gel stage, turn off the heat. Quickly skim the foam from the jelly and put the jelly in sterilized jars. Then process pints or half-pints in a boiling water bath for five minutes (0–1,000 feet), ten minutes (1,001–6,000 feet), or fifteen minutes (above 6,000 feet).

Once you've gone to all this trouble to extract juices from fruit to make jelly, eventually you're going to get the bright idea that you can skip all this boiling and straining, and just purchase the juice already processed from your grocery store. **There is no law that says you can't do this. In fact, after you've done it the old-**

fashioned way you may decide that as far as you're concerned, making jelly from professionally processed juice is the only way to do it. However, if this is your option you need to be aware that commercially-processed juices no longer have enough pectin to allow the jelly to set. If you want to use commercially processed juices, throw away your old recipe and use the recipe that's inside the container of pectin.

Pickled Products

A generation ago, pickles used to be one of the staples of an American dinner. Mustard pickles were passed around the table for adults, and gherkins were a childhood favorite. But in the past twenty years, as American tastes have veered away from tangy foods to the point that honey is being added to mustard and even tomatoes are being re-engineered to lower the acid content, pickles have waned in popularity. You can still find dill slices on a hamburger or relish in ham salad, but a lot of the other pickles linger on the grocers' shelves, unloved and forgotten.

This may not be a good time to be buying stock in Heinz's 57 Varieties. But not all pickles are in a slump. Pickled jalapeños are taking the place of relish in tuna fish. Pickled okra sells for more money than pickled cucumbers ever did. Pickled baby corncobs are considered a delicacy. The taste for tangy products still exists—Americans are just eating fewer tangy foods, and choosing more exotic fare. And home canning can accommodate our changing tastes. Instead of bread and butter pickles, it's perfectly acceptable to pickle string beans or Bermuda onions or even watermelon rind, as long as your family will eat it.

Tomato Stuff

The information in this little section is a rerun, so if you've read every word of this chapter it may sound familiar to you. However, it bears repeating because we have to assume some people are reading this book who have canned lots of things in the past. These people may have skipped around in this chapter, and may have missed this vital news. **We do not want these people to die. After all, they have the good taste to buy our books.** It is for them that we include this information again. (Also, it won't hurt you to be reminded of it.)

Although all recipes that are older than 1988 should be thrown away or at least checked against new recipes to make sure they're still the same, that goes double for tomato recipes. Modern tomatoes are so low in acid that they are no longer acidic foods. Many tomato recipes can't be processed in a boiling water bath at all; even the ones that can be processed in a boiling water bath have changed so drastically that the processing time is greatly increased.

With one exception, recipes containing tomatoes will be listed in the pressure canning area, because instructions will be given for them to be pressure canned as well as (or instead of) processed in a water bath canner. Remember—if you have pre-1988 recipes for canning tomatoes, throw them out. *All* your old recipes should be thrown out, but tomato recipes should be thrown out first.

> **Recipes that are older than 1988 should be thrown away.**

Boiling Water Bath Recipes

Here are a few recipes to get you started in your canning experience. Some of these are fairly unusual recipes, because we figure you're going to be buying cookbooks of your own that will contain the standard canning fare.

Remember—don't can something just to be canning. If you don't like pickled okra from the store, you're not going to eat it just because you bottled it. Only bottle things your family would enjoy. And yes, you'd think this information is a no-brainer, but the authors of this book have a basement full of bottled green tomatoes and green tomato jam and lots of other stuff they have never even thought about eating, after canning it just because the ingredients were on hand. Thus we're including this obvious piece of information for the rest of you out there who have no brains.

Apple Butter
(yield: 8–9 pints)

8 pounds apples*

2 cups apple cider

2 cups vinegar

2 ¼ cups white sugar

2 ¼ cups packed brown sugar

2 tablespoons ground cinnamon

1 tablespoon ground cloves

*Good apple varieties to use are Jonathan,
Winesap, Stayman, Golden Delicious, Macintosh, and others.*

Wash, remove stems, quarter, and core fruit. Cook slowly in cider and vinegar until soft. Press fruit through a colander, food mill, or strainer. Cook fruit pulp with sugars and spices, stirring frequently. To test for doneness, remove a spoonful and hold it away from steam for 2 minutes. It is done if the butter remains mounded on the spoon. Another way to determine when the butter is cooked adequately is to spoon a small quantity onto a plate. If a rim of liquid does not separate around the edge of the butter, it is ready for canning. Fill, hot, into sterile half-pint or pint jars, leaving ¼ inch of headspace. If you use quart jars, you do not need to presterilize them. Process in boiling water bath 5 minutes (0–1,000 feet), 10 minutes (1,001–6,000 feet), or 15 minutes (above 6,000 feet). If using quart jars, add 5 minutes to processing times.

Marinated Mushrooms
(yield: about 9 half-pints)

7 pounds small whole mushrooms
½ cup bottled lemon juice
2 cups olive or salad oil
2 ½ cups white vinegar (5%)
1 tablespoon oregano leaves
1 tablespoon dried basil leaves

1 tablespoon canning or
   pickling salt
½ cup finely chopped onions
¼ cup diced pimento
2 cloves garlic, quartered
25 black peppercorns

Mushrooms should be fresh and small, with unopened canopies (caps less than 1¼ inch in diameter). Wash. Trim stems, leaving ¼ inch attached to cap. Add lemon juice and water to cover mushrooms. Bring to boil; simmer 5 minutes. Drain mushrooms. Mix oil, vinegar, oregano, basil, and salt in a saucepan. Stir in onions and pimento and heat to boiling. Place ¼ garlic clove and 2–3 peppercorns in each half-pint jar. Fill jars with mushrooms and hot, well-mixed oil and vinegar solution, leaving ½ inch of headspace. Adjust lids and process in a boiling water bath for 20 minutes (0–1,000 feet), 25 minutes (1,001–3,000 feet), 30 minutes (3,001–6,000 feet), or 35 minutes (above 6,000 feet).

Raspberry Peach Jam
(yield: 8 half-pint jars)

1 cup whole, fresh or frozen,
   raspberries
3 cups pitted, washed &
   chopped peaches

3 tablespoons lemon juice
1 ½ packages of dry,
   powdered pectin
7 cups sugar

Combine fruits and lemon juice in large non-aluminum, heavy pan. Bring to a boil, stirring often. Add the pectin and stir well. Return to boil. Slowly add the sugar, stirring constantly to dissolve it completely. Bring to a new rolling boil, stirring often. Put into half-pint jars, leaving ½ inch of headspace. Process in a boiling water bath for 5 minutes (0–1,000 feet), 10 minutes (1,001–6,000 feet), or 15 minutes (above 6,000 feet).

Cranberry Chutney

(yield: 6 half-pint jars)

1 teaspoon grated orange rind	2 tablespoons peeled, grated &
¼ cup orange juice	fine-chopped ginger root
1 bag (12 ounces) cranberries	1 cup red wine vinegar
1 ¼ cups finely chopped onion	1 ½ cups granulated sugar
1 ¼ cups chopped glacé pineapple	1 cup golden raisins
(in the baking section of your	1 teaspoon dry mustard
supermarket)	½ teaspoon cayenne pepper
3 cloves garlic, finely chopped	1 teaspoon ground cinnamon
	1 teaspoon ground cloves

Combine grated orange rind, orange juice, cranberries, onion, pineapple, garlic, ginger, and vinegar in a large saucepan. Bring to a gentle boil, stirring occasionally until cranberries soften (about 15 minutes). Stir sugar, raisins, mustard, cayenne pepper, cinnamon, cloves, and 1 cup of water into cranberry mixture. Boil gently, stirring occasionally to prevent sticking, about 20 minutes. Mixture should be slightly runny and will thicken upon cooling. Ladle hot chutney into a hot jar, leaving ½ inch of headspace. Remove air bubbles with your trusty chopstick and readjust head space to ½ inch. Put lid on jar and place in canner. Repeat for remaining chutney. Cover canner; return water to a boil; process for 10 minutes (0–1,000 feet), 15 minutes (1,001–6,000 feet), or 20 minutes (above 6,000 feet). Remove jars. Cool 24 hours. Wipe jars, label, and store jars in a cool, dark place.

Lloyd & Beth Kidd's Mustard Pickles
(yield: 15 pints)

4 ½ quarts cucumbers, cut into ¾-inch pieces	2 green peppers
1 ½ quarts cauliflower, cut into ¾-inch pieces	2 cups sugar
	⅓ cup dry mustard
1 ½ quarts peeled pearl onions	7 cups cider vinegar
2 cups salt	2 tablespoons celery seed
1 red pepper	1⅛ cups flour
	1 tablespoon turmeric

Cut all vegetables but peppers and soak for 24 hours in a brine made of 4 quarts water to 2 cups salt. Drain and add peppers, which have been chopped into ½-inch pieces. Cover with boiling water for ten minutes. Combine sugar, mustard, cider vinegar, celery seed, flour, turmeric, and 8 cups water. Bring to boil. Drain vegetables thoroughly, add to sauce and cook slightly. Pack in pint jars, leaving ½ inch of headspace. Process in boiling water bath for 10 minutes (0–1,000 feet), 15 minutes (1,001–6,000 feet), or 20 minutes (above 6,000 feet).

Pickled Bread-and-Butter Zucchini
(yield: 8–9 pint jars)

16 cups fresh zucchini, sliced	2 cups sugar
4 cups onions, thinly sliced	4 tablespoons mustard seed
½ cup canning or pickling salt	2 tablespoons celery seed
4 cups white vinegar (5%)	2 teaspoons ground turmeric

Cover zucchini and onion slices with 1 inch water and salt. Let stand two hours and drain thoroughly. Combine vinegar, sugar, and spices. Bring to a boil and add zucchini and onions. Simmer five minutes and fill jars with mixture and pickling solution, leaving ½ inch of headspace. Adjust lids and process pints or quarts in a boiling water bath for 10 minutes (0–1,000 feet), 15 minutes (1,001–6,000 feet), or 20 minutes (above 6,000 feet).

Sher of Seattle's Pineapple Chutney*

3 cans (15 ounces) crushed
  pineapple (with juice)
1 mango, peeled and diced
  (or use 2 peaches instead)
2 apricots (fresh, diced—
  or use 1 peach instead)
1 cup brown sugar
1½ cups white sugar
1½ cups cider vinegar
2–3 tablespoons crystallized
  ginger, finely chopped
  (candied ginger)
⅓ cup lemon juice
½ cup chopped onion

2 small yellow peppers or
  banana peppers, seeded,
  chopped fine
2 cloves garlic, minced
1 teaspoon dried red pepper flakes
¾ cup yellow raisins
½ teaspoon salt
¼ teaspoon each: cayenne
  pepper, powdered ginger,
  cinnamon, cloves, allspice,
  mustard seed, & powdered
  coriander (all optional)
1 package dry pectin powder

There is no right or wrong way to season a chutney. Taste it while it's cooking. Experiment with seasonings, adding the ones that sound good to you and tasting after every addition until it tastes perfect. Add more seasonings if you want, and omit the ones that you don't have in your cabinet.

Mix all ingredients except the pectin powder together in a big pot. Heat over medium heat, stirring almost continuously to prevent burning, for about 1 hour, until the mixture thickens. Only then add the pectin powder. Stir until the mixture reaches a "soft rolling boil." Fill sterilized jars, leaving ½ inch of headspace, and process in boiling water bath for 10 minutes (0–1,000 feet), 15 minutes (1,001–6,000 feet), or 20 minutes (above 6,000 feet).

Tomato Salsa
(from Washington State University Extension Service)

(yield: 13 pints)

7 quarts peeled, cored, chopped tomatoes*	6 cloves garlic, finely chopped
	2 cups bottled lemon juice
4 cups seeded, chopped, long green chilies	2 tablespoons salt
	1 tablespoon black pepper
5 cups chopped onion	2 tablespoons ground cumin
½ cup seeded, finely chopped jalapeño peppers	3 tablespoons oregano leaves
	2 tablespoons fresh cilantro

For best consistency, use "paste" tomatoes such as Roma tomatoes, rather than slicing tomatoes. Regular slicing tomatoes yield a watery consistency.

Combine all ingredients except cumin, oregano, and cilantro in a large pot and bring to a boil, stirring frequently. When boil is reached, reduce heat and simmer 10 minutes. Add spices and simmer for another 20 minutes, stirring occasionally. Ladle into hot pint jars, leaving ½ inch of headspace. Adjust lids and process in a boiling water bath for 15 minutes (0–1,000 feet), 20 minutes (1,001–6,000 feet), or 25 minutes (above 6,000 feet).

Warning: Do not change the amounts of any ingredients other than dry seasonings, and do not thicken salsa with cornstarch. Processing times are based on the proportions of vegetables and lemon juice that are present in this exact recipe. Cornstarch and other thickeners inhibit the conductivity of heat through the salsa.

Jean Mead's Pickled Cauliflower
(yield 3–4 pints)

1 quart vinegar
2 tablespoons mustard seed
1 cup sugar

8 whole cloves
4 sticks cinnamon
2 heads cauliflower

Simmer all ingredients except cauliflower together for 15 minutes. Meanwhile wash cauliflower, cut away all leaves and break into uniform flowerets. Blanch cauliflower by putting it into kettle of boiling water, turn off heat and let stand 2 minutes. Drain and put flowerets into jars. Pour hot syrup over, straining out spices, leaving ½ inch of headspace, and seal. Process in a boiling water bath for 10 minutes (0–1,000 feet), 15 minutes (1,001–6,000 feet), or 20 minutes (above 6,000 feet).

Pressure Canning

Although high-acid foods can be safely processed in boiling water, low-acid foods need the extra protection that pressure canning gives. These foods, which include meat products and vegetables, must be processed at 240°F. in order to kill botulism spores and other bacteria such as salmonella and staphylococcus. This is a higher temperature than can be reached with a regular boiling water bath, so jars are processed in a "pressure canner" that uses pressurized steam to raise the internal temperature of the food to the necessary temperature.

The equipment you'll need to do pressure canning is the same as the equipment you'll need for the boiling water bath—with one major exception. Instead of using the boiling water bath canner, a pressure canner is used. This is a pot that's similar to Mom's old pressure cooker, only bigger. The lid of the pressure canner is tightly secured onto the canner itself, and there's a gauge on the lid to regulate pressure. Because there are several kinds of pressure canners, we won't get into any big discussion of their appearance. When you buy your pressure canner, it will come with a booklet of instructions that will show you exactly how to use it. ***Be sure to read that booklet.***

Before you buy your pressure canner, here's a piece of advice: Buy a big one. If you're going to the trouble to do home canning, don't handicap yourself by purchasing a canner that holds only a few bottles. A big pressure canner doesn't cost that much more than a small one. Besides, you'll save heating costs—not to mention time—if you can process more bottles at once.

Do not be afraid of your pressure canner. Treat it like a beloved family pet that *almost* never bites, as long as you remember not to pick it up when it's trying to eat. Unless you do something really stupid, such as taking off the pressure gauge when the canner is being used, the pressure canner will not explode in your face and bury glass shards in your ceiling. In fact, the only thing your pressure canner asks is that you have the pressure gauge checked once per year. Your county extension service should be happy to handle that assignment for you, and will probably be glad to give you some canning recipes and tips while you're there.

Your First Pressure Canning Experience

If you've never done your own pressure canning, you should approach it the same way as you approached your first experience with a boiling water bath. Start small, with a small amount of an easy recipe. Succeeding at your first easy project will give you the confidence to do something a little harder next time.

Just as we held your hand during your first boiling water bath experience, we're here to do the same thing for you as you pressure can for the first time. We can go only so far, because we don't know what kind of pressure canner you own. But we'll give you the basics and allow you to supplement them with the instruction book that came with your canner. If the instruction manual that came with your canner conflicts with the instructions we give you here, follow the manual that came with the canner!

MUST... GET DONE... BY.... MIDNIGHT!

PRESSURE CANNER

Here is a recipe that we've used countless times as home canners, and have gotten a whole lot of use from. Bottled mushrooms can be used in countless recipes and are easy to make. If you don't like mushrooms, use the one for baked beans or one for soup. It doesn't matter what recipe you use, as much as it matters that you've got a step-by-step tutorial to help you through that first canning project.

❏ 1. Go to the store and purchase whichever of these items you don't already have:

   one case of 12 half-pint canning jars, with lids and rings
   about 10 pounds of fresh mushrooms (domesticated—not wild!)
   about 3 hardboiled egg slicers (available in the gizmo section
   **   of your supermarket or kitchen store)**
   salt
   ascorbic acid powder or 250-mg. vitamin C tablets (optional)

❏ 2. Now that you're home, the first step is to put the jars (not the lids) in your dishwasher and run them through a normal cycle. If you don't have a dishwasher, wash them by hand, making sure to get out all the detergent when you're rinsing them.

❏ 3. While the bottles are washing, trim off the edges of the mushroom stems. Also trim any discolored parts and discard any mushrooms you wouldn't want to eat. (The rule we gave you for boiling water bath canning also applies to pressure canning—*garbage in, garbage out.*) Slice the mushrooms with the egg slicers. The egg slicers are fragile and will break—that's why we told you to buy several of them.

❏ 4. Soak the mushroom slices in cold water for ten minutes to get rid of dirt; then drain the water. Put the mushrooms in a large pot and cover them with clean water. If there's still debris floating in the water, drain the mushrooms again and add clean water. Bring them to a boil and boil five minutes. Watch them shrink! Ten pounds of mushrooms aren't going to go nearly as far as you thought they would.

❏ 5. While the mushrooms are boiling, get your pressure canner ready by placing the rack on the bottom and pouring two to three inches of water over that. In a small saucepan, simmer the jar lids (not the screw tops!) until you'll need them.

❏ 6. Place ¼ teaspoon salt in each half-pint bottle. Also add one vitamin C tablet or ⅛ teaspoon of ascorbic acid powder to each bottle. The salt is necessary for taste, but the vitamin C or ascorbic acid is just to prevent discoloration; you don't need to use the vitamin C or ascorbic acid unless you want to. Then fill the bottle with drained mushrooms, leaving 1 inch of headspace. Add fresh hot water, again leaving that 1 inch of headspace. Use your chopstick to get the air bubbles out of the jar before cleaning off the rim and putting on the lid.

❏ 7. When the jars are full and the lids are in place, pick up the jars one at a time with the jar lifter and place them on the rack of the canner. Try to keep the jars from touching one another, because they're fragile when they're hot.

❏ 8. Following the manufacturer's directions for your particular pressure canner, securely fasten the lid of the pressure canner, and bring the water to a vigorous boil with the vent open to allow steam to escape. When steam starts escaping through the vent, set your kitchen timer for ten minutes and continue allowing steam to escape until the ten-minute period is up. Then close the vent by putting the weight on the vent port or closing the petcock, depending on the type pressure canner you're using.

❏ 9. Here's a handy chart to help you determine your processing information for the mushroom project. Note that we have information for both dial-gauge and weighted-gauge canners, so choose the numbers that are appropriate for your canner:

Dial-Gauge Pressure

Bottled Mushroom Jar Size	Processing Time	0–2,000 feet	2,001–4,000 feet	4,001–6,000 feet	6,001–8,000 feet
Half-pints or pints	45 min.	11 lb.	12 lb.	13 lb.	14 lb.

Weighted-Gauge Pressure

Bottled Mushroom Jar Size	Processing Time	0–2,000 feet	2,001–4,000 feet	4,001–6,000 feet	6,001–8,000 feet
Half-pints or pints	45 min.	10 lb.	15 lb.	15 lb.	15 lb.

❏ 10. Watch the steam gauge until the pressure is reached for your altitude (about three to five minutes). When the dial indicates the right pressure has been reached, or when the weight starts to rock on a weighted gauge, start timing the process. **Make sure the pressure goes no lower on the gauge than the recommended pressure. The pressure can go higher, but not lower. If the pressure goes lower, timing must start from the beginning.**

❏ 11. When the processing time ends, turn off the heat and remove canner from the heating element if you're using an electric range. **Do not open the lid to the canner yet!** Lay an old bath towel on a counter or table, ready to receive the jars when they are finished processing.

❏ 12. Allow the canner to depressurize naturally. **This gradual cooling is part of the canning process, so do not yield to the temptation to help it along by pouring cold water over it, or by jiggling the weight.** Only after the gauge returns to zero or the steam stops escaping from under the weight, even when the weight is gently nudged, is the processing completed. Remove the weight from the vent. Now wait two more minutes before removing the lid from the canner. Be careful when you remove the canner lid, because there is still steam in the canner that can potentially cause burns if care isn't taken.

❏ 13. Using the jar lifter, remove the jars from the canner and place them one by one on the towel. Be careful with the jars, because they're fragile from the canning. You'll notice that jars that have been pressure canned will usually seal a lot faster than jars that have been through a boiling water bath. But if the jar doesn't seal after a reasonable length of time, either refrigerate the contents to be consumed over the next few days, or reprocess the contents with a fresh lid.

There you have it—a whole shelf of mushrooms that can be used to enhance all sorts of home-cooked dishes. Best of all, you've only scratched the surface. Wait till you make your first bottle of baked beans!

Step-by-Step Pressure Canning Checklist

➲   From your first pressure canning project, you can see that using a pressure canner is exactly the same as using a boiling water bath, only different. Here is the same easy checklist we gave you earlier, modified for use with your pressure canner. For your convenience, the changes are in boldface.

❑ 1. Put the rack on the bottom of the canner and then pour about **two to three inches of hot water** over it. At the same time, fill a small saucepan with a few inches of water and leave it on a smaller back burner. You'll turn the heat on under that small pan later.

❑ 2. Thoroughly wash your canning jars, making sure to rinse all the soap from the jars before filling them with food. **Washing your jars in the dishwasher is fine. When you're pressure canning, you do not need to sterilize the jars.**

❑ 3. Place the flat canning lids in the small saucepan of water. Turn on the water until it reaches a low boil, turn down the heat, and leave the lids in the simmering water until needed, checking occasionally to make sure they're still covered in water.

❑ 4. Place food into clean, hot jars, being careful to leave the proper amount of headspace. Pour hot liquid, as the recipe calls for, into the jar, again leaving the proper amount of headspace. Use a chopstick to dislodge air bubbles that may be hiding in the jar of food.

❑ 5. With a moistened paper towel, clean food and liquid from the rim of the jar. Be thorough, because even a single grain of salt or sugar may interfere with the seal of the lid. Then take a lid from the saucepan, put it on top of the jar, and secure it in place with the screw-top. Follow the manufacturer's directions for how tightly to secure the screw-top over the lid. Repeat until you have filled enough jars to load the canner.

❑ 6. Place the bottles into the canner by using the jar lifter. **Securely fasten the lid of the pressure canner. Turn on** the heat, making sure the pressure vent in the lid is open to allow steam to escape.

❏ 7. **Heat at highest setting until steam starts escaping through the vent in the lid. Set the timer for ten minutes and continue allowing steam to escape until the ten-minute period is up. Then close the vent by putting the weight on the vent port or closing the petcock, depending on the type pressure canner you're using.**

❏ 8. **Watch the steam gauge until the pressure is reached for your altitude (about three to five minutes). When the dial indicates the right pressure has been reached, or when the weight starts to rock on a weighted gauge, start timing the process.**

❏ 9. **Make sure the pressure goes no lower on the gauge than the recommended pressure. The pressure can go higher, but not lower. If the pressure goes lower, timing must start from the beginning.**

❏ 10. **When the processing time ends, turn off the heat and remove canner from the heating element if you're using an electric range.** *Do not open the lid to the canner yet!* Lay an old bath towel on a counter or table, ready to receive the jars when they are finished processing.

❏ 11. **Allow the canner to depressurize naturally, without any help from you. Only after the gauge returns to zero or the steam stops escaping from under the weight, even when the weight is gently nudged, is the processing completed. Remove the weight from the vent. Now wait two more minutes before removing the lid from the canner. Be careful when you remove the canner lid, because there is still steam in the canner that can potentially cause burns if care isn't taken.**

❏ 12. Using the jar lifter, remove the jars from the boiling water and place them one by one on the towel. The jars should be close together but not touching, so that air can circulate between jars. Note: Jars that are hot from the processor are fragile. To avoid breakage, be careful not to hit them against any other jars or any hard surfaces.

❑ 13. As the jars cool, the flat lids will be drawn to the jar to form a vacuum. Jars that have been properly sealed will be tightly drawn toward the contents of the jar so that the lid seems to curve downward. Sometimes a jar doesn't seal for several hours. Give the lid time to do its work. If the jar doesn't seal after a reasonable length of time, either refrigerate the contents to be consumed over the next few days, or reprocess the contents with a fresh lid.

❑ 14. Before putting the jars away, use a grease pencil, magic marker, or gummed label to indicate the month and year the food was bottled. As you will find out later, this date is used to rotate your food properly, so that you will be eating the oldest food first.

Pressure Canning Recipes

Here are a few canning recipes to get you started. You'll find more recipes in the instruction booklet that came with your canner, and even more of them on the shelves of your friendly bookstore. (Look in Chapter 9 for reference books and web sites that will help you in your search.)

One thing you may want to consider is that you can process food in a pressure canner even if you're on a salt-free diet. Fermented pickles do require salt, but the foods processed in a pressure canner contain salt for taste only. If you are on a salt-free diet and do not want to add salt to your recipes, feel free to omit the salt. Alternate ways to add flavor would be to add a tablespoon of lemon or orange juice to each pint of carrots, beets, or asparagus. For green beans and peas, you could add one-half teaspoon of mace, nutmeg, or curry powder per pint. Do not substitute salt with a commercial salt substitute, though. Salt substitutes change the color and the flavor of bottled foods in a way you won't expect and don't want.

Chili con Carne
(yield: 9 pints)

2 quarts crushed or whole tomatoes	1½ cups chopped onions
3 cups dried pinto or red kidney beans	5 teaspoons salt (separated)
	3–6 tablespoons chili powder
5½ cups water	1 teaspoon black pepper
3 pounds ground beef	1 cup chopped peppers of your choice (optional)

Wash beans thoroughly and place them in a 2-quart saucepan. Add cold water to a level of 2–3 inches above the beans and soak 12–18 hours. Drain beans, discarding the water. Return beans to saucepan, adding 5½ cups of fresh water and 2 teaspoons salt. Bring to a boil; then simmer for 30 minutes. Once again, drain beans and discard water. Brown ground beef, chopped onions, and peppers in a skillet. Drain off fat and add 3 teaspoons salt, pepper, chili powder, tomatoes, and drained cooked beans. Simmer 5 minutes. Caution: Do not thicken. Fill jars, leaving 1 inch of headspace. Process according to the chart below: Adjust lids and process.

Dial-Gauge Pressure

Chile Con Carne Jar Size	Processing Time	0–2,000 feet	2,001–4,000 feet	4,001–6,000 feet	6,001–8,000 feet
Half-pints or pints	75 min.	11 lb.	12 lb.	13 lb.	14 lb.

Weighted-Gauge Pressure

Chile Con Carne Jar Size	Processing Time	0–2,000 feet	2,001–4,000 feet	4,001–6,000 feet	6,001–8,000 feet
Half-pints or pints	75 min.	10 lb.	15 lb.	15 lb.	15 lb.

Beans with Molasses Sauce
(yield: 7 quarts per 5 pounds beans)

Ingredients for each cup of dry beans:

1 cup dry beans (Great
Northern beans are less
grainy than pinto beans)
pork, ham, or bacon

3 tablespoons dark molasses
1 tablespoon vinegar
2 teaspoons salt
¾ teaspoon powdered dry
mustard

Wash dry beans. Add 3 cups of water for each cup of dried beans or peas. Boil 2 minutes, remove from heat, and soak 1 hour and drain. Heat to boiling in fresh water, and save liquid for making the sauce. Fill jars three-fourths full with hot beans. If desired, add a ¾-inch cube of pork, ham, or bacon to each jar. Fill jars with heated sauce, leaving 1 inch of headspace. Adjust lids and process according to the chart below.

Molasses Sauce: For each cup of dry beans you used, mix 4 cups water or cooking liquid from beans, 3 tablespoons dark molasses, 1 tablespoon vinegar, 2 teaspoons salt, and ¾ teaspoon powdered dry mustard. Heat to boiling.

Dial-Gauge Pressure

Beans with Molasses Sauce Jar Size	Processing Time	0–2,000 feet	2,001–4,000 feet	4,001–6,000 feet	6,001–8,000 feet
Pints	65 min.	11 lb.	12 lb.	13 lb.	14 lb.
Quarts	75 min.				

Weighted-Gauge Pressure

Beans with Molasses Sauce Jar Size	Processing Time	0–1,000 feet	Above 1,000 feet
Pints	65 min.	15 lb.	15 lb.
Quarts	75 min.		

Spaghetti Sauce with Meat

30 pounds tomatoes	1 pound sliced fresh mushrooms
2 ½ pounds ground sausage	(optional)
or beef	4 ½ teaspoons salt
5 cloves garlic, minced	2 tablespoons oregano
1 cup chopped onion	4 tablespoons minced parsley
1 cup chopped celery	2 teaspoons black pepper
or green peppers	¼ cup brown sugar

Wash tomatoes and dip in boiling water for 30 seconds to a minute until skins split. Then dip in cold water and slip off skins. Remove cores and quarter. Boil 20 minutes, uncovered, in large saucepan. Put through sieve or food mill to strain out the seeds.

Sauté sausage or beef, and cook until brown. Add onions, garlic, celery or peppers, and mushrooms, and cook until vegetables are tender. **Do not increase the proportion of onions, peppers, or mushrooms in the recipe!** Add remaining ingredients and bring to a boil. Simmer, uncovered, until thick enough for serving. At this time the volume will have been reduced by about one-half. Stirring frequently to avoid burning, fill jars, leaving 1 inch of headspace, and process in pressure canner according to the following table:

Dial-Gauge Pressure

Spaghetti Sauce Jar Size	Processing Time	0–2,000 feet	2,001–4,000 feet	4,001–6,000 feet	6,001–8,000 feet
Pints	60 min.	11 lb.	12 lb.	13 lb.	14 lb.
Quarts	70 min.				

Weighted-Gauge Pressure

Spaghetti Sauce Jar Size	Processing Time	0–1,000 feet	Above 1,000 feet
Pints	60 min.	10 lb.	15 lb.
Quarts	70 min.		

Tomato Juice Cocktail
(yield: 7 quarts per 22 pounds tomatoes)

22 **pounds tomatoes**
 3 **cups finely chopped**
   vegetables—any combination
   of onions, celery, carrots, or
   peppers (including hot peppers,
   if you're brave)

salt
lemon juice or citric acid

Wash tomatoes, remove stems, and cut off all portions that are bruised or otherwise unappetizing. Quickly cut about 1 pound of tomatoes into quarters and place in a large saucepan, heating to boiling while crushing. (Reliable sources say that doing it this way will keep the juice from separating.) Continue to slowly add and crush tomato quarters to the boiling mush, making sure the mixture continues to boil at a vigorous pace. Add *finely* chopped vegetables to the brew and simmer for 20 minutes. While the mixture is simmering, add 2 tablespoons bottled lemon juice or ¼ teaspoon citric acid to each quart bottle. If you want to add sugar to offset the tartness, you may do so—but do it sparingly. (In fact, it's best to experiment with one bottle on the first batch so you can see how the juice will taste after it has been processed.) Add 1 teaspoon salt per quart as well. (The salt is a flavor enhancer and is not necessary for the safe processing of food.) At the end of 20 minutes, press the mixture through a sieve or other sort of strainer to remove seeds and skins. Heat the juice again to boiling. Immediately fill jars with hot juice, leaving ½ inch of headspace. Adjust lids and process according to the charts below:

Tomato Juice Cocktail by Boiling-Water Bath

Style of Pack	Jar Size	1–1,000 feet	1,001–3,000 feet	3,001–6,000 feet	Above 6,000 feet
Hot	Quarts	40 min.	45 min.	50 min.	55 min.

Note: See Pressure Canner instructions on following page.

Tomato Juice Cocktail by Pressure Canner
Hot Pack Only

Dial-Gauge Pressure

Tomato Juice Cocktail Jar Size	Processing Time	0–2,000 feet	2,001–4,000 feet	4,001–6,000 feet	6,001–8,000 feet
Pints or Quarts	15 min.	11 lb.	12 lb.	13 lb.	14 lb.

Weighted-Gauge Pressure

Tomato Juice Cocktail Jar Size	Processing Time	0–1,000 feet	Above 1,000 feet
Pints or Quarts	15 min.	10 lb.	15 lb.

Dry Pack

Most people will tell you there are two types of canning—boiling water bath and pressure canning. These people would lose if they bet the farm on "Jeopardy." There are indeed two types of canning, but boiling-water bath and pressure canning are both classified as "wet-pack" canning. This means they're packed into jars with some sort of liquid or juice—wet and sticky. The juice is a vital component of wet-pack canning because it conducts the heat that kills the germs. The other type of canning is "dry-pack" canning, which is, well, dry.

Dry-pack canning is designed for foodstuffs that don't lend themselves to wet pack. You couldn't process cocoa powder in a boiling water bath, for example. You wouldn't want to package raisins in a liquid. But wheat, beans, pasta, and rice are among the foods that can be stored indefinitely by using the dry-pack method.

There's at least one great web site on the Internet (glitchproof.com) that specializes in dry pack. This site is recommended in Chapter 9, because it sells equipment that is needed for successful dry-pack canning, and it also has a whole lot of handy information for the home canner. Dry pack can be done in huge containers such as five-gallon plastic drums. It can be done with

See Chapter 9 for more resources.

machines that seal items in aluminum cans, similar to cans that would hold a gallon or so of tomato soup. But a nifty feature for the home canner is that dry-pack canning can also be done in a standard mayonnaise jar. Any container that doesn't allow air to leak in, and that is fit to hold food, is suitable for dry-pack canning.

Not everything needs to be officially dry packed in order to be preserved. For example, cocoa probably isn't going to rot if you just leave it sitting around in a twenty-five-pound bag—although it might attract rodents. But things that are affected by the air, such as raisins or brown sugar, could profit from being packaged in containers that allow for the air to be displaced. Dry-pack canning allows for this.

"Absorber packets" that take the oxygen out of the air in a container are inexpensive and easy to use. For small containers, these are all that are needed to keep the contents of the container free from air-caused damage. Absorber packets create a vacuum in the container, so they will protect the contents of the container only as long as the container remains sealed. The first time it is opened, the vacuum is released and the product will begin its normal deterioration. Thus it would be foolhardy to rely on absorber packets to preserve a twenty-five-pound bag of brown sugar—unless your family consumes a whale of a lot of brown sugar. But you could use an absorber packet to preserve a two-pound sack of brown sugar that had been placed in an airtight container, saving that brown sugar from deterioration until the container is opened sometime down the road.

Here's a list of things that lend themselves to dry-pack canning with absorber packets. This list is by no means comprehensive. Experiment on your own. In fact, dry-pack canning is wonderfully versatile in that you can throw more than one variety of item in a single container and protect them both with the same absorber packet. Imagine putting cocoa mix on the bottom of your container, adding a loose layer of waxed paper to separate the two, and putting miniature marshmallows on top. Such a deal!

- Beans of all types
- Chocolate chips
- Cocoa mix
- Dehydrated apple slices

- Granulated sugar
- Marshmallows
- Pasta
- Popcorn
- Powdered sugar
- Raisins
- Rolled oats
- White flour
- White rice
- White sugar

When you've chosen the item you want to store via a dry-pack method, find a container of the size you're likely to use before it would go stale under ordinary conditions. Pack the item in the container and add the absorber packet according to the manufacturer's directions. Once the lid has been placed on the container, the food should remain good until the package opens. At that point, the food is just as you'd bring it home from the supermarket. Use it within a reasonable length of time.

Because their deterioration is slower, bulk foods such as wheat, beans, pasta, and white rice can easily be stored dry in relatively large containers. There are a number of companies that manufacture or sell large plastic buckets to contain these items. When storing food in these large containers, the recommended way to do it is by using "gas displacement" in addition to absorber packets. Not only does gas displacement slow the normal deterioration of food, but it also acts as a fumigant to rid the food of pests that may infest the food in the form of eggs that may be invisible to the naked eye. Wheat is especially susceptible to infestation by weevils. If you're a wheat storer, you may want to consider using gas displacement to treat any wheat that wasn't already thus treated by the distributor.

Gas displacement uses a gas such as argon, nitrogen, or carbon dioxide to replace the air in a container. A vacuum is not formed, so the contents are not under as much stress as they would be if absorber packets alone were used. When you order gas absorber packets, you should be given information on how to use the particular kind of packet you're purchasing for dry-pack canning. There are so many varieties, and so many sizes of containers, that we could spend fifty boring pages just listing all the various instructions.

⮕   But to give you an example of what's involved in dry-pack canning, here's an explanation of how to store wheat with dry ice (carbon dioxide!) gas displacement.

▶ Dry Ice Fumigation

❑   1. Obtain 5-gallon buckets that are safe to use as food containers. (It's important to get containers that are specifically designed to be safe for food use, because other containers may deteriorate and contaminate your food.) Choose a day with low humidity to get the best effectiveness from your fumigation.

❑   2. Place 3–4 inches of clean wheat or other grain on the bottom of the bucket. Add approximately 2 ounces of dry ice and then fill the container with clean grain. (For larger quantities, use ½ pound of dry ice per 100 pounds of grain, or 1 pound of dry ice for each 30 gallons.)

❑   3. Put the lid ajar over the container for about a half hour, until the dry ice vaporizes. Then put the lid tightly on the bucket. The system will be effective only as long as the lid is air tight. The dry ice will not kill eggs, but should control most adult and larval insects.

If you've done this properly, a single dry ice treatment should protect the grain until it's opened. Once the grain is open, it can be sprouted or used in recipes. The moment the container is open, the timer starts ticking and normal deterioration of the grain will begin.

There aren't a whole lot of dry-pack recipes for us to give you. In fact, we can think only of one—and it may not even qualify as a dry-pack recipe because it uses canning jars and no oxygen absorbers. But if you want a way to keep raisins fresh and soft for years, this is how to do it:

```
┌─────────────────────────────────────────────────────────┐
│                                                         │
│                       Raisins                           │
│                                                         │
│    Loosely pack raisins into mason jars which are clean and dry. Bake in │
│    225°F. oven for 15–20 minutes. While the raisins cook, heat the lids in │
│    boiling water, just as you would for a normal canning project. When the │
│    raisins come out of the oven, make sure the inside of the lid is dry. Then │
│    screw on bands firmly tight.                         │
│                                                         │
└─────────────────────────────────────────────────────────┘
```

Okay, Any Questions?

?   *Is home canning really worth my time?*

Here's a short answer for you: It sure beats watching television.

Here's a longer answer for you: It depends on how you value your time.

You may decide you can purchase food in cans more cheaply than you can bottle it. (In fact, that may indeed be the case unless you have a garden or have slain Bambi or have an apricot tree in your backyard.) A lot depends on the size of your family. If you're a two-person family who can be satisfied sharing, say, a 59 cent can of baked beans from the supermarket, canning will not be nearly as economical for you as it would be for a family of eight who'd be eating those beans by the half gallon.

But self-sufficiency is a big part of the equation. Something that is not economically feasible may be worth your time if you enjoy doing it, or if it teaches you new skills, or if seeing your own finished work gives you a sense of accomplishment, or if you can do something that helps make you independent from the rest of the world. When you add those factors to the mix, you may want to consider canning. It's an enjoyable hobby—and it's also a good excuse for your family to gather around the kitchen table and work together, and visit.

?   *Should I really be that paranoid about following the processing instructions to the letter, and not altering any recipes?*

A few years ago, we would have shrugged and told you we'd never met anyone who died from eating home-canned food. Now we have—or at least we've met their survivors. We've heard the horror story often, but it never fails to give us the creeps. If we were doing home canning today, we'd be a lot more stringent about not altering the recipes than we used to be. It doesn't make any sense to take chances with the lives of your family members. There are enough good recipes on the market that you don't need to take liberties with experimenting on your own. If you *must* experiment, take your recipe to your state extension service and ask if they'll check out the recipe for you.

?   *I'd like to do pressure canning, but aren't the canners quite dangerous?*

If you grew up with a pressure cooker in your home, the odds are that your parents told you all kinds of horror stories to make sure you kept away from it. You probably wondered why your parents would keep such a dangerous device in the kitchen, and breathed a sigh of relief whenever dinner was cooked without the loss of life and limb. But now that you're an adult, it's time for you to realize that when it is used properly, the pressure cooker or canner is no more dangerous than any other household appliance. Treat it with respect and common sense, just like you would a power lawnmower or a chainsaw, and you should be fine.

CHAPTER 4
You're Under Arrest

★ **IN THIS CHAPTER**
- ✔ Giving foods the cold shoulder
- ✔ Choosing the best freezer for your needs
- ✔ Becoming a wrap star
- ✔ Freezing all kinds of stuff
- ✔ Preserving foods by drying
- ✔ Making jerky and fruit leather
- ✔ Answering common questions

The beauty of home canning is that it preserves food by stopping microorganisms in their tracks, but canning isn't the only way to do that. Freezing and drying are both excellent ways to store food. Like canning, both drying and cold storage prolong the life of foods by arresting the life process of microorganisms that would cause food to go bad. But where canning kills those microorganisms, freezing and drying only put those bugs in suspended animation. These processes arrest the growth of bacteria, but only as long as the products remain frozen or dried. Once the food is brought to room temperature or rehydrated, the process of decay will begin all over again.

Of all the ways to preserve food, cold storage provides food with the shortest additional shelf life. Milk that is stored in the refrigerator may be good for a week, with butter stored in the freezer being good for up to about a year. Drying is at the other end of the spectrum, with dehydrated foods lasting longer than any other foods that have been preserved. Both methods have their advantages, however. This chapter will explain in detail how to use cold storage and dehydration to your advantage. In fact, the section on dehydrating just may provide your family with a lifelong hobby.

Chill Out with Cold Storage

It's a cold fact—the refrigerator/freezer can be a valuable asset to your food storage program if you manage it wisely. Unless you're interested in "astronaut" ice cream, which is neither cold nor wet, keeping ice cream in your freezer is the only way you're going to have frozen desserts on hand when you get that craving in the middle of the night. If you don't have refrigeration you don't have ice cubes, either. Going entirely without a refrigerator/freezer would be a real hardship for a nation that's as dependent on cold soft drinks as ours is, especially in the summer.

And don't forget dairy products and meat. It's refrigerator/freezers that have changed the whole structure of modern life by allowing men and women to go to the supermarket weekly instead of daily. We can refrigerate milk and cheese, we can freeze the Sunday roast beef when we buy it on Tuesday, and we can put our fruits and vegetables in compartments that are similar to Grandma's root cellar. The refrigerator/freezer has made a huge impact on our daily lives.

Not only do refrigerators and freezers retard spoilage, but they also preserve taste. Few people who have tasted canned green beans prefer them to the frozen variety. Freezer jam is far and away better than the best commercially-bottled jam or jelly on the market. And when given a choice between canned corned beef and a fresh one that has been kept in the "icebox," no Irishman worth his shillelagh would eat his St. Patrick's Day dinner out of a can.

The refrigerator/freezer is so indispensable to modern life that many of us are tempted to get a full-sized freezer so we can increase those benefits. As the popular television jurist Judge Judy might say, "That would be your first mistake." Unless freezers are judiciously used, they can be a big drain on your money. They can also cause serious wastage of food, because so many people throw food items in the freezer and then forget about them until they suffer freezer burn and have to be thrown out.

At the beginning of this book, we assured you that the authors have made all the food storage mistakes that are possible to make, so you won't have to make them. This goes double for the way we've used our freezer. We bought an upright freezer because it would be easier for us to get things off the shelves rather than out of a deep chest. A chest freezer would have been better, because the chilled air pools in the bottom of the freezer rather than leaking out every time the door is opened. But that was the least of our freezer-related blunders.

As many people do, we stuck our freezer in our basement. This was probably the smartest freezer-related move we made, because temperatures are naturally cooler in basements, and there's no seasonal fluctuation. (People who put their freezers in garages can expect to pay huge seasonal power bills, as the freezer works overtime to keep interior temperatures down during the summer.) There's a downside to putting the freezer in the basement, though. Unless you're young and spry, you may take so many pains to stay out of the basement that food which is stored in your freezer might as well be at the supermarket. Kathy is old, and her knees are decrepit. She bought food for the freezer, having the best of intentions that the food was going to be judiciously used. But the only time she went to the basement was when she put the food inside the freezer. Somehow, she never remembered to take it out.

Today, our freezer is full. This is another good thing, because electricity bills are much cheaper when the freezer is on the full side than when there are dead spots of air. But the food in our freezer is food in name only, because for several years the only usable items in our freezer have been the bottles of freezer jam that are in the freezer door, and the turkeys we buy every autumn when prices are low. The turkeys are too big to be forgotten, so we actually use them. But everything else in our freezer with the exception of the freezer jam was purchased during the Dark Ages, and is no longer fit for human consumption.

Here lies the problem with frozen food: It just isn't permanent. Freezer shelf-lives depend on the item being stored (see Chapter 8 for a handy table that will give you rough estimates), but there's precious little of anything that will last more than one year in a freezer. And that's even if you do everything else right.

Here, for your edification, are the Seven Commandments of Cold Storage. Engrave them in stone, because if you plan on freezing food, or if you just want to purchase an extra refrigerator to serve as a family root cellar, these things will make the difference between success and failure.

I.

**THOU SHALT LOCATE
THY FREEZER OR
SPARE REFRIGERATOR
FORTUITOUSLY.**

Freezers and refrigerators are extremely susceptible to the surrounding temperature. Putting a freezer or even a refrigerator in a spot where the temperature changes from season to season will cost you many dollars in electricity bills, to say nothing of wearing out the motor years earlier than it would wear out if you tucked the unit away from temperature fluctuations. If you have a basement, that's where the extra freezer or refrigerator belongs—far away from the heat-generating washer, dryer, furnace, and water heater, and away from nearby windows that might cast sunlight on the appliance. If you don't have a basement, put the unit in some part of the house that is away from direct sun, and that is protected by your home air-conditioning systems. If the only place you have for your freezer is a porch or unattached garage, do not even think of purchasing a freezer.

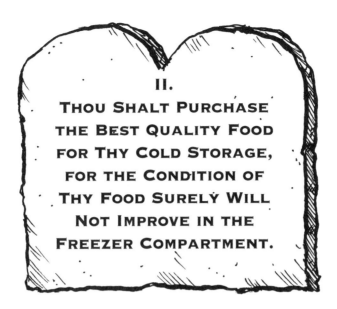

II.

THOU SHALT PURCHASE THE BEST QUALITY FOOD FOR THY COLD STORAGE, FOR THE CONDITION OF THY FOOD SURELY WILL NOT IMPROVE IN THE FREEZER COMPARTMENT.

Although you want the food you take out of the refrigerator or freezer to be just as fresh as the food you put there, it's a sad fact that no means of preserving (with the possible exception of dehydration) will keep your food from deteriorating in quality. Foods that have been subjected to cold storage are particularly susceptible to deterioration. If there's a soft spot in a piece of fruit when you stick it in cold storage, that soft spot will still be there after storage—only softer and mushier and even less appetizing than before. In fact, with apologies to Donny Osmond, "One bad apple *does* spoil the whole bunch, girl." The unseen moldy spot on a single tangerine can cause the contents of the whole refrigerator compartment to go bad. Thus you should buy only top-quality items for your freezer or refrigerator storage, and you should inspect each item before you put it in the refrigerator or freezer to make certain it wasn't damaged on the way home. Meats should be trimmed of their fat, and everything else should be in tip-top condition. Then, allowing for the normal deterioration caused by the freezing process, the food will be appetizing and healthful when you take it out of cold storage for your family. Perhaps not as perfect as it was when you put it in, mind you, but nonetheless acceptable.

III.

**THOU SHALT WRAP EACH
ITEM IN THY FREEZER
AS CAREFULLY AS IF
THOU WERT ENTERED
IN A FREEZER
WRAP CONTEST.**

This information is so important that we have a whole section, "Wrap Session," devoted to it below. Suffice it to say that an item that has been properly wrapped can last more than twice as long as one that was just tucked into the freezer the way it came from the supermarket. You've already invested money in a freezer—now invest just a little effort in properly preparing the food you entomb there. You wouldn't want your neighborhood cryogenics lab to freeze you any old way and hope to thaw you later, would you? No, you'd make sure you went to a cryogenics lab that would take the best possible care of you, so that when you were unfrozen you'd be as fresh and chipper as you were the day you were put into cold storage. The least you can do is to show the same consideration to your filets mignon.

Wasted space means lost money. If you're already going to the expense of buying and operating a freezer, don't make it any more expensive by allowing good freezer space to go to waste. If you don't have any food to put in the freezer, leave it unplugged until you get the food. As you're filling the freezer, it's better to stuff the empty spots with bags of ice or wadded-up newspapers than to leave all that dead space. Newspapers and ice cubes conduct the cold; empty space doesn't. It may look silly for you to have a freezer that's filled with three turkeys, ten pounds of butter, and a wadded-up Sunday newspaper, but it's somewhat more economical than if you had the turkey and the butter without the comics section. Be careful not to overfill your freezer, though. Look in the text below for advice on how to fill your freezer—and how full to fill it.

V.

THOU SHALT KNOW THE CONTENTS OF THY FREEZER AS SURELY AS THOU KNOWEST THY CHILDREN'S NAMES.

You may be one of those people who is so aware of time that he doesn't need to wear a watch, or so cognizant of your children's schedules that you never even look at a calendar. But a refrigerator/freezer that is stored in your basement isn't going to remind you of the passage of hours by cueing you with a setting sun, or remind you what day it is with such subtle hints as weekends or television shows. Indeed, unless you have some sort of continual reminder that your freezer exists, and what's in that freezer, you're going to forget about it just long enough for those expensive tenderloins to turn into cat food. It doesn't matter how you keep your inventory. One way might be to put an erasable board on the refrigerator in your kitchen, listing everything in the freezer and the date by which it should come out. But whatever way you choose, do something. You can afford to keep your sock drawer unorganized, and you don't have to have your spices in alphabetical order, but the contents of your freezer should be rigorously accounted for. Otherwise, you might as well save your money and give the unit to Goodwill.

VI.

THOU SHALT USE THE FOOD IN THY FREEZER BEFORE THE EXPIRATION DATE, THUS AVOIDING THE DREADED FREEZER BURN.

It's not enough to know what's in your refrigerator/freezer. You also have to make use of it. The shelf life of refrigerated and frozen foods is not infinite, and is in fact considerably shorter than the shelf life of foods that have been processed in other ways. You may find yourself cooking a turkey in July in order to use a particular food item before it goes bad, but once you get a little practice you'll be able to gauge how long specific foods will last in your particular freezer after being wrapped by your particular hands. When that happens, you can take advantage of sales on such exotic items as frozen berries, such household staples as butter, or such seasonally inexpensive foods as that ever-popular turkey.

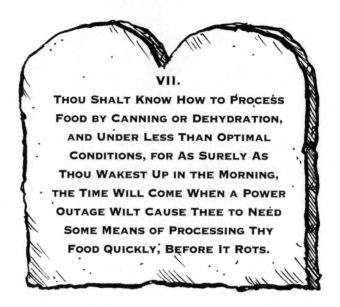

VII.

THOU SHALT KNOW HOW TO PROCESS FOOD BY CANNING OR DEHYDRATION, AND UNDER LESS THAN OPTIMAL CONDITIONS, FOR AS SURELY AS THOU WAKEST UP IN THE MORNING, THE TIME WILL COME WHEN A POWER OUTAGE WILT CAUSE THEE TO NEED SOME MEANS OF PROCESSING THY FOOD QUICKLY, BEFORE IT ROTS.

Picture this: You've won the Omaha Steak Sweepstakes, and your freezer is full to the brim with enough cut-'em-with-a-fork steaks to choke a convention of the Cattlemen's Association. Then the power goes out—and stays out. Even though Omaha Steaks are packaged so well that they'll keep for a couple of years under ordinary conditions, everything thaws. You have three choices: Hold a big barbecue and feed the neighborhood, wait a few days and feed the neighbors' cats, or find some way to bottle or dry that meat without electricity. Option three is your best bet. Beef jerky may never be "fork tender," but it's a snack that will keep your family alive. Perhaps Dian Thomas, author of *Roughing It Easy* and other books of that ilk, will one day turn her attention to *Processing It Easy*. Until she does, you're on your own. Find a way to turn those steaks into jerky or some variety of "bottled surprise," so all that expensive protein does-n't wind up down the drain. (And if you're a sieger, look in Chapter 9 for a source of gas-powered freezers and canners that are designed to be used over wood-burning fires.)

To Freeze, or Not To Freeze

The Seven Commandments of Cold Storage should have awakened you to the pitfalls of refrigeration and freezing. If after studying the commandments you haven't been scared away from cold storage, the first thing you need to do is to decide whether you'd get more use out of a freezer or a second refrigerator.

If your family is heavily carnivorous, your hands-down choice should be a freezer. Such varied meats as roast beef and Swiss steak can be bottled, but your family will probably prefer the taste of "fresh" meat—or at least meat that has been so recently thawed that it appears to be fresh. For a carnivore, nothing takes the place of seared animal flesh. Whether that animal is beef or venison or something else, a freezer is what will guarantee your family has a year-round source of animal protein.

If your family isn't heavily carnivorous, the choice isn't so clear-cut. You may have to do a little detective work to figure out whether a second refrigerator or a freezer will work better for you. Many families subsist heavily on frozen vegetables. Others are cheese and dairy eaters. Others rely on items from the root cellar. All these things make a difference in deciding whether to go for a second refrigerator or a full-sized freezer unit.

If you live in a family of dairy eaters, you may not be pleased with what freezing does to cheese. Cheese can be frozen, if you're not interested in shredding it or melting it afterwards. Freezing changes the texture of cheese so that your old recipes

Advice for Carnivores

Many people who subsist on vegetables and grains are so vocal in their preferences that carnivores are starting to feel guilty that they eat meat. There's no doubt that Americans have consumed too much meat in past decades, but every human body is different. It's not a matter of virtue: Some people's bodies are able to subsist on little or no animal protein; others aren't. As you plan your food storage, try to determine how much meat your family needs versus how much they actually want. (This may vary from one family member to another.) Then store your food according to what each member of your family needs rather than what is politically correct or nutritionally trendy. (In fact, the most recent theory is that the carbohydrate gurus were wrong, and that we should be eating more protein and fewer carbohydrates—but that could change tomorrow.)

may not work if the cheese has been frozen. (Before you freeze large quantities of cheese, freeze a small amount of each variety and then use it in a favorite recipe to determine if the results will be acceptable. You may find you'd rather not eat cheese at all than to eat cheese that has a funny texture.)

Even though cheese doesn't freeze particularly well, an unopened block of cheddar has a shelf expectancy of at least six months in the refrigerator. Other hard cheeses may last even longer. Containers of yogurt are often good for months after the expiration date, if the packaging is unbroken. Butter lasts for months in the refrigerator, but this is one dairy product that can be frozen indefinitely without any deterioration in the quality. If your family consumes a large quantity of dairy products, a spare refrigerator may work better than a freezer for you.

A spare refrigerator may also benefit people who use a lot of onions, potatoes, carrots, and apples. These things keep for months in cold storage if they've been stored properly. After all, the apples you eat in July were part of last September's crop. The most important thing about storing root vegetables is that they give off gases in storage that may affect their shelf life. Although they aren't root vegetables, apples are particularly bad about this. They give off gases that cause other fruits and vegetables to ripen more quickly and then deteriorate, thus greatly reducing their refrigerator longevity.

Oils are another thing that are helped by refrigeration. This may be a boon and a blessing for people who find they'd need a whole lot more oil eating under food storage situations than they could ordinarily consume in the course of the year. The authors of this book eat a low-fat diet, and during the course of a normal year we go through about three bottles of mayonnaise—a good portion of which is consumed during artichoke season. But when Kathy recently looked in the food storage area, she realized she had acquired more than a hundred cans of tuna, with another fifty cans of assorted chopped meats that would be used in chicken, turkey, or ham salads. Three bottles of mayonnaise wouldn't begin to make all those sandwiches, assuming we could eat that many sandwiches without dying from appetite fatigue. Kathy realized she was going to have to start storing a much higher amount of oils than the non-emergency year's supply. Having a second refrigerator would help make sure the oils would survive long enough to be consumed. Creamed honey should also be stored in the refrigerator, as Kathy learned several years after storing a case of it in the basement. If you have a lot of oils and creamed honey, a refrigerator may be the best bet for you.

Later in this section we're going to give you a list of things that freeze well, along with a primer on how to put them in the freezer so they'll keep longer. But first, here's a list of things that don't do so well in the freezer. (You didn't really *think* you could freeze lettuce, did you?) This list may contain no surprises, but it may help you choose which method of cold storage best meets your family's needs:

➥ (Foods that don't freeze well include any food with a high water content. Before you freeze a quantity of any of these, experiment with small amounts to see if the deterioration in texture or taste is acceptable to your family.)

- *apples, whole*—can be stored in refrigerator for long periods

- avocados—only people with no taste buds think guacamole can be frozen; others realize there's absolutely no way to preserve an avocado for long-term storage. But for those who insist on trying, you will find instructions later in the chapter

- *carrots, whole*—can be stored in refrigerator for long periods

- *cheese, blocks*—can be stored, unopened, in refrigerator for long periods

- cheese, cottage

- cooked egg white

- cream, whipped—can be whipped and then frozen in dollops for later use, but not suitable for long-term storage

- cream pies

- cucumbers

- custards

- egg yolk

- egg, whole—see text below for instructions to freeze eggs

- gravy

- green onions

- *honey*—can be stored in refrigerator for long periods

- lettuce—resists all attempts to preserve it

- *mayonnaise*—can be stored, unopened, in refrigerator for long periods

- milk—skim milk can be frozen, but the texture changes to the point that you might as well just buy the powdered stuff.

- milk sauces

- mushrooms, raw—but fresh mushrooms can be canned or dried, and sautéed ones can be frozen

- *onions*—can be stored in refrigerator for long periods

- *oils*—don't freeze, but keep indefinitely in the refrigerator

- *potatoes*—can be stored in refrigerator for long periods

- radishes

- sour cream

- squash, whole

- tomatoes, whole—need you ask?

- *yogurt*—can be stored, unopened, in refrigerator for longer than you might think

We've marked in italics the products on the above list that don't do well in the freezer, but that can be refrigerated for long periods. That's an impressive array of foods, but the list isn't at all complete. If you'll do a little experimenting on your own, you'll find that some of the foods you eat on a regular basis will last indefinitely in your refrigerator. (The operative word here is *your* refrigerator, because not all refrigerators are created equal. Different families use different temperature settings, or open the refrigerator door more or less frequently, or wrap their food differently, or do any number of things that may increase or decrease the shelf life of refrigerated food.)

In our house, we've found that the particular brand of flour tortillas we buy will last for months if kept unopened in the refrigerator. We also use a brand of shredded potatoes that claim to have a shelf life of only a week or two, but that actually last for months on end without any deterioration in quality. Needless to say, brown rice lasts for considerably longer if it's refrigerated than it does when it's sitting on your kitchen shelf, and

we're working on a large bottle of olive oil that's been in the refrigerator for nearly two years. If similar items are big staples in your family's diet, perhaps a storage refrigerator would fill your needs better than a freezer.

If you choose to use a second refrigerator rather than purchasing a freezer, look in Chapter 8 for information on storing foods in the refrigerator for long periods. Otherwise, be guided by common sense. A storage refrigerator shouldn't be a common household refrigerator that the kiddies will search through when they're hungry. If you store apples in that refrigerator, for example, rotate a few to your regular refrigerator so they'll be on hand for snacking. A storage refrigerator should be opened as seldom as possible, so you may want to allow access only to adults—or at least to the family members who are responsible for preparing meals. And remember to follow those Seven Commandments of Cold Storage, paying particular attention to numbers five and six. If you don't know what's in your refrigerator, and approximately how much longer those things are going to last, your cold storage isn't going to do you a bit of good.

After looking at the above information, you may decide that a freezer—not a second refrigerator—is exactly what you're looking for. If that's the case, the rest of this section is for you.

Choosing a Freezer

There are two different kinds of freezers, and they have entirely different functions. One of them, the *chest freezer*, is better for your food but is a pain in the neck (or back) to use. The other one, the *upright freezer*, is as convenient as your friendly refrigerator—but it doesn't do great things for the food you put in it.

You've seen chest freezers. They're big and clunky boxes that open from the top. When you want to remove one thing from a chest freezer, it's invariably the thing that is hidden on the bottom. That means you almost have to crawl into the freezer to remove everything from chest until you find what you're looking for—then you have to put everything back in its proper place.

Chest freezers work on the gravity principle. Cold air is heavier than unrefrigerated air. When you open a chest freezer, the cold air pools at the bottom. This means you can open and close that freezer door without causing a major temperature change in the freezer compartment. This saves money, because you're not constantly having to bring back down the temperature of your freezer to the temperature you want. But it also saves your food. Because there's not a lot of air circulation in the chest compartment, humidity isn't brought in from the outside when the freezer door opens. Humid air dries out frozen food, causing freezer burn that makes food inedible. Protected from fluctuations of temperature and humidity, food that is kept in a chest freezer should keep longer than food that is held in an upright unit.

After reading all those advantages, you'd think nobody in his right mind would buy an upright freezer. On the contrary, it's upright freezers that most consumers prefer. Upright freezers take up less floorspace than the chest models, but floorspace is the least of it. What consumers like is the convenience of a freezer that has shelves, just like a regular refrigerator. You don't have to bend over and root through a hundred assorted packages to find your pound of frozen chicken livers. Instead, you can organize your freezer shelves just as you might organize the things in your refrigerator—keeping things in the same place so you'll know exactly where to look when you open the door.

Speaking of doors, the door is the Achilles' heel of the upright freezer. The door opens from the side, just like doors in a basic refrigerator. But gravity is still gravity, and as soon as the door is open, the heavy air from the freezer will drop to the bottom and cool the feet of whoever opened the door. The cold air that escapes the freezer is replaced by warm and humid air from outside the freezer. Every time your frozen food is exposed to this warm and humid air, the shelf life of those precious packages decreases. And needless to say, every time that freezer door opens, your freezer is going to consume vast quantities of precious and expensive electricity as it valiantly struggles to cool the warm air that has been introduced into the freezer compartment.

Before you choose a freezer, think. Will you go for efficiency, or convenience? Convenience will probably win out—but you can't say we didn't warn you.

Once you've decided to go against all logic and buy that upright freezer, the next thing you'll need to determine is what size freezer to purchase. This requires a little bit of elementary math. *Keeping Food Fresh*, a nifty book we'll tell you about in Chapter 9, recommends that you allow five cubic feet of space for every person in your family, plus an additional five cubic feet of total extra space if you're planning on using the unit for food storage purposes. (And what other purpose would you have in buying a freezer?) If you have a family of twelve, face it—you're not going to find a freezer that's as large as the book recommends. But if you have a family of two, you may not want to spring for a freezer that holds twenty cubic feet of food.

> ### Freezer Space
>
> • 5 cubic feet per person
> • 5 additional cubic feet of total space
>
> For a family of four:
>
> 4 x 5 cubic feet = 20 cubic feet
> + 5 additional cubic feet
> = 25 cubic feet

After you decide how many cubic feet you want, you need to do a little research. Check out *Consumer Reports* to see which freezers work best, or take the lazy way out and do your research at the appliance store. Appliances that are sold in the United States must have a label that shows how much it will cost to operate the unit. There can be significant differences in power usage, so read the tag before you make your purchase.

Once you buy your freezer, read the Seven Commandments of Cold Storage to determine where to put it. If you follow the first commandment, Thou Shalt Locate Thy Freezer or Spare Refrigerator Fortuitously, you'll be on your way to a good experience.

Wrap Session

If you make your beds with military corners or wrap your Christmas presents with scientific precision, you have an advantage over the rest of the world as far as successful freezing is concerned. That's because in the art of freezing, packaging is everything. If you're ever tempted to doubt this, order a steak from Omaha Steaks. The Omaha

Steak people are the people to imitate as far as freezing is concerned, because they do everything right. As you'll see from this photograph, each piece of meat is individually wrapped in a way so that the only thing inside the wrapping is meat. Air is the biggest enemy of frozen food, and the Omaha Steak people have found a way to make such a tight seal around each individual steak that there isn't any way the meat can be contaminated by air. The steaks in this photograph were recently found in the back of the authors' miserable freezer. They were at least two years old at the time this photograph was taken, and perhaps considerably older than that—but they tasted like they had been packaged yesterday. Considering that steaks normally keep no longer than a year in the freezer, you've got to concede that the Omaha Steak people are doing something right.

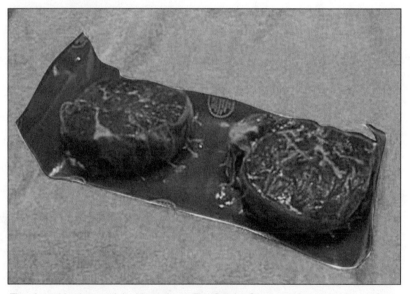

There's nothing but steak in this package. The Omaha Steak people are masters at freezing, and their attention to detail pays off big in the shelf-life of their products.

Unfortunately, you and I don't have access to whatever machine the Omaha Steak people use to wrap each individual item that leaves their processing plant. But the wrapping job you do will make the difference between whether your own pot roast survives six months or a year in your freezer—and if you're rotating your food the way you should be rotating it, a year in the freezer should be good enough.

There isn't just one way to wrap food for freezing. You may have grown up in a family where white freezer paper was used to wrap everything, and there's nothing wrong with that. But this is a new generation, and as long as we have space-age materials available to us, we might as well use them. Don't get locked into one means of wrapping your frozen food. Experiment with different materials and processes until you decide what works best for the food you're storing in your own freezer.

Choosing Your Packaging

No matter how you prepare your food for freezing, your packaging should always meet these criteria:

- Your packages should be easy to seal—and by "seal" we mean to keep the air out. Some materials are more porous than others. Remember: Air is the enemy. Do what you can to keep air away from your food.

- Your packages should be waterproof. There are three excellent reasons for this. First, it guarantees that the contents of your package will stay in your package, despite any surprise power outages. During a power outage, things are liable to leak. Leaking foods may contain bacteria that could contaminate packages of food that remain frozen, and you don't want that to happen. Second, if your food has been securely sealed in waterproof packaging, cold will be trapped in the package and ice crystals will stay intact longer. This will help save some or all of your valuable food. Last, but not least, using waterproof packaging prevents moisture from evaporating out of your foods. Evaporated moisture is the main cause of freezer burn, which is the bane of your freezer's existence. This is why food that is packaged in those handy paper milk cartons doesn't exactly taste garden fresh when it's thawed six months later.

> **Packages should be:**
>
> ❑ easy to seal
>
> ❑ waterproof
>
> ❑ able to withstand freezing
>
> ❑ carefully labeled

- Your packages should be made of materials that can withstand freezing temperatures without cracking or becoming brittle. There are plastics that work perfectly well at room temperature, but that develop hairline cracks when they're exposed to below-zero conditions. Hairline cracks allow air in and moisture out. That's a recipe for freezer burn.

- Your packages should be carefully labeled, with both the name of the item and the date it was put in the freezer. You can't rotate food if you don't know what it is and when it was produced. If you're not willing to label your food, save yourself a lot of money and don't buy a freezer.

Although you may think it's hard to find packaging that will meet all the above criteria, there are really a lot of options you'll have when determining how to package your food for freezing. Here's a sample of some of the varieties that are available to you:

❑ 1. Rigid containers have the advantage of stacking well in a freezer, if they are flat on both the top and bottom. Avoid round containers, because they waste space. Straight-sided containers have an additional advantage because the frozen contents can be removed without being thawed first. Some of the rigid containers available for freezing include the following, but before you invest heavily in any one method, make sure it works in your freezer, on the food you eat, with the packaging methods you use:

  - Freezer-proof glass. (Canning jars are suitable for the freezer, as long as the food isn't packed in liquid.)

  - Freezer-safe plastic. Even though plastic is specifically designed for the freezer, air may still penetrate tiny holes in the plastic.

  - Metal

  - Cardboard, heavily waxed to make it less porous

❑ 2. Non-rigid containers have the advantage that it's easier to keep air away from your food. You can put chili in a plastic freezer bag, squeeze all the air out, and seal it without worrying that the expanding chili will break the bag—unless you've forgotten to leave room for expansion. There are nifty items on the market that will suck the air out of porous plastic bags and then seal the bags, assuring a longer shelf-life for your food. Non-rigid containers also take up less shelf space when they aren't being used. The major disadvantage of non-rigid containers is that they take the shape of the food and are thus harder to stack in your freezer. You can get around this by putting your non-rigid containers in cardboard boxes that will provide the necessary rigidity. Some of the items used to wrap food for freezing include:

- Freezer bags (can be used for liquid as well as dry pack)
- Freezer wrap (plastic or plastic-laminated paper)
- Freezer grade aluminum foil
- Polyethylene

How to Prepare Your Food

Once you've decided what kind of material to use to package your food, it's time to prepare that food for packaging. The following charts will help you decide how to prepare some foods before putting them in the freezer. Some foods should be packed in liquid or syrup. Some foods are better off packed dry. Some should be blanched first. (We have detailed blanching instructions in both the freezing table and the dehydrating section, later in this chapter.) Foods will have a different shelf life—and a different taste—depending on the way they're prepared to go in the freezer. The more care you take with the food that goes in, the better your food will taste when you put it on the table for your family to eat.

If you're packing fruit in the freezer, there are numerous ways the chart will tell you how to process it. Here they are, in all their excruciating detail. (You may fall asleep while you're reading this, but it'll help you out when you do your first freezing project.)

- Some fruits need to be protected from color and flavor loss by being dipped in ascorbic acid or citric acid. You can add one teaspoon of crystalline or powdered ascorbic acid or citric (found in drugstores) to a little bit of water and dip the fruit in it. The lazy way out is by dipping the fruit in lemon juice, but this doesn't work quite as well as the professional stuff.

- Some people recommend steaming fruit before you pack it for freezing, as a way to control darkening. This results in cooked fruit rather than raw fruit, so you'll have to decide what kind of fruit you want to come out of the freezer before you decide how you're going to put your fruit into the freezer.

- A "sugar pack" is made by sprinkling sugar over the fruit and then stirring the whole mess together—very, *very* gently. The stirring pulls juice out of the fruit, which mixes with the sugar to make a sweet juice.

- An "unsweetened pack" is made by putting the fruit into containers and freezing it without adding any sugar or liquid.

- A "tray pack" involves freezing small fruits such as blueberries or blackberries on a cookie sheet and then packing the frozen berries into containers.

- A "syrup pack" is made by packaging the fruit with syrup. Syrups that are used in freezing aren't the same as syrups used in canning. For one thing, the freezing syrups don't need to be heated to the boiling point! To make freezing syrup, choose the type that suits your family's tastes. Then simply dissolve the sugar in the water. You can use hot or cold water, although if the water is hot you might as well simmer it to get rid of all those sugar crystals. If you heat the water, chill it in the refrigerator afterwards so the hot water won't damage the fragile fruit.

Freezing Syrup

Type of Syrup	Cups Water	Cups Sugar	=Cups Syrup
Very Thin	4	1 ½	4 ½
Thin	4	2	5
Medium	4	3	5 ½
Thick	4	4 ¾	6 ½
Very Thick	4	7	7 ¾

Now that you know how to make your syrup, here's a table of fruits and vegetables you may want to freeze, together with options for doing so (if nothing appears in the third column, food can be frozen as prepared):

Preparing Fruits and Vegetables for the Freezer

Fruit/Vegetable	Preparation	Freezing/Using
Apples	Use only crisp and firm fruit. During preparation, place slices in a salt brine made from 2 tablespoons of salt added to a gallon of water. Then drain.	Use sugar, syrup, or unsweetened pack. Dip in an ascorbic acid solution, if desired, to reduce browning during storage.
Applesauce	Wash, core, and slice apples, and remove peels if desired. Cook until tender in ⅓ cup of water for each quart of slices. Cool and strain until desired thickness is achieved. Sweeten to taste.	
Apricots	Use only firm, ripe, uniformly colored fruit. Wash, then dip in boiling water for 15–25 seconds to loosen skins. Peel, halve, remove pits, and then slice if desired.	Use syrup or sugar pack. Dip in an ascorbic acid solution, if desired, to reduce browning during storage.
Asparagus	Select young stalks. Wash and remove tough segments. Leave whole or cut into 1–2 inch lengths. Blanch 2–4 minutes, then cool.	
Avocados	Select avocados that are soft and free from rind blemishes. Peel, halve, and remove pit. Mash or puree the avocados before freezing.	Pack one quart of puree with one cup sugar if you plan to use it in desserts such as ice cream or milk shakes. Otherwise, use an unsweetened pack.

Fruit/Vegetable	Preparation	Freezing/Using
Beans	Select young, tender, stringless beans of the green, snap, or wax varieties. Wash, remove tips, and cut lengthwise or into slices. Blanch 3 minutes, then cool.	
Beet Greens	See Spinach. Blanch for 2–3 minutes.	
Beets	Select young, tender, smaller beets. Wash, remove tops, and sort by size. Cook until tender, 25–50 minutes, depending on size. Cool. Peel beets and then slice or dice them.	
Blackberries	Select firm, ripe berries with glossy skins. Wash and drain.	Use tray, sugar, or syrup pack.
Blueberries	Select ripe berries with soft skins. Wash and drain. Optionally, steam for one minute and then cool to tenderize skin.	Use tray, sugar, or syrup pack.
Boysenberries	See Blackberries.	
Broccoli	Select smaller, dark-green heads. Wash and remove leaves and woody stem ends. To remove insects, soak for 30 minutes in a brine of 1 gallon water and 4 teaspoons salt. Rinse and drain. Cut through stalks lengthwise to produce heads about an inch in diameter. Blanch for 3 minutes, or steam blanch for 5 minutes. Cool.	Pack heads and stems alternately in the same container.

Fruit/Vegetable	Preparation	Freezing/Using
Brussels Sprouts	Select smaller, green, firm heads. Wash and remove leaves and stems. If insects are present, soak for 30 minutes in a brine of 1 gallon water and 4 teaspoons salt. Rinse and drain. Blanch 3–5 minutes, depending on size of heads. Cool.	
Cantaloupe	Select firm, ripe, well-colored melons. Halve, remove seeds, and peel. Cut into slices or cubes.	Use syrup pack.
Carrots	Select young, tender carrots. Wash, remove tops, and peel or scrape. Dice or slice, or leave smaller pieces whole. Blanch 2 minutes for slices or 5 minutes for small, whole carrots. Cool.	
Cauliflower	Select firm, smaller, white heads. Wash, trim, and cut into one-inch pieces. If insects are present, soak for 30 minutes in a brine of 1 gallon water and 4 teaspoons salt. Blanch 3 minutes. Cool.	
Cherries (Sour)	Select fruit that is ripe and well colored. Wash, drain, remove stems and pits.	Use tray, syrup, or sugar pack.
Cherries (Sweet)	Select fruit that is ripe and well colored. Wash, drain, and remove stems. Optionally, remove pits.	Use tray or syrup pack. Dip in an ascorbic acid, solution if desired, to reduce browning during storage.

Fruit/Vegetable	Preparation	Freezing/Using
Corn (Cob)	Select young, tender ears. Husk, remove silk, then wash and trim. Blanch 7–11 minutes, based on size of ears. Drain and cool.	Wrap each ear separately, and then combine meal-sized portions in large freezer bags.
Corn (Kernel)	Select young, tender ears. Husk, remove silk, then wash and trim. Blanch 4–5 minutes, based on size of ears. Drain and cool. Cut kernels from cob and package.	
Crookneck Squash	See Zucchini.	
Currants	Select ripe, well-colored fruit. Wash and remove stems.	Use tray, sugar, or syrup pack.
Figs	Select soft, ripe fruit. Wash and remove stems. Peel if desired. Slice or leave whole.	Use tray or syrup pack. Optionally, dip in an ascorbic acid solution to reduce browning.
Gooseberries	Select slightly under-ripe fruit for jelly, otherwise, use ripe fruit. Wash and remove stems and blossoms.	Use tray or syrup pack.
Grapefruit	Select ripe fruit with no soft spots. Remove all membranes and seeds, and slice if desired.	Pack in syrup or water. Optionally, dip in an ascorbic acid solution to reduce browning.
Huckleberries	See Blueberries.	
Kale	See Spinach. Blanch for 2–3 minutes.	
Loganberries	See Blackberries.	

Fruit/Vegetable	Preparation	Freezing/Using
Melons	See Cantaloupe.	
Mushrooms	Select small, edible mushrooms free from spots. Wash, and remove base of stem. Slice larger mushrooms into quarters. Blanch 3–5 minutes in a solution of one quart water and 3 teaspoons lemon juice. Optionally, slice mushrooms into ¼-inch pieces and sauté in butter until almost done. Cool.	
Mustard Greens	See Spinach. Blanch for 2–3 minutes.	
Nectarines	Select ripe, well-colored fruit. Wash and pit. Remove peels if desired. Cut into halves, quarters, or slices.	Pack in syrup, orange juice, or water. Optionally, dip in an ascorbic acid solution to reduce browning.
Onions	Select fully mature onions. Peel, wash, section, and then chop. Optionally, blanch for 1–2 minutes. Cool.	
Oranges	See Grapefruit.	
Peaches	Select ripe fruit with no green color in the skin. Wash, peel, and pit. Cut into quarters or slices if desired.	Pack in sugar, syrup, orange juice, or water. Optionally, dip in an ascorbic acid solution to reduce browning.
Pears	Select ripe and firm fruit. Wash, peel, and remove cores. Cut into quarters or halves. Heat in boiling syrup for 1–2 minutes. Drain and cool.	Pack in syrup. Optionally, dip in an ascorbic acid solution to reduce browning.

Fruit/Vegetable	Preparation	Freezing/Using
Peas (in Pod)	Select young, tender pods. Wash, and remove stems and strings. Blanch 1–2 minutes, based on size of pods. Cool.	
Peas (Shelled)	Select young, tender pods. Remove peas from pod. Blanch 1–2 minutes. Cool.	
Peppers (Chili)	Select firm, smooth peppers. Wash and dry, then make a small slit in each pepper for escaping steam. Broil for 6–8 minutes to loosen skin. Remove peel, seeds, and stems. Wear rubber gloves to protect hands.	
Peppers (Sweet)	Select crisp red or green peppers. Wash, remove seeds and stem. Dice, or cut into halves or slices. For easier packaging, blanch 2–3 minutes.	
Plums	Select ripe, firm fruit. Wash. Optionally, cut into halves or quarters.	Use tray or syrup pack. Optionally, dip in an ascorbic acid solution.
Potatoes (Fries)	Wash, peel, and remove eyes and bruised portions. Cut into fry-sized strips. Fry in deep fat until light brown. Drain and cool.	To serve, bake in a 400° F. oven for 10–20 minutes.
Potatoes (Sweet or Yams)	Select medium to large potatoes. Wash and peel, and then mash, slice, or cut in half. To avoid browning, dip for 5 seconds in a brine of 1 quart water and ½ cup lemon juice.	Before freezing mashed potatoes, add 2 table-spoons orange or lemon juice to each quart of potatoes.

Fruit/Vegetable	Preparation	Freezing/Using
Potatoes (Red or White)	Wash, peel, and remove eyes and bruised portions. Cut into 2-inch cubes and blanch for 5 minutes. Cool.	
Prunes	See Plums.	
Pumpkin	Select well-ripened, tender pumpkins that are not stringy. Wash, dry, remove seeds, and cut into uniform pieces. Bake or steam until tender. Cool. Remove rind and put pulp through a sieve or blender.	
Raspberries	Select ripe, juicy berries. Wash and drain.	Use tray, sugar, or syrup pack.
Rhubarb	Select firm, well-colored stalks. Wash, trim, and cut into 1–2-inch pieces.	Use unsweetened or syrup pack.
Rutabaga	See Turnips.	
Spinach	Select young, tender leaves. Remove tough stems, then wash. Blanch 1–2 minutes. Cool.	
Strawberries	Select firm, red, ripe berries. Wash, drain, and remove.	Use tray, sugar, or syrup pack.
Summer Squash	See Zucchini.	
Swiss Chard	See Spinach. Blanch for 3–4 minutes.	
Tomatoes	Select ripe tomatoes free from blemishes. Wash, peel, remove stems, and quarter. Cook until tender. Stew or puree for best results.	

Fruit/Vegetable	Preparation	Freezing/Using
Turnip Greens	See Spinach. Blanch for 2–3 minutes.	
Turnips	Select young, tender turnips. Wash, peel, and cut into ½-inch cubes. Blanch for 2 minutes, then cool.	
Winter Squash	Select well-ripened squash with hard rinds. Follow instructions for Pumpkin.	
Zucchini	Select young squash with small seeds and tender rind. Wash and slice into 1 ½-inch pieces. Blanch for 6 minutes. Cool.	

Vegetables and fruits are a large part of freezing, but they don't tell the whole story. There are other foods you may be tempted to drop into the old deep freeze. Hints for freezing some of these foods are listed in the table below. In general, it is often a challenge to preserve the taste and texture of these foods by freezing, so some experimentation on your part may be needed.

Preparing Non-Produce Items for the Freezer

Food	Technique
Bacon (Cooked)	Frozen bacon will keep longer if it is cooked first. Slightly undercook an entire package of bacon. Drain on paper towels. When cool, wrap several strips gently in a paper towel, and then place in a freezer bag. To serve, remove strips and reheat in a frying pan or microwave.

Food	Technique
Bacon (Raw)	Wrap in heavy-duty foil or freezer wrap. Thaw completely in the refrigerator before cooking.
Biscuits	See Breads. Thaw by heating in the oven until ready to serve.
Breads	Make baked goods as usual, but do not overcook. Cool, and then package in aluminum foil. Before serving, either thaw at room temperature or bake at approximately 300°–400° F. Experiment with different temperatures and thawing methods until you find the one most acceptable for the product you are freezing. Thawing at room temperature works better for items containing frosting.
Butter	Double wrap packages in plastic or foil to reduce odor absorption. Freeze. Thaw in the refrigerator before using.
Canapé s (Crisp)	Cover bread or toast base with butter to prevent soggy consistency. Prepare and arrange on a single layer in metal pans. Freeze, and then package separately. Place individual packages in shallow, airtight containers. Separate multiple layers with moisture-resistant paper. Thaw at room temperature, and don' t unwrap until ready to serve.
Canapé s (Other)	Prepare and arrange on a single layer in metal pans. Freeze, and then transfer to shallow, airtight containers. Separate multiple layers with moisture-resistant paper. To serve, arrange first on serving trays, and then thaw at room temperature.
Candies	Prepare or purchase, then package for freezing. To serve, keep in packaging and thaw at room temperature. Cracks and other imperfections should disappear as the candy thaws.

Food	Technique
Casseroles	See Stew.
Cheese	Cut into sections no larger than ½ pound. Double wrap in plastic or heavy aluminum foil, and seal airtight. Thaw in the refrigerator for 1–2 days.
Chicken (Pieces)	Remove from packaging, then wash and dry. Remove inedible portions, such as fat and feathers. Optionally, remove the skin. Wrap each piece in plastic wrap, and then place meal-sized portions in plastic bags or freezer wrap. Place the packages away from each other in the freezer (so they will freeze faster), and directly on top of the freezer shelves. Thaw in the refrigerator before use, or use immediately in cooking.
Chicken (Whole)	Remove from packaging, then wash and dry. Remove inedible portions, such as fat and feathers. Optionally, remove the skin. Wrap in freezer paper, aluminum foil, or a freezer bag from which the air has been removed. If the chicken weighs more than 7 pounds, divide it into multiple packages. Place the packages away from each other in the freezer (so they will freeze faster), and directly on top of the freezer shelves. Thaw in the refrigerator before use.
Eggs (White)	Break eggs and remove yolks. Put egg whites in freezer containers without beating. Do not attempt to cook whites before freezing.
Eggs (Whole)	Break eggs into a bowl. Add ⅛ teaspoon salt or sugar for each egg. Beat well, and place into freezer containers.
Eggs (Yolk)	Follow instructions for whole eggs, but remove whites from bowl. Yolks may also be cooked before freezing.

Food	Technique
Fish (Fresh)	Keep fish on ice after catching, and freeze it as soon as possible. Clean fish and remove all scales, entrails, and bones. Wash in cold running water. Cut into serving-size portions. Package each portion in glass or plastic containers, thick freezer wrap, or with a vacuum-sealing machine. Put several individually-wrapped portions into larger freezer bags. For more tender fish, wait 6–8 weeks before consuming.
Flour	Whole-grain flour will not keep for long at room temperature. To freeze it, place it in airtight containers in the freezer. To use the flour, measure out the amount that you need, and let it warm up to room temperature.
Ham	Select whole over sliced, because it will keep longer. If possible, store in a vacuum-sealed package. Otherwise, wrap securely in plastic or freezer wrap. Thaw in the refrigerator before using.
Hors d' oeuvres	See Canapé s.
Ice Cream	Store in the original, unopened packages. The colder the temperature, the longer it will keep.
Macaroni & Cheese	Make as usual, but cool quickly. Freeze in a foil-lined casserole dish, but then remove from the dish and package it. To serve, unwrap, place in an oven-proof dish, and heat in the oven.
Margarine	See Butter. Diet margarine may change texture when frozen, but the flavor should be unaffected.
Meat (Raw, Ground)	Mold meat into burger-sized patties, even if you wish to mold it into another form before cooking. Stack patties on top of each other, separated by a piece of freezer or plastic wrap. Package a meal-size portion into a freezer bag or a wrapped freezer package. You can thaw in the refrigerator, or cook the meat while it is still frozen.

Food	Technique
Meat (Raw, Stew)	Trim to remove fat and connective tissue, then cut into cubes. Wrap a small portion of cubes in plastic wrap or aluminum foil, no more than one layer deep. Seal several packets in a large freezer bag, or in freezer paper. You can thaw in the refrigerator, or cook the meat while it is still frozen.
Meat (Raw, Whole)	Trim off excess fat, and cover sharp bones with aluminum foil to prevent holes in the packaging. Place a piece of freezer or plastic wrap between each piece of meat, so they will not stick together. Package several pieces of meat into a large freezer bag. You can thaw in the refrigerator, or cook the meat while it is still frozen.
Muffins	See Breads.
Pizza	Make as usual, but don't cook. Freeze and then package. To serve, unwrap, place it immediately in the oven, and cook for 15–20 minutes at 450° F.
Ravioli	See Stew.
Sandwiches	Avoid using lettuce, tomatoes, cooked egg whites, jams, jellies, and mayonnaise. Use butter or salad dressing instead. Wrap. Thaw at room temperature for 3–4 hours.
Shrimp	Shrimp that is pink has already been cooked, and is ready to freeze once it has been placed in the appropriate containers.
Soups	Omit potatoes, and use less water if the soup is made from concentrate. Heat and then cool quickly. Package in a freezer container with ample head space. To serve, heat without thawing. Heat cream soups over boiling water, stirring occasionally to keep them smooth.
Spaghetti	See Stew.

Food	Technique
Stew	Reduce fat from recipe, if possible, and substitute other vegetables for potatoes. Slightly undercook the vegetables. Cook, and then cool rapidly. Make sure all meat is covered with sauce. Package in wide-mouth freezer containers, with plenty of head space. Thaw partially in the package, and then transfer to a double boiler.
Turkey (Pieces)	Individually wrap each piece, and then combine meal-sized portions in airtight freezer bags, no larger than 4 pounds in weight. Place the packages away from each other in the freezer (so they will freeze faster), and directly on top of the freezer shelves. Thaw in the refrigerator before use, or use immediately in cooking.
Turkey (Whole, Fresh)	Whole turkeys cannot safely be frozen in a home refrigerator because of their size. Cut them into pieces first, and follow the instructions for turkey pieces.
Turkey (Whole, Frozen)	Transfer whole frozen turkeys to your freezer within one hour from the time they were purchased. Thaw in the refrigerator before use.
Waffles	See Breads. Thaw by placing in the broiler or the toaster oven.
Yeast	Freeze in tightly-wrapped containers for up to six months.
Yogurt	Keep in the original containers or transfer to freezer containers. Flavored yogurt may freeze better, because the fruit and sugar stabilizes the yogurt. Thawed yogurt may taste more acidic. Thaw for three hours at room temperature, or 1–2 days in the refrigerator.

How to Pack Your Containers

No matter what kind of container or freezer wrap you choose, you should pack your food tightly enough to keep air out and water in. But this can be somewhat of a challenge if you're packing foods in liquid, or if you're freezing foods that have a lot of natural liquid in them. Foods that are high in liquid tend to expand when they freeze, so you'll have to take that into account when you're putting foods in a container to go in the freezer.

➡ Now that you've chosen your containers and prepared your food to be packaged away for the freezer, here are some tips that may help you out.

- The most important tip comes first: *Freeze only as much as your family will eat in one meal.* If you're cooking for four, it makes no sense to freeze ground beef in ten-pound blocks. When you're storing food, conservation should be your constant goal—and the best way to conserve frozen food is to freeze meal-sized portions.

- *Food should be cold when it's packed into containers.* Any warm food you put in your freezer will cost you extra money in electricity, as your freezer works overtime to cool the items you're adding to the compartment. In addition, cold packs will preserve the flavor of the food you're freezing. Flavorful food is always a plus.

- *Allow for ample headspace if you're using rigid containers.* Most food that is frozen will expand as it freezes. If you don't allow for this expansion, your glass containers will break and your plastic or metal containers will bulge. At the least, bulging containers are harder to stack in your freezer space. At the other end of the spectrum, all you *don't* want to have to do is clean out your freezer after a glass jar has shattered inside it.

- *Pack your food to minimize freezer space.* Ground beef is a good example to show how creative you can be, because we all know approximately how much ground beef equals one pound. Instead of freezing your ground beef in those clunky blocks, put a pound in a zipper bag that is suitable for the freezer, squeeze out the air, and then roll it flat with a rolling pin. Then seal the bag. Presto! You have a ground beef Frisbee®. Not only does this take up less space in your freezer, but it's also a whole lot easier to thaw. A third advantage is that the rolling pin squeezes out so much extra air that the meat is less likely to develop freezer burn. And of course, those Frisbees® are a lot easier to stack than those irregular blocks. Be creative, and you might be able to come up with ideas that are just as fresh and helpful.

- *Make sure your packages are wrapped securely enough to keep the cold out.* It never hurts to double-wrap anything. If you're wrapping meat, for example, you may want to wrap the meat in plastic wrap, making sure to squeeze out as much air as possible, and then put the wrapped meat in a zippered plastic bag, getting as much air out of *that* as possible. The more barriers there are between air and your food, the longer your food will keep in the freezer. In any case, having a layer of plastic between your individual pork chops will allow easier separation when they're frozen.

- *Make sure your packages are sealed before you put them in the freezer.* This is especially important for those handy zippered plastic bags, which work wonders if they're sealed all the way, and that don't work at all if there's even a tiny gap in the plastic. We've read that one way to make sure the bag is sealed and to force all the air from the bag is to zip it most of the way shut and then zip it the rest of the way when the bag is immersed in water. Needless to say, be careful not to get any water in the bag! From what we've read, the water immersion will force any residual air out of the bag, creating a more freezer-friendly environment. If you're using rigid containers, remove as much air as possible from the container, "burping" the lid if you can to get rid of the last bits of air. You may need to use freezer tape or wax to make the seals on your cardboard containers waterproof. Do what you have to do to keep the liquid in and the air out of your frozen food. And make sure those sealing edges are clean: Food that is trapped on a sealing edge will keep the seal from being air- and water-tight.

- *Label each package with the name of the food and the date it was processed.* You may think it's obvious that the plastic container is full of sliced peaches, but you never know what the contents will look like after they've been sitting in the freezer for a year and a half. If each package is prominently labeled, you won't be serving a 1996 meat loaf to your family in September of 2003.

How to Load Your Freezer

In freezing, there's a rule for everything. You have to prepare your food the right way, and then package it the right way. But even that's not enough. You can't just throw your packaged food in the freezer. There's a science to this as well. If you're going to use the freezer at all, you might as well do what you can to get the best possible results.

Fortunately, the rules for loading the freezer are pretty easy. Read the rules the first time you freeze. The second time you freeze, the information should be second nature.

- If you're going to be putting a large quantity of food into the freezer at once, turn the freezer to its coldest setting the day before. According to the people at Ziploc®, who are in the business of knowing how to freeze foods, most frozen foods should be kept at 0°F. Too cold is better than too warm.

- Don't waste any time between packaging your food and freezing it. Your food will deteriorate in quality if it's left sitting on the counter.

- Add only enough food to a freezer that can freeze in a twenty-four-hour period. This translates to no more than three pounds of unfrozen food to each cubic foot of the freezer's capacity. The longer the food takes to freeze, the more the quality will deteriorate.

- In order to facilitate quicker freezing, separate the packages so air can circulate freely between them. Also, place the new packages directly on the freezer shelves, and not on top of other frozen packages. Once the food is frozen, the packages can be moved and stacked on top of each other.

- Don't underfill the freezer, but don't overfill it either. If a freezer is about 75 percent full, this allows cold air to circulate between the packages. If the freezer is packed, the air can't circulate. If the freezer is too empty, you'll be wasting electricity. When you're first putting food into your freezer, you can fill the dead spaces with loosely crumpled newspapers.

- Place a list of the contents of your freezer somewhere that you can see it often. The front of the freezer may not be the best place for this list, unless you visit the freezer every couple of days. Perhaps the refrigerator is a better place for the list—if you can push aside some of your children's artwork. You may want to consider doing your list on a white board with a marking pen, so you can change the list as foods are taken from or added to your freezer.

Curl Up and Dry

Some foods are well suited for preservation by means of drying. You simply remove all the moisture from the item, and then there is nothing left to spoil. When you are ready to consume the food, you can add water again, or sometimes just eat it the way it is. Dried fruits have become popular in the grocery stores over the past few years, but you can make your own at a fraction of the cost.

In this section we will try to make you experts at drying food. We will show you the basic techniques, provide some hints, and even share some more recipes.

Advantages of Drying Food

The very night we were going to start work on this chapter, we got home from a restaurant to find a message on our answering machine from a good friend who said she had something she wanted us to taste. Kathy was looking for any excuse not to write, so she gladly invited the friend over for a visit.

The friend arrived with a bowl of soup that had been made from dehydrated vegetables and other food storage items. Kathy (who is an obnoxious food snob) could immediately tell from the taste that dehydrated vegetables had been used, but the soup was perfectly acceptable.

But Judy's excitement over the soup was all out of proportion to the fact that it had been made from food storage items. As soon as the soup had been pronounced worthy, Judy pulled out the container of dehydrated mixed vegetables that had been opened just that day, and from which the soup had been made. Judy had written the date of purchase on top of the can. The vegetables had been sitting under her stairwell, forgotten, for more than twenty-four years.

Kathy had been doing enough research on dehydrated foods that she wasn't surprised to learn that the vegetables were still good. But it's one thing to know something from an intellectual standpoint, and quite another to see (or taste) it firsthand. In nearly a quarter of a century, those vegetables hadn't crumbled or faded. Indeed, from the appearance of the brightly colored vegetable bits, the can might just as well have been sealed yesterday.

> **If dehydrated food can be kept from contamination, it will keep indefinitely.**

There you have the advantage of drying food. If dehydrated food can be kept from contamination, it will keep indefinitely. Yes, Judy's dehydrated mixed vegetables had been commercially processed, but she could have gotten similar results by drying her own vegetables and then packaging them with dry-pack canning.

The Incredible Shrinking Foodstuffs

When you learn that twenty-five pounds of onions yield about three pounds of dried onion chips, you see some of the advantages—and disadvantages—of drying. First, dried food is easy to store because it takes so little space. Water is what provides bulk and weight to food; remove the water and what's left is light and compact.

Not all food that has been dehydrated must be rehydrated again. Dried fruits are terrific snacks; indeed, one of Kathy's favorite foods in the world is dehydrated fruit cocktail, "Fruit Galaxy," that's available from several bulk food storage suppliers. But when you're eating that dehydrated food, keep in mind that a small amount of the dried stuff equals a warehouse full of non-dehydrated food. You wouldn't think of sitting down to eat twenty-five pounds of apples, would you? Not unless you were a horse! Nor would you eat an entire pot roast at one sitting. But over the course of a day or two, you could easily eat four pounds of dehydrated apples or devour a package of beef jerky—which is the same thing. When you're dealing with dehydrated food, appearances are deceiving. A slice of dried apple may not have any more calories after it's dehydrated than it did before it was dried, but you can potentially

IT LOOKED SO MUCH SMALLER WHEN IT WAS DEHYDRATED!

consume so many more slices when it's in the dehydrated state that you should always watch what you're eating when you snack on dehydrated food.

Even if you never eat a piece of dehydrated food without rehydrating it first, there are still potential problems. Water is a big one. Before you can eat most dehydrated food, it must be rehydrated. That means you must have enough water on hand to do the rehydrating. During times of extreme emergency, when water is at a premium, you may not be able to spare the water to rehydrate your food unless you've stored extra water for that purpose. Nor will you have enough extra water to satisfy a thirst that has been whetted by eating food that is in dried form. Thus dried foods should never be the only foods in your food storage supplies. They're a terrific supplement, but they shouldn't comprise your entire food storage investment.

Although you're losing water when you dehydrate foods, that's just about all you lose. As we already said, the calories remain the same. Fiber remains the same, too. Minerals may be lost when dehydrated foods are soaked for rehydration (the jury is still out on that), but no minerals are lost in drying.

As for vitamins, it's a mixed bag. Vitamin B remains stable during the drying process. Vitamin A is retained better if vegetables are blanched before they're dried. Vitamin C loss may vary, depending on whether the food was dried quickly and away from the light. Speed and darkness keep the ascorbic acid content high.

As with other means of food storage, the quality of your dried food will depend on the food you started out with. You'll want to choose foods that are at the peak of their freshness, with no bad spots. Don't assume underripe food will ripen as it dries; it won't. Fruit will be no sweeter after it's dried than before, and beef will certainly be no less fatty or more tender. Remember that the moment a fruit or vegetable comes off the plant, it starts losing quality. Don't buy a flat of mushrooms and let them sit around for a couple of days, even in the refrigerator, until you can get around to the dehydration process. Always start out with top-quality food, and that's exactly what you'll end up with.

Choosing a Dehydrator

How you choose to dry food—or even whether you choose to dry food at all—is largely dependent on where you live. Kathy grew up in a climate that was so damp that it was possible to bend potato chips in half, once they'd been exposed to the air for half an hour or so. She had no idea it was humanly possible to dehydrate food, and indeed thought the SunMaid people made raisins by some arcane chemical method that was denied to ordinary citizens. Sort of like baking bread.

When she was nineteen years old, she rode from Phoenix to central Utah with friends who sliced apples before the trip began and put the slices in the rear window of the un-air-conditioned car. Later that day, everyone feasted on dehydrated apples. This was a miracle to someone who'd grown up in the semi-tropics. If Kathy had done the same thing on a trip from New Orleans to Miami, the smell of rotting fruit would have assailed everyone's nostrils within the hour. By the time the car reached Pensacola, the apples would have devolved into fly-infested sludge. Long before the car reached Miami, the flies would have subdued the human occupants and commandeered the vehicle.

Proper dehydration using the sun as your dehydrator calls for several days of temperatures that are approaching 100°F., with low humidity, and no chance of rain. If you live in an area with excessive humidity, you may want to consult your local county extension service before you decide how to dehydrate food, or even *whether* to dehydrate food. Even if dehydration is possible, the food may have to be stored afterwards in some way that will keep the humid air out—perhaps via dry-pack canning in small containers with oxygen absorber packets. (This is a good suggestion even in dry climates, because sealed containers keep out pests.)

If drying foods in the heat of the sun is out of the question in your area, it's possible to dry foods in electric dryers. If you're handy with that sort of thing, you can make your own food dehydrator. Dehydrators are simple mechanisms, with only a few requirements:

- A cabinet that can be shut to keep the bugs out;

- A heat source that can provide a uniform temperature of 140°–160°F.;

- A fan to remove moisture that evaporates from the food that is being dried, along with a venting system to allow that moist air to escape; and

● Shelves that are made of a material that will allow air to freely circulate around the food that is being dehydrated.

Of course, there's another way to get your own food dehydrator, and that is to buy one. There are lots and lots of them on the market. You can even buy dehydrators from your own easy chair by watching them being demonstrated on infomercials. A good dehydrator doesn't have to be expensive. At least, that's what gizmo inventor Ron Popiel says on his television shows.

When you're choosing a food dehydrator, decide how you want to use it. We bought the mother of all food dehydrators years ago. It is so large and unwieldy that Clark has to move it from one place to another. Because of its size, it is almost never used. Our two-person family would have been far better off with a smaller model that could fit on a countertop or inside a cabinet, so we could have dehydrated small amounts of leftover food whenever we got the urge to do so. On the other hand, a gargantuan dehydrator may be just the ticket for a large family that wants to dehydrate a bushel of apples in one fell swoop.

You don't even need to purchase a food dehydrator, though. If you don't have young children at home, you can dry food in your own oven by propping open the oven door a few inches and setting the temperature to 150°F. This isn't the most ideal situation, for two reasons. First, you'll have to make sure to aim a fan into the oven to remove the moisture from the air as it evaporates from food. Second, and more important, the last thing you may want during those hot summer months is to run your oven with the door open for days on end. The cost to run the oven is prohibitive, to say nothing of increased energy bills to cool your house if you're drying in the summer. But oven drying is possible in a pinch. In fact, you may find it so convenient that you'll do it that way all the time, instead of investing in a real, live food dehydrator.

Your First Project

No matter what sort of food dehydrator you use, the procedure is roughly the same. Choose the food you want to dry, pretreat it if necessary (more on that later), slice it in uniform pieces (same approximate size and thickness), and lay the pieces on the shelves of the dehydrator. The dehydrator does the rest.

Let's assume you've purchased a bunch of apples and want to dehydrate them. Apples are good things to dehydrate, because they can be rehydrated and turned into pies or (much more common) they make great snacks just the way they come out of the dehydrator.

Although we've had great success dehydrating apples without peeling them first, the apples do have better "mouthfeel" if they've been peeled before being dehydrated. In addition, getting rid of the peel will eliminate the waxes that are often commercially applied to apples—to say nothing of the pesticides that may have been sprayed on those beautiful skins.

The idea of peeling your apples probably raises a red flag in your alert little mind, as you realize that as soon as the air hits that pale apple flesh, it's going to start turning brown on you. This is where pretreatment comes in. In the case of apples, they need to be treated to retain their color. You can do this by steam blanching the slices for ten minutes, but why make that much work for yourself? Instead, buy yourself some orange or pineapple juice and soak the slices in that for five minutes before you lay them on the dehydrator trays.

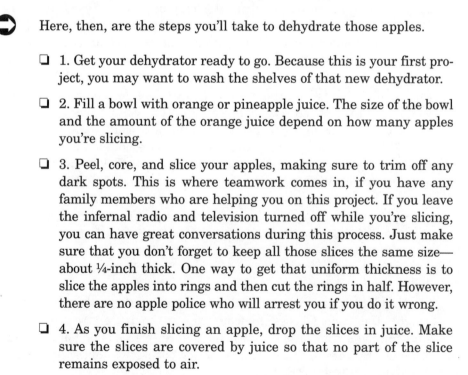

Here, then, are the steps you'll take to dehydrate those apples.

❏ 1. Get your dehydrator ready to go. Because this is your first project, you may want to wash the shelves of that new dehydrator.

❏ 2. Fill a bowl with orange or pineapple juice. The size of the bowl and the amount of the orange juice depend on how many apples you're slicing.

❏ 3. Peel, core, and slice your apples, making sure to trim off any dark spots. This is where teamwork comes in, if you have any family members who are helping you on this project. If you leave the infernal radio and television turned off while you're slicing, you can have great conversations during this process. Just make sure that you don't forget to keep all those slices the same size— about ¼-inch thick. One way to get that uniform thickness is to slice the apples into rings and then cut the rings in half. However, there are no apple police who will arrest you if you do it wrong.

❏ 4. As you finish slicing an apple, drop the slices in juice. Make sure the slices are covered by juice so that no part of the slice remains exposed to air.

❏ 5. After all the apples are peeled and have been soaking in that juice for at least five minutes, remove the apples from the juice.

How you do this will determine whether you can use the juice later. If you have your five-year-old removing the slices with his sweet little hands that have been who-knows-where, you may want to jettison the juice afterwards. However, if the juice has been used judiciously and then drained from the apples in a sanitary way, you may be able to use that juice as part of a fruit salad dressing or a flavoring for frosting, or you may even want to drink it. The choice is yours.

❏ 6. Lay the apple slices on the dehydrator trays, making sure they don't overlap. Good air circulation is essential for successful drying, so put the slices close to but not on top of one another.

❏ 7. Let the dehydrator do its work, leaving your apple slices in the sun for 3–4 days, in the oven for 8–15 hours, and in a real dehydrator for 6–12 hours. When the apples are finished, they should be dry but flexible.

❏ 8. When the apple slices are finished, store them in a container that is airtight, insect-proof, and moisture proof. Yes, you may eat a few slices when you're packing them away.

More About Pretreatment

As we saw with the apple project, pretreatment of a food is often necessary to prevent it from changing color during the dehydration process. But preserving the color is only one reason to pretreat foods before dehydrating them. There are several reasons to pretreat food, and two ways to do it. Okay, we lied. There's a third major way to pretreat food, and that's with sulfur compounds. We're not recommending them. As far as we're concerned, there are only two acceptable methods of pretreatment at home, and those are the ones that are described here.

▶ Dipping

Dipping is the easiest way to pretreat products before dehydration. All you need is a bowl to hold the liquid. There are numerous dipping compounds, which we'll list in a table below. The big advantage of dipping is that it helps retain the flavor and the appearance of the fruit. Dipping may also preserve vitamins A and C.

In addition to the solutions listed below, it is also possible to use a powdered ascorbic acid that is found in the canning section of the supermarket. This does not produce as good results as the harder-to-find crystalline form of ascorbic acid, which may be available behind the pharmacy counter in drugstores.

If you're interested in the syrup option, be advised that this produces a candied fruit instead of a traditional dried product. If you use the syrup, make sure to put a thin coating of oil on dehydrating trays. Otherwise, the fruit will stick to the trays.

Dipping Solutions

Agent	Mixture	Procedure	Soaking Time
Ascorbic acid (crystalline)	1 teaspoon per cup of cold water (for apples, 2½ teaspoons)	Place fruit in plastic bag, add solution, and shake well	No soaking needed
Fruit Juice	high-acid juice (orange, lemon, pineapple, etc.)	soak in undiluted juice (juice can be used twice)	3-5 minutes
Vitamin C	one 500-mg. tablet per 1 quart water	crush tablet & dissolve in water	3-5 minutes
Salt	4-6 tablespoons salt to 1 gallon water		10 minutes
Honey	½ cup sugar to 1½ cups water and ½ cup honey	dissolve sugar in boiling water and add honey	3-5 minutes
Honey Lemon	½ cup honey, juice of 1 lemon, ½ cup water	dip only	No soaking needed
Syrup	1 cup each corn syrup, sugar, water	boil ingredients, add fruit	simmer 10-15 minutes

▶ **Heat treatments**

Some items, particularly vegetables, are heated to reduce enzyme activity—which in turn stops the ripening process and reduces spoilage in the finished product. Heat treatments have the happy side effect of killing some of the more easily killed microorganisms that happen to be inhabiting the food product, while at the same time preserving the vitamin content. The process also helps moisture escape more easily from the product that is being dried. This hastens the drying process and also makes the food easier to rehydrate later.

Heat treatments have two disadvantages—one, it's more work for you, and two, it might leach the flavor out of foods, particularly fruits. This is why, in the table on fruit dehydration, heat treatments are rarely, if ever, suggested. Vegetables are hardier and can withstand heat treatments. In fact, heat is the pretreatment of choice when dehydrating vegetables.

Here are some of the methods used to pretreat with heat, along with some quick and easy instructions for each method:

▶ Steam Blanching

There are two primary forms of blanching—**steam blanching** and **water blanching** (also called **scalding**). Steam blanching is the preferred way to go, because foods that are steamed instead of immersed don't lose the nutrients that would be washed away if the food were soaked in boiling water. Even if you don't care about the nutrients, the flavor often floats off when the nutrients do. If you choose to blanch, at least consider using the steam method.

If you're going to blanch using the steam method, you should have a large pot or kettle that has a lid that will keep the steam inside. There should also be a wire basket that can fit inside the kettle so the steam will circulate freely around the food. The food should not touch the water, which can be a logistical problem.

While you're bringing the water to a boil, fill the wire basket to a depth of no more than about 2½ inches. (Otherwise the steam won't reach all the vegetable pieces.) The water should be boiling at a rapid pace before you lower the basket of food into the kettle.

Steam the vegetables until each piece is heated through and wilted—but not long enough to cause the colors to fade away. If a vegetable from the center of the wire basket is done, you can be certain all the vegetables have cooked long enough. Then quickly remove the wire basket from the heat and lay the vegetable pieces on paper towels to absorb the steam. The vegetables are now ready to be spread out on trays and put into the dehydrator.

▶ Microwave Blanching

Small quantities of vegetables can also be steam blanched in a microwave oven. Trim them and prepare them exactly as you would to blanch them, but instead fill quart-sized microwave bags with about four cups of vegetables, and a little bit of water. Seal the bags except for an inch-long slit where steam will escape. Then microwave on the highest setting for the duration specified on our handy chart. Be careful not to burn yourself when you open those hot bags!

▶ Water Blanching (scalding)

We're realistic enough to know that unless you choose the microwave option, the whole process of steam blanching can be a pain in the neck. Where are you going to get a container that has a wire basket that can be lowered into the kettle so the lid can be firmly placed on the kettle, but that will still keep the vegetables from being immersed in the water? Yes, there are steamers that do this—but a good number of you aren't about to go out and buy a steamer after you've already sprung for a dehydrator. If you're one of those stubborn (or frugal) people, water blanching may be your option.

Water blanching (let's just call it scalding) is just like steam blanching, but without the steam. You have the same big kettle, but you don't have to worry about the wire basket. You just bring a kettle of water to a boil, drop in the vegetables, and they'll be ready in a flash. You'll have lost some of the nutrients and a little of the taste along the way, but at least you didn't have to mess around with a steamer.

▶ **Crazing**

Crazing is different from the other forms of heat treatment because it's the only heat treatment where you do not want to heat the food all the way through. Crazing is only used to penetrate the natural waxiness of the skin of such fruits as cranberries, plums, grapes, and blueberries. The fruits are dipped in boiling water for just a few seconds, and then plunged into cold (and that's icy cold) water. The heat followed by the cold causes the water to "craze" the waxy coating on the fruit. This allows the moisture to escape during drying.

Frankly, we never even heard of crazing until we did research for this book. It was the "crazy" folks at the USU Extension Service whose document on food dehydrating told us that crazing existed. We've made lots and lots of raisins in our time without ever using the crazing process, and our results were just fine. Who knows, though. If we'd crazed those grapes first, maybe our raisins would have been prize-winners. Try it and see what you think.

Endless Information

Now that you know all about dehydrating, you want to know exactly how to prepare every fruit and vegetable under the sun. This is a whole lot of trouble for us, your authors, but once again we've been bailed out by the people at the USU Extension Service. We've adapted a few of their charts and have added information from other sources to create the following gargantuan table. You may think this list is unending, but it could have been worse. We had *lots* more information than we actually used. By the way, drying times are based on the experience you'd have in a low-humidity environment.

Dehydration

Food	Preparation	Pretreatment	Average Drying Time
Apples	Peel, trim, core, and cut into slices or rings ¼-inch thick. Treat with ascorbic acid solution or fruit juice containing vitamin C to prevent browning.	(choose one) – Fruit juice dip – Steam blanch 10 minutes	3–4 Days (Sun) 8–15 Hours (Oven) 6–12 Hours (Dryer)
Apricots	Wash, do not peel. Cut in half and remove pit. Treat with ascorbic acid solution or fruit juice containing vitamin C to prevent browning.	(choose one) – Fruit juice dip – Blanch in hot	2–3 Days (Sun) 24–36 Hours (Oven) 18–24 Hours (Dryer)
(Globe)	Cut hearts into ⅛-inch strips.	Boil 6–8 minutes in a solution of ¾ cup water and 1 tablespoon lemon juice.	10–12 Hours (Sun) 2–3 Hours (Dryer)
Asparagus	Wash well, and cut large tips in half.	(choose one) – Steam blanch 4–5 minutes – Water blanch 3–5 minutes	8–10 Hours (Sun) 1–3 Hours (Dryer)
Bananas	Peel, slice, and pretreat. Spray trays. Cut in slices or lengths.	(choose one) – Fruit juice dip – Honey Dip	1–2 Days (Sun) 8–12 Hours (Oven) 6–10 Hours (Dryer)
Beans (green)	Wash and cut lengthwise, or in short pieces.	(choose one) – Steam blanch 4–6 minutes – Water blanch 3–4 minutes	8 Hours (Sun) 3–4 Hours (Dryer)

Food	Preparation	Pretreatment	Average Drying Time
Beets	Cook as usual, then cool. Peel and cut into shoestring strips ⅛-inch thick.	None required	8–10 Hours (Sun) 2–3 Hours (Dryer)
Berries	Wash and cut larger berries in half.	(choose one) – No treatment – Steam blanch 45 seconds	1–2 Days (Sun) 3–6 Hours (Oven) 2–4 Hours (Dryer)
Broccoli	Trim and cut as for serving. Wash, and cut stalks into quarters.	(choose one) – Steam blanch 4–5 minutes – Water blanch 2–3 minutes	8–10 Hours (Sun) 3–4 Hours (Dryer)
Brussels Sprouts	Cut in half lengthwise through stem.	(choose one) – Steam blanch 6–7 minutes – Water blanch 4–6 minutes	9–11 Hours (Sun) 2–3 Hours (Dryer)
Cabbage	Remove outer leaves, quarter and core. Cut into ⅛-inch strips.	(choose one) – Steam blanch 3–4 minutes – Water blanch 1–2 minutes	6–7 Hours (Sun) 1–2 Hours (Dryer)
Carrots	Wash, cut off roots and tops, and peel. Cut into ⅛-inch slices.	(choose one) – Steam blanch 3–4 minutes – Water blanch 3–4 minutes	8 Hours (Sun) 2–4 Hours (Dryer)
Cauliflower	Prepare as for serving.	(choose one) – Steam blanch 4–5 minutes – Water blanch 3–4 minutes	8–11 Hours (Sun) 2–3 Hours (Dryer)

Food	Preparation	Pretreatment	Average Drying Time
Celery	Wash, then trim and slice stalks.	(choose one) – Steam blanch 2–3 minutes – Water blanch 2–3 minutes	8 Hours (Sun) 2–3 Hours (Dryer)
Chard	See Spinach.		
Cherries	Wash, leave whole or remove stem and pit.	(choose one) – No treatment – Craze 15–20 seconds – Blanch in hot syrup	8–10 Hours (Sun) 3–4 Hours (Dryer)
Corn (cob)	Husk and trim ears.	(choose one) – Steam blanch 6–9 minutes – Water blanch 5–8 minutes	9–11 Hours (Sun) 2–3 Hours (Dryer)
Corn (kernel)	Leave on cob until after blanching, then cut off.	(same as above)	6 Hours (Sun) 1–2 Hours (Dryer)
Cranberries	Wash well.	Craze 15–30 seconds, or no treatment	2–3 Days (Sun) 8–12 Hours (Oven) 6–8 Hours (Dryer)
Eggplant	Wash, trim, cut into ¼-inch pieces.	(choose one) – Steam blanch 3–5 minutes – Water blanch 3 minutes	6–8 Hours (Sun) 2–3 Hours (Dryer)
Figs	Wash fully ripened figs with a damp cloth. Cut larger pieces in half.	Craze 30–45 seconds	3–5 Days (Sun) 9–15 Hours (Oven) 6–12 Hours (Dryer)

Food	Preparation	Pretreatment	Average Drying Time
Grapes	Wash, and remove stems. Leave seedless grapes whole; otherwise, cut in half and remove seeds.	(seedless only) Craze 15–30 seconds, or no treatment.	2–4 Days (Sun) 10–16 Hours (Oven) 8–12 Hours (Dryer)
Horseradish	Wash, and remove small rootlets and stubs. Peel or scrape root, then grate.	None required.	7–10 Hours (Sun) 1-2 Hours (Dryer)
Kale	See Spinach.		
Mushrooms	Make sure to use only edible varieties. Clean, and remove any tough stalks. Cut into slices with an egg or mushroom slicer.	Steam blanch 2–3 minutes.	6–8 Hours (Sun) 3–4 Hours (Dryer)
Nectarines (Halves)	Peel if desired. Cut in half and remove pit.	(choose one) – Ascorbic acid dip – Steam blanch 10–20 minutes	3–5 Days (Sun) 20–30 Hours (Oven) 15–20 Hours (Dryer)
Nectarines (Slices)	Peel if desired. Cut in half and remove pit. Slice.	(choose one) – Ascorbic acid dip – Fruit juice dip – Steam blanch 5 minutes	3–5 Days (Sun) 10–18 Hours (Oven) 8–16 Hours (Dryer)
Okra	Wash, trim, and slice into ¼-inch sections.	(choose one) – Steam blanch 4–5 minutes – Water blanch 2–3 minutes	8–11 Hours (Sun) 2–3 Hours (Dryer)

Food	Preparation	Pretreatment	Average Drying Time
Onions	Wash, trim, and remove outer skin. Cut into ¼-inch slices.	None required.	6–8 Hours (Sun) 1–2 Hours (Dryer)
Parsley	Wash, separate clusters, and discard tough stems.	None required.	6–8 Hours (Sun) 1–2 Hours (Dryer)
Peaches	See Nectarines.		
Pears	Peel, cut in half, and remove core.	(choose one) – Ascorbic acid dip – Steam blanch 5–20 minutes – Blanch in hot syrup	3–5 Days (Sun) 20–30 Hours (Oven) 15–20 Hours (Dryer)
Peas	Remove from pod.	(choose one) – Steam blanch 3–4 minutes – Water blanch 3 minutes	6–8 Hours (Sun) 3–4 Hours (Dryer)
Peppers	Wash, stem, core, and remove interior partitions. Dice into pieces ⅜-inch square.	– Water blanch 2–3 minutes	6–8 Days (Sun) 3–4 Hours (Dryer)
Persimmons (Quarters)	Peel fully ripe fruit and cut into quarters using a stainless steel knife.	(choose one) – No treatment – Blanch in hot syrup	3–5 Days (Sun) 15–24 Hours (Oven) 12–15 Hours (Dryer)
Persimmons (Slices)	Peel fully ripe fruit and cut into slices using a stainless steel knife.	(choose one) – No treatment – Blanch in hot syrup	3–5 Days (Sun) 8–12 Hours (Oven) 6–8 Hours (Dryer)

Food	Preparation	Pretreatment	Average Drying Time
Plums (Halves)	Wash, sort, and dry. Cut larger plums in half.	(choose one) – Craze 30–45 seconds – Steam blanch 15 minutes	3–4 Days (Sun) 15–24 Hours (Oven) 12–15 Hours (Dryer)
Plums (Slices)	Wash, sort, and dry. Cut plums into slices.	(choose one) – Craze 30–45 seconds – Steam blanch 5 minutes	3–4 Days (Sun) 8–12 Hours (Oven) 6–8 Hours (Dryer)
Potatoes	Wash, peel, and cut into ⅛-inch slices.	(choose one) – Steam blanch 6–8 minutes – Water blanch 5–6 minutes	8–11 Hours (Sun) 2–4 Hours (Dryer)
Raspberries	See Berries.		
Spinach	Trim and wash well.	(choose one) – Steam blanch 2–3 minutes – Water blanch 1–2 minutes	6–8 Hours (Sun) 2–3 Hours (Dryer)
Squash (Banana)	Wash, peel, and slice into strips ¼-inch thick.	(choose one) – Steam blanch 2–3 minutes – Water blanch 1 minute	6–8 Hours (Sun) 2–4 Hours (Dryer)
Squash (Hubbard)	Cut into 1-inch pieces. Remove seeds and pulp. Peel rind, then cut squash into ⅛-inch strips.	(choose one) – Steam blanch 2–3 minutes – Water blanch 1 minute	6–8 Hours (Sun) 2–4 Hours (Dryer)

Food	Preparation	Pretreatment	Average Drying Time
Squash (Summer)	Wash, trim, and slice into strips ¼-inch thick.	(choose one) – Steam blanch 2–3 minutes – Water blanch 1–2 minutes	6–8 Hours (Sun) 2–3 Hours (Dryer)
Strawberries	See Berries.		
Tomatoes (Stewed)	Craze to loosen skins, then peel. Cut into slices ¾-inch wide.	(choose one) – Steam blanch 3 minutes – Water blanch 1 minute	8–10 Hours (Sun) 3–5 Hours (Dryer)

I'm into Leather

As any mother can attest, fruit leather is a popular treat for children of all ages. But as anyone who reads labels can testify, commercially-produced fruit leather is not as healthy as you'd think it should be. If anyone has any idea what Vaseline (listed under its generic name, petrolatum) is doing as a main ingredient in a popular name brand children's snack, please let us know. Somehow feeding petroleum products to toddlers just doesn't seem kosher.

Fortunately, making fruit leather in a dehydrator (or even in your oven) is so easy a child can do it. (Make sure the child is supervised, of course!) All you need to do is puree the fruit, put it on shelves that have been lined with plastic wrap, and turn on the dehydrator. We can assure you that the recipes you'll see here do not contain petroleum products. If you want to add Vaseline, or Band-Aids, or Elmer's glue to your fruit leather, fine—but you're going to have to do it without our help.

In the last chapter, you saw that canning is a science. In contrast, making fruit leather is an art. There's a lot of room for creativity here, so experiment and see what you like. Blend different fruits. Add your favorite seasonings. (Hint: this might not be a good time to try garlic powder.) Throw in some powdered drink mix or gelatin desserts (without adding any water first, of course!). Frozen juice concentrates work well, but don't add water to those, either.

If you want to experiment with other ingredients, you can add coconut, chopped dates, bits of dehydrated fruit such as cranberries or raisins, granola, miniature marshmallows, and chopped nuts or seeds. Prepare the leather for drying and then sprinkle the added ingredients on top. The Utah State Extension Service suggests that you can make a fruit leather and then lightly frost it with cream cheese. Then you can roll it up and slice it "for a pinwheel effect." (Hint: If you're going to do this, remove the plastic wrap before you roll it, and store the fruit leather in your refrigerator.)

Jell-O Leather

Make a puree of two cups of applesauce and one small box of fruit-flavored Jell-O. Dry and store. (Kiddies love this stuff.)

Applesauce Leather

applesauce
caramels (optional)

Spread homemade (or homestyle) applesauce onto plastic wrap and dry until rubbery. Roll up and place in zipper lock bags for air-tight freshness. A great addition to this is to melt down caramels and spread a thin layer over the apple leather. This will be sticky, so when you're rolling it up you should leave the plastic wrap in place. Another option is to cut the caramel treats into coins or strips.

Peach Leather

Peel soft, ripe peaches. Mash and remove juice. To every cup of peaches, add ¼ cup sugar. Simmer 15 minutes. Pour into shallow pan and cool. Dry on plastic wrap until leathery. Cut in thin squares, or roll and slice. Sprinkle with powdered sugar. Store.

Apricot Leather

3 ounces dried apricots
¾ cup water
1 tablespoon sugar

2-inch piece vanilla bean, split
    lengthwise
3 tablespoons fresh lemon juice

Combine all ingredients in a casserole dish. Cover tightly with microwave-safe plastic wrap. Cook on high 8 minutes and then uncover carefully, to avoid being burned by the steam. Discard the vanilla bean and puree everything else in the blender to remove the lumps. Pour onto dehydrator trays that have been lined with plastic wrap. You know what to do from there.

Berry Rollups

Blend **frozen berries** in blender until smooth. Cover dehydrator shelves with **plastic wrap** and pour berry mixture on shelves to a depth of no more than ¼ inch. Sprinkle **powdered sugar** on top. Dehydrate until leathery. Peel off or roll up in the plastic wrap until you're ready to eat it.

Christmas Leather

32-ounce can applesauce
(or 2 quarts home bottled)
6-ounce can frozen cranberry
juice concentrate (thawed
but not reconstituted)

3–4 tablespoons of sliced
almonds (optional)
powdered sugar (optional)

Combine applesauce and juice concentrate. Pour on dehydrator trays that have been covered with plastic wrap, to about ¼-inch thickness. Sprinkle on almonds and, if you're adventurous, dust with a light coating of powdered sugar. Dehydrate until it's dry enough that it can be peeled from the plastic wrap. It will still be sticky due to the high sugar concentration. Roll up inside the plastic wrap. If you choose to use nuts, either eat in a few days or refrigerate—fruit leather is forever, but nuts go rancid pronto.

Pumpkin Leather

2 cups pumpkin, canned
or cooked & pureed
½ cup honey

⅛ teaspoon nutmeg
⅛ teaspoon powdered cloves
¼ teaspoon cinnamon

Blend ingredients and dry.

What a Jerky!

Making jerky is one of the joys of using a food dehydrator. There are a lot of jerky recipes floating around these days—so many of them that everyone seems to have a favorite. Most of these favorite recipes use uncooked meat, and the people who tout the recipes on computer bulletin boards are apparently not dead yet. However, in the interest of public safety we should tell you that the U.S. Department of Agriculture says that jerky that has not been precooked is unsafe for human consumption. The USDA recommends that red meat, fish, and game that are used for jerky be baked or simmered until they reach an internal temperature of 160°F., and poultry to no less than 180°F., before putting it in the dehydrator. If you have any questions about this, there's a USDA Meat and Poultry Hotline at 1-800-535-4555.

If you choose to bake the microorganisms out of your beef jerky, here's how to do it. Prepare the jerky strips just as you'd get them ready for the dehydrator. Then place the strips over wire cake racks that have been laid on top of baking sheets. (The wire racks will raise the meat out of its own juices and begin the drying process for you.) Bake in a 325°F. oven, and cook to an internal temperature of 180°F. for poultry or 160°F. for anything else.

If you'd prefer to marinate and simmer your jerky, here are the directions. Make a marinade using your own preferred recipe, or choose one of the marinade recipes given below. If you want to create your own marinade, you should use oil, salt, and some sort of acid product (vinegar, lemon juice, soy sauce, or cooking wine). After the meat strips have marinated one to two hours or overnight, place the meat in a saucepan with the marinade and simmer to an internal temperature of 180°F. for poultry or 160°F. for anything else.

When the proper temperature has been reached, either through baking or through simmering, move the jerky to your dehydrator and follow the recipe from there. Jerky that has been precooked will not need to dehydrate as long as the recipe says, for obvious reasons!

You can continue processing your jerky in the oven, if you don't have small children at home who may be tempted by the open oven door and get burned. Prop open the oven door a couple of inches and continue drying at 170°F. (Don't forget to place that fan outside the oven, near the door!)

Whether cooked in an oven or a dehydrator, jerky is done when a test piece cracks but does not break when it's bent. When the proper rate of doneness is reached, remove the jerky from oven or dehydrator, blot away any beads of oil that may have formed on the individual pieces. Remove the strips from the drying racks and then cool before packaging as you would any other dehydrated product. Store in a cool, dry, dark place.

Here are some sample marinade recipes for you to try, followed by jerky recipes. These recipes aren't carved in stone, so feel free to experiment with them. Don't forget that you can never go wrong adding garlic or pepper, and that fresh ginger or liquid smoke will enhance many recipes.

Jerky Marinades

Recipe #1:

1 cup soy sauce
⅛ cup lemon juice
½ teaspoon salt
2 fresh-squeezed garlic cloves
1 teaspoon black pepper

Recipe #2:

1 cup dry red wine vinegar
1 teaspoon Italian herbs

Recipe #3:

1 cube beef bouillon
1 cup boiling water
1 teaspoon chili powder
1 cup soy sauce
4 teaspoons freshly grated ginger root
2 tablespoons sugar
4 teaspoons salt

Recipe #4:

1 teaspoon pepper
1 cup soy sauce
¼ cup Worcestershire sauce
2 teaspoons onion powder
1 teaspoon garlic powder

Recipe #5:

4 teaspoons liquid smoke
1 cup red cooking wine
¼ cup fresh lemon juice
1 small onion, chopped fine
1 clove garlic, mashed

Recipe #6:

1 cup catsup
1 cup soy sauce
1 tablespoon brown sugar

Deli Meat Jerky

To start you off in your jerky experience, here's the world's easiest jerky recipe. All you need is meat from your deli—cured meat such as pastrami, ham, or corned beef. You'll want it lean (trim off that excess fat!), and sliced about ¼-inch thick. But you don't need to cook it, because it's already cooked.

Spread the slices in your dehydrator so they don't overlap and dry them until they're tough and leathery. Allow to cool, blotting away any beads of oil with a paper towel. Then store as you would any dried food.

Jerky for Refrigerator and Smoker

25 pounds of beef, sliced against the grain, 2 inches wide x ½–¾ inch thick
1 pound salt (not iodized)

½ pound coarse ground or cracked pepper (Montreal Steak Seasoning is great, if you can find it)
½ cup minced garlic (fresh, not bottled)

Slice meat into large plastic container and add garlic. Cover with salt until the meat is well covered. Mix well. Refrigerate for about 2 days, until the meat has released most of its water (about 2½ days). Dip meat in boiling water just long enough for the meat to turn gray. (Don't cook the meat!) Roll the meat in the cracked pepper or Montreal Steak Seasoning. Bake slices as described in instructions earlier, until the beef reaches an internal temperature of 160°F. Put slices in a smoker or in your dehydrator, or continue drying in the oven at 140°F. until the proper consistency is reached. Cool and store.

Turkey Jerky Teriyaki

large turkey breast
teriyaki marinade (use from store or make your own)

Have the grocery store butcher slice that raw turkey breast as thin as possible. Marinate the slices for 6 hours or overnight in a zippered bag, refrigerated, turning occasionally. Drain marinade, place strips in dehydrator, and dehydrate. Occasionally blot off beads of oil with a paper towel. When jerky is done, bake for 1 hour at 180°F. to kill off any unwanted microorganisms.

Ground Meat Jerky

10 pounds lean ground meat
½ cup salt
2 tablespoons black pepper
5 teaspoons garlic powder
1 tablespoon Worcestershire sauce

¼ teaspoon red pepper (cayenne)
3 tablespoons sugar
1½ tablespoons liquid smoke

Mix all ingredients together with an electric mixer (this assures that all the spices will be evenly distributed). Place meat on a sheet of **waxed paper** on a cookie sheet. Cover with another sheet of waxed paper and roll to a thickness of ¼ inch or less. Remove top sheet of waxed paper. Dry uncovered in an oven or directly on the shelf of your dehydrator at 160°F. When meat is almost dry, remove from cookie sheet and turn upside-down onto the dehydrator shelf, so the waxed paper bottom is now on the top. Remove the waxed paper and continue drying. After drying, slice in strips.

Beef Jerky

1 pound flank steak	¼ teaspoon pepper
1 teaspoon seasoning salt	⅓ cup soy sauce
½ teaspoon garlic powder	⅓ cup Worcestershire sauce
½ teaspoon onion powder	2 tablespoons liquid smoke

Pat flank steak dry and slice thinly across grain of meat. In a large zipper bag, combine the rest of the ingredients. Place meat in the bag, making sure each slice is coated with marinade. Refrigerate overnight. Drain marinade off the meat, blotting with paper towels to remove pools of moisture. Bake slices to an internal temperature of 160°F., as described above. Continue dehydrating in 140°F. oven with the door open, or place slices in food dehydrator and dehydrate until done. Cool and store.

Other Dried-and-True Recipes

By now your head should be swimming with all the potential you have with your trusty dehydrator. You probably didn't think there was anything else to contemplate, but just in case you want some icing on the cake, we've got a couple of recipes for you to consider.

Instant Soup Mix

Place into saucepan any combination of your favorite dried vegetables. Add dry rice and your favorite dried meat. Place in airtight container until ready to use. Preparation: Pour 2 cups of Instant Soup Mix into 2 cups of boiling water. Cover and simmer until tender. Add seasonings to taste.

French Onion Soup

1 cup dried onion
1 cup water

1 beef bouillon cube or ½ cup
beef stock

Mix ingredients in saucepan over medium heat for 15 minutes or until onions are soft. Drain liquid and retain. Brown onions in **2 tablespoons butter**. Add **2 tablespoons flour** and $1/4$ **teaspoon salt**. Stir, then add broth to pan. Add an additional **3 cups water**. Simmer. To serve, pour soup into individual oven-safe bowls. Top each with toasted **croutons**. Sprinkle with **Parmesan cheese,** cover with a slice of **bread**, and top it with a slice of **provolone cheese**. Bake at 375°F. to melt and brown cheese. Serve hot. Makes 4 servings

Sun-Dried Tomatoes*

plum (Roma) tomatoes
salt

Choose tomatoes that are at the peak of ripeness. Cut them in half lengthwise. Sprinkle a pinch of salt on each half and arrange them seed side up on the drying trays. When done, the tomatoes will have shrunk to half their original size and will be the consistency of a dried apricot. These keep best in the refrigerator, covered in olive oil. However, experiment with storing them in a cool, dry place with an oxygen absorber.

*Note: Making your own sun-dried tomatoes sure beats paying $9 a pound for the ones that have been sun-dried for you. Besides—commercial food processors often use tomatoes that are beginning to rot. Not only will your tomatoes be lots cheaper, but they'll also taste much better than the store-bought variety.

Dried Watermelon

Cut watermelon in large chunks, take out the seeds and cut off the rind. Dry it and eat. A novelty item that reputedly tastes surprisingly good.

Pineapple Cherry Rings

Place slices of pineapple (canned) onto trays with a maraschino cherry in the center. Dry until rubbery. Store in zipper bags for freshness.

Banana Variations

Slice bananas directly onto tray (no overlapping) and let dry completely before removing. Puree bananas, either plain or with tart fruits, to make leathers. Add spices for variety.

Glazed banana chips: Slice bananas into ¼-inch slices, soak in lemon juice for a few minutes, drain, then place on trays. Sprinkle with a mixture of sugar and cinnamon. Dry until crisp and shiny. For best results, use almost green bananas.

Honey-glazed banana chips: Dip banana slices into mixture of ¼ cup water and ¼ cup honey. Soak for a few minutes, drain, then place on trays to dry. Sprinkle with cinnamon or pumpkin pie spice to add an extra touch.

Okay, Any Questions?

? *What happens if the power goes out and the food in my freezer thaws?*

This is a question you should answer for yourself long before you purchase a freezer. Eventually, a power outage will occur; it's a fact of life. If you're going to own a freezer, you need to be prepared for it.

One option if you're serious about being a freezer owner is to keep a gasoline-powered generator on hand to keep that freezer running if the power goes out. Of course, freezers use a whole lot of juice. If your power goes out, you may have better places to use that gasoline than to keep your freezer running.

As mentioned earlier in this chapter, there are other alternatives. Freezers that are powered by natural gas do exist, although they're prohibitively expensive and they have such small capacities that they're almost not worth thinking about. There are also pressure canners that can be used over wood fires, so you can process freezer food before it goes bad. Food dehydrators are another option. Look at the resources in Chapter 9 to give you ideas where you can find these treasures.

But from a practical standpoint, most of the above options cost more than it would take to replace a freezer full of food. Most people who own freezers (or second refrigerators) don't have any back-up plan. They just hope for the best.

If you're caught with a power outage, here are some freezer facts for you. A fully packed freezer will stay at freezing temperatures for up to two days if you don't open the door. Partially-packed freezers should have their foods grouped together, with wadded-up newspapers filling the empty spots. This will help the freezer conduct the cold.

Food is safe to be refrozen or used as long as there are still ice crystals in it. Once the ice crystals are gone, the food is pretty much useless. Some things such as butter or freezer jam can be safely refrozen once they've reached room temperature, assuming they're uncontaminated by juices from thawed foods, but almost everything else should be thrown out uneaten. Once the power has been restored, you should clean out your freezer and start over.

As for refrigerators, food that is kept in a refrigerator will be safe for about six hours. After that, everything except condiments and fruits or vegetables should be thrown out. Use your judgment—you know what's bad. If you have any doubts about anything in your refrigerator, throw it out. You know the old adage about "safe" being better than "sorry." Food poisoning is the last thing you need when you're already experiencing a stressful situation such as an extended power outage.

By the way, if food is unappetizing but still safe, it can be recovered. Look at the section in Chapter 8 that tells you how to recover old food.

? *I've heard that the best way to dehydrate fruits is to pretreat them with sulfites. Why don't you recommend this?*

Call us old-fashioned, but we believe food should be kept in as natural a state as possible. The average American eats fourteen pounds of artificial food additives every year, and that can't possibly be good for us. In fact, we theorize that the epidemic of autoimmune diseases that is plaguing our country in these modern times is at the very least aggravated—if not directly caused—by the toxins in our environment.

Many people are allergic to sulfites. Some have died from reactions to food that has been treated with them. Do you know exactly who's going to be eating your dehydrated fruit? Can you guess beforehand which, if any, of your children or grandchildren or their little friends are already allergic to sulfites? Would you bet their lives that they won't develop such an allergy in the future?

If there were no other alternative than sulfite treatment, we'd recommend sulfites—with grave reservations. But since there are other treatments that are virtually as good, we'd forego the sulfites and use one of the other methods. You wouldn't use nuclear weapons to kill a mouse, would you? Nor would a prudent person use a potentially dangerous chemical to pretreat fruit when a fruit juice dip will do the trick.

? *Because you don't like sulfites, I've heard that the second-best way to dehydrate foods is to treat them with plain old sulfur. Why don't you recommend this?*

Good grief, but you're persistent! If it's not one poison, it's another. Very well, here's your answer. Get comfortable. This might take some time.

First of all, we exaggerated. Sulfur isn't really a poison. In fact, it's a real, live chemical element that's a component of many of your favorite foods. Cabbage, for instance. Wheat germ. Clams.

But just because sulfur may not be bad for you, that doesn't necessarily mean that large quantities of it are good for you to eat. The big reason we don't buy the sulfur concept is that it adds a chemical to your food that you just don't need. Sure, sulfuring will retain vitamins A and C better than unsulfured food. It also keeps the bugs away, and there's a clue for you.

There's a reason insects have survived for millions of years, while human beings have barely refrained from killing themselves off in their brief history. It's because bugs have common sense. Bugs smell chemicals and say to themselves in their little buggy voices, "Bad stuff. Stay away." Humans, on the other hand, are not as intelligent. It takes a human to believe the Food and Drug Administration's arbitrary decision that any of the hundreds of chemicals that were added to foods before 1958 can be "generally recognized as safe." Any self-respecting bug would roll over on his back laughing at such an absurd notion. (In fact, that's exactly how those dead bugs you see on their backs got that way—laughing at the foibles of humankind.)

We suspect you eat MSG-laden potato chips, and drink soft drinks that have been laced with Nutrasweet, and stuff your cheerful little faces with luncheon meats that have been preserved with nitrates. Why not? Everyone else does it! If that's the kind of diet you eat, a little extra sulfur in your food certainly isn't going to hurt.

So here's an argument that you may listen to, which is that sulfur is hard to come by. You can't just pick it up at the good old 7-Eleven. It's also hard to use, because you have to make a sulfur box in order to treat your food. This strikes us as a whole lot of extra work—which is pointless, when the good old fruit juice dip works almost as well.

CHAPTER 5

Grow, Grow, Grow Your Oat

★ **IN THIS CHAPTER**
- ✔ Gardening indoors with sprouts
- ✔ Learning the secrets of the sprouting masters
- ✔ Rising to the occasion with sourdoughs and starters
- ✔ Growing some culture with yogurt
- ✔ Putting your new knowledge to work: recipes
- ✔ Answering common questions

If canning, freezing, and drying cause all life processes to cease, there's another facet of food storage that is at the opposite end of the spectrum. In fact, a good food storage program will feature growing things as well as the preservation of things that are in suspended animation.

Sprouting is quite popular, because it is easy to grow your own greens that may be used to garnish salads and sandwiches. The growing of cultures will also enhance your food supply, when you can produce such items as yogurt and sourdough bread. Sourdough is uniquely suited to food storage because it's a way for you to be able to use all that wheat you have tucked away in your basement without having to rely on yeast.

If you want to sprout a new interest or get cultured, this chapter will teach you how to do it. Sprouting and culturing include some of the most fascinating aspects of food storage, and we hope to make you a convert by the time you're through with this chapter.

Sprout-Hearted Men

When Clark was in elementary school, his teacher had the students perform an interesting science experiment. They each wrapped a handful of dry wheat in cheesecloth, and suspended the pouch of seeds just inside the opening of a bottle. Twice each day, they would pour water over the seeds and down into the bottle. Within a week, large healthy green stalks were growing up out of each jar. In the dark ages before children were jaded by computers, video recorders, and home game systems, these were the kinds of tricks that really impressed students.

Clark may have thought his teacher had discovered a great trick, but she was actually teaching her students an art that had been practiced for thousands of years. Almost 3,000 years before the birth of Christ, the Chinese were writing about the health properties of sprouted seeds, more commonly known today as "sprouts."

Although sprouts have a long history in the oriental cultures, they have only become popular with other cultures in the past few years, as people have moved away from processed foods and towards more natural "health" foods. It is not uncommon to walk into most grocery stores and find several varieties of sprouts, both fresh and canned.

As their popularity has increased, it has become common to find sprouts listed as an ingredient in many recipes, and not just as a staple in Chinese food or as an interesting garnish for sandwiches and salads. Their flavor, texture, color, and nutrients are a welcome addition to many foods.

There are many reasons for including dry seeds for sprouting as a food storage item. The dry seeds used in sprouting are one of the best foods for long storage life. Seeds that are kept in a dry and cool storage area can retain their potency for twenty years, if not longer. When you finally decide to sprout them, they change from a dry seed into a moist vegetable, and increase their weight by a factor of four or more. Thus, every pound of seeds will produce at least four pounds of sprouts. So, you could think of seeds for sprouting as dehydrated vegetables. They are compact and store well, yet they can be rehydrated in only a few days. Apartment and condominium dwellers can grow fresh vegetables without needing a garden plot, and they can grow them without regard to the weather outside. You can have all the advantages of having a vegetable garden, but without needing good weather, expensive tools, or a lot of time. With very little effort, you can add some living food to your diet, which may be a boon and a blessing if you're otherwise subsisting on canned food storage supplies.

The process of sprouting seeds destroys many of the enzymes that make raw seeds difficult to digest. Thus, someone who has a difficult time digesting raw wheat might not have the same problem with wheat sprouts.

Another advantage is that sprouts are healthy foods. Because of the added water, sprouts are lower in calories than the seeds from which they sprouted. The process of sprouting converts fats and starches into vitamins, proteins, and sugars. Thus, sprouts provide vitamins, minerals, and proteins, while being low in fat and cholesterol. Foods that are typically stored for emergency use tend to be low in vitamins B and C. You can compensate for this by also storing sprouting seeds, which are rich in these same vitamins. Sprouts that are green and leafy are also good sources of vitamin A.

The final advantage of sprouting is the low cost. Compared with the grocery store prices you pay for fresh vegetables, you can stretch your grocery budget farther by including sprouts as a complement to other vegetables in the family diet.

The Need for Good Seed

The Bible advises that "whatsoever a man soweth, that shall he also reap." That is probably good advice for sprouters as well, because the success of sprouting is often related to the quality of the seeds being used. Seeds will keep their potency for many years, but the prudent sprouter will make an effort to obtain the freshest seeds possible. There are some seeds developed expressly for sprouting, although regular grains and beans sold as food items in grocery stores will often work just as well. Experiment a little and see if the custom seeds are worth the extra cost, or if dried seeds found in the grocery store give you the results you want.

In general, avoid seeds that are designed for growing in the garden. These are often treated with chemicals to make them more resistant to pests and disease. These chemicals are not transmitted to the full-grown plant, but they are concentrated enough to cause harm if the treated seeds are used for sprouting rather than for gardening. In some cases, these chemically treated seeds are dyed red to alert you that they should not be eaten raw. But this is not always the case, so be careful.

When locating a source of seeds to be used for sprouting, you have several options. Factors to consider when selecting a seed source include price, convenience, and the variety of seeds available. Consider the following:

- The local grocery store is the most convenient place to buy seeds, but you probably will not find the prices or selection that may be available from other sources. Also, don't expect to find a lot of knowledgeable help from the staff if you have detailed questions about the types of seeds available, and the advantages of each.

- Local health food stores will probably carry a wider variety of seeds from which to choose, and a more knowledgeable staff to answer your questions. Expect to pay about the same as you would at the grocery store, if not slightly more.

- If price is your main consideration, determine if there are any farm supply stores in your area. These usually sell several types of seeds and grains that may be acceptable for sprouting. Don't expect the staff to be sprouting experts, but they should be able to tell you if the seeds they carry are safe for sprouting.

- Another alternative is to use a mail order company that sells seeds for sprouting. If you look carefully, you should be able to find one that has a good variety and a staff that can answer your questions. Expect to pay a little more if you get your seeds here, because you will have to pay for shipping. Many of these stores can be reached easily through toll-free phone numbers and Internet web sites. Refer to Chapter 9 to get you started.

You might want to buy your first seeds at the grocery store, until you decide that sprouting is something you want to do. Once you make that decision, you can become more adventurous and move on to the more exotic suppliers.

When storing sprouts for emergency use, plan on about 125 pounds of seed per person, assuming you are planning to get all your vitamins from the sprouts. If you have other sources of vitamins, this can be reduced by half. Plan your meals so that you eat about half of your sprouts cooked and the other half raw, because this will give you the proper balance of vitamins.

Plan to rotate through your sprouting seed so that it is stored no longer than about five years. It will keep longer than this if you have a storage location that is dark and less than 60°F. Seeds stored in vacuum-packed cans will keep as long as fifteen years. If you attempt to sprout seeds that are too old, fewer seeds will sprout, and those that do will take longer and not grow as large.

Sprouting Secrets

As you would expect, the key to successful sprouting is controlling the environment in which the seeds germinate. You need to provide the proper temperature and moisture level, plus you need to account for the fact that the seeds will grow in size as they germinate. To remove waste products that are produced by germination, you will need to rinse the seeds regularly. Try to keep the seeds at a temperature between 70°F. and 80°F., and also use rinse water that is within this range. In general, use slightly cooler rinse water in the hot months, and slightly warmer rinse water in the cool months. Keep the seeds away from direct sources of drafts and heat.

To prepare the seeds, wash them thoroughly and then manually remove any foreign matter and broken seeds. Place the seeds in a container with an amount of water equal to four times their volume. For example, you would soak one cup of seeds in four cups of water. When determining the amount of seeds to sprout, remember our previous rule of thumb that seeds will expand to about four times their dry volume. Half of this increase will occur during soaking, and the remainder will occur during sprouting. Some report better success when using bottled or filtered water that does not have the chlorine found in municipal systems. Soak seeds for approximately eight to twelve hours, depending on the size of the seed. This soaking time should also be increased when the weather is colder. When soaking is complete, rinse the seeds with fresh water and then drain all the water off.

Seed Preparation

• Wash
• Soak
• Rinse
• Drain

Although any sprouting method will work that provides the proper environment for the seeds, listed below are five methods that are common and easy to do with the supplies found around most homes:

▶ Bottle Method

This is the most common method, and it works well with most types of seeds. Try it first before using the other methods. This requires a wide-mouth quart canning bottle, a small amount of coarse-weave cloth, and a string or rubber band for fastening the cloth to the mouth of the bottle. If you can't find cheesecloth, use nylon net or plastic screening or even a discarded but clean nylon stocking. Anything that will hold the seeds in and let the water out should work fine.

Either soak the seeds directly in the bottle, or place them in the bottle when soaking is complete. Cover the mouth of the bottle with the cloth or net, stretched tight, and secure it with the string or rubber band. Another option is to hold the cloth in place with the metal canning ring designed to fit on the bottle. Find a place to store the bottle where it can sit on its side, with the mouth end slightly lower than the bottom of the bottle. You want it in this position so that any excess moisture can drain out the mouth of the bottle. Store the bottle in a warm, dark place, or cover it with a cloth or piece of paper to keep the light away from the sprouts. Store in a place with good ventilation, and yet away from drafts.

Sprouting Options

• Bottle Method
• Towel Method
• Sprinkling Method
• Pressure Method
• Screen Method

Rinse and drain the seeds several times a day, depending on the type of seeds being sprouted. See the table below for more details. Remember to rinse more often when the weather is warm. If the seeds produce a foul odor, they have been kept too damp and have started to rot. Throw the seeds away, clean up, and try again.

Rinse the seeds by pouring water in through the cloth, and then inverting the bottle and pouring it back out again. As before, rest the bottle with the mouth down so that water can continue to drain. But also make sure air can get in.

You know that the sprouting is complete when the stalks of the sprouts have reached a certain length. Suggested lengths are also shown in the table below, although you need to experiment for your own tastes. If the resulting sprouts have a bitter taste, they were grown for too long. When sprouts are the desired length, place the bottle in artificial light or indirect sunlight to cause the sprouts to turn a darker shade of green. This last step is optional, but most people find that green sprouts are more appetizing than white ones. Also, as the sprouts turn green the amount of vitamin A they contain will dramatically increase, making them even more healthy.

▶ Towel Method

This method requires a stainless steel draining rack, such as those used for cooling cookies. You also need some paper towels, and a tray or pan into which the draining rack can be placed. Place the rack into the pan, and cover it with a two-layer damp paper towel that has been soaked in water, squeezed out, and then unfolded again. Cut down the size of the towels if they cover the sides of the rack, as the air needs to circulate around all the sides.

Scatter the soaked seeds evenly over the paper towels. Then cover the seeds with another two-layer damp towel prepared in the same manner. While keeping the pan horizontal, slip it into a plastic or paper bag, and store the bag in a dark, dry place, such as a closet or cupboard. To encourage air circulation, leave the end of the bag open, and leave the door to the closet or cupboard partially open.

When rinsing the seeds, remove the pan from the bag and remove the top layer of paper towels. Replenish the moisture in the top layer of towels by soaking and squeezing them again. Sprinkle water on the seeds until the bottom towel is moist all over, but not dripping wet. Cover the seeds again with the freshly moistened towels, and return the pan to the bag and then the bag to the cupboard.

As with the previous method, you can optionally expose the final sprouts to light until they are a pleasant shade of green.

▶ Sprinkling Method

This method should be used for chia and garden cress, and a few other species of seeds that should not be soaked before they are sprouted. These seeds tend to cling together when wet, so they don't drain well, and are more subject to spoilage.

Start with an equal amount of water and seed. Pour the water into a pie plate, or a similar container made of glass or stainless steel. Sprinkle the seeds evenly over the water. After about an hour, check the moisture level of the seeds. If the seeds appear too dry, sprinkle more water on them until they are moist. Tip the container slightly, and remove any excess moisture that runs off to the side. The seeds should be jelled together, and should not move if you tip the container gently.

Cover the container with a piece of aluminum foil. Or, place the container in a large plastic bag, leave the end of the bag open, and place the covered container in a dark place.

You need check the seeds only once per day, although you may need to do it more often if you live in a hot, dry climate. If the seeds appear dry, sprinkle on just enough moisture to keep them wet, but not enough so that pools of water form.

When the sprouts have reached their mature length, put them in the light and let them acquire the proper shade of green.

▶ Pressure Method

This method can optionally be used when sprouting mung beans. It causes the sprouts to have longer and thicker stalks than any of the other methods.

Place the soaked and drained beans in a small colander, and put that colander in another container. Cover the top of the beans with several layers of thick cloth, such as burlap. Place a 3–5 pound bag of marbles or small stones on top of the cloth.

Every 2–3 hours, pour water on top of the cloth until it is damp all over.

Unlike other sprouts, keep them in the dark at all times, and do not green them when they are ready to harvest. They should be harvested when the sprouts are 2–3 inches long.

▶ Screen Method

This is for people who want to get into sprouting in a big way, and produce large quantities of sprouts. Make one or more wooden frames and then nail window screen material to one side of the frame. Thus, what you have when you are done will be one or more trays with wooden sides and window screen for the bottom.

Soak the seeds and then transfer them to the trays. Stack the trays on top of each other in a warm, dark, dry place, that is well ventilated but free from drafts. When rinsing the seeds, hold each tray under running water and then make sure the excess water has drained off before stacking them again.

Storing and Using Sprouts

Regardless of the method used for sprouting, all sprouts should be cleaned and stored after the sprouting and greening processes are complete. Place the sprouts in a large bowl and cover them with water. Stir them gently, and keep them covered for several minutes. This will clean away any remaining waste products from germination, as well as seed casings that are present for some types of seeds. These will usually float to the top of the rinse water. After rinsing, place the sprouts in a colander and let them dry thoroughly. Inspect the sprouts and remove any unsprouted seeds or broken sprout pieces. These usually sink to the bottom of the rinsing bowl.

The method just described may not be practical for some of the smaller seeds. For these seeds, omit the first rinse and place the seeds directly in a colander with fine wire mesh. Rinse the seeds with running water, and pat them dry with a paper towel.

Wrap the sprouts loosely in a damp paper towel, and place them in a plastic bag that can be sealed tightly. Refrigerate. If the sprouts begin to wilt or get dry, rinse them again in cold water, wrap them again in the moist paper towel and the plastic bag, and return them to the refrigerator. Sprouts will remain fresh for seven to ten days if refrigerated. Discard the sprouts if they look, smell, or taste funny. Even if they don't spoil, sprouts start to lose their nutritive value when stored for longer than a week. Rather than preparing a large amount of sprouts, make multiple smaller batches that can each be consumed in less than a week. Consider starting a new batch when you harvest the old batch, as this will ensure that you always have fresh sprouts.

> *Sprouts will remain fresh for seven to ten days if refrigerated.*

When using sprouts in cooking, they can be added directly to salads, sandwiches, and most stir fry recipes. They are good in some Mexican foods, such as tacos, and can also be added to soups and stews just before serving. You can add up to a cup of sprouts to most popular casseroles without affecting the recipe or the cooking time. Substitute bean sprouts in any recipe calling for beans, but reduce the cooking time by about one-third.

There is no law stating that certain types of sprouts have to be eaten raw versus cooked. In general, sprouts from beans are generally better cooked. Conversely, alfalfa, radish, mung bean, sunflower, clover, and cabbage sprouts are most often eaten raw. Sprouts from lentils, soy beans, green peas, and wheat are tasty either cooked or raw.

Heat kills some of the nutritive properties of sprouts, so simmer them or steam them slowly, and avoid cooking for too long. Simmering and steaming cause the sprouts to lose about 25 percent of their vitamin C, but boiling them and then discarding the water will cause you to lose up to 60 percent. So avoid boiling, if at all possible.

For recipes that call for a specific amount of sprouts, press the sprouts lightly into a measuring cup until the proper quantity is reached. In most cases, you can substitute a different type of sprout in a recipe without affecting the taste.

When adding sprouts to a bread recipe, add one cup of sprouts and then reduce the flour by half a cup and also the liquid by half a cup. Experiment with chopping the sprouts or leaving them whole. When adding sprouts to a recipe that contains yeast, add them as late as possible in the mixing process, as the enzymes in the sprouts will sometimes affect the action of the yeast.

Sprouting Table

Use the table on the following page as the starting point for your sprouting adventures. This does not list all the seeds that may be sprouted, but it lists the most common ones. Take care not to try to grow tomato or potato sprouts, which are toxic to humans.

Seeds that have a "normal" temperature requirement should be kept at a temperature of 70°– 85°F. For other seeds, use the range listed.

The "Rinse Days" column indicates the number of times that rinsing or sprinkling of the sprouts should be done each day.

See
Chapter 9
for more
resources.

The "Sprout Days" column indicates the approximate number of days it will take the sprouts to reach the stage where they are ready to harvest.

The "Length/Inches" column tells you the approximate length the sprouts will be when they are mature and ready to harvest. Use this as a guide for when the sprouts are ready. In general, sprouts that are going to be cooked should be harvested slightly before they reach this length, while sprouts that will be eaten raw should be harvested as per the table.

The "Volume" column indicates the amount that each dry seed will increase in volume when it is sprouted. For example, a seed with a value of four will see its volume increase four times. In other words, one cup of dry seeds will produce four cups of sprouts.

By the way, much of this information came from the Oregon State University Extension Service, which is a good food storage resource. Find out more about them in Chapter 9.

Sprouting Table

Seed Type	Temperature	Rinse Days	Sprout Days	Length in Inches	Volume
Alfalfa	Normal	3–4	3–5	½	6
Barley	Normal	2–3	3–4	¼	2
Beans	Normal	3–4	3–5	1–2	4
Buckwheat	Normal	1	2–3	¼–½	3
Chia	Normal	1	4	1½	28
Corn	Normal	2–3	2–3	½	2
Garden	50°–68° F.	2	3–4	1½	24
Fenugreek	Normal	1–2	4–5	3	16
Garbanzo Beans	68°–72° F.	4–6	2–3	½	3
Lentils	Normal	2–3	3–4	½–1	5
Mung Beans	Normal	4–5	3–4	½–1½	4
Mustard	Normal	2–3	2–3	½–1	4
Radish	Normal	2	3–5	1–2	6
Rye	50°–68° F.	2–3	3–4	¼–½	4
Soybeans	Normal	6–8	3–4	½–1½	3
Triticale	Normal	2–3	2–3	⅛	3
Wheat	Normal	2–3	2–3	¼–½	3

Recipes for Sprouts

As you might have already noticed, we are not shy about sharing our opinions. Well, here's another one we'd like to share. We think that sprouts should be used more as a garnish than as a cooked ingredient. After all, the main benefit of sprouts is the variety they give your diet with their freshness. Why dilute that benefit by cooking them until they aren't fresh anymore?

In previous sections of this chapter, we have explained how sprouts can add zest to any number of foods, including:

- Sandwiches and Burgers

- Salads

- Casseroles

- Mexican Foods

- Pizza

We also explained how any number of recipes could be modified slightly to include sprouts. But we know that some of you demand recipes, and would feel cheated if we didn't give you a few recipes that included sprouts. So here are your recipes—now please quit whining.

Tuna Sprout Summer Salad

1 can tuna	grainy mustard
1 cup chopped sprouts	1 tablespoon sugar
1 cup chopped vegetables	lemon juice
balsamic or rice vinegar	

Break or chop the tuna into bite-sized pieces. Chop the sprouts and the other vegetables (consider using combinations of red and green peppers, tomatoes, zucchini, and onions).

Make a thin paste out of the other ingredients. The amount of paste you need depends upon your taste and the amount of sprouts and vegetables you are using. Mix all ingredients together and season to taste.

Chicken Fried Rice

1 pound chicken breast	1 cup bean sprouts
½ teaspoon cornstarch	½ cup sliced mushrooms
1 teaspoon salt	½ teaspoon salt
1 dash white pepper	3 cups cooked rice
5 tablespoons vegetable oil	2 tablespoons soy sauce
2 slightly beaten eggs	2 chopped green onion tops

Remove bones and skin from chicken breast, and cut into small pieces. Mix together the chicken, cornstarch, salt, and pepper. Heat wok until very hot, then coat the sides with 1 tablespoon oil. Cook and stir the eggs until they are thick but still moist, and then remove from wok and set aside.

Clean, dry, heat wok again, and coat sides with 2 tablespoons oil. Add chicken mixture and stir fry until chicken turns white. Add bean sprouts, mushrooms, and ½ teaspoon salt. Stir fry for 1 minute, then remove from wok and drain. Clean, dry, heat wok again, and coat sides with 2 tablespoons of oil. Add rice and stir fry for 1 minute. Then stir in soy sauce, eggs, chicken mixture, and green onions, and stir fry for another 30 seconds.

Veggie Bean Burgers

1 cup dried pinto beans	sprouts
1 chopped onion	2 tablespoons chili sauce or catsup
2 tablespoons vegetable oil	½ teaspoon prepared mustard
2 tablespoons bread crumbs	dash salt
dash cayenne pepper	cheddar cheese

Cook the beans. Sauté the onion in the vegetable oil until golden brown. Mash together the beans and the onion, then stir in all of the other ingredients except for the cheddar cheese and the sprouts. Mix well and moisten with water if the mixture is too dry. Form mixture into four burgers. Fry. Top with cheese, sprouts, and other toppings of choice. Serve with or without buns—the choice is yours!

Stir Fry Flank Steak

1 tablespoon soy sauce

1 tablespoon rice vinegar

1 teaspoon vegetable oil

1 teaspoon cornstarch

½ teaspoon sugar

¼ teaspoon black pepper

¼ teaspoon salt

1 pound flank steak

1 clove chopped garlic

1 teaspoon minced ginger

2 sliced green onions

½ cup bean sprouts

½ cup snow peas

½ cup mushrooms

Slice the flank steak into thin strips, cutting across the grain of the meat. In a shallow bowl, make a marinade using the first seven ingredients. Add the meat and allow the mixture to sit at room temperature for 30 minutes.

Heat a large skillet or wok and coat it with non-stick spray. Add the steak mixture, garlic, and ginger. Stir fry the ingredients for two minutes or until the steak is still a little pink. Transfer to a separate bowl and set it aside. In another bowl, dissolve 1 tablespoon of cornstarch in 3 tablespoons of water.

Heat skillet again and add more vegetable spray. Add salt, bean sprouts, snow peas, and mushrooms. Stir fry for about 1 minute. Cover and cook for about 1 minute. Uncover and add the beef mixture to the cornstarch mixture. Stir fry until slightly thickened. Then add the green onions and heat thoroughly. Serve immediately over rice or noodles.

Sprout Rollups

chopped vegetables	thin-sliced turkey or ham, or
tortillas	flaked tuna
mayonnaise	sprouts
mustard	shredded cheese

Chop whatever vegetables you have available into ½-inch pieces. (Green onions, tomatoes, and avocados all work well.)

Warm tortillas in the oven or microwave just until they're flexible. Meanwhile, make a dressing by combining the mayonnaise and a small amount of mustard. Put a thin layer of dressing on each tortilla, followed by a thin layer of meat and a thin layer of sprouts. Sprinkle on the chopped vegetables and the shredded cheese. Roll up each tortilla. Either serve it whole as a long sandwich or slice it into 1½-inch pieces secured with a toothpick. Make sure children remove the toothpick before eating!

The number of servings depends on how many tortillas you use. One per person would make an acceptable summer entree, especially if you had a soup or other side dish.

Ginger Vegetable Stir Fry

1 cup pearl onions or onion slices	1 tablespoon vegetable oil
¼ cup orange juice	1 clove minced garlic
¼ cup water	2 tablespoons chopped ginger
1 tablespoon rice vinegar	1 chopped red or green pepper
2 teaspoons grated orange peel	2 cups broccoli florets
1 teaspoon cornstarch	cooked rice or noodles
½ cup sprouts	

Prepare onions and chop into pieces. Make a sauce using orange juice, water, rice vinegar, orange peel, and cornstarch, and set it aside. In a large skillet, heat the oil, and then add garlic and ginger and stir fry for 30 seconds. Add onions, pepper, and broccoli and stir fry for 2–4 minutes. Remove the mixture from the skillet and set it aside. Stir the sauce again, and heat it in the skillet until it is thickened and bubbly. Add the cooked vegetables, and stir well to coat them with the sauce. Cover and cook for 3 more minutes or until heated through. Uncover, stir in sprouts and serve over rice.

Making Your Own Sourdough Bread

A couple of years ago, a popular Christmas present was a "virtual pet." If you slept through that Christmas or were hiding in the Gobi Desert, a virtual pet was a battery-operated gizmo that represented a specific animal—a dog, a cat, a baby chick, a dinosaur, or something else a child would want to have on hand. (Many adults also owned virtual pets, but we're not even going to get into that.) This obnoxious toy beeped when it wanted attention for any reason whatsoever. If the child didn't pay attention to the pet when the pet wanted attention, the virtual pet died. Allegedly, virtual pets were a great way to teach responsibility to children—although not entirely successful because the virtual pets generally "died" long before the batteries gave out.

Sourdough starters are virtual pets without the batteries—always demanding attention or they'll die, but at least they don't call you out of a board meeting.

Clark was astonished to learn we were including sourdough recipes in this book. He thought the only people who could make sourdough were people who had inherited starters from their great-grandfathers. Clark was starterless, because his great-grandfathers apparently had other interests.

What Clark didn't know is that you can make your own sourdough starter in the privacy of your own home. You can look at your sourdough starter and feel the pride of creation, just as Dr. Franken-stein did after the lightning storm. In fact, *you* can be the great-grandparent who passes a sour-dough starter down from generation to generation. All you have to do is to keep your starter alive once you create it.

(And thanks to the information in Appendix B, even dead starters can usually have life breathed back into them. Now you understand the Frankenstein analogy!)

Sourdough purists will tell you that the only true starters are made without yeast. To an extent, they're right. If you're serious about being a sourdough person, make sure to read Appendix B for a wonderful explanation of sourdough starters. But just in case you're lazy, we're going to supply one or two yeast-based recipes as well as non-yeast ones. You can choose which one suits your taste and your degree of commitment. You can also choose how tart you want your sourdough starter to be, based on the information in that handy appendix. Some people like a lip-puckering astringency to their sourdough; others just want a product that tastes a little different from what they eat every day. The choice is yours.

See Chapter 9 for more resources.

In case you haven't already considered sourdough, there's a huge advantage to getting cultured. That is, if you get hooked on sourdough you'll never again have to worry about whether your yeast is still good. Yeast dies awfully fast, and its short shelf life is one of the many weak links in a food storage program that relies on homemade grain products. But if you have your own sourdough starter, you'll no longer have to rely on yeast. There are multitudes of sourdough recipes. We'll give you some here, and Chapter 9 will include at least one web link so you can download zillions of free sourdough recipes from the Internet. Once you get excited about sourdough, it can become a great family hobby. We have one friend who brings his world-famous sourdough pancakes to our annual Fourth of July church breakfast. Sourdough pancakes are among his claims to fame.

A Sourdough Primer

An evangelist for sourdough, Ty M. Bittner, has cheerfully spread the sourdough word on the Internet—for free. He is a proponent of the yeast school of sourdough, which means that purists may want to take what he says with a grain of salt. Nevertheless, he has good ideas for beginners. We've adapted his information here for your convenience.

1. **Equipment.** Some of this equipment is optional, but don't skimp on the bowls. Sourdough does not *like* metal bowls. Do not use metal bowls (or even metal measuring cups) when you're working with sourdough. Other equipment may include:

- a good clean jar with a clean lid (a mayonnaise jar does fine)

- a large pottery, ceramic, or glass bowl (you may want a small one, too)

- a large rubber spatula

- an assortment of bread pans

- cheesecloth or dish towel

- plastic or glass measuring cups; plastic measuring spoons

- whisk

- cooling rack

- a work space

- sense of humor and patience

2. *Flour.* The best flour to use is **unbleached all-purpose flour**. It has a better flavor in breads and has an off-white color. Unbleached flour has obviously not been bleached or chemically whitened. It has been aged to naturally oxidize or whiten. Other flours include **bread flour**, which is a high-protein flour with a high gluten content; **all-purpose bleached flour**, which is flour with chemical additives; **self-rising flour**, which is combined with baking powder and other ingredients that could be out of date. It should not be used in bread baking. Once you learn the basics of sourdough, feel free to experiment with whole wheat flour or rye flour or even cornmeal. (By the time you've gotten to that point, you should have abandoned this primer and should be working from Appendix B.) Remember that the quality of your flour influences the quality of your sourdough products. If you can keep your flour frozen, this isn't a bad alternative. Otherwise, consider storing it in a large plastic container that has been labeled so you'll know what kind of flour you're using. Then keep it in a dark cool place.

3. *Starter.* If you don't have a friend who will cheerfully give you some starter, you'll need to make your own. We've included a bunch of starter recipes after this primer. Choose one you'd like to try, or use Mr. Bittner's authentic (yeastless) recipe, which consists of **2 cups unbleached all-purpose flour, 2 cups warm water**

(preferably not from the tap), and **1 tablespoon honey**. Assemble the ingredients and mix them in a glass or ceramic bowl that has been sterilized to kill off the microorganisms. Clean the sides of the bowl with a spatula and cover it with a cloth. Place the bowl in a warm space that has plenty of air flow. Twice a day, stir the contents of the bowl. In a few days, you should start to notice a sour aroma. If it's not a *nice* sour aroma, throw the batch out and start over. But if it's a nice sourdough aroma, you've got your starter. Congratulations!

4. ***Care and feeding of your starter.*** A properly cared for starter will last quite a long time. But starters evolve as time passes, due to the microorganisms in the air. If you have a starter you like just the way it is, go to Appendix B to learn ways you can preserve the flavor you have now in case your starter becomes corrupted. In the meantime, here are ways to care for the starter you're using right now.

- First, use clean equipment. This keeps out germs, as well as unappetizing globs of hardened dough.

- Stir your starter daily, or preferably twice a day. This helps keep the mixture like a pancake batter consistency, which is what you want. It will also stir in the amber liquid that floats to the top.

- Refrigerate your starter when not baking with it. (That's why you have that handy glass jar!) You can even freeze it if you put it in a container that won't crack with the expansion of the liquid. You may want to even try to dry it by spreading it out on a cookie sheet. (See Appendix B for all sorts of spiffy ideas.)

- Most of the time you will feed your starter by replacing what you took out to bake with. You replace it by adding 1 cup of warm water and 1 cup of flour and mixing it in. You can feed it if you have not used it in a while just by taking a cup of starter out and giving it to a friend or the trash can. If you want to increase the amount of starter just keep adding 1 cup of flour and water per day till you have what you need. If the starter is slow, or does not perform well when baking, look for help in Appendix B.

- After you use your starter and replace it with new "food," let the mixture work for a day or so to catch up before you store it again. Also let it work at least overnight before you use it for baking.

Homemade Sourdough Starter Recipes

Basic Starter

1 cup flour   2 tablespoons sugar
1 cup water

Mix very well and let stand for several days or a week at room temperature, stirring every day. This gets quite pungent, but don't cover it tightly. After the mixture has sat for as many days as you have patience for, add **1 cup flour** and **1 cup water**. The next day, the starter should be ready to use. Now add an additional **1 cup flour** and **1 cup water** every time you take some out. But make sure that you stir it every day. If you get tired of it freeze a piece and when you are ready to start again let it come to room temperature for 1 day before using it. Then proceed as before.

Cheater's Sourdough Starter

1 package yeast   1 cup sugar
1½ cups warm water   6 tablespoons instant potato
                                         flakes

Mix together (always use a wooden spoon). Stir well. Then pour into a mason jar and poke about 3 holes in the top of the lid or tin foil.

Refrigerate 3–5 days. When you remove it from your refrigerator, FEED it first using the following: Mix this in a separate bowl and add to starter:

¾ cup sugar   1 cup warm water
3 tablespoons instant potato flakes

Wait a day or two after a feeding before using the starter again.

10-Day Starter and Lemon Pudding Bread

Day 1:

1 cup flour   **1 cup milk**
1 cup sugar

Mix in a container with tight lid. Use only a wooden spoon. Do not use a metal bowl or metal spoon. Do not refrigerate.

Days 2–4:

Stir mixture with wooden spoon.

Day 5:

1 cup sugar   **1 cup milk**
1 cup flour

Add ingredients above. Stir. At this point, transfer to a large container with an air-tight lid.

Days 6–9:

Stir mixture with wooden spoon.

Day 10:

1 cup sugar   **1 cup milk**
1 cup flour

Add ingredients above. Pour 1 cup of mixture into 3 containers and give away with a set of instructions. To the remaining batch, add:

¾ cup oil	**½ teaspoon baking soda**
3 eggs	**1 small box instant lemon**
1 teaspoon vanilla	**(or banana) pudding**
1 cup chopped nuts	**2 cups flour**
1¼ teaspoons baking powder	**1 cup sugar**
½ teaspoon salt	**1 teaspoon cinnamon**

Mix all together well. Pour into 2 well-greased and sugared loaf pans. Bake at 350°F. for 50–60 minutes. Cool before removing from pans.

Prospector's Starter

In an earthenware crock place **4 cups flour**, **2 tablespoons sugar**, **1 tablespoon vinegar**, add enough **water** to make a light, creamy batter, cover loosely with a **cheesecloth** and leave in a warm spot. This mixture should be ready for use in 7 to 10 days. If properly working, the starter will bubble and "work," giving off a pleasant and slightly sour smell.

Yogurt Sourdough Starter

2 tablespoons natural plain yogurt   1 cup white flour
1 cup lowfat milk

Heat milk to 100°F. Remove from heat and stir in yogurt. Pour into scalded glass jar or bowl, cover with plastic and place in a warm location for 18 hours. Consistency will be like thin pancake batter. Stir in flour until well blended, cover again with plastic and pierce with fork to release gases. Place in a warm, draft-free location at an even 85°F. for 2 days; stir several times each day. The mixture should have a strong sourdough smell and show bubbles. Refrigerate until ready to use. When replenishing starter, add lukewarm milk instead of water.

Sourdough Recipes

Amish Oatmeal Bread
(yield: 12 servings)

1 cup active sourdough starter	3 eggs
½ cup vegetable oil	2 teaspoons baking powder
1 cup light brown sugar	½ teaspoon baking soda
¾ cup all-purpose flour	1½ teaspoons cinnamon
¾ cup quick oats	½ teaspoon nutmeg

Mix all ingredients together. Bake at 350°F. for 40 minutes.

Sourdough Applesauce Cake
(yield: 4 servings)

1 cup active sourdough starter	½ teaspoon allspice
¼ cup nonfat dry milk	½ teaspoon ground cloves
1 cup unbleached flour	2 teaspoons baking soda
1 cup applesauce	½ cup white sugar
(homemade, if possible)	½ cup brown sugar
½ teaspoon salt	½ cup butter
1 teaspoon cinnamon	1 large egg, well beaten
½ teaspoon nutmeg	raisins or nuts (optional)

Mix together the starter, milk, flour, and applesauce, and let stand in a covered bowl in a warm place. In another bowl, cream together the sugars and butter. Add the beaten egg and mix well. Add soda and spices. Add a half cup of raisins or chopped nuts, or a mixture of the two. Add starter mix and beat by hand until well mixed and without lumps. Bake at 350°F. for half to three quarters of an hour. Test for doneness with a knife when half an hour is up. Allow to cool until cold before cutting and serving.

Ty Bittner's Sourdough Bread The Easy Way

1½ cups lukewarm water
1 tablespoon sugar or honey
1 tablespoon active dry yeast
  (one package)
1 tablespoon olive oil

5½ to 6½ cups unbleached
  all-purpose flour
1 tablespoon salt
1 cup active sourdough starter

The Sponge: In a large mixing bowl, dissolve the sugar or honey in the water, (try not to use tap water); then add the yeast. Let it sit for 10 minutes or until it activates. Add the starter and stir. Gradually add 3 cups flour, stirring until smooth. Cover the sponge and let it sit in a warm draft-free place for 2 to 3 hours. It may not take that long but you are looking for at least double the volume. Try placing it in the oven with the door propped open and the temperature turned off.

The Dough: Stir down the sponge with a spatula. Stir in the salt and olive oil. Gradually add the flour until the dough no longer sticks to the side of the bowl, or at least till you can dump it out on the counter and work in the flour by hand. After you turn the dough out onto a floured counter, knead for a few minutes. Let the dough rest. Clean out and grease the bowl with a little more olive oil. Continue kneading until the dough becomes firm and elastic and you have put in most or all of the flour (I've never been able to use all the flour). Place the dough ball into the greased bowl and flip it around to cover the entire ball with oil. Cover it with a towel and let it rise in a warm place for about an hour or so, or until it has almost doubled in bulk. Back to the unheated oven with you!

Baking: Turn the dough out and shape into 2 loaves. I do this by inverting the bowl onto the counter and letting the dough fall out. Cut the dough ball in half with a knife or dough knife. Then gently shape into 2 loaves. Place into loaf pans that have been greased with yet more olive oil. Let the loaves rise for 1–1½ hours covered with a cloth (back again to the unheated oven). Be careful towards the end of the last rising to take the loaves out of the oven and preheat it to 375°F. With a sharp knife and being careful not to let the loaves fall, score them down the middle lengthwise (it looks pretty). Brush the top of the loaves with water and bake for 30 minutes or until the loaves are golden brown and are hollow when thumped. Check at about 20 to 25 minutes to see that the loaves are not too done on top. If they are getting too brown for your liking, cover the tops with foil and continue to bake. Cool on racks. Then slice off a piece and load it with butter!

Bran Date Bread
(yield: 12 slices)

1¼ cups unbleached flour, sifted
1½ teaspoons baking powder
1 teaspoon salt
¾ cup firmly packed brown sugar
1 cup All Bran cereal
1 teaspoon grated lemon peel

¾ cup buttermilk or sour milk
2 large eggs, beaten
¼ cup vegetable oil
½ cup active sourdough starter
1 cup finely chopped pitted dates

Sift the first three ingredients together. Dust dates with 1 tablespoon of the flour mixture, then add to the bowl. Then add the brown sugar, All Bran, and grated lemon peel. Combine buttermilk, beaten eggs, and vegetable oil. Stir in dates. Add all at once to flour mixture with the sourdough starter, stirring until well moistened. Pour into a greased loaf pan about 9x5 inches. Bake at 350°F. for 1 hour. Allow to stand 10 minutes in pan and then remove from pan and cool until cold. Wrap in plastic wrap or foil and refrigerate. To serve, spread with butter or cream cheese.

Sheepherder Bread

1½ cups sourdough starter
4 cups unbleached flour
1 teaspoon salt

2 tablespoons sugar
¼ teaspoon baking soda
2 tablespoons shortening

Place sourdough starter into a large (non-metal) bowl. Form a well in the center of the starter. In a second large bowl, blend dry ingredients. Add dry mix into the starter from the edges with enough flour and knead with the melted shortening until smooth and shiny. Place in greased bowl and let rise until almost double. Shape into 2 loaves and place in greased bread pans. Bake at 375°F. until done.

Two-Day Sourdough Waffles
(yield: 6 waffles)

Mix, and let stand overnight:

2 cups flour   ½ cup starter
2 cups water

The next day:

2 cups of the overnight mix   2 tablespoons sugar
2 eggs   ¼ cup corn oil
1 teaspoon salt   1 teaspoon soda
½ teaspoon cinnamon

In the morning save 2 cups of the overnight mix for waffles. Feed the rest to your starter jar and return your starter jar to the refrigerator. Mix all ingredients well. Add oil just before baking. If waffles stick, add a little more oil. Because sourdough is relatively unpredictable, it is hard to judge how much oil to use. Use a hot waffle iron.

Sourdough Pancakes
(yield: 4 servings)

3 large eggs, beaten   1 teaspoon baking soda
1 cup sweet milk   2 teaspoons baking powder
2 cups active sourdough starter 1½ teaspoons salt
1¾ cups unbleached flour   ¼ cup sugar

Beat eggs. Add milk and starter. Sift together the flour, soda, baking powder, salt, and sugar. Mix together. Drop onto hot griddle by large spoonful. NOTE: If ungreased griddle is used, add ¼ cup melted fat to the above recipe. Bacon fat tastes great.

Sourdough English Muffins
(yield: 12 muffins)

½ cup active sourdough starter
1 cup milk
2¾ cups unsifted all-purpose flour
1 tablespoon sugar

¾ teaspoon salt
½ teaspoon baking soda
about 3 tablespoons cornmeal

In a large mixing bowl, combine starter, milk, and 2 cups flour; mix together, cover loosely and set aside at room temperature overnight. Mix ½ cup flour, sugar, salt, and baking soda; sprinkle over dough and mix thoroughly. Turn this very stiff dough onto a floured board with the remaining ¼ cup flour; knead 2–3 minutes or until no longer sticky, adding flour if necessary. Roll dough out to a ¾-inch thickness. Using a 3-inch cutter, cut out 12 muffins. Place muffins 1-inch apart on a cookie sheet covered with waxed paper which has been sprinkled with cornmeal. Sprinkle more cornmeal over top. Cover with a cloth or waxed paper; set aside in warm place to rise (about 45 minutes). Bake on a lightly greased electric skillet set at 275°F. or in a frying pan over medium heat for 8 to 10 minutes per side, turning once. Serve warm from griddle, or split and toast.

Sourdough Biscuits

1 cup sourdough starter
1 cup flour
¾ teaspoon soda

¼ teaspoon salt
⅓ cup butter or oil

Mix all ingredients well. Use a large spoon to drop clumps of dough on a greased baking sheet. Bake each batch at 350°F. for 10–12 minutes.

Mendenhall Sourdough Gingerbread
(yield: 4 servings)

1 cup active starter	½ cup hot water
½ cup molasses	½ teaspoon salt
1 teaspoon baking soda	½ cup firmly packed brown
1 large egg	sugar
1 teaspoon ginger	1½ cups unbleached flour
½ cup shortening	1 teaspoon cinnamon

Cream brown sugar and shortening. Then add molasses and egg, beating continuously. Sift dry ingredients together and blend into hot water. Then beat this mixture into creamed mixture. As the last step, add the sourdough starter slowly, mixing carefully to maintain a bubbly batter. Bake in greased square pan at 375°F. for about 30 minutes or until done. Serve with ice cream or whipped cream while still hot if possible.

Baked Stuffed French Toast
(yield: 4 servings)

4 large slices sourdough bread, cubed (without crust)	6 eggs
	1 cup milk
8-ounce package cream cheese, cut into cubes	1½ teaspoons ground cinnamon
	2–3 tablespoons powdered sugar
1 large Granny Smith apple, peeled & chopped	Maple or fruit syrup

Preheat oven to 375°F. Place half the bread cubes in an ungreased 11x7-inch baking dish. Cover with the cream cheese cubes, distributing evenly. Sprinkle with the chopped apple. Top evenly with the remaining bread cubes. Beat together the eggs, milk, and cinnamon until well blended. Pour over the bread mixture in the dish. Bake for about 35 minutes or until set. Sprinkle with the powdered sugar. Serve with syrup.

Bread Machine Sourdough

¾ cup active sourdough starter
5 ounces water or milk
¾ teaspoon salt

2–3 teaspoons sugar
2½ cups unbleached flour
2 teaspoons yeast (optional)

For this recipe, your starter should be the consistency of thin pancake batter. If it's not, thin it down by starting with about ½–⅔ cup starter and then adding water until the right consistency is reached. Bake at a medium setting. This is a loose-crumb bread that is very tasty. (Note: Sourdough bread tastes more sour if you're using water instead of milk in the recipe.)

49er Christmas Bread
(yield: 2 loaves)

2 cups active sourdough starter
1 teaspoon salt
½ cup melted butter
1 cup milk
2 eggs, beaten
½ cup sugar

1 cup raisins or dried cranberries
½ teaspoon mace
½ teaspoon cinnamon
5 cups flour
powdered sugar (optional)

Add salt, sugar, milk, eggs, melted butter, raisins, and spices to the starter and mix well. Add the flour a cup at a time until too stiff to mix by hand. Then turn onto a floured board and knead in remaining flour. Divide in half. Form two loaves, place in greased loaf pans, and let rise in a warm place 1½–3 hours (until the dough rises 1–2 inches above the top of the pan). Bake in preheated 400°F. oven for 55–60 minutes. Cool on racks. If frosting sounds appealing, make a glaze with powdered sugar and milk, and dribble over the top of the cooled loaves.

Pumpkin-Mincemeat Bread

4 cups all-purpose flour	4 eggs
1 teaspoon baking powder	½ cup active sourdough starter
1½ teaspoons baking soda	⅔ cup water
1½ teaspoons salt	1 cup vegetable oil
2 tablespoons pumpkin pie spice	2 cups canned pumpkin
1½ cups granulated sugar	½ cup prepared mincemeat
1½ cups packed brown sugar	1 cup chopped pecans

Grease three 9x5-inch or five 7½x4-inch loaf pans, and set aside. Preheat oven to 350°F. In a large bowl, stir together flour, baking powder, baking soda, salt, pumpkin pie spice, granulated sugar, and brown sugar; set aside. In a medium bowl, beat eggs. Stir in sourdough starter, water, oil, and pumpkin. Pour all at once into flour mixture. Stir until dry ingredients are just moistened. Stir in mincemeat and nuts. Pour evenly into prepared pans. Bake in pre-heated oven 1 hour or until a wooden pick inserted in center comes out clean. Turn out of pans. Cool top side up on a rack. Wrap each cooled loaf in plastic wrap or foil as a gift or to freeze. Thaw wrapped frozen loaves at room temperature 2 hours. Makes 3 large loaves or 5 medium loaves.

Sourdough Pizza Shells
(yield: 1 shell)

1 cup active sourdough starter	1 teaspoon salt
1 tablespoon shortening, melted	1 cup flour

Mix ingredients, working in the flour until you have a soft dough. Roll out into a flat shape. Dash oil over a dough sheet and place dough on it. Bake about 5 minutes at 375°F. It doesn't take long, so watch carefully. Have pizza sauce and topping ready and make pizza as usual.

Sourdough Cinnamon Rolls

1 cup active sourdough starter
½ cup powdered milk
2 teaspoons salt
3 tablespoons sugar

2 tablespoons shortening
½ cup whole milk
2½ cups unbleached flour
1½ teaspoons baking soda

Mix ingredients together, working in the flour until a good dough results. Divide the dough into two parts, rolling each out into large rectangles about ¼-inch thick. Do the following with each half: Dot with **butter**, sprinkle with ¼ to ½ cup of **brown sugar** mixed with 1 teaspoon **cinnamon** or to your taste. Also add soft **raisins** or chopped **nuts**, if that's the way you like your cinnamon rolls. Roll each rectangle into a long tube, cut off 1-inch slices and place in pan in which has been prepared with a mixture of **2 tablespoons of melted butter, 3 tablespoons of brown sugar, ½ teaspoon of cinnamon, and a dash of salt**. Let dough rise about an hour and bake at 325°F. Serve with sticky side up.

Sourdough Banana Bread
(yield: 12 servings)

½ cup shortening
1 cup sugar
1 large egg
1 cup mashed bananas
1 cup active sourdough starter
2 cups unbleached flour

1 teaspoon salt
1 teaspoon baking powder
½ teaspoon baking soda
¾ cup chopped nuts
1 teaspoon vanilla OR
1 teaspoon grated orange peel

Cream together the shortening and sugar, add egg and mix until blended. Stir in bananas and sourdough starter. Add orange peel or vanilla. Stir flour and sift together with salt, baking powder, and soda. Add flour mixture and nuts to the first mixture, stirring until just blended. Pour into greased 9x5-inch loaf pan. Bake in 350°F. oven for 1 hour or until toothpick comes out clean. Slice when cold.

Norman's Sourdough Cornmeal Cakes
(yield: 1 family breakfast)

4 cups flour
2 cups cornmeal
½ cup milk

½ cup active sourdough starter
3 eggs
2 teaspoons soda

Mix all ingredients together the night before and let rise in a warm place. Bake on a griddle the next morning, just as you would pancakes. This is a tasty pancake alternative, and the cornmeal provides roughage.

Sourdough Soda Bread
(yield: 1 round loaf)

2 cups whole wheat flour
2 cups all-purpose flour
1 teaspoon baking powder
1½ teaspoons baking soda
1 tablespoon sugar
1 pinch salt
1 cup active starter

1 cup buttermilk
1 tablespoon honey
1 tablespoon pure maple syrup
1 teaspoon dried basil
¼ teaspoon dried thyme

In a large bowl combine the flours, the baking powder, the baking soda, salt, and sugar. Stir well. Mix the sourdough starter and buttermilk in a 1-quart cup and blend in the honey, syrup, basil, and thyme. Pour the liquid mixture into the flour mixture. Knead until a dough forms. Turn onto a floured surface and continue kneading. Form into a round loaf and slit the top several times. Place a pan of water on the lowest rung of the oven. Preheat the oven to 400°F. Place the dough on a non-stick cookie sheet or pizza pan that has been sprinkled with **cornmeal** and place it in the oven directly above the pan of water; bake for 30 minutes.

Sourdough Cornbread
(yield: 4 servings)

½ cup sourdough starter
2 tablespoons butter, melted
½ cup cornmeal
1 teaspoon salt
1 tablespoon sugar

½ cup yogurt or sour cream
2 large eggs, stirred
1 cup unbleached flour
½ teaspoon cream of tartar
½ teaspoon baking powder

Mix ingredients in the above order, stirring only enough to blend the mixture. Pour into a buttered pan. Bake in a 375°– 400°F. oven for about 15 minutes.

Sourdough Sam's Doughnuts
(yield: 4 servings)

½ cup active sourdough starter
½ cup sugar
2 tablespoons shortening
2 cups unbleached flour
1 teaspoon baking powder
1 large egg

½ teaspoon nutmeg
¼ teaspoon cinnamon
½ teaspoon baking soda
½ teaspoon salt
⅓ cup buttermilk or sour milk
powdered sugar (optional)

Sift dry ingredients, stir into liquid, roll out, and cut with regular doughnut cutter. Then heat some oil in a deep fryer to 390°F. and fry. Makes about 17 doughnuts with holes. Just before serving, dust with powdered or cinnamon sugar. (**Note: These doughnuts are virtually greaseless. You can also make extra batches and freeze after frying. Just thaw, dust with powdered sugar, and eat.**)

San Francisco Sourdough Bread
(yield: 2 loaves)

1 tablespoon active dry yeast	2 tablespoons apple cider
1½ cups warm water	vinegar
1 cup sourdough starter	5½ cups white flour
1 tablespoon sugar	½ teaspoon baking soda
½ tablespoon salt	yellow cornmeal

In a large warmed bowl, sprinkle yeast over water, stir to dissolve and let stand until bubbly. Blend in starter, sugar, salt, and vinegar. Gradually beat in 3 cups of the flour and continue beating at least 3 minutes. Turn batter into a large, oiled glass or ceramic bowl, cover with towel and let rise in warm place 1 hour or until double in bulk. Combine 1 cup of the remaining flour with baking soda. Stir batter down and add flour-baking soda mixture. Gradually add remaining flour to make a stiff dough. Turn out onto floured board and knead, adding additional flour only as needed to prevent sticking (approximately 300 strokes of folding and turning). Sprinkle a greased baking sheet with cornmeal. Form dough into 2 oblong loaves and place on sheet. Cover with towel and let rise in warm place 1–1½ hours or until not quite double in size. With sharp razor, slash the tops of loaves diagonally. Mist with water and bake in 450°F. oven 10 minutes. Reduce heat to 400°F. and bake 35 minutes longer or until bread tests done. For a harder crust, place a pan of hot water on bottom of oven and mist with water several times during baking. Remove pan of water after 15 minutes of baking. Turn out onto wire rack and cool. **(Note: If you like your sourdough very dark, remove the baked bread from the pan or sheet and place under broiler about 2 minutes, or until rich brown in color.)**

Flatbread

2 cups active sourdough starter
½ cup water
1 teaspoon salt

1 teaspoon sugar
3 cups white flour

Add water, sugar, and salt to the sourdough starter and mix well. Add flour, one cup at a time, until it's almost too stiff to mix by hand. Knead until satiny. Divide dough into 6 equal balls. Roll each ball into a 6-inch round, and place under a floured cloth. Let rise for 30 minutes at 85°F. Preheat oiled heavy griddle or baking sheet to 550°F. in the oven. Carefully transfer 2 rounds at a time to the oiled griddle with a hand board or large spatula. Bake 5 minutes or till they puff in the middle and start to brown.

Pat's Sourdough Chocolate Chip Cookies
(yield: 70 cookies)

4½ cups flour
2 teaspoons baking soda
1 teaspoon salt
1 cup butter
1 cup shortening
1½ cups sugar

1¼ cups brown sugar
2 teaspoons vanilla
1 cup sourdough starter
4 eggs
1¾ cups chopped nuts
2 12-ounce packages
    chocolate chips

Preheat oven to 375°F. Soften butter and shortening. In a large bowl, combine butter, shortening, and sugars. Mix well. Add eggs and beat until all are blended. Add vanilla and sourdough starter. Beat in flour, soda, salt, and mix well. Stir in nuts and chocolate chips. Drop by tablespoons onto greased cookie sheet. Bake 10–12 minutes.

Sourdough Raisin-Oat Bread
(yield: 2 loaves)

1 cup lukewarm evaporated milk	½ tablespoon salt
1½ cups sourdough starter	1 teaspoon ground allspice
½ cup molasses	2 cups unprocessed rolled oats
½ cup honey	¾ cups raisins
4 tablespoons butter, melted	2½ cups white flour

In a large warmed bowl, combine milk, starter, molasses, honey, butter, salt, and allspice. Gradually add oats, a small amount at a time, mixing in well. Then stir in raisins, which have been tossed lightly with a little flour to keep them from sliding to the bottom of the loaf. Beat in flour, ½ cup at a time, to form a stiff dough. Turn out onto floured board and knead 5–7 minutes, adding additional flour only as needed to prevent sticking. Form into smooth ball, place in oiled bowl, turn to coat all surfaces, cover with dampened towel and let rise in warm place at least 2 hours or until double in bulk. Punch down, turn out onto board and knead briefly. Cover with towel and let rise 10 minutes. Divide dough into 2 equal portions, form into loaves and place in two #2 loaf pans. Cover with towel and let rise in warm place 1½ hours or until almost double in size. Bake at 375°F. for 35–40 minutes, or until bread tests done. Turn out onto wire rack, turn right side up and cool.

Making Your Own Yogurt

Yogurt is milk you can eat with a fork. It is made with milk that is fermented with bacteria that convert some of the milk sugar into lactic acid. Depending on who you talk to, yogurt is either one of the finest elixirs on Earth, or it's just another snack food. We'll let you decide for yourself.

If you've grown up in America, and have only seen yogurt in those little plastic containers, you may not realize that a third of the world's population eats yogurt on a regular basis—and has been doing so for more than 4,000 years. There are all sorts of health benefits that are claimed from yogurt. It's dense in nutrients, and is digestible by people who are normally intolerant of milk products. It also has a high water content, and water is always good for us. People claim that yogurt can reduce the risk of cancer, decrease your serum cholesterol, and boost your immune system (something we can all use in such a toxic environment). If you're interested in doing a little research, we've included some Internet sites in Chapter 9.

Yogurt itself is a low-calorie food, which means many people use yogurt as a mainstay in a weight-reducing diet. They may be sabotaging themselves when they do so. Plain yogurt can be made from whole milk, from low-fat milk, or from skim—but yogurt's calories don't lie in the milk. It's the added fruit and sugar (and sometimes even chocolate!) that turn yogurt from a diet food into a snack food. If the only reason you're eating yogurt is to lose weight, make sure you know what you're eating.

Even yogurt's biggest fans admit it's the live cultures in yogurt that make all the difference. If your yogurt doesn't have the live cultures, you might as well be eating—well, junk food. And the yogurt that's sold in those little plastic containers may or may not contain live cultures. It all depends on whether the yogurt has been heated to prolong its shelf life. If you buy your yogurt from the supermarket, *read the labels*. If the label doesn't say the yogurt contains live cultures, buy another brand.

If you want a family of yogurt-eaters, the best time to start is when the children are young. If you start eating yogurt as an adult, you may never develop a taste for it. In our own family, Clark could eat yogurt every day of his life. Kathy has tried, sometimes valiantly, to enjoy yogurt—but it just hasn't worked. There is a reason for this. Kathy grew up on raw oysters, which are not part of your basic food storage program. Clark, on the other hand, was fed yogurt as a young child. He can't remember a time when he didn't eat yogurt.

Because yogurt is an acquired taste, don't just jump with both feet into yogurt-making until you're sure your family is going to eat the yogurt you've produced. But if you can get your family members to enjoy yogurt, perhaps by starting them off with some of the great recipes we'll provide in this section, you'll also find that yogurt is easy to make and is a terrific supplement to your food storage. You can also sneak yogurt into other recipes without your family ever being the wiser. The bacteria in yogurt work particularly well with baking soda, so feel free to use yogurt as part or all of the oil in cakes, waffles, pancakes, and muffins.

There are numerous yogurt-making machines on the market, and they don't cost a whole lot of money. But you don't have to buy a machine. You can make yogurt in your oven . . . or in your clothes dryer. In case you don't believe us, a recipe for clothes dryer yogurt follows:

Clothes Dryer Yogurt

2 tablespoons plain yogurt (Dannon is a good brand)
3 cups milk

Boil the milk and then reduce the heat to a simmer. Keep it boiling gently. If it burns slightly on the bottom, make sure not to scrape the burned portion off. Cook the milk for about 5 minutes, until it is still slightly warm but so that you can handle the pot with your bare hands.

Heat up your clothes dryer by running the empty dryer for 5–10 minutes on high. Mix the yogurt culture into the milk and pour into a glass bowl or casserole dish with a lid. Turn the dryer off and put the covered bowl in the dryer and close the door. The low heat of the dryer should culture the yogurt in 8–12 hours. Refrigerate when finished.

As an alternative to a clothes dryer, keep the mixture in the oven, using no heat but the oven light. For a gas oven, the pilot light for the oven will often be warm enough.

Your First Yogurt Project

If you're nervous about making yogurt, let's walk you through a project. First, assemble these supplies:

1 glass quart jar, with a lid
cooking thermometer
powdered milk

1 carton Dannon unflavored yogurt
an insulated lunch carrier (optional)

❏ 1. First of all, clean your supplies to kill germs that may be lurking in your quart jar or on your equipment. This is the hardest part about making yogurt, so you can tell how easy yogurt making is.

❏ 2. When your equipment is clean, fill your jar about ¾ full of hot tap water. (Measure your hottest tap water with that handy cooking thermometer. If the temperature doesn't reach 130°F., heat it until it does.)

❏ 3. When you have a jar that's ¾ full of that hot tap water, add enough powdered milk to make a quart of milk. (Use the recipe on the box to determine how much that is for your brand.)

❏ 4. Put the lid on the jar and shake it like crazy until the powder is dissolved and the milk is thoroughly mixed. (If you're a musical person, you have permission to dance around the kitchen.)

❏ 5. Add 2 *heaping* tablespoons of yogurt to the jar. Stir it in until it is dissolved in the milk.

❏ 6. If you have an insulated lunch carrier, put the jar in the carrier, close it, wrap the whole thing with towels, and let it sit overnight. If you don't have an insulated lunch carrier, you can improvise by going to the recipe for Clothes Dryer Yogurt and following the directions for storing your yogurt in the clothes dryer or oven.

❏ 7. After the jar has been sitting for 12–18 hours, your yogurt should be ready. If it isn't thick enough or tart enough, let it sit in a warm place for a little longer. Don't fret if your yogurt isn't perfect the first time around. The ingredients are cheap; try again, or use a different recipe. Refrigerate it or eat it warm, according to your personal taste.

Yogurt by the Gallon

7 cups powdered milk
1 cup plain Dannon yogurt
large glass container with a lid
   (it must have a capacity greater
   than a gallon)

2 measuring cups
a large, sturdy spoon for stirring
a cooking thermometer
an insulated cooler that's bigger
   than the large glass container

Wash all your equipment in hot, soapy water to kill the germs. Put 1 gallon of water (105°–110°F.) in your large bottle. Add powdered milk and yogurt. Stir until the yogurt is dissolved (about 2 minutes). Seal the container and place inside the insulated cooler. Fill the cooler with 105°–110°F. water. Close the cooler and let it sit for about 20 hours. (It may take anywhere from 8–24 hours, but that first batch takes longer to ferment.)

Handy Yogurt-Making Tips

➡ Now that you're all excited about making yogurt, here are some handy tips to make your project a successful one.

● Successful yogurt making depends on bacterial growth, but you only want the right bacteria growing in your yogurt. Thus, you should work with glass or ceramic containers (metal inhibits bacterial growth, and plastic has little crevices in it where nasty things can hide). Your containers should be germ-free when you start your yogurt-making process. You can kill the germs by running your bowls through the dishwasher (with the hot drying cycle), or by boiling water in them. As long as you kill the germs, that's all that matters.

● Some people who make yogurt insist that as long as you're killing germs, you should also kill the germs that are in the milk you'll be using. These germs are the ones that make milk go bad, and you don't want those germs in your yogurt. If this makes sense to you, scald your milk by bringing it to a boil before you make your yogurt. As you'll notice, our recipe for Clothes Dryer Yogurt calls for this—but our other yogurt recipes don't. You choose.

● Once you start making yogurt, you need to maintain a proper incubation temperature. This doesn't have to be as precise as the temperature when you're creating a sourdough starter. Any temperature that is between body temperature (98.6°F.) and about 130°F. should be sufficient. As long as you stay within that range, though, the higher temperatures are better. Increasing the temperature can halve the time the yogurt will take to cook—but just don't make that yogurt *too* hot!

● The starter should be protected from contamination. As soon as you finish your first batch of yogurt, set aside enough of that batch to start a second batch. Keep your starter in the refrigerator, tightly sealed in a clean glass container, until you're ready to make your next batch. By the way, yogurt cultures are like sourdough cultures in that they have a tendency to snatch bacteria from the air and evolve over time into something that was quite different from what you started out with. If you notice that the flavor of your starter has drifted, begin with a new starter. (And if you produce a starter that is so beloved by your family that you develop an emotional attachment to it, starter can be frozen for later use. Just put it in an ice-cube tray and store your "yogurt cubes" in bags. A cube should equal at least one of the two tablespoons of yogurt starter that you'll need to produce a quart of fresh yogurt.)

- When you make your first batch of yogurt, it may not be as thick as you're accustomed to. It will get thicker (and more tart) if it sits longer. After you've made that first batch and are using it as starter, you may not have to let it ferment as long. Conversely, for a blander yogurt, make it quickly!

- The acidity that turns milk into yogurt is also helpful for keeping your yogurt fresh. If you keep your yogurt containers tightly closed and refrigerated, they should keep a couple of months (or maybe more) in the refrigerator. If a layer of white mold grows on your yogurt, you can still skim off that mold and use the yogurt in baking recipes. (If the very idea of eating moldy yogurt turns your stomach, you may be reassured to know that mold only grows where it has access to the air. This means that top layer is the only contaminated part of your yogurt.)

- Make **yogurt cheese** by placing yogurt on a piece of cheesecloth. Draw the sides of the cheesecloth up to make a bag and hang the bag over a container overnight. What drips out is "whey," as in the Little Miss Muffett story. *You* figure out what to do with that! What's left is yogurt cheese. It has the consistency of cream cheese and can be used as cream cheese. Try doctoring it up with garlic or chives or even pineapple. It's a great spread for crackers or bread.

Useful Recipes for Cultured Folk

Faygie's Lemon Yogurt Bundt Cake

Cake:

3 cups flour	½ cup milk
2 cups sugar	½ cup vegetable oil
2 teaspoons baking powder	1 [8 ounces] container low-fat
½ teaspoon salt	lemon yogurt
3 eggs	½ cup fresh lemon juice
1 egg yolk	grated peel of 1 lemon

Glaze:

½ cup strained fresh lemon juice	2 tablespoons grated lemon peel
½ cup sugar	

Preheat oven to 350°F. In a large mixing bowl, stir together flour, sugar, baking powder, and salt. In separate bowl, beat eggs and yolk, milk, oil, yogurt, lemon juice, and peel with mixer on medium speed. Beat the liquid mixture into the dry ingredients just until blended. Transfer batter to greased and floured 8-cup bundt pan and bake 50–60 minutes or until a toothpick inserted in the center comes out clean; cool about 10 minutes, then invert cake onto a rack, remove pan, and let cool completely.

In small saucepan over medium high heat, heat lemon juice, sugar, and peel until it barely starts to boil. Stir to combine ingredients. Remove from heat and let cool 10 minutes. Use a long skewer to poke numerous holes into the warm or cool cake; drizzle warm glaze over top of cake so it has time to slowly soak in.

Hanging Yogurt Pudding

1 quart plain yogurt   2 ounces pistachio nuts, chopped
6 tablespoons sugar

Put yogurt onto a large piece of cheesecloth. Tie like a bag. Hang over a bowl overnight, so excess liquid drips off. Throw away the liquid. (What's left is called "yogurt cheese," and it's good to use as a vegetable dip. Experiment with yogurt cheese on another occasion!) Getting back to the pudding, add sugar to yogurt, blend, and chill. Garnish with nuts. This is a basic recipe. If you like this one, come up with variations on your own.

Frozen Yogurt
(yield: 4 servings)

8 cups yogurt   4 egg whites
½ cup sugar   1 cup fresh fruit, thinly sliced
1 tablespoon vanilla

Make yogurt cheese by hanging yogurt in a cheesecloth bag over a bowl overnight, squeezing the yogurt occasionally to drain out the liquid. Don't stop until yogurt is about the consistency of cream cheese. Mix yogurt cheese, sugar, and vanilla. Whip egg whites until stiff, fold into yogurt mix. Add fruit. For best results let the mix stand overnight in refrigerator. Freeze according to ice cream maker instructions.

Fantasy Cheesecake
(yield: 8 servings)

2 cups yogurt cheese*
vanilla to taste
4 tablespoons sugar

1 tablespoon cornstarch
2 eggs, lightly beaten

*If you don't remember where you read the instructions for making yogurt cheese, look at the recipe for frozen yogurt. **Note: Yogurt cheese may be kept in a covered container in the refrigerator until you have enough for the recipe.**

Combine yogurt cheese, sugar, and cornstarch. Add vanilla to taste. Add eggs, and mix gently with a fork or wire whisk. Pour into an 8-inch pie pan or 7-inch springform pan. Bake in a pre-heated 325°F. oven for 20–25 minutes (pie pan) or 55 minutes (springform). Cool slightly and refrigerate, uncovered, for 24 hours.

Applebake with Granola and Yogurt
Woods Hole Passage Bed and Breakfast Inn
Falmouth, Massachusetts
(yield: 8 servings)

8 medium apples, peeled, cored,
   & sliced into ½-inch bits
1 tablespoon water
¼ cup sugar

2 teaspoons cinnamon
½ teaspoon nutmeg
1 cup granola cereal
1 carton vanilla yogurt

Put apple bits and water in a covered 2-quart microwave dish. Microwave on high for 3 minutes. Stir, return to microwave, cook another 2 minutes on high. Combine sugar and spices, fold into apples. Microwave on high one minute. Spoon into bowls, crumble granola cereal over apples, then spoon yogurt on top. Serve warm. (From www.virtualcities.com—1st Traveler's Choice Internet Cookbook.)

Fresh Fruit Yogurt Drink

½ cup milk
1 cup yogurt

2 teaspoons honey
⅓ cup peeled, coarsely diced
fresh fruit

Combine all ingredients in a blender container in the order listed. Whirl until the fruit is pureed. Suggested fruit: Strawberries, blueberries, peaches, apricots, pitted cherries, or banana. Makes about 1¾ cups.

Quaker's Lemon Yogurt Cookies
(yield: 4 dozen)

½ cup butter, softened
1¼ cups sugar
½ cup plain yogurt or lemon
low-fat yogurt
2 egg whites or 1 egg
1 tablespoon grated lemon peel
½ teaspoon vanilla

2 cups Quaker Oats, uncooked
(quick or old fashioned)
1½ cups all-purpose flour
1 teaspoon baking powder
½ teaspoon baking soda
¼ cup powdered sugar

Lightly spray cookie sheet with non-stick cooking spray or oil. Beat butter and 1¼ cups sugar until fluffy. Add yogurt, egg whites, lemon peel, and vanilla; mix until well blended. Gradually add combined remaining ingredients except powdered sugar; mix well. Cover and refrigerate for 1–3 hours. Heat oven to 375°F. With lightly floured hands, shape dough into 1-inch balls; place on prepared cookie sheet. Using bottom of glass dipped in sugar, press into ⅛-inch thick circles. Bake 10–12 minutes or until edges are lightly browned. Cool 2 minutes on cookie sheet; remove to wire rack. Sift powdered sugar over warm cookies. Cool completely. Store tightly covered.

Yogurt-Pecan Coffee Cake

Graycote Inn, Bar Harbor, Maine

(yield: 12–18 servings)

Topping:

¾ cup firmly packed brown sugar   2 tablespoons butter
1 tablespoon flour   1 cup chopped pecans
1 teaspoon cinnamon

Cake batter:

½ cup butter   1 teaspoon baking soda
1 cup sugar   ¼ teaspoon salt
3 eggs   1 cup plain yogurt or sour cream
2 cups flour   ½ cup golden raisins
1 teaspoon baking powder

Prepare topping first: Mix together brown sugar, flour, and cinnamon. Cut in butter until mixture has the consistency of cornmeal. Finally, mix in chopped pecans. Set aside.

In an electric mixer or food processor, cream together butter and sugar. Add eggs, one at a time, beating well after each addition. Mix flour thoroughly with baking powder, soda, and salt; add to creamed mixture alternately with yogurt, making 3 equal additions of each and blending. Sprinkle raisins over the top and stir in. Spread mixture in a greased baking pan (9x13x2 inches). Sprinkle with pecan topping. Bake at 350°F. for about 30 minutes. Cut in squares and serve hot or cold.

Raspberry-Lemon Yogurt Muffins

Bed & Breakfasts on North Main Street
Breckenridge, Colorado

2 cups flour
½ cup sugar
2 teaspoons baking powder
½ teaspoon baking soda
8 ounces lemon yogurt
½ cup oil

1 teaspoon lemon peel, grated
2 eggs
1 cup fresh or frozen
raspberries, not thawed
½ cup pecans, finely chopped

Topping (combine with fork until crumbly):

⅛ cup sugar
¼ cup flour

2 tablespoons butter

In large bowl, combine flour and all dry ingredients except for topping. In small bowl, combine yogurt, oil, lemon peel, and eggs, mixing well. Add to dry ingredients; stir just until dry ingredients are moistened. Gently stir in raspberries. Fill muffin cups ¾ full. Sprinkle topping over batter. Bake at 400°F. for 18–20 minutes.

Yogurt Ambrosia

1 banana
1 red apple
1 orange, cut into chunks
1 cup seedless grapes

1 cup canned crushed pineapple
1 cup yogurt
sugar or honey
vanilla extract

Peel and slice banana. Core and dice apple. Combine in a bowl. Cut orange over the bowl to catch any juice. Add orange chunks; stir well (the juice will delay the browning of the apple and banana). Drain pineapple. Slice grapes in half. Stir in pineapple, grapes, and yogurt. Add vanilla extract and sweeten to taste. Chill at least 1 hour before serving.

Yogurt Primavera
(yield: 4 servings)

2 cups chicken broth
1 tablespoon cornstarch
1 package frozen peas
about ½ cup diced carrots
about ½ cup diced zucchini
about ½ cup diced golden squash
½ cup sliced mushrooms
cooked noodles

1 cup yogurt
1 ounce grated Parmesan cheese
2 tablespoons fresh parsley,
  chopped
2 tablespoons fresh basil
  leaves, shredded fine
freshly ground pepper

Reduce the chicken broth by boiling 2 cups down to one. Pour ¼ cup of the broth into a small bowl or cup, and stir in the cornstarch until dissolved. Set aside. In a medium saucepan, bring the remaining broth to a boil over moderate heat. Add the vegetables, except for the peas, and simmer until tender-crisp, about 3 minutes. Stir in the broth-cornstarch mixture, the yogurt, Parmesan, and herbs, and simmer just until thick, 1–2 minutes. Add the peas, and pour the sauce over cooked pasta. Season to taste with black pepper.

Potato Raita
(yield: 4–6 servings)

3 potatoes
1 teaspoon butter
1½ teaspoons cumin seeds
1 teaspoon coriander

1 teaspoon salt
½ teaspoon cayenne pepper
1 pint yogurt

Boil the potatoes, peel them, and chop rather coarsely. Heat the butter in a small pan and add the spices. After a few minutes, add the yogurt, remove from the heat, and stir well. Pour the yogurt mixture over the potatoes, mix thoroughly, and chill before serving.

Diana Rattray's Baked Yogurt Chicken
(yield: 4 servings)

2½ pounds chicken pieces (or boneless breasts)	2 cups plain yogurt
6 tablespoons butter	¼ cup fresh mushrooms, sliced
2 tablespoons flour	2 tablespoons fresh lemon juice
1 tablespoon paprika	2 tablespoons fresh parsley, chopped

Wash chicken and pat dry. Add salt and pepper. In a large pan, melt 4 tablespoons of butter; fry the chicken until golden brown. Remove to buttered shallow baking dish. Sprinkle flour and paprika into pan juices and cook, stirring for 1 minute. Stir in yogurt and mix well. Spoon over the chicken. Sauté the mushrooms in the remaining butter and lemon juice for 1 minute and spoon over the chicken and yogurt. Sprinkle with the parsley. Bake, covered, in a preheated 325°F. oven for about 1½ hours, or until chicken is tender (less for boneless breasts).

Stephen Ceideburg's Mourgh (Afghani Chicken)
(yield: 6 servings)

2 large cloves garlic	½ teaspoon cracked black pepper
½ teaspoon salt	
2 cups yogurt	6 boneless, skinless chicken breasts
juice and pulp of 1 large lemon	

Put the salt in a wide, shallow non-reactive bowl with the garlic and mash them together until you have paste. Add yogurt, lemon, and pepper. Add the chicken breasts to the yogurt and turn so all surfaces are well coated. Cover the bowl tightly and refrigerate. Allow to marinate at least overnight, up to a day and a half. Turn when you think of it. To cook, remove breasts from marinade and wipe off all but a thin film. Broil or grill about 6 inches from the heat for 6 to 8 minutes a side, or until thoroughly cooked. Meat will brown somewhat but should not char. Serve at once with soft **pita** or **Arab flatbread** and fresh yogurt.

Okay, Any Questions?

?   *Other than those handy recipes you've supplied, is there any-*
thing you can actually do with yogurt?

Yogurt fans assure us the possibilities are endless. We've already told you that yogurt can be substituted for fat in baked goods. Yogurt can also be substituted for cream in recipes, so that you can have fettuccini Alfredo even during lean times. We've even given you foolproof instructions for making yogurt cheese, so you can substitute that for cream cheese. (Do some research on the Internet for exciting things to do with the whey.) And yogurt can be substituted for sour cream, so you can put it on baked potatoes or whip it into mashed potatoes or add it to casseroles without all that fat.

We saw one suggestion that says if you substitute ⅓ cup plain yogurt for the milk and butter in packaged macaroni and cheese, it greatly improves the taste. (Frankly, if anything can improve the taste of packaged macaroni and cheese, this may be reason enough to think about yogurt.) You also can make yogurt pops by stirring fruit or granola into some yogurt, putting the yogurt in paper cups, putting Popsicle sticks in the paper cups, and freezing the whole mess. (Popsicle sticks are available at craft stores.) And don't forget frozen yogurt! On the whole, yogurt is a whole lot more versatile than, say, all the wheat that's cluttering up your basement. Now, if you can only cultivate a taste for it. . . .

CHAPTER 6
Power Shopping

★ **IN THIS CHAPTER**
- ✔ Stretching that dollar through savvy shopping
- ✔ Learning the rules for brilliant bulk buying
- ✔ Paying less for food
- ✔ Answering common questions

Kathy recently went to a going-out-of-business sale at a local sneaker emporium. Every pair of shoes in the store was on sale for $19.99. She normally wears name-brand leather walking shoes that cost around $50 per pair at discount stores, and indeed she found exactly what she was looking for. The sticker said the suggested retail price was $65, but that this store normally sold the shoes for $49.99.

Most shoppers would have bought a pair of shoes and been satisfied, but Kathy was working on this book at the time, so she was being constantly reminded that when you find a bargain, you buy in bulk. She took her Christmas money and bought four pairs of shoes for a total of $83.19. She'll wear these shoes every day until the last pair falls apart, which should be three to five years after the original purchase.

Assuming the four pairs of shoes only last for three years, Kathy will have spent $27.73 per year on shoes, instead of the $66.67 she would spend at the discount store under normal circumstances. This represents a savings of approximately 58 percent. Translate that into financial terms, and Kathy got a return on her investment slightly exceeding 140 percent. If you dabble in investments, you know it's a rare investment that garners that good of a return on your money.

This isn't a book about walking shoes. It's a book about food storage. But the same principle applies to food storage as it does to walking shoes. As we mentioned in Chapter 1, it's hard to find a better return on your investment than if you invest your money in food storage.

Just as with any investment, there are handy guidelines that will keep you from going astray when you spend your money on food storage. Commit these rules to memory, grab your checkbook, and run toward the nearest bargain.

Rules for Buying in Bulk

▶ Make sure you're getting a bargain

Don't go to the store thinking, "I'm going to stock up on Mediterania spaghetti sauce," unless you know it's on sale for a great price. Either do research ahead of time by checking the grocery ads, or go to your favorite low-price store with an open mind. Look for pasta sauce or canned fruit or your favorite soup or toilet paper, or something else you're going to want to put in storage. Something's bound to be on sale at a great bargain. (If there isn't, find another place to shop.) The item you should buy in quantity is the item that's on sale. Don't be tempted to diversify and buy a little of that spaghetti sauce even though it's being sold at the regular price. Buy the bargain; maybe the spaghetti sauce will be on sale when you return next week.

By the way, your favorite supermarket may not be the best place to go when you're buying food in bulk. Supermarkets advertise their goods the same way other products are advertised, which means that some stores feature discount prices, others may feature occasional discounts, and still others focus instead on "quality," or "convenience," which is store-speak for saying, "We're charging top dollar for our groceries, and we're proud of it."

Do some investigating. One store in your neighborhood may have the best prices on paper products. Another one may have a greater variety of canned goods. Still another may feature in-store coupons that can save a lot of money for the shopper who buys in bulk. (Many is the time that Clark has stood by a coupon dispensing machine in a local supermarket, waiting for the machine to spit out enough coupons at forty-five-second intervals to allow him to buy a few dozen cans of soup.)

Check out each store in your vicinity to see where its advantages lie. Then watch your local newspaper to see which store has the best sales on items you want to buy.

One good place to look for good food bargains is in the sale ads for stores that aren't primarily food stores. Drug stores or discount stores will occasionally have "loss leaders" in food items, drawing customers into the store by offering cans of chunk tuna for fifty cents or cans of turkey chunks for a dollar. But whether you shop in a supermarket or a hardware store, look at the ad carefully. If there's a limit of two items per customer, the investment isn't worth your time. Your time and energy are worth enough to you—or *should* be worth enough to you— that you shouldn't be running around from store to store picking up two cans of this and three bottles of that.

Some areas of the country have "case lot sales," where shoppers can buy cans or bottles of food products by the case. (A case usually consists of twenty-four cans, although it may be forty-eight cans for smaller items such as tuna, or twelve pint-sized bottles.) Case lot sales represent terrific savings, and if your area features them, take advantage of them.

If you live in an area where case lot sales are common, you've probably heard rumors that the stuff that goes on sale is last year's stock. Who cares? Canned goods should last seven years. If you're rotating your food the way you should be (see Chapter 8 for more on that), you will have eaten the food years before it even thinks of expiring.

▶ Buy what you'll use

We've mentioned it once or twice in this book, but it bears repeating: If you like a food only marginally during good times, you won't like it at all during times of stress. And *during times of stress, if you don't like something you will not eat it*. This is a maxim you should write on your hand before you go power shopping for food. Buy only your favorite foods, your favorite brands of those foods, and your favorite flavors of those foods. *Nothing else will do.*

This might take a little detective work on your part. If your husband says he likes chicken corn chowder, for example, watch and see how often that's the can of soup he chooses from the shelf. If he says he's crazy about chicken corn chowder but he always chooses minestrone, don't even think of buying chicken corn chowder for your food storage. If the two of you are shopping together and he finds chicken corn chowder on sale at a great price and loads the shopping cart with it, find some diplomatic way to divert him. Unless you yourself are crazy enough about chicken corn chowder to consume every can of it, money your family spends on chicken corn chowder will be money down the drain.

Food that won't be eaten isn't a bargain for you no matter how cheaply you can buy it. So pass up the temptation to buy smooth peanut butter if little Mazie prefers chunky. Don't buy a case of generic chili if your family always eats Hormel. But *do* experiment with house brands, a can or package at a time.

Some supermarket house brands are as good as the name brands, but without name brand prices. If you find that the house brand of evaporated milk tastes just like Carnation, by all means buy it and save yourself that 11 cents a can. But before you buy a bunch of it, test the house brand from that particular grocery store. Not all house brands are created equal, and you don't want to be stuck with something your family won't eat.

▶ Buy what you like—not what you *should* like

Sardines may be packed with protein and energy, but they're not going to do you any good in the can. If you don't like them, you're not going to eat them. And if you're not going to eat them, pass them up even if you see them at an unbelievable price. Remember, any food that isn't eaten is money wasted. Even if the sardines cost only 33 cents per can, buying them is a bad investment unless somebody in your household is going to eat them.

Nobody is going to inspect your food storage and grade you on the quality of food you have there. Nobody *can*, because no two families eat alike. On your next visit to the supermarket, take a look in the carts of shoppers who are in line near you. Some people buy whole foods and no processed foods whatsoever. In some people's carts, the food is so highly processed it looks like it probably came from a chemical factory rather than a farm. Some people live out of cans; some live exclusively off TV dinners.

Perhaps you feel guilty because your family eats junk food rather than bulgur wheat, but if you don't like the way your family eats, the time to change their habits is before you buy food storage, not afterwards. If your kids are addicted to canned spaghetti, you'd better have canned spaghetti in your food storage despite the nagging suspicion that bulgur wheat would be better for them. All the nutrients in the world aren't going to sustain your family unless they're eaten.

▶ If all other things are equal, buy food according to its nutritive value

This may sound like a no-brainer, but there's a huge difference between different varieties of food. Beans are a good example. Once green beans have been processed with any sort of heat, almost all nutritive value has been destroyed. People think they're virtuously eating their vegetables when they sit down to a plate of canned green beans, but they're really consuming bean-shaped pieces of water. In contrast, baked beans are loaded with nutrition and they'll fill your stomachs. If your family likes baked beans and green beans equally, go for the baked beans. You'll get more bang for your food storage buck if you go for the item that keeps your family strong and healthy.

▶ Buy a variety of foods

This may seem like a direct contradiction of the previous advice in this chapter. We've already said that if your husband always eats minestrone soup, that's the only kind you should buy for him. But man does not live by soup alone. When your minestrone-lover isn't eating soup, he's eating some other sort of food. He needs vegetables, even if the only vegetable he'll eat is Green Giant creamed corn. He needs fruit, even if the only kind he'll accept is Del Monte Very Cherry Fruit Cocktail.

Don't focus on one food group to the exclusion of all others. It's fine to spend this week's food storage budget on canned tuna, especially if you found it at an incredible price. But next week look for some other food group. Maybe it's time to concentrate your energies on pasta or applesauce or refried beans.

Although the recommendation is for each of us to have a year's supply of food, most of us probably won't need food for a whole year. Unemployment may last only a couple of months. Back surgery may take your breadwinner out of commission for six weeks. A snowstorm may keep you trapped in the house for a few days until the power is back on and the roads are clear. If you've concentrated all your efforts on entrees, your family is going to get awfully tired of chili and beef stew when the emergency strikes. But if you've supplemented that chili and beef stew with apple slices or Jell-O or even Cream of Wheat, you'll be better prepared to ride out the crisis—whatever it is—for its duration.

And when you're choosing your food groups, don't forget the all-important comfort foods or sick foods. If your family is addicted to chocolate chip cookies, and if your five-year-old always drinks 7-Up whenever she's sick, chocolate chips and 7-Up are a vital part of your food storage. (But be sure to follow the rules in Chapter 8 so you won't end up with moth-eaten chocolate chips, or dead 7-Up all over your storage shelves.)

▶ Buy food that won't go bad before you eat it

In 1998, one of the major soft drink companies launched an idiotic campaign based on putting expiration dates on its products. Nobody had ever considered that soft drinks were going bad in their cans, so the ad campaign probably didn't win any converts to that particular brand. But there are some items that don't stand the test of time as well as other products do. Knowing what those products are may influence your shopping decisions, and it should definitely influence the way you store and rotate your food.

Food that is exposed to air will harden and eventually be unpalatable. Granulated sugar turns rock hard over time. It can be reclaimed by using a good old cheese grater and a little elbow grease. Brown sugar is harder to reconstitute, but it can be done by sealing it in a jar with an apple slice. Marshmallows turn into tiny bricks that nevertheless soften up acceptably well in hot cocoa. Having candy turn hard may be the least of the reasons for not including a whole lot of candy in your food storage, but it's a consideration.

Food that is exposed to humidity may eventually get soggy. Have you ever bent a potato chip in half? It happens if the air is humid enough. Even though crackers and cookies are sealed in sacks inside their boxes, they weren't designed for long-term storage. Think about other foods that should be dry, such as cereal and potato flakes. If a food is supposed to be kept dry, either make sure it stays dry or don't store it.

Anything that contains oil is a candidate for rancidity. This includes items that have never been opened, such as bottles of salad dressing or cooking oil, boxes of crackers or cereal, or cans of shortening. It's rumored that you can keep a bottle of cooking oil from going rancid by pouring the contents of a vitamin E capsule into the bottle. But since you have to break the seal of the bottle in order to insert the vitamin E capsule, you may break even just by leaving the bottle untouched. A better rule is to make sure you don't purchase any bottles of oil that won't be consumed within the year. Date the bottles when you buy them and use the oldest bottles first so you won't be in for any unpleasant surprises.

Rice mixes aren't a great investment because they may go rancid before you'll have time to eat them. Bread stuffing cubes or mixes pose a similar problem. The more nutritional value there is in a particular food, the faster it's going to rot on you. Brown rice may start showing rancidity a month after the package has been opened, and not much beyond that even if the package has been kept sealed. White rice will keep considerably longer, but it doesn't last forever the way wheat and dried beans do. "Helper"-type mixes will go bad fairly quickly because of the ingredients such as bouillon that are combined in the box with the rice.

Exposure to sunlight may discolor bottled items such as ketchup or hot sauce. All food storage should be kept in a cool, dry, dark place, but food that is stored in bottles is particularly sensitive to sun damage.

Even food that's stored in cans isn't immune from going bad. We're going to assume you don't keep food around after the cans have started to bulge, but canned milk can go bad a lot faster than that. If you're keeping canned milk on hand, the cans need to be shaken monthly. (See Chapter 8 for advice on how to shake your cans without the work.)

These are just a few examples of the things that can go wrong with your food storage. Most things you buy, with the exception of rice products and bread products, should keep for a year, but you may have some unpleasant surprises when you store food on your own. Chapter 8 will tell you how to minimize the chance of losing your precious food storage to the dreaded, and ofttimes unspecified on the label, expiration date.

▶ Gauge your purchase by the amount of a product you anticipate using in a year

If the previous information didn't convince you that you should store only a year's worth of food because it's likely to go bad if you store it for longer, there are other reasons to store only a one-year's supply.

First, there's no getting around it: Food storage takes a lot of space. If you've found such a good bargain on canned salmon that you've bought three years' worth instead of only one, the odds are that you're going to be storing that extra salmon at the expense of something else you could be storing. Salmon is good for you, but you're going to find yourself unhappy if you've cut down on your toilet paper or bottled water in order to find a place to keep your salmon.

Second, your tastes may change without warning. Kathy once mortgaged the farm to buy twenty bottles of marinated feta cheese at $3.99 per bottle. Then Clark announced he was tired of feta cheese and didn't want to eat it anymore. Kathy didn't have enough energy to eat all that feta cheese by herself before it expired, and it wasn't long before the contents of all the pretty little hexagonal bottles had gone bad and she had to throw the contents away.

Third, your tastes may be changed *for* you, also without warning. Say you start to take a calcium-blocker blood pressure medication. All of a sudden, that grapefruit juice you've stored in the basement may kill you if you drink it. Or you may develop an intolerance to wheat—which, as you've learned from Chapter 2, is highly possible even for experienced wheat-eaters. Bingo!—the wheat you've got in all those fifty-gallon containers is no longer edible as far as you're concerned.

Clark read a book about Mad Cow Disease and decided overnight that he was no longer going to eat beef. This threw Kathy into a tizzy when she thought of all the beef stew and chili in the basement, but at least she didn't have a three-years' supply of it. Or you may find out your migraine headaches are caused by monosodium glutamate. If you have cases upon cases of Rice-a-Roni in your storage, you could lose all the money you invested in that particular food.

Because human needs change so quickly and so often, storing a whole lot of food isn't a good investment of your energy or your money. Figure out what you'll need for one year and store that. If you have any extra money, sock it away for other emergencies.

The Ten Commandments of Paying Less for Food

As a summary to this chapter, here are the Ten Commandments of Paying Less for Food. Some of this advice has been mentioned earlier in this chapter, and the rest is common sense. Even so, every power shopper should live by these rules:

I. Use Coupons

Food coupons are one of the oldest tricks for saving money on food, yet they still work as well as ever. Some people have made a science out of clipping, filing, and using coupons, often reducing their total grocery bill by 20 percent or more. One problem with coupons is that they often seem to be for convenience or snack foods that are high in price and low in nutrition. But there are still bargains to be had if you manage coupons carefully.

II. Use Rebates

More and more manufacturers are starting to offer rebates on food items, particularly when you buy them in large sizes. A rebate is similar to a coupon, except that you get a partial refund at a later time, rather than an immediate reduction in the price of the item. Manufacturers like rebates because a certain percentage of the population will never get around to sending in the forms to claim the rebate after they've purchased the products. If you plan to use a rebate, make sure you have all the necessary items before you leave the store, such as a rebate coupon and a cash register receipt. Read the fine print carefully to make sure you qualify for the rebate. Make a rule that you will fill out the rebate forms as soon as you get home. This is especially important if you are the kind of person who tends to procrastinate such things. When you get the rebate check, take note that you usually have a limited time to cash the check. These guys know all the tricks to keep you from getting your discount, but you can beat them at their own game with just a little bit of organization.

III. Shop the Sales

The nice thing about living on your food storage is that you can take your time and not restock food items until they go on sale. But just because an item is on sale doesn't mean it's a good bargain. Some stores are so overpriced that their sale prices may still be higher than what you would pay at another store. You should be familiar enough with the items you store to know a good price when you see one. In many cases, good sale prices on food items will be found at drug and specialty stores, rather than grocery stores. These stores often stock a limited supply of food items in addition to the items that are the mainstay of their business. When these food items go on sale, they are often used as "loss leaders" to get you into the store to buy other things. This means that the store will be selling you the food item at almost their cost, or even slightly below cost. But it is still a great bargain for you, and is often deeply discounted from the best price you would find in a grocery store.

IV. Do Comparison Shopping

Forget all that nonsense about one store having lower prices than the others. We live in an area that has a half dozen grocery store chains, and they all claim to be cheaper than the other guys. In our experience, each store is cheaper on some items, but more expensive on others. So, where we shop is determined by what items we intend to buy. For paper products and cleaning supplies, one chain is lower. Another chain is the better choice if we are buying primarily vegetables or canned goods. It doesn't make sense to do your weekly shopping at six different stores to make sure you get the absolute lowest price on every item. Gasoline and your time are more valuable than the few pennies you will save. But know the character of each store in your area, and pick the one that will be the best for you based upon what you are buying on a particular day. This is especially important when buying in bulk. Paying five cents more is unimportant when buying one can of soup, but starts to add up when buying a case of forty-eight cans.

V. SHOP AT
WAREHOUSE STORES

Most areas of the country have at least one chain of warehouse stores, such as Costco, Sam's, or BJ's. These stores cater to families that buy in bulk, and can often offer substantial savings when compared to grocery stores. But as noted above, you need to do some comparison shopping and make sure you really are getting a good price. One caution when using warehouse stores is that they usually carry far fewer items than a typical grocery store. It is not uncommon to buy something you really like, only to find that the item is no longer in stock on a return visit. If you find something you like, you'd better go back the next day to buy it in bulk or you may never see it again. There are some who object to warehouse stores because they require an annual membership fee of $20–$50. But depending on the amount of merchandise you buy, it is not uncommon to recover the cost of the membership fee in the first month of membership.

VI. TRY THE HOUSE BRANDS

Most grocery store chains carry a house brand, which is a brand of product that is made specifically for that grocery store chain, and is found only under that name in that chain. House brands tend to be several cents cheaper than the known brands, yet often they are made by the same companies that make the better known brands. You can often determine this by reading the label on the product. Some house brand products are obviously inferior to the better known products, and you will not want to buy them again even if they are cheaper. But other products you will find to be of equivalent quality, if not better. Try the house brand, and then come back later if it meets your needs.

VII. LOOK FOR DISCONTINUED GOODS

Sometimes a store will decide to stop carrying a particular brand or size of product. When this happens, the price will often be reduced on the remaining items so the store can clear them out of stock. Before buying the discounted items, make sure they have not outlived their freshness date, and will not do so before you consume them. If the products are fresh and you like the brand, then help yourself to a bargain. The ultimate bargain on discontinued goods occurs when a store goes out of business, or moves to a new location and wants to reduce the inventory. If you watch for these kinds of situations, you can often find incredible bargains on a whole array of products. We are still using shampoo that we bought five years ago when a major drugstore closed up shop. And Clark recently visited a store having a moving sale, where everything was reduced by 90 percent.

VIII. LOOK FOR NEW BRANDS

New brands are often sold at a lower introductory price in order to get a lot of people to try them. If you buy one or two and like the product, you can go back later and buy larger quantities, often saving a considerable amount of money.

IX. LOOK FOR DAMAGED GOODS

We have a friend who is a successful attorney. From his nice house and his fancy cars, you would never guess that he was once a struggling law student. While he was in law school, he and his wife would buy canned food where the labels had been accidentally removed. They did this to save money, because the unmarked cans were much cheaper than the cans with the labels. Every evening they would cook dinner and open a can of mystery food. This food was incorporated into the family dinner, and a lot of money was saved. Just about every grocery store will have a cart of damaged goods. Although you should inspect the packaging carefully to make sure the quality of the food has not been compromised, you can save a lot of money on these occasional deals.

X. Consider Seasonal Goods

Have you ever noticed the prices of Halloween candy on the day after Halloween? Stores will often reduce the price of such seasonal goods by 50 percent or more. Halloween candy is probably not a good example of something to tuck away in your food storage, because it would be pretty stale by next Halloween. But nonfood items such as Christmas cards and Christmas wrap can be bought and stored until the next year. Some food products will fluctuate in price throughout the year, as they go in and out of season. You can consider this in your budgeting, and plan to buy certain goods when their availability is good and their prices are low. We recently got a whole bag of high quality Easter chocolates for 90 percent off the original price. As any wise shopper can tell you, Easter candy that is purchased on sale does not contain calories.

Okay, Any Questions?

? *You've made it all sound so easy. Is buying in bulk a no-risk proposition, or could I lose my shirt?*

Just as there's a risk in the stock market, risk takers are also able to gamble when they power shop. When Kathy visited the sneaker store, an employee told her the store would be open for five more days, and that before the store closed the price of shoes would probably drop to $14.99. At this point Kathy had to decide whether to take the 140 percent return on her investment and be satisfied with it, or to wait and see if the size she wanted would still be in stock when the price dropped. Even though she could have saved an additional 25 percent over the $19.99 price if her size were in stock, the condition of the shoes she was wearing convinced her the risk was too great. She was so happy to pay $83.19 for three years' worth of footwear that when the price dropped to $14.99 the next day, and to $10.99 before the store went out of business, she still felt satisfied with her purchase.

Even though Kathy could possibly have gotten a better deal on the walking shoes than she did, she couldn't have lost money on the purchase once she paid her money. The moment she paid for the shoes, she locked in a 140 percent return on her investment. If the new owners of the sneaker store sold the same brand of shoes for the suggested retail price of $65, she wouldn't have had to return to the store and pay the difference. In that respect, buying in bulk is considerably better than investing in the stock market, where your investment is worth only what the stock market says it's worth at the close of business today.

➲ Here are some of the risks of power shopping. These risks are small compared to the benefits you'll gain by buying your food on sale and in bulk, but it's best to be fully aware of what you're getting into before you make your first investment at the discount store:

▶ The price may go down after you buy it

Walking shoes are not the only items that fluctuate in value. Many years ago, Clark and Kathy bought armloads of blank video tapes when they went on sale for $10 per tape, "because they'll never get any cheaper than they are now." Even more painful was their decision to buy sterling silver flatware when silver was selling for $50 per ounce. They paid a small fortune on silverware that is worth a fraction of that amount today.

Fortunately, the price of food doesn't fluctuate as much as the price of silverware does. You may see tuna advertised for 69 cents a can one week and buy a bunch of cans because you usually pay 79—only to see it for 50 cents a week later. You're allowed to wince over this, but it isn't going to kill you. **Remember—the return on your investment should be calculated not on the basis of the price you *could* have gotten for the product, but on the basis of how much you would normally have spent for that product if you had bought it a can at a time at the supermarket.**

If you read the grocery ads and pay attention to the prices, you'll learn when something is an okay bargain, and when it's a bargain you can't afford to pass up. The more you practice, the better you'll get. Soon you'll reach the point where all your purchases are excellent ones.

▶ A natural disaster may destroy it

Chances are, if a catastrophe destroys your house it's going to wreak havoc with your food storage. A flood may cause dry or dehydrated foods such as wheat and beans to be waterlogged. An earthquake could break your glass bottles. A tornado could carry your food storage to who-knows-where. A fire could melt your cans of food into lumps of aluminum and tin. Extended power outages could cause frozen food to spoil.

Damage can be mitigated by storing your food in a variety of different containers, using a variety of different methods. You also may want to store food in different places throughout your home, so that you'll be able to reach some of your food even if access to the rest of your storage has been blocked. If you do these things, you'll increase the odds that you won't lose *all* your food storage, even if some of it is destroyed.

If your home is one of a community of homes that are destroyed by some natural calamity, disaster relief may help you get back on your feet. Even more likely is the possibility that people whose food storage is intact may help you out by sharing their own food supplies. This happened in Idaho in 1976, when the Teton Dam broke and homes were flooded and destroyed. Members of the LDS Church who lived in areas that were undamaged by the flood rallied to help those who had lost their food storage to floodwaters.

Remember—you're storing food against an emergency. After learning of the damage that a natural disaster can wreak on a neighboring community, you may determine that this constitutes enough of an emergency for you to give at least some of your precious foodstuffs to others. After all, you'd want them to do the same for you.

▶ You may develop an allergy to something, or a distaste for it, after you've filled your basement with it

This is always a possibility. People's tastes change over time. But if you've followed the rules outlined in this chapter, even if you do lose a taste for a particular item, you won't be out a whole lot of money, and you'll still have a whole lot of other supplies in your food storage that you *can* eat. Perhaps you can trade the product you don't eat anymore for something a friend may have on hand.

If you learn you've purchased a lemon, make lemonade by finding a good use for that food before it goes bad. There are food banks all over the place that will be glad to take unopened canned goods, or even boxes or other packages that have not been damaged or tampered with. The sardines you bought on sale even though you hate sardines will never be eaten by you, but they could be a valuable source of protein (and a prized gourmet delicacy) to a homeless person. If you make a mistake in your power shopping, you can at least do what you can to make your mistake a blessing to others. If you do that, even the investments that you consider to be your mistakes will be money well spent. And given that many such food banks qualify as charitable organizations, you can deduct the fair market value of the donated goods from your income when tax time rolls around.

CHAPTER 7
Not by Bread Alone

★ **IN THIS CHAPTER**
- ✔ Considering useful nonfood items to store
- ✔ Storing cleaning and food preparations supplies
- ✔ Including clothing, medicines, and personal items
- ✔ Living without power or water
- ✔ Becoming more self-sufficient
- ✔ Answering common questions

Although the majority of this book has focused on edible items, provident people will also pay attention to nonfood items that should be included in their home storage. In fact, when people use the words "food storage," what they often mean is all of the household items needed to carry on a comfortable life without depending on others. After pondering this for a bit, the average person can come up with a list of dozens of nonfood items that should also be stored as part of a storage program. As an extreme example of the importance of this, consider the person who stores hundreds of cans of soup, but then forgets to include any extra can openers!

Although the main focus of this book must remain the storage of food, we wanted to devote one chapter to those other items that you really need to consider for your storage.

Here's a personal example that will be the theme of this chapter— and indeed, it should be one of the prevailing themes of this whole book. You'll hear the message several times in these pages, with one illustration or another. If it sinks in, you're going to be a step ahead of most of the other people who have ever started a food storage program.

When our publisher called us and asked us to write this book on food storage, we said to each other, "This will be a piece of cake. We've been the food storage king and queen of North America. Not only that, but we have the best food storage books that have ever been written, which we can use as references to supplement our vast and impressive knowledge."

Our smugness didn't last long. Clark spent an entire weekend looking for our food storage books. We used to have them, when we lived in Utah. We never would have given them away when we moved to Virginia. But after twelve years in Virginia we still haven't unloaded all the boxes we brought with us when we moved to the state. Perhaps our treasured food storage books are still tucked away in one of those boxes. But one thing is certain—wherever they are, we can't put our fingers on them.

Here's the lesson from that. You may want to engrave it in stone and post it in a prominent place wherever you keep your food storage:

IF YOU CAN'T FIND SOMETHING, OR IF YOU CAN'T USE IT, YOU DON'T OWN IT.

That may seem harsh, but it's true. If you don't know how to cook with wheat, the wheat is useless to you. If your family can't digest powdered milk, it's in your house only for decoration. If you keep your food storage in such a haphazard manner that it rots before it's eaten, it does you no good at all.

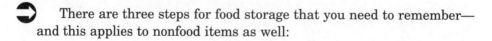 There are three steps for food storage that you need to remember—and this applies to nonfood items as well:

1. You have to know what your family will eat, and how to prepare it.

2. You have to have those foods in your possession, along with the utensils you'll need to cook them.

3. You have to store your food in such a way that it can be easily retrieved and rotated, so that you won't be tempted to use the food you've just bought at the supermarket and leave the food storage food in the basement. If your food is easily accessible, the items you've purchased will be consumed rather than thrown away.

In the next chapter we'll give you some ways you can store your food and nonfood items in a way that will allow you to find things when they're needed. But as you read this chapter and decide which items you want to purchase for your own use, be thinking about places you can store these items so you'll always know where they are. If you do that, you'll truly own the things you buy. Otherwise, your storage supplies will be as useful to you as our food storage books are to us. We can't find them, so we don't own them. Money spent on those books, as valuable as those books would otherwise have been, is money we threw down the drain. And even worse, those books—wherever they are—are adding to the clutter of our house and making it harder for us to find other things we can't put our hands on today.

Food Preparation Supplies

The food preparation supplies you store will depend on the food preparation supplies you use. If you don't bottle your own food, for example, you'll have no need for canning lids or pectin. If you don't like yogurt, you'll have no need for recipes on how to make yogurt from scratch.

But living under emergency conditions does strange things to your priorities. You may have no need of a food dehydrator now, but you may want a non-electric dehydrator pronto if the power goes out and the food in your freezer would otherwise spoil. You may shudder at eating off a paper plate, until the day comes when the water supply has been shut down and you have no way to wash your dishes.

When you're looking at this list of items, don't dismiss one until you've thought of alternate reasons why you might need it.

- Dutch oven that can be used over charcoal or wood fires
- Frying pan, heavy duty

- Heavy-duty aluminum foil
- Cast iron cook set—like the Dutch oven, it does you no good if you don't know how to use it
- Utensils—both metal and disposable
- Paper plates and cups—if you get paper rather than plastic, you can burn them to recycle them and get a few moments of warmth out of each meal
- Wheat grinder (if your primary grinder is electric, you'll need a non-electric backup)
- Can openers
- Utility knife
- Food dehydrator, or instructions and materials to build one
- Plastic storage bags with zippers
- Large drawstring trash sacks
- Home canning supplies such as pectin, jars, and lids
- Plastic wrap

Cleaning Supplies

The cleaning supplies you store depend on the cleaning supplies you use. Don't go out and buy a year's supply of Brillo Soap Pads if you never use Brillo. See what you have under your counter, and then notice what items under your counter you actually use. Those are the items that should be in your storage.

Here's a list of possible items. You don't have to have all of them. There isn't a team of food storage police who are going to search your basement and mark you down if you don't have a year's supply of scouring powder. In fact, with the exception of antibacterial disinfectants, cleaning supplies—like many of the items in this chapter—are a low-priority purchase. Get your food supplies into shape before you lay down money on extra belts for the vacuum cleaner.

- Antibacterial dish soap

- All-purpose cleaning spray

- Scouring powder

- Dishcloths, scrubbers, and sponges

- Food storage bags (locking variety); snap-top containers

- Laundry soap. "Soap" may be the operative word here. If you're planning on ordinary emergencies, your regular detergent is fine. But if you're a sieger who expects to lose the use of your washing machine when the power goes out, those detergents contain caustic materials that could damage your skin if you wash clothes by hand. In that case, look for laundry soap instead.

- Fabric softener or dryer sheets

- Dishwasher soap

- Glass cleaner. This is a real frill. If your breadwinner is unable to work for a year, the last thing you may be worrying about is how clean your windows are. But if it's a big deal to you, buy a bottle or two for storage.

- Vacuum cleaner bags and belts

Clothing

Although some people recommend having a year's supply of clothing on hand, it's not prudent to run out and purchase extra outfits just to go in your emergency essentials. Clothing storage should come from your closet. Most Americans already have a year's supply of clothing lying around the house. Our closets are bulging, but how many of those clothes actually fit? Children spring up like weeds. Adults grow outward rather than upward. Even shoe sizes change, as adult feet broaden after years of walking and running on them. It's foolish to invest big money in disaster clothes, because you don't know what sizes you'll be when and if "the big one" hits.

When you're thinking about a year's supply of clothing, the clothes that should come to mind first are clothes that will protect you. Every member of your family should have a warm coat on hand before winter hits. You should have a good supply of mittens, gloves, and hats that will protect your family members in the cold. You should also have a good supply of underwear—perhaps not 365 pairs of socks, but enough pairs of socks that if you learned today that you wouldn't be able to buy socks for another year, you wouldn't panic. The same is true for other undergarments. What you put in your clothing storage doesn't have to be pretty. Functionality is the word of the day. If the time were ever to come that you couldn't shop for a year, think about the things you'd need before the year is up and make sure you have enough of those items on hand to tide you over.

When you're thinking of emergency conditions, "comfort clothes" may be just as important as comfort food. If your son has a favorite shirt that you've retired from his regular rotation because it's just too ratty to wear, clothing storage may be the place to put it. The jeans your husband wears on Saturdays may not be appropriate for the office in today's society, but they'll be far more practical than a closetful of suits if a life-altering catastrophe strikes.

Toiletries

Toiletries may not sustain life, but they do sustain civilization. Imagine how you'd feel if you knew you couldn't buy soap or deodorant for a year. Fortunately, toiletries are easy to store, because you can buy them when they're on sale and put them away until they're needed. In fact, an old bar of soap will last longer in the shower than a new bar. If you really want to get the maximum bang for your soap buck, buy your bars of soap, unwrap them, and let them harden for weeks or months before you use them.

Toilet paper should be a foremost consideration for people who store food. If you don't know how much your family uses in a given year, start out with new packages in each bathroom at the beginning of the month and see how many rolls you go through. If you've been using cut-rate brands, this may be your opportunity to see that the money you think you've been saving has literally been going down the toilet. Some rolls of toilet paper last considerably longer than others, and you may want to experiment before you invest in your toilet paper supply. If you've consistently ignored our advice throughout this book and have determined to store siege food without incorporating it into your diet first, you may want to have a whole lot of extra toilet paper on hand in your storage. You're definitely going to need it.

A sense of normalcy is extremely important in times of stress, and that goes double for young people. A child whose favorite color is pink may accept a yellow barrette under normal circumstances, but if she's under stress anyway she may allow only a pink barrette to touch her hair. A teenager may completely fall apart if she runs out of the Only True Hair Rinse. If you think of these things as *things*, they'll be so far down your priority list that you won't ever get around to buying them. But if you think of them as peace of mind for your children, they'll climb higher up the priority scale.

 Here's a list of supplies you may want to consider:

- Toilet paper

- Diapers, baby wipes, and other baby-specific items

- Feminine hygiene products

- Toothbrushes and toothpaste

- Mouthwash—preferably an antibacterial one that can be used as a disinfectant

- Hairbrushes, combs, and accessories

- Facial tissues, ear swabs, and cotton balls

- Soap—your best bet is an antibacterial variety, such as Safeguard

- Shampoo and cream rinse

- Towels and washcloths

- Deodorant

- Razors

- Shaving cream

Medicines

Medicine is an important part of your family food storage plan—especially if your family relies on prescription medicines. It doesn't take a global calamity for you to have a medical crisis, either. After Hurricane Mitch devastated Central America in 1998, friends of ours in Tennessee found they were unable to get their son's seizure medication because whole shipments of Dilantin were destroyed by the hurricane. For weeks, there was a shortage of the drug in the United States. Fortunately our friends had a stock of Dilantin on hand. If they hadn't learned the need to store medicine, their son could have been in serious jeopardy.

If you order prescription drugs through the mail, you may be able to have a ninety-day supply on hand. That's good, but it may not be good enough. If you speak with your family physician, you may be able to get a year's prescription for vital medications. Just be sure to rotate them, because drugs do expire and lose their potency.

If your physician won't give you a year's prescription, there may be other avenues. If you have a friend who lives near the Mexican border, he may be willing to go across the border and get a year's worth of your prescription drug for you. (Medicine is sold without prescriptions in Mexico.) If you have a friend who lives near the Canadian border, he may be able to go across the border and get a year's worth of A.C.&C. for you. A.C.&C. stands for acetaminophen/caffeine/codeine or acetylsalicylic acid/caffeine/codeine, depending on whether you prefer Tylenol- or aspirin-based pain medication. This mild codeine preparation is sold without prescription in Canada, and is stronger than aspirin for short-term emergency pain situations.

Although it's usually unwise to prescribe antibiotics for yourself, you may want to have a year's prescription of broad-spectrum antibiotics on hand in case of a dire emergency. Ask your doctor to give you a prescription for each member of your family, and make sure he prescribes one that has a long shelf-life. These should never be used except during emergencies when you can't visit a doctor or a pharmacist, and they should be scrupulously thrown away and repurchased when they reach their expiration date. Always keep in mind that Americans have over-used antibiotics to the point that they aren't as effective as they used to be. You should never use an antibiotic unless there's no other alternative. In addition, you or some family member may become allergic to certain antibiotics (specifically, penicillin or its derivatives). Make sure you account for this when you get your prescription, and be sure to throw out medications as they expire.

Your home storage would not be complete if you didn't keep at least one book of medical information somewhere in your library. Your first choice of books should be one that describes medical symptoms and tells you what to look for. The best book we've ever found is a huge blue paperback book, *Complete Guide to Symptoms, Illness & Surgery*, by H. Winter Griffith, M.D.[1] No home should be without this book.

> **Keep at least one book of medical information somewhere in your library.**

Several years ago, we had a housekeeper who was sick for several months. She thought at first she had the flu or a case of mononucleosis, but she never seemed to get better, and she didn't want to spend money for a doctor. One day, after much prodding, she told Kathy what her symptoms were. Kathy looked up those symptoms in the *Complete Guide to Symptoms, Illness & Surgery*. Blanca's symptoms were vague enough that Kathy couldn't decide whether she had an ulcer, a problem with gallstones, or pancreatitis, but she knew that whichever of the three it was, Blanca needed to see a doctor immediately. She sent Blanca home to find a doctor. Several days later, Blanca called from the hospital. She had undergone emergency surgery to have her gallbladder removed and her bleeding ulcer treated, and the doctors were keeping her in the hospital until her pancreatitis was under control.

Kathy isn't the hero of this story. Kathy doesn't know anything unless she looks it up. But if you could have a book in your house that would help you to that extent when you had a medical emergency, wouldn't you buy such a book? Of course you would.

Other books you may want to consider are one of the many books that tell you about prescription and nonprescription drugs; a book on how to treat common conditions with alternative medicine; a book on healing with herbs, and whatever else seems important to you. The extent to which you build your medical library depends on how bad you think the situation is going to be. If you're not preparing for anything more serious than a short-term calamity, you'll naturally want fewer resources on hand than if you're getting ready for "the big one."

Here is a list of other items you may want to have on hand to round out your medical supplies. Make sure to throw away these and all medications when they have passed their expiration date.

- Cold medication

- Aspirin

- Ibuprofen

- Tylenol

- Cough syrup and other cough preparations

- Chloraseptic

- Betadine (similar to iodine, only it's surgical strength)

- Antacids or other stomach medication—especially important if you're learning how to eat siege food!

- Antibacterial ointment

- Cortisone cream (for itching)

- Ben-Gay or other compound for muscle aches

- Rubbing alcohol

- Insect repellent

- Vitamins—whatever your family normally uses. If your family doesn't take vitamins now, you may want to have a multivitamin in your food storage to supplement your emergency rations, especially if you're storing siege food.

- Prescription glasses or contact lenses.

- Bandages, gauze, and other dressings for wounds

- Tweezers

- Whatever over-the-counter medications your family uses on a regular basis

- Over-the-counter allergy medicine. If you don't have allergies now, eating siege food could give them to you.

Emergency Care

If you live in an area where you may have to evacuate your home quickly due to a flood, tornado, or other disaster, you may want to keep a "seventy-two hour kit" as part of your home storage. Seventy-two hour kits contain everything a person would ostensibly need during a three-day period—from food and water to blankets and other survival tools.

The concept of seventy-two hour kits is not infallible. For one thing, most people store those kits at home. If some or all of your family members are away from home when the emergency strikes, they'll be out of luck. Furthermore, an unforeseen calamity could bury your kits under rubble or destroy them with floodwater. Nevertheless, a seventy-two hour kit could be a great help to your family in some circumstances.

There are two kinds of items that are needed for seventy-two hour kits—items that are required by every member of the family, and items where only one of a kind is needed to be shared by the group as a whole. Every family member needs food and water, for example, but there's no reason you'd need more than one hatchet in a family's three-day survival kit. In fact, one of the hallmarks of these kits is that they should be easily portable by your family members. They should contain the bare essentials needed for survival for those three days, chosen and packed to be as lightweight as possible.

Here are items that you may want to consider for *each* family member for your seventy-two hour kit.

- Food for three days, preferably in a lightweight form such as Meals Ready to Eat (MREs)

- Drinking water for three days (estimate a gallon per person per day)

- Plate, bowl, cup, and utensils

- Minimal medical supplies (aspirin, prescription drugs, plastic bandages)

- Toilet paper

- Diaper material for babies, and feminine supplies for women

- Emergency blanket

- Hand/body warmer

- Prescription glasses or contacts (outdated prescriptions are fine to get you through the emergency period, as long as you can still see when you're wearing them)

- Flashlight, extra batteries, spare bulb. May prefer three twelve-hour light sticks.

- Large, long-life candle

- Matches or a butane lighter (for adults only)

- Paper and pencil

- A small number of one-dollar bills per person

- A change of clothes, including shoes

- One bar of soap or a plastic bottle of waterless washing gel

- Toothbrush, toothpaste, and other toiletries

- Sleeping bags

- Coats, hats, gloves, and boots

Here are items that you'll need only one of for your entire family. They're listed here in no particular order. This list is by no means all inclusive—you may want to add other items as they occur to you.

- First-aid kit (the size of the first-aid kit should depend on the size of your family)

- Cash for the family ($200 for a family of four; plus a roll of quarters)

- Laundry/dish soap

- Hatchet

- Utility knife

- Roadmap, stored in a plastic zipper bag to keep it safe from water damage

- Pot for cooking

- One gallon of cooking water per day

- Folding shovel

- Cooking stove and fuel

- Potholders

- Compass

- Sewing kit

- Nylon rope (at least 100 feet)

- Radio with fresh batteries. There are also solar and hand-cranked radios on the market, which would eliminate the need for batteries.

- Duct tape (you may never need it, but the men in your group will feel safer just knowing it's there)

- Cord, twine, or string

- Portable toilet

- Personal documents: genealogy records, legal papers, passports, checkbook, personal phone book, etc.

- Can opener

- Emergency flare

- Salt

The ideal way to have a seventy-two hour kit is to package it in a way that each family member can carry his own. However, the ideal way isn't exactly practical. It's a strong child who can carry three gallons of drinking water, to say nothing of the other items your family may deem important for that three-day emergency. And once you add the one-per-family items, you may need a packhorse to move all the items on the list.

Here's where you have to make a decision between comprehensiveness and portability. It's entirely possible to assemble a seventy-two hour kit in a backpack, and many people choose to do so. These kits won't have all the amenities of the larger ones, but they'll be a lot easier to grab in the case of an emergency. If you color-code a kit for each family member and store the kit where that family member can grab it on the way out of the home, you won't have to worry about renting a moving van when the crisis hits.

If you'd rather have a seventy-two hour kit with all the amenities, you may want to consider packing all the kits together in one or two large containers. A huge rolling garbage can may be the solution that works for you. However, make sure that either Mom or Dad can lift the container into the family car—and indeed, that the container will fit into the family car. The idea is to be able to move quickly in case of an emergency, and you won't be moving quickly if you're unloading the contents of that garbage can into the family Toyota.

Speaking of cars, people who live in areas that are struck by sudden snowstorms should have some sort of stripped-down seventy-two hour kit in every vehicle during winter months. The amenities you'll need are food, water, warmth, and emergency flares. Many a life is lost every year when drivers get stuck in a snowdrift and aren't found by emergency workers until several days after the occupants of the car have died of exposure.

If you have children or teenagers, you may want to consider assembling a small package of personal items for each child, which can be tucked into the seventy-two-hour kit for short-term emergencies. Teenagers may want a certain brand of creme rinse. Pre-teens may want hairclips. Adolescents of both sexes may need rubber bands for their braces. A small game or a puzzle book may while away many long hours. You may think that if a hurricane hits your town and you're sleeping in the gymnasium of the local high school, the last thing on your mind will be whether Susie brushes her teeth with a green toothbrush. But if that green toothbrush is going to make the difference between normalcy and panic for Susie, everybody in the gymnasium will be happier if you've prepared ahead of time for that contingency.

If your children help prepare these personal packs, they'll have something to distract them and to comfort them in times of extreme emergency. In fact, your family can set aside one night a year to inventory these packs, decide which items are no longer needed, and determine which items should be added. Doing this annual inventory as a family will give you the opportunity to talk with your children about possible emergencies and to drill them on what to do in case of fire or flood or some other sort of disaster. This yearly review may be a lifesaver if your children are caught away from home when an emergency strikes.

Although this is specifically a non-food chapter, we've enclosed one recipe here for "Over My Dead Body Survival Bars." These bars can be put in your seventy-two-hour kit to sustain life in the event of the direst emergency. This recipe got its name because both authors tasted the bars once and swore never to eat them again. This is exactly the kind of recipe we did not want to include in this book, because we believe that food storage doesn't have to taste nasty to sustain life. However, a friend with no taste buds described these as "not bad—pretty good, actually," so we're including the recipe here— solely to be used as part of your seventy-two-hour kit. This recipe is included only for survival purposes, and even then the authors do not recommend you use it unless your family has taste-tested it first and is absolutely crazy about the bars. Remember that people are *more* choosy about what they eat during times of stress—not less. After all, when Chapter 9 gives you resources where you can buy MREs (Meals Ready to Eat) for only about a dollar apiece, why choke down something as noxious as these?

"Over My Dead Body" Survival Bars

3 cups cereal (oatmeal,
barley flake or wheat
flakes)
1 cup powdered milk
4 tablespoons honey

¾ small package citrus-
flavored gelatin
¼ cup white sugar
optional: chocolate chips or
mixed dried fruit

Place all dry ingredients (except gelatin) into mixing bowl. Add 3 tablespoons water to the honey and bring it to a boil. Dissolve the gelatin in the honey-water mixture, then add it all to the dry ingredients. After mixing well, add water a tablespoon at a time until the mixture is barely moist enough to be molded. (You'll be adding approximately ¼ cup of water.) Pack into freezer dish or cookie sheet. This recipe makes six bars (about 3 by 5 inches). You can also drop on cookie sheet for bite-size eating.

Three bars will provide about 1,000 calories. This is sufficient for one person for one day. The bars can be eaten raw (if you can choke them down), or you can cook them by placing them in the oven and drying them under very low heat (250°F. for 40 minutes). Then wrap them in foil and store indefinitely in a covered container. It is best to rotate them every six months to a year.

Alternate Light, Heat, and Power

In the closing days of 1998 and the early days of 1999, the Middle Atlantic States experienced several crippling ice storms that knocked out power to hundreds and thousands of homes. We escaped the one in Williamsburg, Virginia, by driving through corridors of downed trees until we reached Virginia Beach. But when we drove back to our house near the Virginia-Maryland border, the first thing we heard was that an ice storm was predicted for our own vicinity the following weekend. This ice storm was supposed to be so severe that several of the men at a church party we attended decided to go to the discount store the following day and buy generators for their homes.

We didn't need a generator—or so we thought. We had a large fireplace in our home, along with nearly a cord of wood that had been sitting in our garage for nearly a decade. The wood was well seasoned, because a pair of chimney swifts had been using our chimney as a breeding ground for all those years, raising two broods of extremely loud offspring during each summer season.

As we thought about it, we realized that despite our precautions, we didn't dare light a fire in our own fireplace. There were ten years' worth of bird nests in that chimney, and the chance of a chimney fire was just too great. At that point we realized that as much as we'd enjoyed those chimney swifts, our enjoyment of the birds had taken away our source of emergency heat. Until that chimney was cleaned, we didn't have an alternate source of energy—even though the fireplace and the firewood were plainly visible for all to see. This was yet another reminder for us that if you can't find something, or if you can't use it, you don't own it. Realizing that we'd be helpless if an ice storm caused a power outage, we reluctantly made an appointment with the chimney sweep.

Here is a list of items you may want to include in your family's backup power supply. But before you rely on these things, test them. We bought a kerosene heater that worked fine for Clark, but Kathy couldn't be in the same room with the heater because her lungs reacted to fumes that Clark couldn't smell. Buy a variety of things; never put all your eggs in one basket.

- Candles—find or make long-burning candles

- Safety matches

- Flashlights—battery powered, rechargeable, or crankable. If they're rechargeable, keep them charged. If they're crankable, you'd better have strong hands.

- Batteries for flashlights

- Flashlight bulbs

- Kerosene lanterns or propane lamps

- Fuel for kerosene lanterns or propane lamps (take precautions against fire)

- Mantles for propane lamps; wicks for kerosene lamps

- Fireplace

- Kerosene heater

- Wood-burning stove

- Wood for fireplaces and wood-burning stoves

- Firestarters of choice—starter tube, Duralog, etc.

- Sterno cooking fuel cans

- Temporary heat sources for hands and feet

- Warm clothes and blankets

- Barbecue grill (not the electric variety!) or Coleman stove

- Propane tanks or bags of charcoal to fuel barbecue grill or Coleman stove

- Butane lighters

- Generator—only if it's hooked up and ready to go

- Fuel for generator—do not store fuels inside or adjacent to home!

Water

Water storage is an important part of food storage, and it has been mentioned several times in the text of this book. Not only can culinary water supplies become contaminated from flood or sabotage, but power outages can also shut off the water for people whose drinking wells deliver water to the home by means of electrical pumps. Members of the LDS Church are counseled to store two weeks' worth of water for every member of the household, to be used in times of emergencies. (If you store a gallon per day per person for drinking and another half gallon to one gallon per day for non-drinking purposes, you should be fine even during hot summer days.) Anyone who stores food that relies heavily on wheat or beans should also store two to three cups of water for every cup of wheat or beans that will be consumed during the period of need.

You may wonder what you'll do with a whole gallon of water per person per day—but that's only because you've never had to ration your water. As this book went to press, the county where the authors live

How Much Water Do I Store?

•1 gallon of drinking water per day
per person

+

• ½ to 1 gallon of non-drinking water per day
per person

For a family of four:
4x1 gallon of drinking water = 4 gallons
4x½ gallon non-drinking water = 2 gallons

=

6 gallons per day

was in the midst of a drought, and voluntary water restrictions went into effect. We learned that under these voluntary water restrictions, citizens of the county were asked to consume no more than seventy gallons of water per person, per day. If mandatory water restrictions went into effect, county residents would then be forced to subsist on thirty-five gallons per day. Even the idea of using thirty-five gallons of water per day would horrify people in many parts of the world, who survive on less water than you and I should have in our food storage. When you're tempted to skimp on your water rations, consider how hard it's going to be to limit yourself to two gallons when you're accustomed to using more than seventy.

There are two different kinds of water—drinking water, and water that's used for non-drinking purposes. Although you may not realize you have any stored water on hand already, your water heater contains water that is suitable for drinking. Learn how to reach that water in case you need it.

If you have a swimming pool, don't even think of drinking the water unless you have water purification supplies. However, you can use that water to flush your toilet till the cows come home. Another ideal place to store non-drinking water is a waterbed. In emergencies, the water from waterbeds can be used to flush toilets or for other occasions when the water doesn't have to be appetizing or germ free.

A little scouting around in some of the other resources we'll list for you in Chapter 9 will give you some ideas for where to purchase plastic containers that will hold as much as fifty-five gallons of water. Be advised that not all plastic containers are created equal. Milk cartons biodegrade, and if you choose to store your water in those, be prepared for a major water leakage in about a year. We lost a lot of valuable papers to the basement flood that raged when our milk bottles went the way of all biodegradable plastics.

Two-liter soft drink bottles are considerably sturdier than milk cartons, and should be sufficient for your purposes if you replace them every couple of years. An even better bet, though, is the bottled water that's so popular now. Not only are the bottles sealed for your protection, but the water inside them should be considerably freer of chemicals than the water you'll get out of your own tap. If you plan on long-term water use featuring commercially bottled water, however, be warned that one of the chemicals you won't find in bottled water is fluoride. If you have young children and want them to have the benefits of fluoride, you may want to invest in fluoride tablets to store with your bottled water.

We have enterprising friends who own a water cooler. Every few weeks, a deliveryman brings five-gallon bottles to replace bottles the family has emptied. This family figured out how many five-gallon bottles they'd need over a two-week time frame and purchased that many additional bottles for their food storage. Even if you don't have your own water cooler, you may want to consider buying a few of those five-gallon bottles for your own purposes. Five-gallon bottles are considerably easier to carry than the fifty-five-gallon containers. They may be more practical for your family's uses.

If you have any doubts about your drinking water, purify it before you drink it. One good way to do so is to boil it. Boiling won't kill every microorganism, but it may save your life if you're unsure of the purity of your water supply. Because boiling temperatures change with the altitude, a good rule of thumb is to boil water for at least ten minutes—and fifteen minutes may even be a better bet.

When Kathy was growing up, she and her family used to go to Mexico for family vacations. They scrupulously avoided the drinking water, but their soft drinks often had ice cubes floating in them—and those ice cubes had not been imported from the United States. They also brushed their teeth with water right out of the tap. They knew all along they shouldn't be doing this, but they decided as long as they were *mostly* following the rules, they'd be protected.

Needless to say, they were wrong. You don't have to drink contaminated water by the gallon. All it takes is one bacterium on your toothbrush to kill you, as Kathy's cousin learned when he and a group of friends went across the border for a restaurant meal that killed several members of the group. Don't play games with your safety. If you have any doubts whatsoever about the water you're drinking, boil it for at least ten minutes before you even think about putting it in your mouth. A little work now may save your family's life.

Water may be purified by adding bleach to it. To one gallon of questionable water, add sixteen drops of bleach. However, not all bleaches are created equal. Your family would probably be safer with water purification tablets, which are available for a modest cost at outdoor supply stores.

Although boiling, bleach, or water purification tablets may make your water safe, they won't do anything to improve the flavor. If you're planning on a time when you'll have to drink water that you have purified, you may want to invest in a pitcher that has a water filter that will improve your water's taste. (Be sure to purchase a supply of extra filters, too.)

Water tastes flat after it has been boiled. One thing you can do to restore life to it is to pour it back and forth between two containers or by shaking it in a partially-filled bottle to aerate it. Don't do this with hot water; wait until the water has cooled. Another avenue is to buy powdered drink mixes to mask the taste of water that has an edge. These powdered drink mixes are especially popular with the kiddies— and indeed, they may be the only reason your kids will drink water that has an unpleasant taste to it.

➡ Here are some other supplies you may or may not want to include in your food storage program, depending on how severe you think the crisis is going to be. Siegers will necessarily want a whole raft of water purification supplies to get them through the big one. People who are preparing for smaller catastrophes may prefer to concentrate their time and energy on other things:

- Pool water testing kit

- Water chlorinating granules (for pool)

- Pool tarp

- Water can—five gallon size

- Water bag (collapsible)—five gallon size

- Water/gas funnels

- Water filter

- Water pump (hand-operated, to remove water from fifty-five-gallon containers)

Tools and Garden Supplies

Most of the tools you have around the house already can do double duty as home storage equipment. You probably already have a hammer, a saw or two, and an assortment of screwdrivers. Unless you're especially hard on your tools, you probably won't need to buy extras to tide you over in case of an emergency.

Other items may need to be replenished, though. Think about furnace filters, light bulbs, and other equipment that wears out or expires. You may want to determine equipment you own that is battery-operated, and keep a supply of extra batteries on hand. Nails and screws may be in short supply in times of emergency, so you may want to stock up on an assortment of those and other repair items. If your house is kept in good repair, it will last longer than if you allow things to deteriorate.

If you're a gardener, you already have a shovel and a trowel. You probably don't have a year's supply of vegetable seeds, though. Be sure to purchase seeds that are specific to your area. You don't want to store seeds for hybrids, because hybrids don't make seeds of their own. A good gardening book can tell you what kinds of seeds to buy, or take a trip on the Internet to some of the sites mentioned in Chapter 9.

Along with seeds, you may want to buy soil conditioners such as manure or topsoil or mulch. Fertilizers may come in handy. Again, don't panic over this. The first priority should be to get your food storage. After you've made plans for feeding your family during times of crisis, you can take care of feeding your plants.

Self-Help Books

Many years ago, we read a great science fiction book by Larry Niven and Jerry Pournelle, *Lucifer's Hammer*.[2] This book, which predates any of the comet-hitting-Earth disaster movies (and is far better than any of them), is worth reading because it shows what could happen in the kind of life-altering scenario that siegers are preparing for.

One of the intriguing parts of this book was that it illustrated how important certain information would be if modern people had to return to a primitive society. Most of us have no idea how to generate power from wind, or churn butter, or tan leather, but books have been written that can teach primitive skills to modern people. In *Lucifer's Hammer*,

See Chapter 9 for more resources.

these books were so essential to human life that they were more valuable than diamonds.

If you're of the mindset that something big and horrendous is going to happen to the world during your lifetime, you should have at least a small library of books you can use to teach you these lost home arts. Even if you aren't of that mindset, the books make for interesting reading. Look in Chapter 9 for a few suggested titles, or even better, scout some out on your own. But don't just *buy* the books. Keep them where you can put your hands on them, and where they won't be damaged by disasters. Remember, no matter how often you purchase an item, *if you can't find it, or if you can't use it, you don't own it.* These books, like all your emergency essentials, should be put in a place where they'll be easily accessible in an emergency situation.

Money

So many of us live on a shoestring that the idea of storing a year's supply of money seems ludicrous. But if the time comes when your breadwinner is flat on his back for a year, you'll be mighty glad you set money aside for the necessities of life.

Even when you don't have any money, there are things that must be purchased anyway. Gasoline for the car is one of them. Medicines are another. Birthdays and holidays will still roll around for your young children, as will school field trips. Taxes will still be due, and so will insurance premiums. And don't forget rent and utilities.

If the concept of saving money is out of your reach at the present time, the least you can do is to do what you can to get out of debt. Credit card companies don't care whether your breadwinner is incapacitated— they want their money anyway. If you don't have any credit card debt, that's one less worry you'll have if your family situation changes and you don't have any money coming in.

If you can't even get out of debt at the present time, there are other things you can do to improve your situation. We have a friend whose husband left his job looking for greener pastures—and then was out of work for several years. This family faced hard times, and they still haven't completely recovered. But the wife helped considerably by watching all the credit card offers that came in the mail. Whenever she saw a credit card offer that carried an extremely low interest rate, she'd get that card and transfer the balances from all her other credit cards onto the new one. She'd keep that card until the interest rates went up, and then she'd scout around for a new credit card at the lower interest rate. Even though her family would have been better off without any credit card debt, they had no option but to live on credit cards while her husband was seeking work. By continually shopping around for credit cards with lower interest rates, this prudent consumer saved her family thousands of dollars that they would have otherwise spent in credit card interest during that four-year period.

These same friends have also refinanced their mortgage every time the rates have gone down, taking advantage of the lower interest rates. Because of the attention they paid to the family finances during lean times, the family was able to keep their home.

Getting out of debt should be your family's primary financial goal. After you're out of debt, then think about setting aside a year's worth of money. This money should be in a form that is easily liquidated. If won't help your family tomorrow if your T-bills don't mature for five years.

If you're anticipating a global catastrophe rather than a family emergency, you may want to set aside extra items to use for barter. Toilet paper may be worth its weight in gold one day. A can of beef stew could sell for a hundred dollars. If your estimation is wrong and the crisis is family oriented rather than worldwide, you can always use that toilet paper or that beef stew for your own family. Money used in prudent or provident food storage is never lost, as long as your supplies are properly maintained.

Okay, Any Questions?

? *Throughout this book I've been looking for something on how to store food for pets. What about Rover and Fluffy?*

Many years ago, after a generalized plea from our church leaders, we sponsored a family of Vietnamese teenagers whose parents had sent them to this country to find a better future for themselves. We looked forward to their first trip to an American supermarket, and we had a good time showing them all the aisles of food. Our enjoyment came to a screeching halt, however, when the three young adults wandered onto the pet food aisle. The oldest of the three stopped cold in the middle of the aisle, after seeing only half the assortment of chew-toys, leashes, and gourmet food for animals. She turned to us with tears in her eyes and said in halting English, "All this—for *dog?*"

After viewing America's obsession with pets through the eyes of a girl who had grown up with no food on her own table, the whole concept of spending money on pets is so fraught with guilt for us that we can't even think about telling you how to store food for a dog or a cat. If you want to purchase a year's worth of pet supplies, you're on your own. (We do give you some sources in Chapter 9, however.)

The average pet owner spends hundreds of dollars per animal, per year, just for food. Kitty litter, chew toys, medical expenses, and all the frills that most Americans consider essential for pet ownership drive the bill even higher. Once you monitor your pet expenses for a month, the cost may convince you that when Rover or Fluffy flies off to Pet Heaven, you may not want to replace him. Unless you're a sieger, of course. If you're a sieger who is waiting for Armageddon, you may want a vicious and hungry guard dog to help you fend off scavengers who are bent on obtaining your wheat and powdered milk. If that's your plan, remember to sock in huge amounts of dog food to feed your animal so he doesn't have to wonder what a good meal *you'd* make if times are lean.

Notes:

1. H. Winter Griffith, *Complete Guide to Symptoms, Illness & Surgery* (Los Angeles: The Body Press, 1989).
2. Larry Niven and Jerry Pournelle, *Lucifer's Hammer* (New York: Ballantine Pub., 1998).

CHAPTER 8

Where the Sun Don't Shine

★ **IN THIS CHAPTER**
- ✔ Helping food last longer
- ✔ Understanding the shelf life of common foods
- ✔ Dealing with older foods when cooking
- ✔ Reduce waste through rotation
- ✔ Finding storage space in cramped quarters
- ✔ Protecting family and food from Mother Nature
- ✔ Answering common questions

This is the stuff of which nightmares are made. You have just spent five years building up your food storage until it's a work of art. It consists of bags of flour and sugar, gelatin dessert, and saltine crackers. (Okay, so you're not a gourmet). Then you take the kids for a week at Disneyland. You return, only to find that your washing machine hose sprang a leak, and there is a foot of water on the basement floor. Like most families, you also put your food storage in the basement, so now you have 500 pounds of mystery glop. Your tears add an inch to the water level.

The provident person needs to be concerned not only with what is stored, but also how and where it is stored. In this chapter we will teach you how to protect your food storage from the disasters of life, and to minimize the effects of spoilage. We will also provide tips for those who are challenged by having a minimum of space for their storage.

To the Losers Go the Spoils

One of Clark's favorite cartoons shows a man opening his refrigerator, only to find a bowl of potato salad pointing a tiny gun at several condiment jars. The caption on the cartoon reads, "When potato salad goes bad." Failure to plan your food storage properly can result in a lot of bad food that must be discarded. This not only is a waste of food and money, but also a waste of the time you spent in obtaining or preserving the food, and the time you'll spend to throw it away. This wastefulness can be avoided or minimized if you understand a little about the perils that can befall a can of food while it's sitting on the shelf waiting to be eaten.

➲   Consider the following problems that can occur if you fail to plan and store your food supply properly:

▶ Loss of Nutrients

Although some aged foods may still taste fine, they may have lost a great deal of the valuable vitamins and other nutrients that were present when the food was originally canned, bottled, or packaged. This is a minor annoyance when your food storage supplements your regular diet, but is more serious if you are living on your stored food.

▶ Loss of Quality

Have you ever been in the mood for a bowl of ice cream, only to find that the only carton in the freezer is a half-empty carton that has been hiding behind a frozen turkey since your last birthday party? You think it might be fine, so you pull out the carton and open the lid, only to find a half pound of ice crystals covering a substance that has the consistency of rubber cement. Even though such a find probably would not make you sick, it will more likely find itself in the garbage can rather than your stomach.

Food stored improperly will often undergo changes that make it unpleasant to consume. These changes will affect the food's color, flavor, look, smell, or consistency. Although these foods will sustain life, they will still usually be discarded unless you are in the middle of an emergency where every crumb of food is precious.

▶ Loss of Potency

Products such as yeast and baking soda will lose their potency if they are stored too long or under the wrong conditions. Even though they will look fine, any product made with them will not produce the results you expected. Breads and cakes will not rise, and will be more suitable as doorstops than desserts.

This problem also affects products such as popcorn, as Clark learned when he bought a carton of microwave popcorn on sale. After about six months, the size of the popped bag was only about half what it should have been, and most of the kernels would not pop.

▶ Spoilage

This is the worst of all the calamities that can befall food, and it usually gives you no option but to discard the food rather than risk illness from eating it. We give this term a rather broad meaning, and apply it to any foreign body that contaminates a food to the point where it can no longer be eaten. Using this definition, food can be spoiled due to the action of microorganisms, insects and rodents, or chemical contaminants.

The Hall of Shame

Although even the experts have to discard food on occasion, careful planning will help you avoid spending your hard-earned dollars on food that will be discarded before it is eaten. In this section we will give you some tips that should help minimize this type of waste. All your efforts in this area should be targeted against five enemies that will cause your food to lose its appeal and nutrition. These should be easy to remember, because they start with the letters S-H-A-M-E. Just remember that it is a SHAME to waste good food.

▶ Sunlight

Exposure to sunlight may cause chemical changes in the food that will affect its taste, appearance, or potency. The warmth of sunlight will also cause heat, which is another enemy of your food storage.

Direct sunlight is the worst, but even a moderate amount of indirect light can cause similar problems. That is one reason why basements are so good for the storage of food, and why products that have been commercially canned in metal containers are appealing for longer than the ones preserved in glass jars.

▶ Heat

Let's say it's summer and you bought two cases of soup for your food storage. The first one you took down to the basement where it is a cool 65°F. But then you got a little lazy, and just left the other case in the garage where the temperature gets up into the 90s. What would be the difference? Surprisingly, the soup in the garage would last only about half as long. High heat can decrease the life of foods by 50 percent or more. Each 10°F. rise in temperature will double the number of chemical reactions taking place in the food, and these reactions are what cause the food to spoil over a period of time.

Your ideal food storage area should have a temperature between 32°F. and 70°F. If the area gets warmer than this, the food will not last as long. If the area gets colder than this, the food could freeze and rupture the storage containers.

Select an area away from appliances that produce heat. Those little spaces next to the furnace or on top of the freezer may look tempting, but they should be avoided.

If you live in a area with a hot, humid climate, you will have additional challenges. In addition to the heat, you will be fighting against humidity, mold, and insects.

▶ Air

Not only will the air dry out your food, but it will also expose your food to a whole bunch of critters that are intent on having your carefully stored food as their main course.

Bacteria, yeast, and molds are the three types of microorganisms that will infect your food. When food is canned, the heat kills the microorganisms inside the can, and the can itself keeps out new infection. Obviously, this protection is lost when the can is opened and the food is again exposed to the air. Unfortunately, metal cans are not designed for long shelf life. Studies have shown that most spoilage of canned foods can be traced to a problem with the integrity of the can rather than with the food. Bottles are better than cans for long-term storage, but are more subject to breaking. One option is to retain the original cardboard boxes that held the bottles, because they protect from light and breakage.

Drying and freezing food does not kill microorganisms, but it does prevent their continued growth. This protection lasts as long as the food is dried or frozen; once it is thawed or rehydrated, bacterial growth resumes.

Leaving food open to the air also exposes it to larger pests, such as rodents and insects. Rodents eat the food and then show their gratitude for your hospitality by leaving behind their waste products. Insects leave eggs, which hatch and produce larvae. Although food with a slight contamination problem caused by such pests can often be saved by filtering out the foreign matter, most of us just don't have the stomach for this, and simply discard the food.

Well-sealed containers will keep insects and rodents out. Storing food in smaller containers will also reduce the possibility of contamination by such pests after the food has been opened. Never store food in open containers, and clean up any food particles that spill in the storage areas. Keeping the temperature between 35°F. and 65°F. will also make these pests feel less welcome. When you are designing your storage area, avoid cracks and small places where pests could hide. If you have a separate room that is dedicated to food storage, use caulk to seal all the cracks around the floors and the ceiling.

A final class of air contamination is the damage done to food by chemicals. These could be chemicals such as cleaners or bleach that are stored near the food and contaminate them when they are accidentally spilled. Make sure any such chemicals are stored in a different area from the foods.

You don't have to see a chemical spill, however. You may have noticed that baggers at the supermarket make a big effort to separate food items and non-food chemical items because the food items pick up the taste of the chemical products. Food can pick up those chemicals from the air, just as your lungs can. If you can smell something, you're taking it into your lungs. If you can taste something, you're eating it.

Chemical contamination also occurs when you store food in an improper container, and chemicals leach out of the container and into the food. We previously mentioned the danger of storing wheat in plastic trash bags for this reason. Don't use trash bags as food containers, and avoid bottles and cans that originally contained such toxic products as paint. Also stay away from industrial plastics and fibers. If the original packaging of the product is not adequate for storage, place it in a container that is certified as "food grade." These are tested to make sure they are adequate and safe for the storage of food.

Some people expose their food storage to chemicals that claim to prolong the life of the food being stored. If you do this, make sure the chemical treatment is approved and has been proven safe.

▶ Moisture

Excessive moisture in the storage area will make your food more susceptible to destruction by mold and mildew, and can also change the consistency of powdered foods so that they are no longer appetizing.

Do not store food directly on the floor of a basement, where moisture will seep into the food from the concrete. Place the food on top of wooden slats, which will keep the food from making direct contact with the floor.

If you live in an area where there's a chance of flooding, make sure to store all food two to three feet above the floor, so that it would not be covered in the event of a flood. If you don't have the luxury of letting that space go to waste, store canned goods there, because they would have a better chance of surviving after being covered by water. If the basement ever does get flooded and the cans are covered by water, make sure to wash them with soap, water, and bleach, and then rinse and dry the cans thoroughly as soon as the flood waters have receded. Floodwaters are notorious for carrying disease-causing bacteria.

If possible, try to keep the humidity in your storage area at less than 15 percent. Also, the area should be well ventilated so condensation does not form on the containers.

▶ Entropy

Entropy is a fancy scientific term that describes the tendency of all systems to decay. In a biological sense, it means that all living organisms are doomed to die and then to deteriorate into nothingness, given enough time. In a living system, this breakdown is partially offset by the production of new cells that replace the cells that are destroyed each day. But when the animal dies or the plant is harvested, production of new cells ceases, and the existing cells will continue to deteriorate until nothing is left. This thought may not be very appetizing, but you should consider that all food storage represents dead plant and animal cells that are involved in the process of breaking down. Existing methods of food preservation are designed to slow this degeneration, but nothing will stop it from taking its eventual course.

You can fight entropy by rotating your food supplies so that they are consumed before they have lost too much of their nutritional value. There are a number of food storage shelves that are designed to rotate food, so that older cans are brought to the front, and the newer cans you buy are loaded in at the back. This works well for cans, but for other containers you may have to resort to that old trick of dating each package when it is placed in storage and then using the package with the oldest date first

You need to consider the age of food when buying new supplies as well. Be cautious that you are not buying old food that has been sitting in a hot warehouse for the past year. Be careful of canned goods where the cans are dusty, scratched, or rusty. Examine labels on food for signs of fading, tearing, staining, or discoloration. Be cautious of food that comes in boxes that are crushed or faded. In short, no matter how good the price, avoid buying food that shows any signs of being too old or being stored incorrectly.

A later section of this chapter contains some tables that will help you determine how long certain foods may be stored without losing their nutritional value. Take care that you don't buy more than you can eat before the product reaches its shelf life. For example, packaged cookies have a shelf life of about two months, or eight weeks. If your family eats about a package of cookies per week, you should avoid storing more than eight packages at a time.

We Have Met the Enemy

Despite the perils outlined in the previous section, there is one creature that is responsible for more discarded food than any other. You don't need to call an exterminator or set traps to find this beast; you just need to go look in your closest mirror. Although the adverse conditions described previously have to be considered accomplices to the crime, the main perpetrators of food waste are Mom and Dad, and the bad habits they have developed towards stored food.

➜   So before you curse the environmental conditions that are taking their toll on your food, ask yourself if you are guilty of the following bad habits:

- Do you store "emergency only" food that isn't part of your regular diet? If we accomplish nothing else with this book, we want to break you of this wasteful habit.

- Do you have the skills to use the foods you store? How many people are storing wheat with no idea how they would ever grind it or incorporate it into recipes? If you don't know how to prepare it, the odds are pretty good that you will never eat it. Either learn how to prepare it, or replace it with something you can use in your cooking.

- Do you store food based on someone else's plan? You may have thought just duplicating Aunt Gwendolyn's storage plan was a great idea, but what are you going to do with twenty quarts of pickled rhubarb? Take the time to design your storage around your own diet.

- Do you buy food you don't like just because it's cheap? If you ever catch yourself saying, "We would never eat this for dinner—but at this price, we can put it in food storage," just walk away and save your money.

- Do you buy low-quality food for storage? Not only will you be less likely to eat it, but it will probably spoil in a shorter period of time. Adopt the rule that food for storage should meet or exceed the quality of your regular food.

- Do you store your foods in inconvenient locations? We do this all the time, and then ask ourselves, "Should we have tuna fish sandwiches using the tuna we have upstairs, or do we go down to the freezer and get steaks?" Sad to say, the tuna usually wins. If the storage is too inconvenient, the odds are you will not use it.

- Do I rotate my foods regularly? It's difficult to be religious about rotating foods. There are better things in life to do than to make sure we always grab the oldest can of soup. As a result, sometimes old food sits at the back of the shelf for years, while two or three generations of new food cycles through on the shelf in front of it.

To some degree, we are all guilty of wasting food. Make an honest evaluation of the foods you have discarded over the past five years. You will probably find most of the waste was caused by human factors rather than adverse conditions. If so, work on changing your habits before you worry about storage conditions.

Actually, adopting good habits will help to mitigate the damage caused by poor storage conditions. If you use and rotate the food regularly, it will not have time to spoil, even under the worst of conditions.

Shelf Life Tables

Use the tables below to approximate the shelf life of the foods you plan to store. The last column gives additional suggestions for extending shelf life and making sure the food is safe to eat when it is consumed. As noted above, the shelf life of food can vary greatly based on the storage conditions. The numbers shown in this table are extremely conservative, and would apply to an area where there is a lot of heat and humidity. *Never, ever throw away food according to a date on the calendar.* You may find that your foods will have either a longer or shorter shelf life based upon your particular conditions. Sometimes a food can last years longer than the shelf life specified in one of these charts—or it may not last till the expiration date. Storing foods for longer than shown in the tables will usually not result in spoilage, but it might result in some of the less-serious problems described previously such as loss of quality or nutrition.

Cooking and Baking Supplies

Food Item	Storage Life	Conditions
Baking powder	18 months	Keep dry and sealed
Baking soda	24 months	Keep dry and sealed
Bouillon cubes	24 months	Keep dry and sealed
Bread crumbs	6 months	Keep dry and sealed
Chocolate (milk)	12 months	Keep cool
Chocolate (semi-sweet)	24 months	Keep cool
Chocolate (unsweetened)	18 months	Keep cool

Food Item	Storage Life	Conditions
Cornmeal	12 months	Keep tightly closed
Cornstarch	18 months	Airtight container
Flour (white)	12–24 months	Airtight container
Flour (whole wheat)	8–12 months	Refrigerate
Honey	36 months	Airtight container
Molasses (unopened)	18 months	Keep cool
Molasses (opened)	6 months	Keep cool
Mayonnaise (unopened)	4–6 months	
Shortening (solid)	12 months	
Sugar (brown)	6 months	Airtight container
Sugar (confectioners)	18 months	Airtight container
Sugar (granulated)	24 months	Keep tightly closed
Vanilla extract (unopened)	24 months	Keep tightly closed
Vanilla extract (opened)	12 months	Airtight container
Vinegar (unopened)	24 months	Airtight container
Vinegar (opened)	12 months	Ignore cloudy appearance
Wheat (whole raw)	25 years	Airtight container
Yeast (dry)	Use by expiration date	Refrigerate or freeze for longer life

Vegetables, Fruits, and Condiments

Food Item	Storage Life	Conditions
Apples (fresh)	6 months	Store at 32° F. separated
Beans (dry)	12 months	
Beets (fresh)	6 months	Store at 32° F. in mesh bag
Cabbage (fresh)	6 months	Store at 32° F. in mesh bag
Carrots (fresh)	6 months	Store at 32° F. in mesh bag

Food Item	Storage Life	Conditions
Catsup (unopened)	12 months	Refrigerate for longer life
Coconut (packaged; unopened)	12 months	
Coconut (packaged; opened)	6 months	Refrigerate after opening
Fruits (canned)	24 months	
Fruits (dehydrated)	6–12 months	Airtight container
Fruits (frozen)	12 months	Freezer
Fruit juice (canned)	24 months	Keep cool
Fruit juice (dehydrated)	12 months	Airtight container
Fruit juice (frozen)	12 months	Freezer
Jam and jelly (unopened)	18–24 months	
Jam and jelly (opened)	12 months	Refrigerate
Lentils	12 months	Airtight container
Mustard (unopened)	12 months	Refrigerate for longer life
Onions (fresh)	6 months	Store at 32° F. in mesh bag
Oranges (fresh)	2 months	Store at 32° F. in mesh bag
Pears (fresh)	4 months	Store at 32° F. in mesh bag
Peas (dried)	12 months	Airtight container
Pickles (bottled)	12 months	
Potatoes (canned white)	30 months	
Potatoes (canned sweet)	30 months	
Potatoes (dehydrated)	30 months	
Potatoes (fresh white)	6 months	Store at 40° F. in mesh bag
Potatoes (fresh sweet)	6 months	Store at 60° F. in mesh bag
Potatoes (frozen)	8 months	Freezer
Pumpkin (fresh)	6 months	Store at 55° F. in mesh bag
Spices (ground)	6 months	Avoid sunlight
Spices (whole)	12–24 months	Airtight container
Squash (fresh)	6 months	Store at 55° F. in mesh bag

Food Item	Storage Life	Conditions
Tomato products (canned)	24 months	
Vegetables (canned)	24 months	
Vegetables (dehydrated)	6–12 months	Airtight container
Vegetables (frozen)	12 months	Freezer
Vegetable juice (canned)	12 months	

Breads, Rice, Pasta, Nuts, and Cereals

Food Item	Storage Life	Conditions
Bread (frozen)	6 months	Freezer
Bread (frozen dough)	3 months	Freezer
Breakfast cereal (unopened)	6–12 months	
Breakfast cereal (opened)	2–3 months	Reseal package tightly
Breakfast cereal (hot)	6 months	
Cake (frozen)	6 months	Freezer
Cookies (frozen)	6 months	Freezer
Cookies (packaged)	2 months	Keep box tightly closed
Crackers	6–8 months	Keep dry and sealed
Nuts (in shell)	6 months	Keep cool and dry
Nuts (packaged)	12 months	Reseal package tightly
Nuts (vacuum can)	12–24 months	
Pasta (dry)	24 months	Airtight container
Peanut butter (unopened)	6–9 months	Refrigerate to extend life
Peanut butter (opened)	2–3 months	
Popcorn (can)	24–36 months	Unpopped
Popcorn (bag)	3 months	Unpopped
Pretzels	3 months	Keep dry and sealed
Rice (white)	24 months	Airtight container
Rice (flavored)	6 months	Airtight container
Rolls (frozen)	6 months	Freezer

Meats and Dairy Products

Food Item	Storage Life	Conditions
Beef (canned)	30 months	
Beef (dried)	18 months	Keep cool and dry
Beef (frozen)	10 months	Freezer
Cheese (dried)	3 months	Keep cool and dry
Cheese (grated; unopened)	10 months	
Cheese (grated; opened)	2 months	Refrigerate after opening
Cheese (natural)	6 months	Refrigerate
Cheese (processed)	8 months	Refrigerate
Chicken (frozen)	8 months	Freezer
Cream substitutes	24 months	Freeze for longer life
Eggs (dried)	36 months	Keep cool and dry
Egg substitutes	3 months	Keep cool and dry
Fish (canned)	18 months	
Fish (frozen)	3–9 months	Varies by species
Lamb (frozen)	8 months	Freezer
Milk (condensed)	12 months	Invert cans occasionally
Milk (evaporated)	12 months	Shake cans occasionally
Milk (unopened nonfat dry)	24 months	
Milk (opened nonfat dry)	6–12 months	Airtight container
Pork (frozen)	4–6 months	Freezer
Shellfish (frozen)	3 months	Freezer
Turkey (frozen)	8 months	Freezer
Variety meats (frozen)	4 months	Freezer
Veal (frozen)	8 months	Freezer

Packaged Foods and Mixes

Food Item	Storage Life	Conditions
Biscuit mixes	9 months	Keep cool and dry
Brownie mixes	9 months	Keep cool and dry
Cake mixes	9 months	Keep cool and dry
Casserole mixes	9–12 months	Keep cool and dry
Chocolate syrup	24 months	
Cocoa mixes	8 months	
Gelatin	18 months	Refrigerate
Gravy mixes	6–12 months	Keep cool and dry
Grits	12 months	Airtight container
Muffin mixes	9 months	Keep cool and dry
Pancake mixes	6–9 months	Keep cool and dry
Pie crust mixes	8 months	Keep cool and dry
Potatoes (instant)	6–12 months	Airtight package
Pudding mixes	12 months	Keep cool and dry
Roll mixes (canned)	18 months	Refrigerate
Salad dressing (unopened bottle)	12–18 months	
Salad dressing (opened bottle)	3–6 months	Refrigerate
Sauce mixes	6–12 months	Keep cool and dry
Soup mixes	12 months	Keep cool and dry
Syrups (unopened)	12 months	
Syrups (opened)	6 months	Refrigerate

There's No Food Like an Old Food

We have all come across cans or packages of food that have seen better days. Then we must make the decision about whether the food should be consumed or discarded. If the food shows obvious signs of spoilage, the decision is easy because the food should immediately go in the trash. But how about food that is just old? Perhaps it won't make us sick, but it might not be very appetizing either. Are there ways we can salvage it, and take steps to make it edible? That's what we'll cover in this section.

⮕   First, here are some guidelines about when food is unhealthy and should be discarded:

- Discard any food that was processed incorrectly. This is more often a problem with home-canned foods than commercial items. Even if the container sealed properly and the food looks good, discard it immediately if you find the recipe was not followed, or the temperatures or cooking times were incorrect.

- Discard any bottle or can with a bulging lid. The sealed lid on a bottle should be concave, and you should not be able to break the seal with your fingers.

- Although it is common for the solids and liquids to separate in older foods, discard any food where the liquid has a milky appearance.

- Discard if there is any mold growing inside or outside of the container.

- Discard if the food has a slimy appearance or texture. (And if you've felt that texture with your fingers, wash your hands *thoroughly* with an antibacterial soap.)

- In food that contains oil of any kind, discard it if it has a rancid odor.

- Although all foods pick up odors as they age, discard the food if the odor is so strong that it ruins the taste of the food.

- Discard canned food if you see corrosion or rust on the inside of the can, particularly on any of the seams.

- Discard foods if they were stored in an incorrect container. Chemicals may leach from the container into the food and contaminate it.

If you conclude that some older food is safe, but the taste, smell, and appearance makes it so unappetizing that you won't eat it, then why allow it to take up space on your storage shelves? It certainly won't get any better if you allow it to age even longer. One solution might be to give the food to a shelter or food bank. But don't insult them by giving them food no one would eat. Consider this an option only if the food has very slight symptoms of age.

When cooking, there are ways you can use older foods that will cover up some of the imperfections that make it unappetizing. Consider the following:

- Older fruit will go dark and mushy, although the taste usually suffers less. Such fruit is good for making fruit leather. You can add sugar or spices to compensate for some of the loss of flavor.

- Older fruit can also be blended with ice cream and yogurt to make shakes and freezes.

- Blend fruits and use them as an added ingredient to some recipes, such as fruit cakes and cobblers. Blended fruits can also be used to replace some of the fats or oils called for in the recipe.

- Bottled vegetables can be used as an ingredient in soups, stews, and casseroles. If the consistency is too mushy, blend them first.

- If the taste of an older added food is too strong, consider using it in a different recipe where less is used, or where the other ingredients have stronger flavor.

- Add strong spices and herbs to recipes to help cover the stronger flavors of older foods. Use spices such as nutmeg, cloves, cinnamon, Creole seasoning, and Italian seasoning.

Here are some recipes that are designed to be used with older foods, particularly with older bottled or canned fruits:

Ancient Fruit Cake
(yield: 16–20 servings)

1 quart fruit with juice
1½ cups sugar
1 cup oil
4 cups flour
4 teaspoons baking soda

1 teaspoon salt
1 teaspoon cloves
1 teaspoon nutmeg
1 tablespoon cinnamon
1 cup raisins, nuts, or coconut
(optional)

Blend fruit and juice in a blender until it is a fine puree. Add sugar and oil to fruit mixture and mix well. Then add remaining ingredients and mix. Pour batter in a nonstick 9x13-inch baking pan. Bake at 350°F. for 1 hour. This cake has the consistency of a rich pudding and is usually eaten plain. If frosting is desired, use a butter cream or cream cheese frosting.

Bottled Fruit Leather

Drain the juice from the fruit and save for later. Puree fruit, adding additional juice back to the mixture, until the consistency is similar to thick applesauce. Sweeten to taste, either with sugar or with more of the fruit juice. You may also add various spices for additional flavor. Be careful when adding more sweetening or spices, as the taste of each will become stronger as the fruit leather dries.

Spread fruit mixture on cookie sheets or dryer racks that have been lined with plastic wrap. Dry in a fruit dryer or in the oven on a setting of 160°F. for 6–10 hours. You know the leather is ready when it can be peeled from the plastic wrap. Even when it is done, it will always be a little bit sticky because of the sugar in the juice it was in. Refrigerate or freeze if the leather will not be eaten within two days.

Fruit Shake

2 cups of drained bottled fruit   1 banana (optional)
1 cup yogurt or ice cream

Combine all ingredients in blender and blend until smooth. The banana will help thicken the mixture. Adding more ice cream will make for a richer shake.

Cranberry Apple Leather

2 quarts bottled applesauce   3 tablespoons chopped nuts
6 ounces frozen cranberry juice   (optional)
    concentrate

Combine the applesauce with the thawed concentrate. Spread the mixture on dryer trays or cookie sheets covered with plastic wrap. Sprinkle nuts or seeds on top of the mixture. Dry and store in the same manner as the Fruit Leather.

Fruit As a Fat Replacement

Older fruit may be blended and used in place of some of the fat when baking. Although the fruit adds moisture to the recipe, because it does not melt it will not act the same way as fat, and the final product will be changed. Experiment by replacing 25 percent to 50 percent of the fat and then testing the quality. Try to maintain at least one tablespoon of real fat for every cup of flour used in the recipe, substituting the remainder with fruit. The final baking time may also need to be increased to compensate for extra moisture in the fruit.

Planning for Easy Rotation

We hope you will never have to use the advice in the previous section, because we hope you will never have food that gets too old. In addition to eating the foods that you store, the other important thing in keeping foods fresh is to rotate them regularly. As difficult as that might sound, rotation is just a fancy word for using foods in the same order as you purchase them. What could be easier? Unfortunately, in the real world, things are never quite that simple. You may have storage shelves

that are difficult to access, or you may have the same items stored several places in the house, such as in the upstairs pantry and in the basement storage area. It soon becomes a little more complicated to figure out which of those jars of peanut butter was purchased first.

Unfortunately, all rotation systems require a certain amount of effort on your part. Rotation does not just magically happen; you must regularly inventory, date, and move your food. But we can give you some suggestions for how to get started, and how to structure your storage in a way that rotation is encouraged:

1. The key to smart rotation is to keep a running inventory of the items you have stored. Not only will creating the inventory remind you of the contents of storage, but the final result will give you a better idea of the total amount of food you have stored, as well as the food areas where you need to enhance your storage. For example, you might find that you have more food in storage than you thought, and that you could survive for six months on it. The bad news might be that you will be eating tuna fish and peanut butter for dinner every evening.

2. Create the inventory in a notebook or on a clipboard that can be placed near the storage itself. Alternately, build the inventory using a computer, and then print out the result and put it in a

small binder. Regardless of the way you do it, try to list the foods by category, and keep enough space between entries so you can add foods that you store later. Off to the right after the name of the item, draw a small circle to represent each of the items you have in storage. For example, if you found five cans of vegetable soup and three cans of tomato soup, that section of your inventory might look like the following:

Soups
    Tomato   **ooo**
    Vegetable   **ooooo**

3. When you are searching for an item of food, check the inventory notebook first to see if you have it in storage. If you do find the item, place a slash or an X through one of the circles off to the right, and then locate the item and remove it from storage.

4. Review the inventory notebook on a periodic basis, just to remind yourself of what you have in storage. One of our unfavorite shopping scenarios is to have to make an extra trip to the store specifically for a certain item, only to realize later we had a twelve-pack of the same item sitting in food storage.

5. Keep a separate page in the notebook or a separate pad in the same area for building a shopping list. There are two ways to do this. Option one is to add an item to the shopping list every time you remove an item from storage. Thus, if you remove a can of peaches, you add a can of peaches to the shopping list. Option two is to add items to the shopping list only when you start to run low. You will know this because of the circles you are marking through next to each item. When you get down to one or two of each item, add it to the grocery list so the supply can be replenished.

6. When you bring storage items home from the store, make sure to update the inventory notebook before placing the new food on the shelves. For an item that already exists on your inventory, just draw a new circle off to the right for every item you bought. If it is a new item, then add it to the inventory in the proper place, and draw the appropriate number of circles.

7. It is important that you use your stored food in the order it was acquired. One easy way to do this is to mark each item with the

month and the year that it was added to storage. Then just select the item with the oldest date first. Many food storage shelves are designed so that cans have to roll down a ramp, and then are removed from the front of the storage shelf. As new items are purchased, they are added on the back of the ramp behind the existing cans. Not only does this type of shelf make sure you eat food in the order it was stored, but it has the added advantage of turning the cans around each time you remove a can. This is useful for products like evaporated milk, which need to be shaken occasionally. The most effective shelves we have seen were on rollers, similar to the book shelves in some library archives. When adding new food, you could roll the shelf to one side and access the back of the shelf. When taking an item from storage, you could roll the shelf to the other side and remove the can from the front.

8. At least once a year, go through and create your inventory again. Do it on a specific day, such as a holiday, so that you remember to do it once a year. Repeating the inventory will remind you again what you have stored, and will get your list synchronized again with the food that you actually store.

9. As an alternative to the empty circles by each item in the inventory, consider using a running total. This involves putting two numbers next to each item. The first represents the number of those items you wish to keep in storage, and the second represents the actual number in your inventory. This makes it easy when first building your storage to identify the items that need to be purchased. As with the other system, decrease the number on hand when you use an item, and increase it when you add more items to storage. Add an item to the shopping list when the actual number falls below the desired number.

Storage for the Space-Impaired

All throughout this book we have talked about storing food in the basement. Maybe each time we have mentioned this, you have said, "You idiots! I live in a one-bedroom efficiency apartment. How does this apply to me?" Well, we are finally going to try to help you. In this section we will give some advice about how you can store food if you live in a situation where storage space is at a premium.

If you have not already done so, read the previous section about rotating food and maintaining a storage inventory. This is even more critical when you have limited storage space, because you will tend to have food scattered all over your living quarters, rather than in one central location. Your neighbor might have a case of tuna fish on his basement storage shelf, but you may have the same case scattered throughout your home—a few in the bedroom closet, some in the medicine cabinet, one behind the couch, and the rest in your underwear drawer. Also, you may have to store foods in less ideal storage places, making it critical that you rotate that food. For these reasons, you need to be almost fanatical about keeping an inventory and rotating your food.

Now here are some tips for finding storage space where you least expect it:

- Many walk-in closets contain a shelf above the area where you hang your clothes. Consider using all or part of this space for food storage. You could stack boxes of goods there, or visit your local lumber yard and build a set of shelves on top of the larger shelf.

- The racks in walk-in closets are usually high enough that they will hold dresses and long coats off the floor. But chances are, you have many shirts and jackets that don't need all that space. Relocate all these shorter clothes to the same area, and then stack food on the floor under them.

- Most people have more clothes than they need, and a lot of their clothing may no longer fit or be in style. If this is the case with you, inventory your clothes regularly, and give unused clothes to charity. Write the donation off of your taxes, and use the newly found storage space for food.

- Store seasonal clothing in a different area, and store food where it used to be. For example, in the summer, move your winter coats to the attic, and store food where the coats used to be stored.

- If you have stairs in your dwelling, and you can access the underside of them, consider this as an area for food storage. It will be a little bit of a challenge because of the shape, but it will usually work well for canned goods, or buckets that can be stacked. When stacking buckets of food, put a piece of plywood between each bucket, so the weight of buckets on top will not crush the lids of lower buckets.

- If you have access to the area under stairs, consider adding a small shelf on the back of each stair riser. This will allow you to store two or three rows of cans on the back of each stair. (Don't do this in a rental unit without written permission from the owner!)

- Some furniture, such as beds, usually has a lot of empty space under it that could be used for storage. Use a long bedspread or decorative cloth to hide the food from sight.

- Consider storing food in large boxes, and then covering each box with a decorative cloth. This type of box can double as a night-stand or a corner table.

- If you have deep bookshelves, store a row of cans at the back of each shelf, and then store the books toward the front.

- A neighbor of ours has a pretty table in her living room, covered with a floor-length tablecloth. If you lift up the cloth, you see that the space under the table is completely filled with boxed food, except for the metal cylinder that forms the hub of the table—which is a new metal garbage can filled with food.

- If you have utility rooms such as a laundry room, consider mounting shelves on all available wall space. Yes, it won't be pretty, but how often do you invite company in to watch you do the wash? By the way, this is only a storage space of last resort. Many foods don't respond well to the heat from a laundry unit. The laundry room may be a better place to store such nonfood essentials as toilet paper and soaps.

- Perhaps you have a good deal of open space, but just not many cabinets or storage shelves. Consider buying stand-alone plastic or metal storage shelves. They work quite well, and can be adapted to fit in a large number of locations within the home.

- Replace your coffee table with a flat-topped chest or trunk. It will function just as well for holding snacks and magazines, plus you can also open it up and store food inside.

- Storage shelves are made that attach to the inside of cabinet or pantry doors. This is usually just wasted space anyway, so being able to add several rows of cans to the back of a door can be quite useful.

- Many homes have a small coat closet near the front door. Most of these are large enough that you could build a shallow storage shelf on the back and sides, and not interfere with the storage areas designed for the coats. Of course, you may want to hang up the coats of party guests for them, rather than have to answer the same question all night.

- Although some locations such as attics and garages are not good for the storage of food due to temperature fluctuations, consider those areas for the storage of nonfood items that will be less affected by extreme temperatures.

- You can even store foods in extreme environments, such as the attic, provided you rotate through it frequently enough that it does not have time to spoil.

- If you live in an area with a moderate climate, consider renting a storage shed in a public storage area close to your home. Move less-frequently used items from your home to this area, and then store food in the areas that were made available. Needless to say, the best storage units are ones that are climate-controlled.

- If your home has windows that can be opened and receive adequate sun, consider installing flower boxes outside the windows, and growing vegetables each summer.

- To minimize the inconvenience of having food scattered all over the house, have a pantry or cabinet near the kitchen that serves as a staging area for the stored food. Keep an assortment of foods there, and replenish the pantry on a regular basis from the other storage areas throughout the house.

- Another way to make stored food more convenient is to store boxes that each contain an identical variety of different foods. For example, you might divide your storage into twenty equal portions, store each portion in a box, and then store the boxes throughout your home wherever you can find the storage space.

Thus, opening any box found in the house will reveal the same assortment of foods. This prevents you from having to dig through your stored items looking for a particular food, as that food will be a part of any box that you open. This technique takes more planning when you store the food, but saves time and frustration when you need to replenish it.

Guarding Against Catastrophes

The only thing worse than having no food storage during a catastrophe would be to have food storage that was destroyed because it was not stored properly. It is probably not possible or practical to create a food storage area that would be protected from all possible disasters, but you can do some basic things that will protect your storage against some of the more common types of calamity.

Some General Suggestions

Before providing specific advice for specific types of problems, let's examine some suggestions that apply to all types of catastrophes. Following these suggestions will help protect family members, as well as your food storage:

- Earlier we talked about a portable emergency kit, more commonly known as a "seventy-two-hour kit." These are designed to help family members survive away from home for up to three days in relative comfort. During many types of disasters, it is common to ask people to evacuate their homes quickly and report to shelters or other public meeting areas. Your family may be given just a few minutes to gather up a few belongings and evacuate your home. With a little bit of luck, you will be able to return to your home within a few days, and will hopefully find everything as you left it. But for the few days you are gone, your emergency kit can provide you with food, medicine, and other comforts that will make you feel a little less displaced. Review the contents of your emergency kit regularly. Keep it in a place that is protected, but also in a place that can be accessed quickly if you need to leave on short notice. Make sure all family members know where the kit is stored.

- Regularly review with family members the procedures for staying in touch during an emergency. What will you do if a disaster strikes in the middle of a weekday, when each family member is in a different place? Make plans to meet at a certain place or to leave messages with certain friends or relatives, particularly those who are some distance away and less likely to be affected by the disaster. For example, you may have an Aunt Helga who lives in another state. Everyone in the family should understand that Aunt Helga should be called if some kind of catastrophe separates the family. She can pass messages between family members, and make arrangements for them to get back together. Her phone number should either be memorized by all family members, or should be stored in a place where it may be available in time of emergency. If the phone lines are down and no calls can be made, an alternate plan should be used. You need to develop all of these plans ahead of time, review them regularly, and make sure they are understood by each family member.

- In many cases, the catastrophe itself causes less damage than some of the effects that follow it. For example, earthquakes can break gas and water lines, resulting in fires and floods that can create more damage than the original earthquake. Everyone who lives in your home should understand how to shut off the electricity, water, natural gas, fuel, oil, and any other systems that could cause such problems. Also make sure that such systems are inspected regularly and kept in good repair.

- We have all heard the adage, "Don't put all your eggs in one basket." This could apply to your food storage as well. If you have the space, consider separate food storage areas on different floors or in different locations within the house. In the event that a disaster strikes your home, at least one of these storage caches may be spared. For example, a flood might ruin your basement storage, but not the storage on the second floor. Conversely, a fire might destroy the upper floor, but spare the basement. If you use the cache method, be sure to store a variety of items in each cache.

- If you have a family pet, keep in mind that Fifi or Fido will probably not be welcome at the local shelter or emergency gathering place. This may seem cruel to animal lovers, but the main priority of the emergency workers will be saving people. Despite your affection for the household dog or cat, pets just aren't as high on the list as people are. Even if the family pet is allowed in the shelter, there may not be any food there suitable for animals. As part of your emergency storage, keep a three-day supply of pet food and some bottles of water reserved for the family pet.

- Teach children how to contact the police and fire departments, and how to locate radio stations that broadcast emergency information.

- Make sure you have a reliable battery-powered radio, and that you test it regularly. This becomes very important during any catastrophe, when emergency management agencies broadcast instructions, suggestions, and other status information.

- Keep a supply of battery-powered light sources, and spare fresh batteries to power them. Candles and lanterns will do in a pinch, but they are more dangerous as a potential cause of fires and fumes.

- Every family should include a good first-aid kit as part of its home storage. A first-aid kit could make the difference between life and death when a disaster occurs.

- With any emergency, remember to be a good neighbor. Look after those who are older, younger, or have physical limitations. Share your supplies with those who did not have the foresight to store their own, or whose supplies were damaged or destroyed. If you were fortunate enough to escape damage or injury, then help those who were not as fortunate. After all, the situation could very well be reversed next time.

Now that we have covered the basics, let's look at some specific types of catastrophes and the things that can be done to minimize the damage they will do to your home and your food storage.

Earthquakes

Unlike some disasters, earthquakes usually strike with no warning. There's little that can be done to minimize the consequences of an earthquake unless you plan for them ahead of time. Your food storage can be damaged in an earthquake by direct movement (such as bottles falling off a shelf) or by collisions (such as your bowling ball collection knocking down your storage shelves like so many pins).

➔   If you live in an area that is prone to earthquakes, consider taking the following precautions:

- If your food storage is in the basement, place it in a corner, or against one of the outside walls. If your food storage is on the main or upper floors, place it next to an interior wall, away from windows if possible.

- Fasten storage shelves securely to the walls so they will not tip over.

- Put large or heavy objects on the lower storage shelves.

- Store breakable items in low cabinets that are resistant to tipping, and that have doors that latch shut. This will keep the items from migrating too far, and from colliding with other items. As an alternative, use large cardboard boxes that can be fully closed and that contain interior padding.

- Avoid storing your food near appliances or other heavy furniture that can fall or bounce into your storage area. Secure such objects by bolting them to the floor or fastening them to the wall.

- Store toxic and flammable items well away from your food supplies. Like breakable food items, store these dangerous solutions in low cabinets with latching doors. If you have a detached garage or shed that can be locked to keep children out, this is a better place to store flammables and toxins.

- Design your storage so that items are less likely to contaminate each other when breakage occurs. For example, storing bottled fruit and soda crackers on the same shelf is not a good idea, because any broken bottles will soak the crackers with fruit juice. It would be better to store the fruit on a lower shelf, and the crackers on an upper shelf. (And considering the short shelf life of crackers, you probably don't want to be storing crackers at all. Use the recipe in Appendix A to make crackers when you need them.)

- Avoid locations too close to windows, artwork, or mirrors, because the glass in these objects can shatter and contaminate your storage.

- Be careful of family pets after an earthquake, because the trauma sometimes causes them to become aggressive and defensive for a few days. Keep them tied up and away from family members until it has been determined that their behavior is normal.

- Aftershocks often occur for several days after the main earthquake. Take caution when entering back into your home, particularly if you're in an area of the home that may have suffered some structural damage. Once inside the home, make sure the electrical and heating systems are free from damage, as well as chimneys, sewer lines, gas lines, and fresh water pipes. If you suspect a problem, don't use these systems until they have been inspected by a professional.

- As soon as it is safe, inspect your storage area and clean up any spills, especially things like bleach, other cleaning supplies, and flammable liquids.

- Open storage cabinet doors carefully. Contents may shift during an earthquake, and that bottle of Aunt Mabel's prize-winning cherries might now be aimed right at your big toe.

Floods

Just as the geography of some areas makes them susceptible to earthquakes, other locations are likely to be affected by flooding during certain seasons or weather conditions. If you live in such locations, you will do well to take some precautions to protect your food storage against the unwanted intrusion of water into your home.

How do you know if flooding is a problem you need to worry about? Contact the Red Cross or the government agencies in your

area that deal with emergency management. They should be able to tell you if your area is subject to flooding. Also, as a requirement for obtaining a home loan, some lenders will require you to purchase flood insurance if you live in flood-prone areas. If you were required to purchase such insurance, you should consider yourself as a candidate for flooding.

In rare circumstances, floods occur from sources other than severe weather. The towns of Rexburg and Sugar City, Idaho, were flooded in June of 1976, when the Teton Dam broke and dumped its contents on the citizens downstream. Few of those hapless folks would have considered themselves living in a potential flood area, until they saw their homes filled with roiling river water.

If you think that flooding could happen to the area around your home, consider taking the following precautions:

- If you don't already own it, consider the purchase of flood insurance. This won't protect your home and your food storage, but it will help replace your home and its contents if there is a disaster. Most standard home insurance policies do not cover damage from floods, so don't just assume that you have this coverage.

- Store items such as shovels, sandbags, plastic sheeting, lumber, wallboard, and construction tools. During minor flooding, these can be used to build barriers that will divert water around your home.

- Have a plumber install check valves in your sewer traps. This will prevent flood water from entering your home by backing up through the sewer drains. If you have not done this, use rags or other materials to block the drains in showers, sinks, and tubs.

- Make sure your storage includes cleaning supplies appropriate for cleaning up from a flood. These would include items such as mops, sponges, detergent, and bleach. Certain types of vacuums are also designed to be used in wet conditions, and these can be used to draw water out of carpet and furniture. Be careful when using any electrical appliance in wet conditions.

- Rather than using the basement, place at least part of your food storage on an upper floor. This may not be as convenient, and may reduce shelf life, but it will protect your storage from all but the most severe floods.

- If your area is under a flood watch, you should keep the radio or television on so that you can keep informed of current conditions. Move any outdoor items (such as toys or patio furniture) indoors, and move any valuable items to the upper floors. You should also fill jugs and bathtubs with water, which can be used if the regular water supply becomes contaminated. Gather up your emergency kit and other items you will need if you are asked to evacuate your home.

- In the event that you evacuate your home, turn off the utilities (electricity, water, gas) if there is time to do so. If you were given instructions or an evacuation route, follow those instructions and use that route. Do not try to drive or walk through flood waters, but turn around and go a different way. If your car stalls or gets stuck, abandon it and proceed on foot. If you are trapped by flood waters, move to higher ground and climb to the top of the highest structure you can locate. Continue to use a portable radio to listen for the latest instructions.

- After an evacuation, do not return until you have been told to do so. Be cautious when entering a home that has been flooded. Inspect the outside of the home for cracks or foundation damage. Wear boots or sturdy shoes, and take a lantern or flashlight if the power is off. Examine walls for structural damage, and examine utility and sewer lines for possible leaks. Do not poke through the debris with your bare hands, because snakes and rodents are often carried in with the flood waters. Do not stay in the home if your inspection reveals any dangers. As soon as possible, have the damage inspected by a plumber, electrician, or utility company representative.

- If your basement is flooded, pump out about a third of the water each day, for three days. Draining the water gradually will reduce the chances of structural damage.

- Because of the toxic materials found in flood waters, it is suggested that all foods that come in contact with it be discarded, including canned goods. If you must use the canned goods, wash them thoroughly in soapy water, then in bleach, then rinse in clean water, and dry the can completely.

Hurricanes

Those who live in coastal areas may be subject to hurricanes during certain times of the year. In fact, hurricanes are so common in some locations that residents tend to underestimate these potentially lethal acts of nature. Kathy grew up in New Orleans, and she earned some of her pocket money during high school baby-sitting for parents who were going to "hurricane parties."

Damage from hurricanes comes from heavy rains, and winds that, by definition, exceed seventy-three miles per hour. If you have not already done so, please read the previous section on floods. Much of the advice in that section also applies to hurricanes, because of the flooding they may cause.

If a hurricane has the potential to strike your area, a hurricane watch will be issued when the hurricane is expected within twenty-four to thirty-six hours. The hurricane watch will be upgraded to a hurricane warning when it is expected in less than twenty-four hours.

Here are some additional suggestions for those of you lucky enough to live in hurricane country:

- Most communities in hurricane areas have developed hurricane preparedness plans, which can be obtained through the Red Cross or the local emergency management office. These plans should provide the addresses of shelters, and suggested evacuation routes.

- Breaking glass is a common problem during hurricanes. To protect yourself, cut panels out of half-inch plywood that will fit over your exterior windows. Drill holes every eighteen inches for screws. Mark each panel so you know which window it fits. Put the panels in place when a hurricane watch is announced. An option that is more expensive but less effort is to have sturdy shutters installed permanently. The quick and cheap way to protect windows is to cover them with strapping tape when a hurricane warning is announced. This won't necessarily keep the windows from breaking, but it may keep broken glass from flying, or it may stop cracked glass from falling into the house.

- Trim branches that are too close to the house, or that appear weakened.

- When hurricanes approach, the best safety procedure is to drive twenty to fifty miles inland. Study maps of your area to determine suitable inland locations, and the best routes to get you there.

- When under a hurricane watch, place some emergency supplies in the trunk of the car, and make sure the tank is filled with gas. Make sure to include items such as blankets, pillows, and extra clothing. Loose objects in the yard should either be taken inside or secured in place with a rope or a chain. Remove large antennas, and other objects that may be damaged by strong winds.

- Turn the thermostat of the refrigerator and the freezer to the coldest setting. This will help foods stay cold if the power is lost. Avoid opening the doors of these appliances if the power is off, because that will reduce the life of the food. If you must open the door, close it again quickly.

- Fill bathtubs, jugs, and other containers with fresh water that may be used for drinking or cooking if the regular water supply is shut off or contaminated.

- During a hurricane warning, avoid things such as elevators, which could trap you if the power were lost suddenly. Stay inside, and away from glass objects that could shatter. If your power goes out, turn off appliances so they will not cause a power surge when the power is restored.

- If you are told to evacuate, turn off the utilities, lock the door, and leave as quickly as possible. Drive inland or to a shelter, based on the instructions that are broadcast.

Tornadoes

Disaster movies were resurrected in the late 1990s, as Hollywood took every opportunity to entertain us at the theater by showing us the destructive power of nature. This made for good entertainment, but it also showed us how dangerous such events can be. Those of us who always thought of tornadoes as nothing more than overgrown winds were treated to scenes of cows, trucks, and houses being blown around like old newspapers. In fact, tornadoes can be deadly and can inflict their damage with very little advanced warning. Those in the path of these monsters must make critical decisions with often just a few minutes of warning.

Tornadoes are rated on a scale from F-0 to F-5. An F-5 tornado has winds in excess of 260 miles per hour. It can lift homes off their foundations, and throw automobiles hundreds of feet away.

→   If you live in an area that is subject to tornadoes, consider the following points that may offer protection for your family:

- Determine the safe places to be in your home if a tornado strikes. These are usually the lowest parts of a building, such as the basement or storm cellar. If there is no basement, choose an inner hallway or an interior room without windows, such as a closet. Try to stay in the center of the room away from corners and windows.

- The safe areas identified for your family will also be the areas where you wish to locate your food storage, or at least the critical parts of it, such as first-aid supplies.

- At the start of each season, conduct a tornado drill with your family. Remind them of the difference between a tornado watch and a tornado warning (see below), and remind them of the safe gathering places within your home. Within the safe areas, have them practice hiding under sturdy furniture, and covering their heads and necks with their arms and hands.

- If there is a possibility of a tornado forming in your area, a tornado watch will be issued. You should turn on the radio or television and monitor storm activity. Gather all family members together, and remind them of the safest places in your home should a tornado actually strike.

- If a tornado is actually spotted in your area, the tornado watch will be upgraded to a tornado warning. If this happens, all family members should assemble in the safe areas, and you should continue to monitor the weather conditions from there.

- For some reason, tornadoes are particularly attracted to mobile homes. Mobile homes are not safe during a tornado, even if they have been tied down and secured. If a tornado warning is issued, leave your mobile home and move to a building with a strong foundation. Avoid gathering in buildings with open wide-spanned roofs, such as auditoriums and shopping malls.

- If you are trapped outside during a tornado, crouch down next to a strong building, or lie in a ditch or area that is low and protected from the wind. Use your arms to protect your head and neck.

- A sign of an approaching tornado will be a cloud of debris, even if you do not see a funnel cloud. Just before the tornado hits, the winds may die down, and the air may become very quiet. Tornadoes often form on the tail end of a thunderstorm, so it is not unusual to see sunny skies behind the tornado.

- Never try to outrun a tornado in a motorized vehicle, such as a car or truck. Get out of the car immediately and find a sturdy building. If no buildings are nearby, stay outside and follow the directions above for protection while outdoors.

- Be aware that tornadoes are often followed by floods. If you are outside, move to higher ground as soon as possible. Take the proper precautions as already outlined in the section on floods.

- If you evacuate your house, do not return home until you have been told it is safe to do so. Be alert for structural damage and broken pipes or utility lines. Clean up any spilled liquids immediately, especially those that are toxic or flammable.

- If you are building a new structure in a tornado area, investigate new building materials, such as reinforced masonry, that provide extra protection from tornadoes.

Landslides and Mudslides

Like most of the catastrophes documented in this section, landslides and mudslides tend to be a problem only in some locations. Certain soil and landscape conditions, combined with environmental factors such as heavy rains, will often lead to the unexpected movement of the earth. Although these disasters usually strike without warning, there are some preparations you can make if you live in an area that is subject to such ground movement.

County geologists and planning officials may be able to tell you the locations that are most subject to such problems. If you live in such an area, it may be worth the money to hire an expert to evaluate your property. The expert will be able to tell you the risk factors, and may also be able to recommend actions you can take that will minimize any damage.

➔   Consider taking the following precautions if you live in an area subject to landslides or mudslides:

- If your property contains steep slopes, plant ground cover on the surface and build retaining walls as needed. Again, ask an expert to supervise the building of these walls.

- You can build channels or walls that will divert flowing mud around your property. Make sure you take into account the neighboring property as well, or you may be liable for any damages to that property.

- Some utility companies can install flexible pipe fittings that reduce the chance of utility and water lines breaking during earth movement.

- Most homeowner's policies do not cover damage by moving earth, although such damage is usually covered with flood insurance. Contact your insurance agent if you wish to add this coverage.

- Recognize signs that the earth may be moving, and that a potential landslide or mudslide is possible. These include windows or doors that start to stick, or new cracks that may appear inside your home. Check also for outside cracks in the ground and on paved areas, or for structures such as fences and stairs that start pulling away from the house.

- In addition to the signs above, more serious signs of significant ground movement include broken utility lines, pools of water forming in outside areas, and new mounds of earth that suddenly form at the base of hills or inclines. Be alert also for fences, walls, trees, and utility poles that may tilt or start to topple.

- If a landslide is approaching your area, you will probably hear it coming. Listen for a faint rumbling sound that gets louder as the landslide nears. You may also feel the ground moving or vibrating.

- As with other emergencies, listen to the radio for instructions. If there is enough warning, you may be told to evacuate. Plan at least two escape routes out of the area, so that you will have an alternate if one road is blocked. If you have enough time, load valuables in your car and turn off all utilities before leaving the house.

- If you are outdoors during a mudslide or landslide, try to get indoors. If you cannot, try to get to high ground, and stay out of the path of the slide. Be alert for sinkholes that may open in the ground. Get to an area that offers some protection, and curl yourself into a ball, protecting your head and face.

- If you are indoors during a mudslide or landslide, get in the corner of a basement or under a large piece of sturdy furniture, such as a desk or table.

- If forced to evacuate, listen to the radio, and do not return until advised that it is safe. Be aware that secondary slides may occur, so you should not return until told to do so. When returning, check for structural damage and damage to utility lines. Replant and repair any damaged ground or structures to avoid future problems.

- Be aware that flooding often follows after a mudslide or landslide. Read the suggestions made previously in regard to flooding, and follow them as needed.

Snowstorms and Ice Storms

As we wrote this chapter, our area had been hit by a surprise winter storm that dumped six to twelve inches of snow across the Midwest and up much of the Atlantic Coast. All the schools closed, and people were being advised to stay at home if at all possible. This is the kind of storm that hits every so often. The best remedy is to make some hot chocolate, open a can of soup, and enjoy an unexpected excuse to just stay home and catch up on the household chores.

But what if the storm continues, and we are trapped at home for two days, or three, or a whole week? What if we get tired of soup, or run out of crackers, or just get tired of staring at the four walls? To make matters worse, what happens if the power goes out? The two real dangers of winter storms are that they trap you in the house, and they often cause the loss of power. The power loss is especially common with ice storms, when the weight of the ice causes power lines to break, or the branches from breaking trees fall across power lines. If such damage is widespread, you may be forced to survive for a week or longer without power.

Although not as dangerous as the previous disasters in this section, snow and ice storms can make us either comfortable or miserable, depending on our level of preparation. And people in Montreal can tell you that ice storms can be more than an inconvenience, having gone without electrical power for up to five weeks after a series of ice storms in January of 1998.

➡ Here are some tips for surviving the winter weather with minimum discomfort:

- Make sure your food storage contains all the items that will sustain your family if an unexpected storm hits and you cannot leave the house for several days. Pay particular attention to such items as medicines, and make sure you always have at least enough on hand to last for a week.

- Consider what will happen if the power is out for an extended period. What will you do for heat? If you have a fireplace, make sure your chimney is clean and your fireplace is usable. Also make sure you have wood on hand so you can use the fireplace without having to break up your fine furniture for fuel. A natural gas burner is also good, as it will operate if the power is out, as will propane and kerosene heaters. (Be sure you have adequate fuel for these heaters, or for electric generators.) Even if you have alternate heat sources, keep a supply of blankets and warm clothing on hand.

- Consider how you will prepare your food if there is no power. Make sure you have the utensils that will allow you to warm food in a fire, or on top of a heater. This should be obvious, but make sure you have a nonelectric can opener in your storage supplies.

- Some homes rely on electric pumps to get water into the house. If this is the case, you will have no water when the power is off. Store bottles and jugs of water, or fill containers with clean water when a storm is forecast.

- If you think a storm will cause you to lose power, turn the thermostat on refrigerators and freezers to their coldest setting. Remember to turn it back up again after the storm threat has passed. If the power does go off, open the doors as infrequently as possible, and then for only short periods.

- If you have small children, keep a supply of games, books, and other non-electrical items that will keep them entertained for long periods without power. Remember also to store lights and lanterns that will provide light when the power is out.

- If you have a sump pump that runs regularly, keep in mind that long periods without power might cause flooding in the basement. Keep a supply of mops in storage, or consider buying a gasoline-powered pump or one that can be operated by hand.

- Long periods without power may cause water lines to freeze if the outside temperature gets too cold. Wrap pipes with insulation if they are next to outside walls. Open kitchen cabinet doors to expose kitchen pipes to the warmer air inside the house. Leave a small trickle of water running from each faucet to prevent freezing. If pipes do freeze, warm them back up with a fan or electric hair dryer after the power comes on again.

- If you have a medical condition that may require hospital attention, take the necessary steps to make sure you can get to a hospital in any weather. Have access to a vehicle that will drive well in the snow, or equip your existing car with snow tires and chains.

- At the start of the winter season, have your mechanic check your cars, and make sure they are ready for winter driving. Replace any tires that are worn. Install snow tires if you have them. Keep the gas tank full during the winter season. Place an emergency kit in the trunk that includes warm clothing or blankets, flares, tire chains, towing ropes, jumper cables, flashlights, tools, quick-energy food items (such as candy bars), bottled water, and a first-aid kit. Keep a small broom and an ice scraper in the passenger compartment.

- If you need to travel, do so during the day, and have another person with you. Check the weather conditions before leaving. Consider using public transportation instead of driving your own car. Dress warmly, in several layers of loose, layered clothing. If you're driving out of town during adverse conditions, don't leave home without survival equipment in your car to keep you warm and fed in case you're stranded.

- If your car is stuck or disabled and it is snowing, do not leave the car for help unless you can see your destination from the car. It is easy to get disoriented in such conditions, and you may not be able to find your way back to the car. Stay in the car, indicate you are having problems (put a bright cloth on the radio antenna, and raise the hood), and wait for help. If you get cold, run the car engine and the heater for about ten minutes of each hour. If it is at night, you may also turn on interior lights while the engine is running. If you plan to run the engine, make sure the exhaust pipe is clear of the snow, and open a window slightly while the engine is running. Do minor exercises to improve circulation and maintain body warmth. If two people are present, they should take turns sleeping, and should huddle together for shared body warmth.

Okay, Any Questions?

?   *Do canned or bottled foods last longer?*

This is the kind of answer you will hate, but the real answer is that it depends. In general, bottles are less subject to the deterioration that inflicts cans, yet they are also more subject to breaking. Also, most bottles are sealed with metal lids, so once again you are at the mercy of a piece of metal that may deteriorate. It may also make a difference whether the food was processed at home, or by a commercial cannery. In general, commercial foods last longer, because there is more exact control over the processing times and temperatures.

The main enemy of cans is rust, which creates tiny holes that will eventually let organisms into the can. Damage such as dents in the cans will also weaken the barrier against outside contamination.

Cans may also be attacked from the inside, as acidic foods like tomatoes and fruit juices will chemically react with the metal in the can. While this usually does not cause spoilage, it will change the texture and taste of the food, as well as lowering the nutritional value.

?   *What are the guidelines again for storing canned foods?*

This is important enough that it bears repeating. Store canned foods in a clean, cool, dark, dry place, where the temperature is in the range 60°F.–70°F. In no case should the temperature be above 85°F. For optimum quality, use high-acid foods within eighteen months, and regular foods within twelve months. In most cases, canned foods kept under these conditions will be good for two to five years. Although foods stored longer than that may experience changes in color, flavor, and nutritive value, they will still be safe to eat as long as they exhibit none of the symptoms listed previously in this chapter.

?   *Can I use a can of fruit that was accidentally frozen?*

We have all placed a can of something in the freezer for "just a few minutes," only to find it days or weeks later. When a can is frozen, the expanding contents break or weaken the seals of the can, allowing small amounts of air to gain access. Once the can is frozen, it becomes susceptible to spoilage. You should never take a can from the freezer and put it back on the shelf as if nothing happened, even if the can looks perfectly intact. But the good news is that the can is now frozen, which is another method of preserving food. Keep the can in the freezer until shortly before you plan to serve it. Then put it in the refrigerator and allow the contents to thaw. Open, and serve immediately.

?   *Should I store guns and ammunition as part of my food storage?*

Some so-called experts recommend a healthy cache of weapons to protect your goods from the marauding hordes that will come to loot your home after a disaster. Call us pacifists, but we don't subscribe to this theory of preparedness. Disasters don't bring out the worst in people—they bring out their true natures. Thus, people who are basically good will be cooperative and seek to help their neighbors. Conversely, those who are bad will look for opportunities to steal or to take advantage of others. Thus, your best protection is to live in a good neighborhood, and to be on good terms with your neighbors. Of course, this assumes that should an emergency happen, you will also be a good neighbor, and be willing to share with those around you.

In the unlikely event that you are threatened physically, don't argue, and give up your supplies willingly. Your life is more important than a shelf of canned goods. Besides, if you have developed the proper relationship with your neighbors, they will probably be willing to share with you.

The only exception to this rule would be if you live in an area where you could hunt for food during an emergency. If you are a trained hunter, and there is game in your area, it might be wise to store some hunting supplies with your storage. But keep in mind that these are for stalking Bambi, and not your next-door neighbor.

Some of the information in this chapter was adapted from the Internet web sites maintained by FEMA and Utah State University. Both of these sites contain excellent information, and can be accessed at the addresses listed in Chapter 9.

CHAPTER 9

Post-Graduate Resources

★ **IN THIS CHAPTER**
- ✔ Finding useful resource books
- ✔ Using the Internet for free information
- ✔ Contacting suppliers using the Internet
- ✔ Turning to the telephone for help
- ✔ Locating suppliers of nonfood items

When you've arrived at this point in the book, you should be just about ready to graduate with your BFS (Bachelor of Food Storage) degree. If we've done our job, and if you've paid attention, you should have a pretty good idea of where you want to go, and how you are going to get there. We hope we have changed your outlook so that you approach the storage of food as something that is exciting and challenging, and not just another thing that you should feel anxious about.

If we have accomplished our goal, then you will probably want to go beyond the basics and start learning about more advanced food storage topics. As we found when researching this book, there are a whole lot of people in this world who are interested in food storage, and they have produced a whole lot of valuable material to assist the rest of us.

In this chapter, we will try to point you toward other sources of information that will be useful as you continue to learn even more about food storage. Although we cannot cover many resources in one chapter, we can point to good resources that also lead you to other good materials. Who knows? After reading all these materials, you will probably be qualified to write your own book. In fact, you'll be better qualified than we were, because we only read the interesting parts.

Handy Tip for Amassing a Food Storage Library

Food storage and self-sufficiency books aren't always available in your local bookstore, and specific titles may be hard to find. If you're connected to the Internet, most of the books mentioned in this chapter are available through amazon.com. If you're not connected to the Internet, discovering amazon.com is as good an excuse as any to get yourself wired. Amazon.com is the Only True Way to get hard-to-find books, usually at discount prices. And no, we aren't stockholders. We only wish we were.

Food Processing Publications

Food storage information is as vulnerable to flood or earthquake as anything in your storage supply. Books and other information should be stored where they are easily accessible—preferably with your other food storage supplies. If your basement is flood prone, you may want to consider sealing individual books in zippered plastic bags. Books stored in this manner may not look pretty on your shelves, but the information contained therein will still be useful if inclement weather or a plumbing catastrophe turns your basement into a swimming pool.

> *101 Essential Tips: Preserving Fruit*, Oded Schwartz, New York: DK Publishing Company, 1998—a slender volume, beautifully illustrated, with emphasis on such exotic temptations as mango butter and pink grapefruit curd, packaged so artfully that you'll either want to give the finished products as gifts or paint them and hang the artwork on your wall.

> *Ball Blue Book: Guide to Home Canning, Freezing & Dehydration,* Muncie, Ind.: Alltrista Corp, 1997—it's great to know that even though the Ball people are no longer producing the canning lids that were far superior to the Kerr lids, at least they're still publishing this terrific (and cheap!) book.

> "Grow Your Own Vegetable Sprouts," N. S. Mansour, Extension Circular 1358, Oregon State University Extension Service, October 1990, reprinted July 1993. 4 pages; 50 cents

> *Keeping Food Fresh*, Janet Bailey, New York: Harper Perennial, 1989—a fat book that will tell you the shelf life of everything,

and how to store it so it will achieve its maximum potential. By the way, the time frames listed in this book are mega-conservative. We've kept food for years longer than some of the recommended times in this book. Nevertheless, this is a handy manual that will give you good ideas.

Mrs. Wages® New Home Canning Guide, Gale R. Ammerman, Tupelo, Miss.: Precision Foods, Inc., 1986—a good basic canning book, with detailed instructions, plus recipes for such diverse home canned products as spaghetti sauce and sauerkraut.

Putting Food By, Janet C. Greene, Ruth Hertzberg, Beatrice Vaughan, New York: Penguin USA, 1991—the book that many home canners consider the Bible of food preservation.

The Classic Wheat for Man Cookbook : More Than 300 Delicious and Healthful Ways to Use Stoneground Whole Wheat Flour, Mabel H. Miller, Dora D. Flack, Vernice G. Rosenvall, Woodbridge Pr Pub. 1975—if your family eats wheat, this is the book for you. If you're a sieger you have to own it, just to say it's in your library.

Internet Resources

The variety and quality of information that can be found on the Internet boggles the mind. The following sources are among the best resources we've found in our food storage searches. There are literally hundreds of thousands of food storage-related sites, however, and we're probably missing a whole lot of good ones. A little searching of your own may be well worth the effort.

Keep in mind that posting information on the Internet does not make it accurate. In general, information from government agencies, university extension services, and other nonprofit agencies is probably reasonably accurate, assuming it is not too old. Information from other sites may reflect the author's personal views, or may seek to promote specific products. Use your own common sense, and cross-check questionable advice with other sources. We have not personally purchased products from all the commercial sites listed here, so let the buyer beware.

If you come across any information in your searches that you just can't live without, you may want to make a hard copy. Internet sites are fluid, and a site that's here today may be gone tomorrow. And if you're a sieger, you may well believe we won't always have an Internet to play with, or electricity to run our handy personal computers. That being the case, a backup of essential information is always a good idea.

If all this Internet stuff is a big mystery to you, may we recommend that you visit your local bookseller and ask for *A Parent's Survival Guide to the Internet*. It is an informative, easy-to-understand book that we can recommend without a trace of bias.

Information

ftp://rtfm.mit.edu/pub/usenet-by-group/news.answers/food/sour dough/starters—the best little document on sourdough starters you can find, designed to make experts out of novices. This is the information included in Appendix B, but the web site promises frequent updates.

http://www.agric.wa.gov.au/agency/pubns/H2H/5a8095b.htm —despite the technical name on the home page, an excellent tutorial for storing fruits and vegetables in refrigerators or other home storage.

http://earth.vol.com/~teri/contents.html—an excellent document about the home preparation and storage of baby food. If you have a baby, this is your site.

http://www.ebicom.net/kitchen/page/souridx.htm—sourdough recipes . . . multitudes of them.

http://eesc.orst.edu/tango/pubsearch/0420.8.qry?function=search —Oregon State University Extension Service, specializes in home storage of fish products (canning, smoking, and even pickling).

http://www.ext.nodak.edu/extnews/askext/canning.htm— North Dakota State University Extension Service canning information.

http://www.ext.usu.edu/publica/foodpubs.htm—Utah State University Extension Service publications, possibly the best source of free information anywhere.

http://www.foodsafety.org/canhome.htm—web site for the *USDA Complete Guide to Home Canning*. All the info, without the cost!

http://www.foodstorage.net/—Preparedness Central, an excellent multipurpose resource out of Salem, Oregon.

http://www.healthgate.com/healthy/eating/1998/yogurt/—a primer on yogurt.

http://idt.net/~wordup/bread/resource.html—lots and lots of bread information, mostly focusing on sourdough.

http://www.innercite.com/~garden/storing.htm—information on vegetable storage.

http://www.justpeace.org/nuggetsindex.htm—"Preparedness Nuggets" Internet newsletters. The only site we've found that recommends we store our own cigarette papers and learn how to make rosaries to barter...but it also has valuable insights on such subjects as how to hook up a generator to your electrical system, and how you can drink rainwater. Great reading, for the information and for fun!

http://www.lis.ab.ca/walton/self/index.html—a whole trove of food storage-related brochures that can be read online, as well as books that can be ordered. Another treat from the Walton Feed people.

http://www.macscouter.com/Cooking/DutchOven.html—Dutch oven cooking, including nine zillion recipes.

http://www.millennium-ark.net/News_Files/Hollys.html—great information for siegers and back-to-basics types, with an Australian flavor (the producer is writing her own food storage book).

http://www.msue.msu.edu/msue/imp/mod01/mod01f.html—good information, particularly on freezing, from the Michigan State University Extension Service.

http://www.nhb.org/index.html—the National Honey Board site features everything you want to know about honey (including storage and recipes).

http://www.oznet.ksu.edu/ext_f&n/hrap/cespub.htm—a site with links to the extension services of every state in the U.S. that has an extension service online, together with a rundown of what each site contains. This is big-time convenient.

http://www.precisionfoods.com/mrswages/links.htm—links to other home canning sites.

http://www.revelar.com/fsp.html—producers of an inexpensive computer program that you can download to do your food storage thinking for you.

http://www.rv-y2k.org/prepstor.htm—general info, plus links to other sites.

http://www.scjbrands.com/ziploc/ziploc.phtml—storage information on the use of plastic bags, from the Ziploc people (who should know whereof they speak).

http://www.scrumptioussourdough.com/recipes/—just what it says: sourdough recipes.

http://soar.Berkeley.EDU/recipes/—more recipes than you'll ever need, free for the asking (at the time this book went to press, there were 46,000 recipes in the archives... and counting). For you acronym buffs, SOAR stands for the Searchable Online Archive of Recipes. Nifty stuff.

http://www.tvsonline.net/~alberts/cooking2/—links to a lot of excellent food storage sites.

http://www.uvol.com/www1st/foodstor.html—basic LDS food storage list, period.

www.virtualcities.com—1st Traveler's Choice Internet Cookbook. Classy recipes for discriminating cooks. Looking at the recipes may also give you a hankering to stay in a bed and breakfast inn. That's exactly what the web site designers are hoping.

http://waltonfeed.com/grain/faqs/—Frequently Asked Questions about food storage; great stuff!

http://www.y2kharvest.com/five_dollar.htm—an interesting site because the information is something Clark wrote in the 1970s, which apparently developed a life of its own. Don't bother to base your food storage on this plan; we're lots smarter now.

http://www.yaourt.org/—everything you always wanted to know about yogurt.

http://www.xmg.com/yogurt.htm—yogurt and cheesemaking on the web.

Vendors of Food Items and Storage-Related Supplies

http://garden.burpee.com/—many varieties of seeds and gardening supplies.

http://waltonfeed.com/—Walton Feed, a locally famous food storage company out of Idaho, has tons of terrific information on food storage subjects, as well as zillions of for-sale items.

http://web2.airmail.net/foodstr2/—a large variety of ready-to-store food, including MREs, dehydrated foods, and freeze dried foods. Also, carries supplies such as sprouters, filters, and grinders.

http://www.1starmy.com/—military surplus and survival supplies, including MREs.

http://www.1stworldwidemall.com/foodstore/—a wide variety of items, including seeds and organic foods.

http://www.americanewsnet.com/—many types of survival supplies, including gas-powered lanterns, heaters, and cooking stoves.

http://www.aqua-sun-intl.com/—water filters and water treatment systems.

http://www.arkinstitute.com/seeds.htm—seeds and gardening publications.

http://www.beprepared.com/—the web site for Emergency Essentials, a large supplier of prepackaged food products and other emergency supplies.

http://www.ccrane.com/—electronic supplies such as radios, flashlights, and telephones.

http://www.cheaperthandirt.com/default.htm—Cheaper Than Dirt has incredibly cheap prices on MRE's and other siege-type items.

http://www.colemans.com/—military surplus and other survival supplies.

http://www.cooksgarden.com/—seeds and gardening supplies.

http://www.dehydrators.com/—the name says it all. They also carry grinders, juicers, and other food preparation appliances.

http://www.eat-it.com/—many varieties of seeds and plants, both edible and decorative.

http://www.foodbanking.com/—dehydrated, vacuum-packed foods with eighteen-year shelf life, for people who are determined not to eat what they store despite the advice in this book.

http://www.fords-mtm.com/—military surplus, survival, and alternative energy supplies.

http://www.frankferd.com/—organic foods and other products.

http://www.frontierherb.com/—spices, herbs, and other natural plant products.

http://www.glitchproof.com/—good prices on oxygen absorbers for dry-pack canning, plus lots of general information.

http://www.gohonda.com/—generators and compressors.

http://www.gourmetgardener.com/—seeds and gardening supplies.

http://www.happyhovel.com/—foods and supplies for becoming self-sufficient.

http://www.healthyharvest.com/—bulk and prepackaged foods, plus other supplies for those wanting to be self-sufficient.

http://www.heirloomseeds.com/—seeds and gardening information.

http://www.imsplus.com/—military surplus, emergency, and survival supplies.

http://www.jademountain.com/—alternative energy, and other products for those who want to be self-sufficient.

http://www.johnnyseeds.com/—seeds and other gardening supplies.

http://www.katadyn.net/—water filters and water treatment supplies.

http://www.lehmans.com/—a terrific place to purchase appliances and other items that run without electricity. If you're looking for a gas-powered freezer, this is the spot for you!

http://www.majorsurplusnsurvival.com/—military surplus and survival products.

http://www.mtmarketplace.com/cookbook.html—sells *Cookin' with Home Storage*, a food storage cookbook.

http://www.northern-online.com/—all types of tools and appliances.

http://www.nutritionlifestyles.com/—natural foods and food storage supplies.

http://www.ornamentaledibles.com/—organic vegetable seeds, some quite exotic.

http://www.parkseed.com/—seeds, plants, and gardening supplies.

http://www.prepare-now.com/index.html—source for solar radios and hand-crank radios, among other nonfood items.

http://www.realgoods.com/—alternative energy supplies.

http://www.rmc.net/kampers/—Dutch ovens and outdoor cooking supplies.

http://www.seedsblum.com/—many types of vegetable seeds and gardening advice.

http://www.seedsofchange.com/—more than 1,500 varieties of seeds.

http://www.shepherdseeds.com/—seeds and gardening supplies.

http://www.shopsite.com/lfs/—many types of bulk prepackaged foods, plus MREs and sprouting supplies.

http://www.sportsmansguide.com/—sporting and outdoor equipment; survival supplies.

http://www.storablefood.com/—plastic storage buckets seem to be their forte.

http://www.superseeds.com/—all types of seeds and gardening supplies.

http://www.survival-center.com/shop/index.htm—"Captain Dave" rates the items he sells; a novel concept for a vendor.

http://www.territorial-seed.com/—many kinds of seeds for growing flowers and edible plants.

http://www.thepowercompanyinc.com/—emergency power generators.

http://www.tlchub.com/seeds/index.shtml—seeds for growing and sprouting, plus other survival supplies.

http://www.usplastic.com/—plastic storage containers.

http://www.vermontcastings.com/—nonelectric heating devices, including wood stoves and gas stoves.

http://www.veseys.com/—seeds, garden supplies, and gardening information.

http://www.vrp.com/—vitamins and health-care products.

http://www.watertanks.com/—water information and water storage supplies.

http://www.wheatmt.com/—grains, flours, and other related baking products.

http://www.windsun.com/—solar systems and other alternative energy sources.

http://www.wizcity.com/—many types of foods and emergency supplies.

Telephone List of Commercial Product Suppliers

If you have access to the Internet, look there before you call these places. Internet shopping caters to individuals rather than other businesses, and you won't have to deal with the large minimum orders. On the other hand, if you want to deal in large quantities, you can always get a group together from church or some other organization to order.

Product	Name of Company	Telephone
Grain & Legumes	Honeyville Grain Lehi Mill Walton Feed Wheat Montana Farms	801/972-2168 800/660-4346 800/847-0467 800/535-2798
Oats	Can Oat Co. Quaker Oats	877/229-1242 800/241-6387
Powdered Milk	Wilfran American Dairy Products Institute	800/336-3247 312/782-4888
Rice	Riceland Riviana Rice	870/673-5823 713/525-9571

Dried Potatoes	Basic American
	   (2000 lb. minimum)
	Idahoan Foods
	   (1000 lb. minimum)
		801/486-0110
		
		208/754-8109

Dehydrated Fruit & Vegetables	Beck Western Harlan Johnson & Assoc., (500 – 1000 lb. minimum)	801/973-6333 612/835-5222
Foods (General)	Country Life Catalog Life Sprouts Long Life Food Depot Mailorder Catalogue Williams-Sonoma	800/456-7694 800/241-1516 800/601-2833 800/695-2241 800/541-2233
Garden Seeds	Carolina Seeds GNLD Products	800/825-5477 888/743-2631

Product	Name of Company	Telephone
Supplies/Containers	Emergency Essentials Harbor Freight Tools Jeffers Northern Ready Made Resources US Plastic	800/999-1863 800/423-2567 800/533-3377 800/533-5545 800/627-3809 800/537-9724
#10 Can Suppliers (Pallets only)	Packaging West Container Supply Ray Slocum (20-pallet minimum)	253/395-3610 714/892-8321 908/730-8455

#10 Can Sealers	Gering and Son (manual)
	Ashco
	   (semiautomatic and
	   manual)
	Ray Slocum
	   (automatic and
	   semiautomatic)
		208/466-9003
		435/257-7752
		
		908/730-8455

Foil Pouches	Xpedx	801/972-2661
Impulse Sealers	Xpedx	801/972-2661
Oxygen Absorbers (cases only)	Mitsubishi Multisorb Tech.	212/605-2577 800/445-9890

Nonfood Resources

Food should be the main emphasis of your storage, but there are other things that should be stored to preserve life. These may be more valuable than gold in a time of true emergency.

Medical & Emergency

Complete Guide to Symptoms, Illness & Surgery, H. Winter Griffith, Los Angeles: The Body Press, 1989—if you have only one secular book in your household library, this should be it.

Vitamins, Herbs, Minerals & Supplements : The Complete Guide, H. Winter Griffith, Tuscon: Ariz., Fisher Books, 1998—the companion book to the book above, it will tell you what to do to cure a charley horse, or how to stop carpal tunnel syndrome in its tracks. This will save you many trips to the doctor's office, because the little aches and pains of life can often be alleviated by knowledge of vitamins and minerals.

http://www.fema.gov/pte/prep.htm—this site tells you how to prepare for such diverse catastrophes as tsunamis, volcanoes, and thunderstorms. If you live in a catastrophe-prone area, you may want to bookmark this area.

Gardening & Householding Skills

http://www.tvsonline.net/~alberts/garden/—amazing amounts of gardening information, including links to top-name vendors.

http://www.tvsonline.net/~alberts/sustain/—an equally impressive fount of information for people who want to return to simpler living.

Roughing It Easy, Dian Thomas, Salt Lake City: The Dian Thomas Co., 1994—if you can't convince her to live in your basement, buy every book this woman writes. She is a self-sufficiency genius.

Backyard Roughing It Easy, Dian Thomas, Salt Lake City: The Dian Thomas Co., 1997.

How to Live Without Electricity—And Like It, Anita Evangelista, Port Townsend, Wash.: Loompanics Unlimited, 1997—reputed to be a greatly practical and highly readable book on alternative power sources, for siegers and nonsiegers alike.

Hoard or Share, and Should You Care?

You've reached the end of a long book. By now you should know what kind of food storage person you are. If you're a sieger, we hope we've inspired you to supplement your siege lifestyle with expanded siege storage, and have given you tips on how your family can be among the few successful siege families. If you're a practical/provident storer, we hope you've been armed with enough resources and information to make your food storage acquisition an adventure.

By now, some of you may have sourdough starters merrily bubbling away in your kitchens, or have newly bottled rows of cherry pie filling or sliced mushrooms gracing your food storage shelves. You may have eaten home-grown sprouts on your sandwich at lunch, or made that sandwich with home-baked bread. Perhaps you've taken your first power-shopping trip, and are already supplementing your food storage with items from your supermarket. If this is the case, we're delighted for you. Food storage can provide you and your family with enjoyable hobbies, and can give your family a feeling of independence that you've never had before.

Until now, this book has focused on the temporal side of food storage. But there's also a spiritual dimension—and we'd be remiss if we didn't end this text by giving you a little food for thought.

In the first chapter, we asked you whether you were planning to feed your food storage to insects and rodents, or to your own family. But there's a third option. The food you've so lovingly put away to sustain your family during hard times may be used to feed a family other than your own. There are many ways this can happen, and as you store your food you should anticipate these situations, and ponder how you will react in each of them.

Throughout this book, we have counseled you to store the foods you eat every day, because most calamities that befall us are everyday adventures. Illness or unemployment can temporarily incapacitate a breadwinner. A winter storm may knock out your power for a day or a week, even over Christmas. A tornado may choose your neighborhood to set down and wreak its havoc. Some other mundane situation may cause your family to be without funds to buy food for an extended period of time. These are crises, but crises such as these are part of life.

However, the possibility exists that the disaster that befalls your family may strike everyone in your neighborhood, your city, your state—or even your region. If such a disaster lasts longer than a few days, everything changes.

As we mentioned previously, we believe that calamity brings out our true nature. If we're good, disaster can make us better. If we're not as good, a threat to our well-being can bring out the worst in us. Thus we see that when times are bad, some people turn into heroes—and others turn into looters.

When the Teton Dam broke in 1976, many people lost their homes and all the contents—including their food storage. Fortunately, the Intermountain West is full of people who store food. Thousands of families gave part or all of their food storage to strangers, to help flood victims survive during their time of peril. Although the breaking of the dam was a tragedy, it fostered heroism in people of several states, who sacrificed their time, their energy, and their food to sustain the flood victims.

> **"Calamity brings out our true nature."**

This experience was a blessing in the lives of the people who received food from the food storage of others. But it was also a blessing in the lives of those who sacrificed their food storage so that others might live. Everyone came out of this situation winning in some way, either as the recipient of kindness or as the giver of kindness.

Unfortunately, not all experiences are so good. Those who gave their food storage to the victims of the Teton Dam did so voluntarily, but people may ask for your food under less voluntary circumstances. Your food may be demanded by the government, or by your neighbors. They may ask you for your food, or they may take it at gunpoint. These are things you should consider so often that you can expect—and plan for— any contingency.

As you visit the survivalist web sites we've listed for you in Chapter 9, you may see that some of them focus as much on defending your food storage as on collecting it. Some families store weapons to defend their food from anyone who may try to take it away. Sometimes weapon storage almost becomes a religion, with people stockpiling guns and ammunition until they have the ability to defend their food storage at the cost of many human lives.

If you start thinking about defending your food storage to this extent, you may want to ask yourself this question: **Do you own your food storage, or does your food storage own you?** There's no denying that food is important, but it may be even more important to raise children who are citizens of a community rather than children who expect the worst from their friends and neighbors, and who are so selfish of their possessions that they would rather kill their neighbors than share with them.

Just as there is more than one way to live, there is also more than one way to die. We can die physically, by starving to death because our food storage has been shared with others or even taken away from us— or we can die spiritually, by becoming so possessed by our possessions that we hoard instead of sharing, and hate when we should be offering love.

There are no easy answers to the question of what you should do with your food storage. In fact, the answer will vary from house to house, and even from situation to situation within the same household. As the people of Montreal learned during their five-week power outage in 1998, sometimes the needs of the few must be sacrificed to the needs of the community. This is a great philosophy if you're one of the grasshoppers who has danced and played during the harvest season, but it may be considerably harder to stomach if you're one of the industrious ants who prepared for lean times.

However, perhaps this is why members of the LDS Church have been asked to store a year's supply of food. Not many catastrophes will incapacitate a community for as long as a year. If the crisis that befalls you lasts for only three months, a year's supply may be enough for your family and for three other families as well. Or your year's supply may last long enough to help feed fifty or a hundred people for ten days, as neighbors pool their collective resources to survive a short-term calamity.

Marion G. Romney, a longtime member of the First Presidency of The Church of Jesus Christ of Latter-day Saints, had this to say about the spiritual side of food storage:

> The Lord doesn't really need us to take care of the poor. He could take care of them without our help if it were his purpose to do so. . . .

It would be a simple thing for the Lord to reveal . . . where the deposits of oil and precious ores are. We could then hire someone to dig them out and we could float in wealth. . . .

No, the Lord doesn't really need us to take care of the poor, but *we* need this experience; for it is only through learning how to take care of each other that we develop within us the Christlike love and disposition necessary to qualify us to return to his presence. ("Living Welfare Principles," *Ensign,* November 1981, p. 92)

Perhaps the reason we are storing food is to save our families' lives in case of an emergency. But the reason may even be bigger than this. As President Romney said, we can only give food if we have food in our cupboards, and we can only offer support and understanding if our souls are full of goodness and compassion.

This book has shown you how to collect your food storage. Now it is up to you to take food storage one step further, and decide what to do with it once you have it.

Improvising with Food Storage

Even though you may not have a gourmet kitchen of ten thousand food items, you will be surprised at the number of foods you can create using just a few basic supplies from your food storage. The recipes in this section are useful when you need to substitute one item for another, or when you don't want to run to the store for that one item you are missing.

Homemade "Hamburger Helper"

Basic Mix:

8 ounces uncooked medium noodles	½ teaspoon paprika
1 cup instant nonfat dry milk	½ teaspoon salt
1 tablespoon dried onion flakes	⅛ teaspoon black pepper

Blend ingredients and store until needed. Make lots of batches at a time. It keeps for months, especially if stored in an airtight container that keeps the light out. Vary the kinds of noodles you use and the seasonings you add to make different recipes, according to your family's tastes. Be sure to freeze a pound of ground meat per batch of Basic Mix you have on hand, or try it with a can of tuna. Rotate the Basic Mix *and* the frozen meat to keep a fresh supply of everything on hand.

To cook: Lightly brown in large frying pan 1 pound lean ground meat. Add 1 cup sliced mushrooms or 1 small can mushrooms with liquid. Then add 4 cups water and 1 tablespoon vinegar. Bring to a boil. Then add 1 batch of Basic Mix. Let simmer, stirring often, for about 20 minutes, or until noodles are done to taste. Serves 4.

Maple Syrup

1 cup brown sugar, lightly packed
3 cups water

5 teaspoons cornstarch
1 teaspoon maple flavoring

Cook sugar, water, and cornstarch until slightly thickened. Stir in flavoring.

Pancake Syrup

2 cups coarse brown sugar
1 cup water

¼ teaspoon cream of tartar

Combine sugar and water in pan. Cook over low heat until sugar dissolves; then strain through a fine strainer or cheesecloth. Return to pan and add cream of tartar. Boil for 3 minutes.

Saltine Crackers (circa 1840 recipe)

8 cups flour
1 teaspoon baking soda
2 teaspoons cream of tartar
1 cup butter (scant)

2 cups water
white of 1 egg
salt or sesame seeds

In bowl, combine flour, soda, and tartar. Cut butter into dry ingredients. Add water until it is the consistency of biscuit dough. Roll out on floured board. Brush with egg white, a little water and salt. A pizza cutter may be used for making square or diamond shapes; a thimble or pill bottle for making oyster crackers. Place on baking sheet and sprinkle with salt or sesame seeds. Bake till golden brown at 360°F. for flat saltines or 400°F. for puffed crackers.

French-Style Mustard

¼ cup mustard seeds
¼ cup red wine vinegar
⅓ cup red cooking wine
¼ cup water
¼ teaspoon ground allspice

½ teaspoon honey
½ teaspoon ground black pepper
1 clove garlic, peeled and mashed
1 teaspoon salt
1 bay leaf, crumbled

Combine mustard seeds, wine vinegar, and cooking wine in bowl and let stand 3 hours or more. Then blend all ingredients together in a blender until coarse texture is reached. Simmer mixture in upper half of a double boiler until thickened. Cool. Store in refrigerator. Yield: 3–4 cups.

Cottage Cheese

16 cups milk
salt to taste

cream

Set milk out to clabber. When clabber is formed, run a long knife through, cutting the curd into cubes about the size of a grain of corn. Place vessel containing clabber in another pan of warm water. Heat to and hold at 100°F. for 30 minutes. Stir frequently to distribute heat evenly. When the whey and curd separate, pour into a cheesecloth and drain out the whey until a dry curd is obtained. There should be about 4 cups of curd. Work curd into small particles with a fork. Add a small amount of cream to soften and season as desired. Yield: 4 cups.

Peanut Butter

2 cups raw peanuts   ½ teaspoon salt
1 tablespoon peanut oil

Spread peanuts on a jelly roll pan and roast at 350°F., stirring occasionally for 15–20 minutes or until golden. Transfer nuts to blender ½ cup at a time, pulverize them, and transfer to a bowl. Stir in oil and salt. Return mixture to blender 1 cup at a time, adding a few more drops of oil if necessary. Blend to desired consistency. Yield: 2 cups.

Cream Cheese

4 cups milk
salt to taste

Pour milk into a glass bowl and cover with several layers of washed, dried cheesecloth. Put near a water heater or other slight source of heat for 24–36 hours. Solids will rise to top and liquids will stay at the bottom. Pour all of this into a strainer lined with damp, clean cheesecloth. Fold ends of cheesecloth over top of clabbered milk and place a plate on top to help force out whey. Put strainer in a bowl to catch dripping whey and refrigerate 24 hours. Now the cheese is ready for use in dips or spreads.

If a thicker cheese is needed, as for cheese cakes, rinse out cheesecloth and return to refrigerator to drain an additional 12 hours. Mash with fork and salt before using. Keeps about 5 days covered in refrigerator or can be frozen for later use. Yield: 6 ounces.

"Miracle Whip"

1 cup vegetable oil
1 egg
4 tablespoons flour
1 teaspoon salt
2 tablespoons sugar

½ teaspoon dry mustard
dash white pepper
⅓ cup white vinegar
1 cup boiling water

Pour oil into blender. Add egg and blend until thickened. In a saucepan combine remaining ingredients and boil until thick. Add boiled mixture gradually to egg and oil in blender and continue blending until fluffy. Store in refrigerator. Yield: 1⅓ pints.

Blender Mayonnaise

1 egg
½ teaspoon dry mustard
½ teaspoon salt

2 tablespoons vinegar
1½ cups oil

Beat egg in blender until thick. Beat in mustard, salt, and vinegar. Add ¼ cup of oil at a time, beating until thick and smooth. Note: Mixture will not become thick until after first 3 additions of oil. The trick here is to keep your spatula out of the blender blades. If you fail to do this, your mayonnaise will be chewy. Yield: 1½ cups. (If your mayonnaise separates while making, place one egg yolk in your blender and start over very slowly, beating the mayonnaise that has separated. It will all come together, like a cheap novel at the denouement.)

Powdered Sugar (Confectioner's Sugar)

1 cup granulated sugar
1 tablespoon cornstarch

Whirl together in a blender until fine.

Yellow (Hot Dog) Mustard

3 tablespoons dry mustard
1 tablespoon sugar
1 teaspoon salt

3 egg yolks
1 cup vinegar
1 teaspoon turmeric

Mix all ingredients together in a saucepan and cook 3 minutes over medium heat, or until thickened. Store in refrigerator. Yield: 1 cup.

Whole Wheat Crackers (Wheat Thins)

3 cups unsifted flour (1½ cups whole wheat and 1½ cups white)
½ teaspoon salt

½ cup oil
¾ cup water

Mix all ingredients together and knead for 5 minutes. Roll out onto cookie sheet (preferably one with sides). This must be paper thin for light, crisp wheat thins. Score, cutting through, and sprinkle with salt. Bake at 350°F. for about 20 minutes.

Egg Substitute (for use in baking only)

1 teaspoon unflavored gelatin

Combine gelatin with 3 tablespoons cold water and 2 table-spoons plus 1 teaspoon boiling water. This equals one egg for baking purposes only.

Vanilla Extract

vanilla beans
vodka or brandy

Cut beans into quarters and then split each section lengthwise. Divide beans evenly among several small bottles with tight screw-tops. For each bean add 2 cups of liquor. Screw on lid tightly and shake well. Every few days shake bottles. Allow to mellow until it smells like vanilla, which could be anywhere from 1–3 months. Fil-ter finished extract through cheesecloth and store in clean bottles with lids. *Yes, vanilla contains liquor. You really didn't think it was rubbing alcohol, did you?*

Cocoa or Chocolate Milk Mix

1 cup cocoa	**¾ cup sugar**
½ teaspoon salt	**4 cups dry milk**

Combine ingredients and store them in a tightly covered con-tainer. For each cup of drink desired, use ½ cup of dry mix and one cup of water. Combine part of the water with the mix to make a smooth paste. Add remaining water and blend well. Heat the mix-ture for cocoa or chill it for chocolate milk.

Brown Sugar

2 cups sugar
1–2 tablespoons molasses

Mix thoroughly and store in tightly covered container. Use 2 tablespoons molasses for darker sugar.

Sweetened Condensed Milk

⅓ cup boiling water
3 tablespoons melted butter

⅔ cup sugar
1 cup instant nonfat dry milk

Combine all ingredients in blender and process until smooth. Store in refrigerator up to one week. Yield: 1 cup

Marshmallows

2 cups sugar
3 tablespoons unflavored gelatin
a bowl of powdered sugar mixed
    with cornstarch

1 teaspoon vanilla
⅛ teaspoon salt

In medium saucepan, combine sugar, gelatin, and salt. Add 1 cup boiling water and stir to dissolve gelatin and sugar. Bring mixture to a boil, then remove from heat and cool slightly (for 5 minutes). Stir in vanilla. Transfer mixture to a large mixing bowl and beat at high speed with an electric mixer for 8–10 minutes until thick. Pour into a buttered 9x13x2-inch pan. Cool in the refrigerator. Dip scissors in hot water and cut into 1-inch squares and roll in the powdered sugar and cornstarch mixture. These freeze well. Yield: 9½ dozen 1-inch squares.

Teething Biscuits

2 tablespoons molasses	¾ cup flour
1 teaspoon vanilla	¼ cup dry milk
1 teaspoon water	¼ teaspoon salt
1 egg yolk, unbeaten	¼ teaspoon baking powder

Combine molasses, vanilla, and water. Add yolk and mix well. Combine dry ingredients and add to egg mixture. Mix ingredients thoroughly. This mixture will be very dry and crumbly, like corn-meal. Work dough into a ball. Roll out on waxed paper about ¼-inch thick, pinching edges with fingers to keep it in shape. Cut into bars 1x2½ inches and place on a cookie sheet. Bake at 350°F. for 15 min., then lower to 140°F. Open oven door slightly and let cookies stay in oven for 30 minutes more. Variation: For babies who can't eat eggs, omit yolk, and add 1 teaspoon more water. Salt can also be omitted, dried soy milk substituted for milk, et cetera. *Note: This is a hard cookie that will not crumble; for a softer cookie, omit the water and add 2 tablespoons shortening.*

Buttermilk

½ cup buttermilk	3 cups warm water
1 cup nonfat dry milk, or	
1½ cups instant nonfat dry milk	

Put buttermilk, water, and nonfat dry milk in a big jar and stir or shake until powder is dissolved. Cover the jar with a lid or clean cloth. Let stand at warm room temperature until it clabbers, about 10 hours in the winter or 5 hours in the summer. After it clabbers, store in the refrigerator. Save ½ cup from each batch to start the next batch. Buy commercial buttermilk occasionally for a fresh start.

Whipped Topping # 1

½ cup ice-cold water
½ cup nonfat dry milk

½ cup sugar
2 tablespoons lemon juice

Put the water into an ice-cold bowl. Add milk and beat with a cold egg beater until stiff. Add sugar slowly while beating. Add lemon juice and beat only until well mixed.

Whipped Topping #2

6 tablespoons nonfat dry milk
1½ tablespoons cold water
1 cup water

¼ cup sugar
2 teaspoons gelatin
1 teaspoon vanilla

Dissolve the milk in the cup of water and scald. Soak the gelatin in cold water. Combine the scalded milk, dissolved gelatin, and sugar. Stir and chill in the refrigerator until it jells. Now beat the mixture until it acquires the consistency of whipped cream. Add the vanilla and whip again.

Homemade Sweetened Condensed Milk

1½ cups instant dry milk or
¾ cup noninstant dry milk
¾ cup sugar

½ cup hot water
4 tablespoons butter

Pour the hot water into a blender. Add the dry milk and the sugar, and then blend. Add the butter and blend again thoroughly. Chill for later use.

White Sauce Mix

2 cups nonfat dry milk
1 tablespoon salt

1 cup sifted flour
1 cup butter

Combine dry milk, flour, and salt in large bowl. Cut in butter with pastry blender until the mixture resembles tiny peas. Store tightly covered in the refrigerator. Makes 5 to 5½ cups of dry mix.

When making the sauce, combine ½ cup White Sauce Mix with 1 cup of water in a saucepan. Cook over medium heat, stirring constantly, until sauce is thickened and bubbling. Makes 1 cup of sauce. For extra rich sauce, substitute milk for the water.

Homemade Pudding Mix

1½ cups sugar
1 teaspoon salt

¾ cup cornstarch
2½ cups nonfat dry milk

Mix all ingredients together well, and store in tightly covered container in a cool place. This makes enough for 24 servings of any of the pudding variations shown below.

Vanilla Pudding

1¼ cups homemade pudding mix
1 tablespoon butter
¾ teaspoon vanilla

2½ cups warm water
1 beaten egg

Combine pudding mix with water in top of double boiler. Place over boiling water. Cook until thickened, stirring constantly. Add butter, remove from heat. Beat half the mixture into the egg. Blend slowly into the remaining hot mixture. Stir in vanilla. Chill. Serves 4–6.

Chocolate Pudding

Follow the Vanilla Pudding recipe, but add ¾ cup cocoa and ¼ cup more sugar to the dry ingredients before stirring.

Caramel Pudding

When preparing the homemade pudding mix, substitute 1½ cups packed brown sugar for regular sugar. Follow the Vanilla Pudding recipe using this modified pudding mix.

Fruit Pudding

Follow the Vanilla Pudding recipe, but add ½ cup of any of the following: Mandarin oranges, drained fruit cocktail, peaches, pineapple, sliced bananas, or other fruit.

Magic Mix

4 cups instant nonfat dry milk   **1 cup flour or ½ cup cornstarch**
1 cup (2 sticks) butter

Combine all ingredients into a large bowl and mix until it looks like cornmeal. Keep mix tightly covered in the refrigerator. This recipe makes 5 cups of Magic Mix, which can then be used to make soups, sauces, and puddings, such as the examples listed below.

Magic Mix Creamed Soups

4 cups water   **2 cups Magic Mix**
1 cube or 1 teaspoon bouillon

Combine all of the ingredients in a saucepan. Stir over medium heat until the mixture is slightly thick. Add one of the following, or develop your own variations:

3 cooked and chopped carrots
1 package of chopped cooked spinach
3 cooked and chopped potatoes, with 1 tablespoon chopped onion
1 can of creamstyle corn, with 1 tablespoon chopped onion

Magic Sauce

⅔ cup Magic Mix
1 cup water

Combine ingredients in a saucepan and stir over medium heat until it starts to bubble. Stir in cheese, cooked meat, or vegetables. This makes approximately one cup of a sauce that may be used in any recipe calling for a white or cream sauce.

Magic Vanilla Pudding

½ cup sugar   **2 cups Magic Mix**
2 cups water   **1 teaspoon vanilla**

Combine in a saucepan Magic Mix, water, and sugar. Stir the mixture over medium heat until the pudding bubbles. Add the vanilla and beat. Cover the pudding and cool until ready to serve.

Magic Chocolate Pudding

Follow the recipe for Magic Vanilla Pudding, but add 3 table-spoons cocoa with the other dry ingredients.

Low-Fat Faux Cream Soup Base

2 cups nonfat dry milk
¾ cup cornstarch
¼ cup instant chicken bouillon
2 tablespoons dried onion flakes

1 teaspoon dried basil leaves
1 teaspoon dried thyme leaves
½ teaspoon pepper

Combine all ingredients, mixing well, and store in an airtight container until ready to use. This mix will make the equivalent of 9 cans of soup. This is a great low-fat substitute for canned creamed soups that can be used in casseroles and as a base for making home-made soups from scratch.

Low-Fat Faux Basic Soup

⅓ cup Low-Fat Faux Cream Soup Base
1¼ cups cold water

Combine ingredients and cook on stove top or in microwave until thickened. You can then add the mixture to any recipe that calls for one can of condensed soup, or use it as the basis for the soups below.

Low-Fat Faux Cream of Mushroom Soup

Obtain a 4-ounce can of mushrooms. Drain the can, and use the liquid when making the Low-Fat Faux Basic Soup. Stir in the drained mushrooms.

Low-Fat Faux Cream of Celery Soup

Add ½ cup of cooked, sliced or pureed celery when making the Low-Fat Faux Basic Soup.

Low-Fat Faux Cream of Cheese and Broccoli Soup

Add 1 cup grated cheddar cheese, 1¼ cups milk, and 1 cup chopped broccoli when making the Low-Fat Faux Basic Soup.

Low-Fat Faux Cream of Potato Soup

Add 1 cup cooked potato cubes and 1¼ cups milk when making the Low-Fat Faux Basic Soup.

Fresh Fruit Pizza

½ cup butter
¼ cup brown sugar
1 cup flour

¼ cup oats
¼ cup nuts

In a large bowl, beat all the above crust ingredients until fluffy. Press dough into a lightly oiled 12-inch pizza pan. Leave a crust rim around the edge, and prick the crust several times with a fork. Bake 10 minutes at 400°F. until crust is golden.

Filling:
1¼ cups condensed milk
½ cup sour cream

¼ cup lemon juice
1 teaspoon vanilla

In a medium bowl, combine the filling ingredients in the order listed above and mix well. Spoon filling onto cooled crust. Top with assorted fruit, then chill and serve.

How to Tell When a Starter Is a Starter

(or, ALL You Wanted to Know About Sour-dough Starters, but Were Afraid to Ask)

Introduction

A sourdough starter is a mixture of liquid and flour that serves as a growth medium for wild yeast and lactobacillus cultures. Using sourdough starters may be tricky at first because a starter is a living medium. But once you get the hang of it, maintaining starters and baking with them is actually quite easy.

When you are getting started, or when you are trying to troubleshoot a starter, then the first thing you need to do is accurately determine what state it is in. Unfortunately, most books do not go into nearly enough detail when teaching us about starters, how they work, and how to care for them. Starting a starter from scratch can require some patience on your part, but if you stick with it, you will (not can, but will) succeed in producing a strong, vibrant starter that can be the joy of your kitchen for years on end. Maintaining and using sourdough starter is really quite easy once you've established an active fresh starter. And once there, then there is never any reason to add commercial yeast as a booster to your recipes. Commercial yeast is not only unnecessary, but it will change the flavor of your sourdough products and will make it difficult to produce a good-tasting stable starter.

Stability of Sourdough Starters

Sourdough starters are about as stable as ticking bombs. When you move a starter to a new area, it will become bombarded by new strains of wild yeast and lactobacillus that are native to the new area. These new strains will change the flavor of your starter, and may even replace the original bacteria that gave your sourdough starter its taste. For this reason, it is suggested that if you wish to maintain a special starter in its original form, that you immediately dry and save much of the original starter before the flavor becomes corrupted (drying instructions are at the end of this document). For example, a starter can be fed once to make it fresh and active, and then dried and frozen in multiple Ziploc® bags. When it is noticed that the flavor is drifting (or any other characteristics are changing), then you can toss the changed starter and restart some fresh from one of the frozen bags. Every so often you should replenish the freezer supply with freshly restored starter. This technique can result in your special starter maintaining its original characteristics for a much longer time. But, since you do need to feed the starter at least once before drying and freezing the stuff, and the drying starter *is* exposed to the local air, even this technique will not guarantee that the special starter will *always* be exactly the same as it was when you first got it.

The best technique is to establish a source for the starter in the area where it originally came from.

Aside: At this time, most home-drying methods are successful only some of the time. Failures usually raise dough but lack the sourness of the original due to the lactobacillus cultures dying during the drying and storing processes. If you want to dry a sourdough starter, ferment it past its time before you dry it and freeze it. This will retain some of the sourness of the original starter.

How to Use This Appendix

Read the definitions of terms for starters in different states [conditions], then from those definitions, compare the different conditions with your starter to see what state *your* starter is in, and follow the directions given there. For example, if you read the following definitions and find that your starter is a "Non-Standard Starter," then read the text supplied at that location. Following the instructional passages below are some techniques for using your starter that should result in fresh, active starter any time you want it.

Also included below is a technique that helps guarantee a consistent, stable, active starter and a way to produce alternative styles of starter on an as-needed basis. For example, if you want a rye starter, or a whole wheat starter, then this technique will allow you the flexibility of having those starters available when you want them, *without* having to maintain separate rye or whole wheat or whatever type of starter in addition to your normal starter.

Definitions of Starter Condition

In all of the following text, I refer to starters using the following terms. These terms are not absolute, and starters can move from one category to another depending on treatment of the starter:

Term	Description/Possible Cause
New Starter	Any starter started from any dry source (commercial or homemade), or the air, that has not yet qualified as "fresh starter." This is not the same as "old" or "dead" starter, because these two conditions do not generally follow the same sequence of recovery stages.
Fresh Starter	Starter that has been recently demonstrated to be vibrant and active. Starter in this category can raise plain white (French or white bread) dough to a "more than doubled" volume in less than 2½ hours after a single proofing (feeding) period, i.e. remove the starter from the refrigerator and proof once, then try using it. Starter that has been refrigerated for less than 5 days or so that was "fresh" before refrigerating is also fresh starter.
Old or Dead Starter	Starter that has been previously demonstrated to be "fresh" but is no longer fresh since it cannot be demonstrated that it can raise dough after a single proof as described above. Risings that take longer than 2½ hours indicate a starter that is either "new" or "old" depending on the prior life history of the starter. Note: in very nearly *all* cases of "old" or "dead" starters, they *can* be revived back into "fresh" starters using the techniques described below. I have heard tell of starters that haven't been fed for six months being successfully revived using the given technique.

Term	Description/Possible Cause
Non-Standard Starter	Starter that contains ingredients other than white flour and plain water. Some starters do use blends or alternative flours, and that's ok. Some starters use other ingredients such as a spoon of sugar (ok, but not suggested). Some starters also use alternative liquids such as potato water or milk. These would all be labeled "Non-Standard Starters" in this appendix.
Polluted Starter	Starter that contains ingredients added by you or by nature, which are not normal to your starter. Examples include baking powder, salt, oils, eggs, or any other baking ingredients. Also, molds and other dark-colored microorganisms not normal to the natural symbiotic relationship that your starter normally maintains. These other microorganisms usually affect appearance, smell, and (especially) flavor. Normal ingredients are flour(s), water, potato water or potatoes, and possibly milk or milk products. Ingredients other than plain white flour and plain water change the habitat you are maintaining for your sourdough microorganisms and may or may not be wanted according to the characteristics you want your starter to exhibit.

New Starters

The most confusing of starters, new starters, go through stages not usually seen in well-established or fresh starters. This one fact is left out of every book I've seen that entertains the topic of sourdough, yet it is the most important thing a sourdough neophyte needs to know! It's confusing for a neophyte to have to compare a new starter to a set of standards written for well-established starters. The least we can do is provide some information that'll help you understand where your starter is, and how well it's doing!

There are basically two ways to produce a "new starter." The first is to revive a dried starter (containing dry lactobacillus and yeast spores) into a living liquid starter. The second is beginning a new starter from the microorganisms in the local atmosphere where you live. When in the situation of having a new starter on hand, it is important to realize that it usually takes some time to transform the starter into a usable, vibrant, fresh starter (which is much more abuse resistant and stable). The process often requires more than a week or two before the starter can be used, and possibly months before it is truly robust, vibrant, and abuse resistant. But just be patient. Very little effort is required on your part. It's primarily just a waiting game! It is also important to realize that it is best to *not* make any bread recipes with the starter until you are *sure* that you have transformed it into the vibrant starter described. But it is perfectly acceptable to use your "new starter" to make pancakes and waffles, or perhaps recipes that use a booster such as baking powder to help raise them—such as most biscuit recipes.

If you have not yet begun your new starter (dried or from the air), instructions for doing so follow near the end of this text. I'm assuming that at this time you have already attempted to start your new starter, but it is not yet a vibrant, fresh starter. Note that it is best to begin a new starter in a clear glass bowl, so you can examine the amount of bubbles present in the starter *below* the surface. Also note that starters that are proofing should be prepared so that the consistency of the starter is not too liquid or too thick. I like to call this the consistency of mud since it most resembles what sloppy mud looks like. This is typically a little thicker than normal pancake batter, but still liquid enough for bubbles to pass through it with no problems.

Since new starters have a somewhat unique set of stages that they go through, the first thing to do is to determine exactly what stage your starter is in. Replenish your new starter using 1 cup of starter, 1½ cups (or so) white all-purpose flour, and 1 cup of 85°F. tap water. Let it proof at exactly 85°F. for 12 hours, then use the following information to determine what stage your new starter is at.

➡ The stages that new starters typically go through are (not necessarily in this order):

▶ Dead

No visible bubbles on the surface or below. The starter may have been subjected to temperatures in excess of 100°F. If your new starter was exposed to these temperatures before the above-suggested 12-hour proof then it is probably what I would call a dead starter. But save it anyway. There may be remnants of the original yeast and lactobacillus still there that can be revived. Don't give up yet!

▶ Flat

No visible bubbles, but you don't believe you have done anything to kill the yeast. You have not subjected your starter to temperatures in excess of 100°F. It's possible that you neglected to feed the starter for so long that it appears that all life has gone out of it. Quite often, starter in this stage is quite sour. And equally as often, starter in this stage may be very mild. The starter may have lactobacilli growing in it (sour smell) but the yeast has not taken off yet, or nothing at all is growing in the flour/water mixture yet.

▶ Barely Living

Visible bubbles exist, but the starter has no frothy layer of bubbles on the surface of the starter. Also, bubbles beneath the surface are not plentiful. It's likely that a layer of *hooch* (a greyish or yellowish, mostly clear, layer of water and alcohol), has formed on top of the starter even though it was not proofed for more than 12 hours. Stirring the starter with a wooden spoon, then drawing the spoon out of the starter and examining the starter clinging to the back of the spoon, shows only a few bubbles in the starter. Note that one of the key symptoms of starter in this stage is the layer of hooch which mysteriously appears "early,"—vibrant, fresh starter usually requires 24 to 48 hours of proofing before any hooch appears. Hooch appearing after being refrigerated is another story, so ignore refrigerator hooch for now. Other symptoms of this stage include slow rise times: 3 to 6 or more hours to raise a bread recipe to double (if it ever does double). Second risings are quite often unsuccessful and the dough appears "dead." The dough may have a dead feel to it and tend to flatten out by itself while rising, even though you kneaded in enough flour and the gluten was well formed. The starter itself may also have a gelatinous feel to it, rather than maintaining a smoother, pancake-batter-like consistency. Starter in this stage has not stabilized the symbiotic relationship among the microorganisms present, i.e. the ratio of yeast and the various lactobacilli has not stabilized and the starter is not ready to use (except for pancakes).

▶ Healthy

The starter has a nice, smooth consistency. It is filled with tiny bubbles throughout the starter above and below the surface. It typically has a layer of frothy foam covering most of the proofed starter. The froth typically appears as early as 8 hours into the proofing period and lasts until about 18 hours of proofing. Stirring the starter obviously releases a lot of gas (smells good). Examining the starter clinging to a spoon shows that the starter is full of little bubbles. The starter quite often appears puffed up when the proof is done and drops down to a lower level upon stirring. As a final check, starter that you expect to be classified as healthy should be able to raise plain white bread dough in 2½ hours or less. It's probably not worth experimenting with raising dough until all of the above characteristics of healthy starter are present. Congratulations! If your starter is like this, you can pronounce it fresh, vibrant, and healthy! It's ready for bread recipes and will now be much more resilient to abuse and mishandling and should be very reliable. Skip the rest of the instructions for "new starters."

What should you do if you have "dead," "flat," or "barely living" starter? Begin the process of transforming it to a fresh, healthy starter. I personally do not believe in throwing away "dead" starter, since it typically *can* be revived from the few yeast and lactobacilli that probably still exist. If restoring dead starter takes longer than a week to see bubbles appearing in it (flat, barely living or otherwise) then you've probably started a new starter from local microorganisms. If so, and your starter was a special strain, you'll probably want some of the original starter to start over with rather than expecting this revived version to be the same as that special starter. Remember that you have probably *not* really killed your starter unless you subjected it to high temperatures for long enough to thoroughly heat the starter above about 100°F. or so.

Here's the "get it going" process I referred to:

▶ The 1-Tablespoon Method

❏ 1. Using 1 tablespoon of starter (discard unused portion or save a little in the refrigerator in case of an emergency), 1 cup 75°F. water, and 1½ cups all-purpose white flour, proof for exactly 24 hours at 72°–77°F. It's very important to maintain these precise temperatures and to proof for exactly 24 hours.

❏ 2. Examine the starter to determine what stage it's in. Assuming you didn't overheat it, it should be "flat," "barely living," or "healthy." Remember the clues to identifying non-healthy starter—low number of bubbles, early hooch, gelatinous consistency, no froth on top, or any 2 or more of these symptoms. If your starter is "healthy," you're done.

❑ 3. If your starter is not healthy yet, stir it well and refrigerate it for no less than 12 hours.

❑ 4. Remove the starter from the refrigerator and go back to step 1. This process needs to be repeated a few times—usually around 4 or 5 times or so unless you were lucky. A lot of the home-dried starters revive *much* quicker than this.

Here's an alternative process you can use (possibly better, if the above process doesn't seem to work well for you):

▶ The 1-Cup Method

❑ 1. Using 1 cup of starter, 1 cup of 85°F. tap water (don't worry about minerals or fluoride), and approximately 1½ cups all-purpose white flour, proof your starter for 12 hours at 85°F. Maintenance of temperature is very important.

❑ 2. Examine the starter to determine what stage it is in. Assuming you didn't overheat it, it should be "flat," "barely living," or "healthy." If your starter is "healthy," you're done. Remember the clues to identifying non-healthy starter: low number of bubbles, early hooch, gelatinous consistency, no froth on top, or any two or more of these symptoms.

❑ 3. If your starter isn't healthy yet, stir it well and refrigerate it for no less than 12 hours.

❑ 4. Remove the starter from the refrigerator and go to step 1. This process needs to be repeated a few times—usually around 4 or 5 times or so unless you were lucky. A lot of the home-dried starters revive *much* quicker than this.

Fresh Starter

Fresh starter is characterized by a nice smooth, pancake-batter-like consistency, lots of bubbles in freshly proofed starter, froth on top of the starter, no hooch at the end of 12 hours of proofing, and rise times for bread recipes of 2½ hours or less. Nothing further needs to be said. This starter is your long-term successful starter and should be protected with your spouse's life! It is now very abuse resistant and you can get away with (although it's not suggested) less accurate temperature control during proofing and for the water added to the starter, and less careful control of the actual proofing period. I believe that the only way to mess up a healthy starter is to heat it up to an excessive temperature (greater than 100°F.) for too long. Nearly anything else will be fine, and even if you seem to have killed it off somewhat, one or two well-controlled proofs should bring it back to life. You can get away with feeding it only once every two weeks or so (but feeding it weekly is better).

Old Starter

Old starter is characterized by a general lack of life due to poor feeding habits or too much time since the last feeding. The cure is simple. If a single, normal proof shows no drastic improvement, do the following:

❏ 1. Using 1 tablespoon of the well-stirred starter (discard the remainder or save a little in the refrigerator in case of an emergency), 1½ cups of 75°F. water, and 2 cups of white-all purpose flour, proof for exactly 24 hours at 72°–77°F.

❏ 2. Examine the starter to determine whether or not it is healthy and fresh. Refer to the section on "fresh starter" or the table of starter stages for a description of fresh, healthy starter. If the starter is healthy, you are finished.

❏ 3. If the starter is not healthy yet, stir well and refrigerate for no less than 12 hours.

❏ 4. Remove the starter from the refrigerator and go back to step 1. Old starter may need to go through this process as many as 5 or 6 times before it becomes healthy again—don't give up even if it takes longer than this. There are very few starters that cannot be restored from this type of abuse.

Non-Standard Starters

If you have a non-standard starter as defined above, and it's healthy, you're doing fine.

▶ Conversion

If you have a non-standard starter that is not healthy, you can convert the starter to a standard starter by using the "Sweetening the Pot with 1 Tablespoon" method described later to create a standard, white-flour-only starter. Use 1 tablespoon of your nonstandard starter to begin the process. If the starter is not very healthy after a single treatment, then refrigerate the starter for no less than 12 hours, and sweeten the pot again. If the starter is very unhealthy, you may have to repeat the process up to 5 or 6 (or more?) times. Each time you repeat the process, use 1 tablespoon of starter from the last run and discard the rest.

Once you've restored the health of your starter by converting it to a standard starter as described, you may pursue either of 2 methods for converting back to the nonstandard starter that you started with.

▶ No Re-Conversion Method

In the first method, you never really do convert back. Rather, you just maintain your standard starter using standard replenishing techniques as later described. Then when you wish to have that special starter for a particular recipe, use 1 tablespoon of your standard starter and follow the directions for sweetening the pot, *but* instead of using plain white flour and plain water, substitute your special flour(s) and liquid(s). For example, a rye starter can be made in one day by taking a single tablespoon of standard starter and mixing it with 1½ cups rye flour and 1 cup water and proofing for 24 hours at 72°–77°F.

▶ Re-Conversion Method

In the second method, you use 1 tablespoon of the newly refreshed standard starter, then blend it with your special flour(s) and liquid(s), and proof for 24 hours at 72°–77°F. *Then* from this time on, continue to feed and replenish your special starter with your special ingredients. If your starter should ever become unhealthy again, then just follow the above procedure to revive it again. Try to determine why your starter is becoming unhealthy. Are you carefully controlling the proofing temperature so the proof is not actually under/over proofing the starter? *Underproofing* prevents the maintenance of high levels of yeast and lactobacilli in your starter. *Overproofing* results in yeast and lactobacilli dying from too much alcohol or acidity in the starter. Are you adding sugar(s) or other simple carbohydrates that cause the starter to proof too fast? The problem with this is that the mixture of "food" (simple and complex sugars and starches) needs to be correct for the blend of microorganisms in the starter. Giving it too much food that is easily metabolized by yeast can cause your starter to proof too quickly, resulting in elevated alcohol levels at the end of the normal proofing time. This can prematurely kill off yeast and result in a weaker starter. Or, if you use the starter as soon as it's ready, you are probably not allowing the lactobacillus to reach maximum population levels. This results in a starter that works well, but is gradually becoming bland over time. I recommend feeding with only plain, unbleached all-purpose flour. Note that you can feed with "best for bread" flours that have higher levels of gluten in them too, but they tend to make the starter clumpier or more gelatinous. I prefer the manageability of a starter fed with all-purpose flour, and use only bread flour for the remainder of the recipe when making bread. If your starter passes these tests, then you may consider the possibility that the mix of flour(s) and liquid(s) that you are using does not sufficiently provide the correct blend of food for long-term maintenance of your nonstandard starter. In that case, I suggest the first method for maintaining your nonstandard starter where you actually just keep a normal white flour and water starter, and convert to your nonstandard type with the 1-tablespoon method when necessary.

Polluted Starter

Polluted starter can be revived, even though it may be all dark, super moldy, or whatever. *Do not stir* polluted starter. If mold exists, carefully scrape or spoon off as much as you can. Remove a couple of tablespoons of the best part of the starter to a clean, scalded container. If you plan to use the original container for starter again, wash it thoroughly with warm soapy water and carefully scald it inside and out by pouring boiling water into and on it. (Be careful to prevent burns! Hot pads or gloves soak up boiling water and hold it on your skin *even longer* than spilling it alone would do.) If your starter only qualified as "polluted" due to the inclusion of any of the baking ingredients listed previously, it will only be necessary to wash the starter container with warm, soapy water. Scalding never hurts (unless you scald yourself!), but it's more optional in this case. In any case, follow the following directions to restore your starter:

❏ 1. Using 1 of the 2 tablespoons you rescued from the polluted starter, add 1 cup of 75°F. water, 1½ cups all-purpose white flour, and proof for exactly 24 hours at 72°–77°F.

❏ 2. Refrigerate for no less than 12 hours, then repeat step 1.

❏ 3.The proof-refrigerate cycle should be repeated at least once. Use your own judgment. If the starter was unusually dark or contained mold, I'd suggest doing it at least 4 or 5 times to be sure the offending organisms are eradicated. If the starter merely contained other baking ingredients, then a single 24-hour proof is probably enough. Each cycle is started by using 1 tablespoon from the last cycle.

Summary on Starter Care and Starter Reviving

I have personally tested many different techniques in replenishing, reviving, and starting new starters, and have found the mentioned techniques to be the most universally successful and easy to perform. The only problem I've had is that sometimes summer temperatures prevent maintaining approximately 75°F. temperatures for a full 24-hour proof period. In that case, the next best thing to do is to follow the same iterative process, but use the 1-Cup Method and 12-hour proofs at 85°F. instead.

Maintaining and Preparing Starters

Always cover proofing bowls with plastic wrap and poke a couple of holes in it so gasses can escape. Always use noncorrosive bowls, containers, and utensils (glass, wood, stainless steel). If the temperature in the proofing area varies much at all, wrap the proofing bowl in a towel to help maintain an even temperature *and* try to find a better place to proof the starter.

➔ To prepare starter for use in nonbread, i.e. pancakes, waffles, or muffins, recipes, here are two practical methods:

● Combine 1 cup starter, 1 cup 80°–85°F. water, and 1½ cups white all-purpose flour in a noncorrosive bowl. For recipes requiring greater lift from the yeast, proof for 8 to 12 hours at 85°F. For noncritical recipes (pancakes and waffles) or recipes using the starter only for flavor, proof at 85°F. for 8 (mild flavor, more active) to 48 (strongest flavor, weaker action) hours. For the non-critical recipes, you may proof at cooler temperatures of 72°–80°F., if that is more convenient. Pancakes work fine using even the longest proofing period.

● Concurrent to the above proofing, replenish the remaining starter in the starter container by adding ¾ cup of 80°–85°F. water and 1 cup all-purpose flour and mix well. Proof at 80°–85°F. for 8 to 12 hours. Refrigerate.

● Note that this method allows the creation of alternative or "special" starters for use in individual recipes. For example, throw some cracked wheat into the starter for the recipe, but replenish the starter in the starter container with plain white, all-purpose flour as usual.

OR

● Combine 1 cup starter, 1½ cups 80°–85°F. water, and 2 cups white all-purpose flour in a noncorrosive bowl. Proof at 85°F. for 8–12 hours.

● Return approximately 1 cup of the starter to the starter container before using the starter in a recipe. Refrigerate the starter in the starter container.

● Note that this method does not allow making alternative starters for individual recipes since the addition of alternative ingredients to the starter (for the recipe) would pollute the starter going back into the starter container.

To prepare starter for use in bread recipes, here are the procedures:

- If the starter has not been used in more than 3 or 4 days, you may wish to replenish the starter once (1 cup starter, 1 cup water, 1½ cups flour, 12 hours at 85°F.) to ensure the starter is really fresh before preparing for a bread recipe. Most healthy starters are fairly flexible, though.

- Use the following table for amounts, and blend together the starter, *bread* flour, and 80°–85°F. water. Measure the starter and water carefully. The suggested amount of flour is only a guideline. Blend enough in to make the starter the consistency of mud (a little thicker than pancake batter).

Bread Flour

Loaves	Flour	Water	Starter
1	1½ cups	1 cup	1 tablespoon
2	2½ cups	2 cups	1 tablespoon + 1 teaspoon
3	3½ cups	3 cups	2 tablespoons

- Proof for exactly 24 hours at 72°–77°F.

- As you're doing the above proof, you can replenish the original starter by combining 1 tablespoon starter (discard most of the rest), 1 cup warm water, and 1½ cups *all-purpose* flour in another bowl or in the starter container itself. Proof for 24 hours at 72°–77°F.

- Refrigerate the starter in the starter container.

- Note that the "1-Tablespoon Method" described allows the instant creation of nontraditional starters such as whole wheat or rye. See "Creating Alternate Starters" below.

OR

- Combine flour, water, and starter using the amounts in the following table according to the size of the recipe you are going to make. Note that because I suggest using *all-purpose* flour in the following proof that you should use *bread* flour for the rest of the flour in the recipe (not counting nonwheat flours). Again note that the starter and water should be measured carefully, but the amount of flour suggested is only a guideline. Blend in enough to make the starter the consistency of mud (a little thicker than pancake batter).

All-Purpose Flour

Loaves	Flour	Water	Starter
1	1½ cups	1 cup	1 cup
2	2½ cups	2 cups	1 cup
3	3½ cups	3 cups	1½ cups

● Proof for 12 hours at 85°F.

● Return about 1 cup of the starter to the starter container before using the starter in a recipe.

● Refrigerate the starter container.

● Note that this method does not allow the creation of alternative starters on an as-needed basis.

 If you are preparing alternative starters for bread recipes:

● If the starter has not been used in more than 3 or 4 days, you may wish to replenish the starter once (1 cup starter, 1 cup water, 1½ cups flour, 12 hours at 85°F.) to ensure the starter is really fresh before preparing for a bread recipe. Most healthy starters are fairly flexible, though.

● Use the following table for amounts, and blend together the starter, *bread* flour (if wheat) and/or other flour(s), and 80°–85°F. liquid (water, milk, or whatever). Measure the starter and liquids carefully. The suggested amount of flour(s) is only a guideline. Blend enough in to make the starter the consistency of mud (a little thicker than pancake batter). It is better to add the specific amount of nonwheat flours that you intend to use, then use wheat flour to adjust the consistency.

Loave(s)	Flour	Liquid	Starter
1	1½ cups	1 cup	1 tablespoon
2	2½ cups	2 cups	1 tablespoon + 1 teaspoon
3	3½ cups	3 cups	2 tablespoons

● Proof for exactly 24 hours at 72°–77°F.

● When you're doing the above proof, you can replenish the original starter by combining 1 tablespoon starter (discard most of the rest), 1 cup warm water, and 1½ cups *all-purpose* flour in another bowl or in the starter container itself. Proof for 24 hours at 72°–77°F.

● Refrigerate the starter in the starter container.

If you are preparing alternative starters for nonbread recipes:

● Combine 1 cup starter, 1 cup 80°–85°F. water, and 1½ cups *all-purpose* flour and/or other ingredients (throw in some cracked wheat, or substitute part of the flour with cornmeal or rye, etc.).

● Proof the starter for 8 to 12 hours (mild flavor, more active) or up to 48 hours (strongest flavor, weakest action) at 85°F. Recipes requiring the yeast action should either use shorter proofs, or cooler (72°–80°F.) proofs if proofing for a longer period.

● Concurrent to the above, replenish the starter in the container with ¾ cup 80°–85°F. water and 1 cup *all-purpose* flour. Proof for 8 to 12 hours at 85°F. Refrigerate.

Using Starter for Commercial Baking

If you are preparing starter for high-volume production, such as in a commercial kitchen, follow these guidelines:

If the starter has not been used in more than 3 or 4 days, you may wish to replenish the starter once to ensure the starter is really fresh before preparing for a bread recipe. For *each* 2 loaves of bread to be baked:

- Combine 1 tablespoon starter, 1½ cups 80°–85°F. water, and 2 cups *bread* flour in a noncorrosive bowl. Remember to measure the starter and water carefully and then to add enough flour to make the starter the consistency of mud. The amount of flour suggested is a guideline for planning purposes.

- Proof for exactly 24 hours at 72°–77°F.

With the original starter,

- At the same time as you're doing the above proof, you can replenish the original starter by combining 1 tablespoon of starter (discard most of the rest), 1½ cups warm water, and 2 cups all-purpose flour in another bowl or in the starter container itself. Proof for 24 hours at 72°–77°F.

- For maintaining larger amounts of starter, use multiples of the above amounts for replenishing the starter. For example, if you normally use 64 tablespoons (4 cups) of starter to produce enough starter for 128 loaves of bread, then you need to maintain at least 4½ cups of starter, so you'd be best off to triple the above replenishing procedure by using 3 tablespoons starter, 4½ cups water, and about 6 cups flour. That's a *lot* of bread from only 4 cups of starter!

Restarting a Culture from a Dried Starter

Restarting a starter from a dried culture qualifies the starter as a "New Starter," so you should refer to the appropriate preceeding section after following the procedure on the next page:

- In a 1-cup measuring cup that has been warmed to around 90°F. by flowing water, combine 1 cup of 90°F. water and the dried culture (1 or 2 tablespoons of powder, more is not necessary).

- Mix well and let the dried culture soak for about 30 minutes.

- Add 1½ cups all-purpose white flour and mix well, being sure to incorporate as much air into the mixture as possible.

- Proof for 12 to 18 hours.

- Refer to the section above on "new starters" to judge the state of your newly revived starter and follow the directions found there.

Starting a New Starter from the Local Atmosphere

When starting a new starter from the local atmosphere (try it, you'll like it!):

- Combine in a *glass* bowl 1½ cups warm water (80°–85°F.) and 2 cups of white all-purpose flour. Use no sugars and especially, use *no commercial yeasts!* Mix well, being sure to incorporate a lot of air into the mixture. Commercial yeasts merely result in the cultivation of commercial yeasts! It won't be sour (unless you're quite lucky) and it won't behave like normal sourdough so none of the above starter usage and maintenance instructions will apply! Some people have reported that their commercial-yeast started starters do get sour eventually, but that just means the starter has finally converted to the natural microorganisms (including the slower growing natural yeast). You might as well start it out right in the first place and avoid months of using so-so starter while you're waiting for it to get good. Your sourdough will be sour only if your starter allows the lactobacillus cultures to reach their highest levels, and that can only happen with wild yeast. Commercial yeast has been bred and crossbred for speed, lack of flavor, and for manufacturability. Just like store-bought tomatoes, it "looks good, but tastes bad."

- Place the bowl in an 80°–85°F. location. Leave uncovered so the natural microorganisms can settle on the surface. Fan air onto the surface using a magazine or something similar. This helps to drive more microorganisms (yeast and lactobacilli) into the surface. Grapes (I prefer red seedless) crushed to remove their insides can also be mixed into the starter. For whatever reason, grapes seem to breed wild yeast and lactobacillus quite well, so their skins tend to carry a lot of it on them.

- Let the mixture proof for 24 hours. Stir the mixture well once or twice during the 24-hour first proof. Before and after each stirring, fan the surface with air again.

- At the end of the 24 hours, examine for bubbles (use a glass bowl). It's unlikely that there will be any yet, but you never know. Stir well and fan again.

- Repeat the 24-hour proof as described, including the brisk stirring and fanning.

- At 48 hours total time, once again examine, stir, and fan the mixture. Continue to leave uncovered. Any skin that forms should be stirred back in *as soon as it is noticed* so no microorganisms will be kept out of the starter by the dry skin. Remove ½ cup of the starter, and replace it with ½ cup warm water and about ⅔ cup white all-purpose flour.

- Continue this 48-hour cycle very carefully until it's obvious that the first bubbles are definitely appearing in the starter. Then, refer to the section entitled "new starter" for further instructions.

It typically takes from 3 to 7 or 8 days for the starter to begin to work. Late spring, summer, or early fall are best times to do this. Winter air may not contain enough yeast spores to get it going, but it's always fun to try. But don't count on having starter for bread when starting a new starter like this because it takes about 3 or 4 weeks *minimum* for the entire process of developing a vibrant, healthy starter suitable for your recipes.

Home-Drying Starters

Drying starters results in a powder suitable for long-term, no-care, storage of starters, or for convenient mailing to friends or relatives.
Dried starters may be kept for long periods of time outside the freezer, and even longer when stored in the freezer. The freezer is the best place for dried starters.

Before relying on any dried starter for maintaining the original starter and all of its characteristics, it is best to test it. That is, dry enough starter so you have numerous 2-tablespoon packets of dried starter, then restore one of the packets and compare its qualities to the original. Taste and smell are good enough tests. Rising time is a tempting test, but remember that given proper feeding, a restored starter can easily resume the raising of bread just as well as it did prior to the freezer storage. No need to prepare an entire recipe. If the "sour" is missing, or the powder doesn't easily restore, then another try at drying is in order. Once you've successfully dried the starter, place it in the freezer or mail it immediately.

The following technique is thought to work in most cases. Note that the technique may actually diminish yeast concentrations while at the same time maximizing lactobacilli concentrations. This will increase the chance that the lactobacilli will survive the drying process.

Here's what to do:

● Using 1 cup of your starter, replenish this starter as described in the instructions above, but rather than proofing for only 8 to 12 hours, proof the starter for about 18 hours at 85°F.

● To restore the starter in the starter container, just follow the normal, unmodified, replenishing directions above.

● Tear off a piece of wax paper about three feet long, and lay it on your working surface, making sure the wax side is *up*.

● Place a few tablespoons of the overproofed starter on the wax paper near one end and spread thinly across the wax paper using a dough blade or flat knife.

- Allow to dry at room temperature overnight.

- When dry, the wax paper will probably have curled up. Just press the wax paper flat to free the dried starter from the paper. Place the flakes of dry starter into a bowl. Scrape or crack-off any remaining starter into the bowl. Using your fingers, crunch up the starter until it is a fine powder.

- Place 2 tablespoons of the dried powder in individual plastic bags. I prefer the zip-type sandwich bags available at most grocery stores.

- Test the newly dried starter by restoring it as described above. If it resembles the original starter fairly closely, then you're in business . . . store the rest of the packages in the freezer. If the starter does not resemble the original, repeat the drying process and try again. I have heard about, but have not tested, people having good success with even longer proofs at lower temperatures. For example, if you're not having good success, you might try proofing at 75°–80°F., for 20 to 24 hours prior to the drying process. If you discover an exceptionally good way to dry starter, please email the idea to me at briandixon@hotmail.com.

This guide is a condensed version of a paper that was written by Brian Dixon <briandixon@hotmail.com> and posted by Darrell Greenwood, Darrell_Greenwood@mindlink.net; website. Unfortunately, the authors of this book were forced at baguette-point by their editors to condense this document, and much interesting material was excised. If you want to read the real document, go to the web.

Cooking with Siege Ingredients

Throughout this book, we've valiantly tried to convince you not to store your food under the siege plan. But we suspect a lot of you are going to do the siege thing anyway, choosing to store food the siege way rather than storing no food at all.

Others of you, who have chosen a better path, also have siege foods as part of your food storage. There's nothing wrong with that. Siege foods were chosen in the first place because they're good for you—assuming, of course, you know how to cook them and your family is able to digest them.

That being the case, we can assume that most people who have a food storage program have at least some siege food on hand. Because you have that food anyway, here's a brief rundown on hints that may help you make those foods more palatable and enjoyable to your families.

The Bean Pot

You may think beans keep forever. In fact, if you store them properly they do keep for years and years. But the longer a bean ages, the more time you're going to have to take to soak it, and to cook it. You'll also need to use more of your precious water to cook old beans. Rotate your beans, just as you would any other item in your food storage. Keep no more than a year's supply on hand, and replenish them as they're used.

Beans are a chameleon food because they take on the flavor of other foods in a dish. This means they can be added to many recipes. We actually possess a recipe for fudge that can be made with pinto beans. We're not recommending that you try this recipe, you understand—it's included here solely to impress you with the versatility of your basic legume.

Pinto Bean Fudge

1 cup cooked soft pinto beans,
    drained and mashed
¼ cup milk
1 tablespoon vanilla
6 ounces unsweetened chocolate

6 tablespoons butter
2 pounds powdered sugar
nuts (optional)

Place beans in a large bowl, stirring in enough milk to give them the consistency of mashed potatoes. Add vanilla and mix well. Melt chocolate with butter; stir into bean mixture. **(Note: If you don't have a bar of chocolate, use 1 cup of chocolate chips.)** Gradually stir in powdered sugar. Knead with hands to make sure all the ingredients are blended. We don't want any pockets of pinto beans that haven't been disguised with chocolate! Butter a square baking dish and spread the mixture in the dish. Chill 2 hours. Enjoy—if, that is, it is at all possible to do so.

Although beans are such chameleons that the foolhardy soul who created the above recipe actually had the courage to combine pinto beans with chocolate, they also have personalities of their own. Red beans have the strongest flavor. Split peas and pinto beans are grainy. Black-eyed peas have a pleasant, musky taste. Black beans add eye appeal to recipes. It's only logical that beans have substantially different cooking times. Lentils are going to cook a lot faster than red beans, just by virtue of the difference in size. Store an assortment of beans to fool your family into thinking they're eating a greater variety of foods, and also to give you an assortment of cooking times to use with various recipes.

Everyone knows that the biggest drawback of beans is their reputation as being the "musical fruit." Throughout the years, many people have found different ways to de-gas beans and reduce the unpleasant side-effects. One way is to bring the beans to a boil, let them sit for ten minutes, and throw out the cooking water. If you do this several times, the beans should be easier on your digestive tract. Another way is to freeze the beans for twelve hours after soaking and before cooking. Apparently, freezing breaks down the starches that make beans indigestible.

Here's a handy rule of thumb when you're preparing beans: **One cup of dry beans weighs approximately one-half pound and produces three cups of cooked beans.** Add three cups of water for each cup of dry beans, bring to a boil, reduce heat, and simmer for about ninety minutes until beans are tender. When you're cooking beans, a tablespoon or so of oil in the water will prevent foaming and reduce the incidence of boiling over.

Be careful at the end of the cooking time, because beans burn awfully fast when they're almost finished cooking. It's always helpful to cook beans in nonstick cookware—not to keep the beans from burning, but to make cleanup easier after they burn. If you burn the beans, they're still edible if you scoop out the beans without disturbing the burned crust on the bottom of the pot. In fact, if you're careful your family will never know by the taste that the beans burned—unless, of course, your house smells like smoke.

Once beans are cooked, they'll keep in the refrigerator for up to five days. (Be sure to keep them covered so they don't dry out.) Small portions of them will keep up to six months in the freezer—but why waste freezer space, when beans are so easy to cook fresh when you need them.

A Honey of a Sweetener

All honey is not created equal. Some of it is mild; some is so strong that you may shudder when you taste it. Honey takes on the flavor of the plant where the bees fed. In the United States, clover honey is the most popular because of its sweet, mild taste. Unless your family has a strong preference for a different kind of honey, clover honey should be used in most recipes. Always use liquid honey in cooking; creamed honey has been whipped, and the measurements would be inaccurate.

When cooking with honey, use level measurements. Don't be tempted to guess when you're adding a cup of honey to a recipe, because you may end up with an inedible glop. The best way to use honey in recipes is to combine it with other liquids and then add all the liquids at once to the recipe. This means you should always use honey at room temperature. This makes it more workable. By the way, you'll have better luck getting the honey out of your measuring cup if you coat the measuring cup with oil before you put the honey in.

Recipes that call for sugar cannot be modified by adding an equal amount of honey, because honey is considerably sweeter than sugar. A cup of honey weighs twelve ounces, but a cup of sugar weighs only seven ounces. This makes honey seem even sweeter than it already is. In baking cakes and quick breads, you can generally substitute half the sugar with honey without having to change any of the other ingredients (ie: if the recipe calls for 1 cup sugar, use ½ cup sugar and ½ cup honey) Hard cookies can take no more than a third of the sugar, although soft cookies can have half the sugar substituted with honey. If you want a sticky fruit bar, you can substitute up to two-thirds of the sugar with honey. Honey may be substituted equally for sugar if you're making baked apples, glazes, lemonade, candied vegetables, pie fillings, puddings, custards, punches, salad dressings, and Oriental dishes.

Another thing you'll want to consider when substituting honey for sugar is that if you're using large quantities you'll have to cut down on the liquid in your recipe. One rule of thumb is that for every one cup of sugar the recipe would call for, use three-fourths cup of honey—and then cut one-fourth cup of liquid out of the recipe. You'll also have to reduce the oven temperature by about thirty-five degrees, because honey burns at a lower temperature than sugar does.

Among the advantages of honey is that sweet sauces are smoother when made with honey than they are when made with sugar. This only makes sense, because honey isn't grainy the way sugar is. Another advantage is that because of the moisture content of honey, baked goods stay fresher longer if they're made with honey than they do if they're made with sugar. If you live in a climate where bread starts drying out as soon as it leaves the oven, this can be a boon and a blessing. A negative when using honey is that items that have been made with honey are so moist that they shouldn't be frozen.

If honey crystallizes, remove the cap from the jar, place it in a pan of hot water taken from the tap, and let it sit overnight. If that doesn't do the trick, put the pan of hot water on the stove and turn the burner on the lowest heat setting. Be patient, and check the water level occasionally; this may take several hours.

Udderly Fine

Powdered milk is one of those things that most people don't have in their cupboards, but that can be a handy item for cooking and even drinking if only your family will learn how to use it.

Not everyone can drink powdered milk. Because of the sugar content (lactose is a sugar), diabetics shouldn't use it. Many adults who aren't diabetics are intolerant to it. Most children aren't lactose intolerant, but young children need the fat that is found in whole milk. If your household uses reconstituted milk, fat should be added in the form of cream or half-and-half to supplement the diet of toddlers.

But once you're aware of the potential drawbacks, powdered milk is a convenient item to have on hand. Some of it tastes so much like milk from a bottle that we have a friend who did a taste test for her husband, and he chose the powdered milk as being real. If your family can be similarly duped—or if they can be trained to enjoy powdered milk by introducing it into their diets a little bit at a time—you'll never again have to make those Saturday midnight runs to pick up a gallon of milk if you realize you don't have milk for your Sunday morning cereal.

Powdered milk is also an ingredient in baking. If you plan on being a bread-baker under your new food storage program, you'll see how many recipes call for milk in its powdered form. You can also reconstitute milk and use it as an ingredient in recipes that call for whole milk, so it's a versatile item to have on hand.

The biggest problem with storing powdered milk is that its shelf life isn't very long. It doesn't store well in its powdered form, and it doesn't keep as long after it has been reconstituted. The fats in powdered milk cause it to go rancid quickly, so nonfat dry milk is preferable to powdered whole milk. "Extra Grade" milk keeps a little bit longer than powdered milk that doesn't have this on the label, because it's slightly lower in butterfat and moisture content than other varieties.

When you buy powdered milk, make sure to look at the expiration date. Don't buy more dry milk than you would expect to use during that time frame. Your powdered milk may last beyond the expiration date, especially if you store it in a cool place. (In fact, temperature is such a big issue that the same container of powdered milk may last only three months at when stored in a 90°F. atmosphere, but four *years* at 50°F.) But cool places are also damp. Make sure you buy powdered milk in metal cans to keep the moisture out. In any case, don't take a chance by investing money in more powdered milk than you can reasonably be expected to use before it goes bad.

If your powdered milk does go bad, the first thing it will do is develop an off flavor. If this happens, you don't need to throw it away. Instead, use it for baking rather than for drinking. The taste is the only thing that has deteriorated, so as long as the flavor isn't *too* rank, the milk should be fine for baking purposes.

Dry milk comes in instant and regular forms. Needless to say, instant milk is easier to make than regular milk. When you're reconstituting instant milk, all you have to do is add the water to the powder and shake it. If you're using regular milk, you may have to add water a little bit at a time.

Here's a table to help you reconstitute your milk. We've got it in cups, quarts, or gallons. In order to make the milk, use the amount of powder called for in the table and then supplement it with enough water to make the amount you want. Remember not to make any more than you'll use before it rots.

Yield	Instant	Regular
1 cup	⅓ cup	¼ cup
1 quart	1⅓ cups	¾ cup
1 gallon	5⅓ cups	3 cups

Here are some handy tips for using powdered milk in cooking:

● In any recipe calling for milk, simply add the dry milk to the other dry ingredients. Sift to blend the milk with the other dry ingredients, then add the water needed to reconstitute the milk when adding the other liquid ingredients to the recipe.

● Add dry milk to meat dishes to make more food and also to bind the meat together. This works well for dishes such as meat loaf and hamburgers. Add ¼ to ½ cup of dry milk per pound of meat.

● To improve the taste of mashed potatoes, mash the cooked potatoes and then add ¼ cup dry milk for each cup of potatoes. Add liquid from the water the potatoes were cooked in until you achieve the correct consistency.

● For cooked cereals, try adding ¼ to ½ cup dry milk to each cup of cereal before cooking.

Rice Is Nice

Although rice is only an afterthought to potatoes in most parts of the United States, much of the world relies on rice as the mainstay of its diet. In the marshlands of Louisiana, which is the rice capital of

America, people are often served rice three times a day—as a breakfast cereal, as a vegetable that's used in place of potatoes or stuffing at dinner, and as a dessert. Indeed, there are seven thousand different varieties of rice. Most of them have considerably more nutritive value than the stuff we buy off our shelves that takes only a minute to cook.

There are five general kinds of rice sold in the United States— brown rice, white rice, parboiled rice, precooked rice, and enriched rice. Here's a comparison to help you choose which rice is for you:

- *Brown rice* is the healthiest of these varieties because it has not been polished. (Polishing removes the inedible hull of rice, but it also removes most of the rice germ and the outer bran.) Brown rice takes longer to cook than white rice, and it uses more water, but that's not its biggest drawback. The biggest drawback is that it goes rancid very quickly. It's quite hard to keep a year's supply of brown rice. It will even go rancid if it has been dry packed with oxygen absorbers. Brown rice may last longer if it is frozen until it's time to open the package. Even so, consumers need to keep in mind that once the rice is opened, it should be consumed within a month.

- *White rice* has had the rice germ and the outer bran layers removed. These are the parts of brown rice that go rancid. Unfortunately, they are also the parts of the rice that account for most of the taste, nutrients, and fiber. Without the rice germ and the outer bran, rice will keep indefinitely in your food storage. There are three grain lengths: long-grain, medium-grain, and short-grain. The grains of long-grain rice remain separate after cooking. Short-grain rice tends to clump together after cooking, and is easiest to pick up with chopsticks. (It also makes a more traditional rice pudding.) As you might guess, medium-grain rice is right in the middle.

- *Parboiled rice*, also known as *converted rice*, has been partially cooked before it reaches your dinner table. It is also treated to retain some of the nutritional value of the rice, which makes it healthier than regular white rice and infinitely healthier than the next type of rice on this list. Even though it has been partially precooked, it takes longer to cook than regular white rice.

- *Precooked rice* is the least desirable of all the kinds of rice on the market. All the flavor has been stripped away, along with most of the nutrients. The best you can say about precooked rice is that it fills you up. Unfortunately, precooked rice is so convenient that most Americans think of this rice when they think of rice at all. After all, as the boxes so cheerfully proclaim, it takes only a minute to cook!

- *Enriched rice* is packed with vitamins and minerals, mostly B vitamins. The individual grains are coated with these minerals, which remain on the rice even after the grains have been cooked.

If you'll notice the above list, all the varieties of rice must be cooked with the exception of precooked rice, which is only dumped in boiling water and removed from the heat. Of the varieties of rice that need to be cooked, there are five cardinal rules of rice-cooking. **Don't ever:**

- **W**ash the rice before you cook it (or rinse it afterwards), because you'll wash the nutrients away;

- **D**rown the rice with too much water, or you'll have soggy rice with fewer nutrients;

- **P**eek when you're cooking to see how it's doing. Peeking removes the steam that cooks the rice;

- **S**tir the rice after it starts boiling, because it makes the rice gummy; or

- **R**est the rice after cooking it by leaving it in the pan for more than five or ten minutes, or the rice will solidify into a pan-shaped doorstop.

These rules should be easy for you to remember, because if you look at the first letter of the first word in each of those rules, you get the letters **WDPSR**, or "**W**hy **D**on't **P**eople **S**tore **R**ice?" This is a good question, because rice is such a valuable addition to our diet that we should be eating more of it. If your family doesn't have the rice habit, there are rice recipes in every cookbook—plus a few of them scattered throughout this book—any number of which can help you teach your family to enjoy this nutritious and versatile grain.

But you can get a start on rice cookery without even using a recipe. One way to do it is to substitute the water that is used to cook the rice with other exotic ingredients. Using broth as the liquid turns rice into an excellent accompaniment for meat dishes. Fruit juices transform rice into a sweet confection. Tomato juice cocktail can make your rice so zesty that it'll raise eyebrows around the dinner table. Add a spice such as cinnamon or garlic powder to the cooking water. Experiment with various liquids and spices. Even more so than beans, rice will take on whatever flavor you lend to it with other ingredients.

Here's a table that will help you cook rice. This is information that comes in handy because the information on the back of the rice container always seems to get torn or misplaced, leaving the hapless cook with rice and no way to cook it.

Rice	Yield	Liquid	Salt	Cook
1 cup brown	4 cups	2½ cups water	1 teaspoon	45 minutes
1 cup regular	3 cups	2 cups water	1 teaspoon	14 minutes
1 cup par-boiled	4 cups	2½ cups water	1 teaspoon	20 minutes
1 cup precooked	2 cups	1 cup water	½ teaspoon	soak 5 minutes in hot water
1 cup regular	3 cups	2 cups broth	1 teaspoon	14 minutes
1 cup regular	3 cups	1½ cups water & ½ cup maraschino cherry juice	1 teaspoon	15 minutes
1 cup regular	3 cups	2 cups fruit juice	1 teaspoon	15–20 minutes
1 cup regular	3 cups	1 cup water & 1 cup tomato or vegetable juice	1 teaspoon	15 minutes

By the way, cooked rice keeps for about five days in the refrigerator. If you don't know what else to do with leftover rice, sauté it with a raw egg and some green onions and pieces of vegetable or meat with soy sauce to make a quick fried rice. Or for a speedy breakfast treat, break an egg or two into the rice, add sugar and a little milk, butter, and cinnamon. Whip it all together so the egg is thoroughly mixed in with the other ingredients. Put in the microwave until the egg sets and voila! You have a quick and dirty rice pudding. It's not suitable for company, but it makes a nutritious and tasty breakfast.

Wheat Is Neat

If you're the proud owner of hundreds of pounds of wheat, you're already so converted to it that all our pleadings have not convinced you to store other things. That's not necessarily a bad thing. Perhaps every member of your family is able to digest wheat, and perhaps you're enthusiastic enough about cooking with it that you're one of the people who can make it work. If so, you're fortunate. Wheat is one of the most nutritious foods on Earth—which is why so many people have recommended that it be used as the mainstay of a food storage program. If your family can digest it, and if you're willing to spend the time to work with it, your family will eat well during fat times as well as lean ones.

If you bought the wheat before you read this book but still don't have any idea what to do with it, we plead with you to make sure your family can eat it before you rely on it and the other siege items to save your lives during hard times. If you're a novice, you're going to need more training than we can give you in this book. That being the case, read *The Classic Wheat for Man Cookbook,* or download some of the extensive wheat-related documents at the Utah State University Extension Service site on the Internet (see Chapter 9 for information on web sites and other resources). But don't just read—practice. If you're going to rely on a wheat-based diet, you need to start using that wheat now. Changing your family's eating habits when they're already under stress due to illness or loss of work or a natural catastrophe is never, ever going to work.

We're not going to bother comparing the nutritive value of white flour versus whole wheat flour in this book: You probably know the numbers better than we do. Face it—whole wheat flour is a whole lot more nutritious than white flour. If your family can eat it, whole wheat flour should be your first choice. But your choices aren't limited to white flour versus whole wheat flour. There's a whole range of flours that are available for your use. Here are the types you can choose. You may want to select one all-purpose family, or keep several different flours on hand for different purposes:

Bleached—white flour that has been left to sit for several months after it has been ground, allowing oxidation to bleach out the natural yellowish color. This makes for a lighter flour in texture as well as in color, so that bread made with bleached flour may rise higher than bread made with unbleached flour. Bleached flour may also be whitened with the addition of chemicals called bleaching agents. Because of this, many health-conscious people don't use bleached flour despite its benefits in baking.

Enriched/Fortified—flour that has had B vitamins and iron added to it. Enriched flour also has added calcium.

Gluten Flour—flour that has been "sweetened" with the addition of gluten, which is the protein in wheat. Because gluten helps bread to rise, it is a desirable component of yeast breads. When using gluten flour, substitute about ½ cup of regular flour with gluten flour per two loaves bread. Needless to say, flour with added protein doesn't have as long a shelf life as flour with all the protein stripped away. Remember the adage, *the healthier the food, the faster it rots*.

Instantized Flour—a fine, granular flour that blends exceptionally well with liquid and is usually sold in shakers for the purpose of making gravy.

Self-Rising Flour—flour with soda, dry acid, and salt added to it. This is a convenient flour for cooks to use because it eliminates having to add extra salt and soda. However, it isn't a good flour to store on a long-term basis because the shelf life of the soda isn't as long as the shelf life of flour. Expired soda won't make the flour bad, but it will keep the flour from rising as it was designed to do.

Unbleached—flour that was packaged after being freshly ground, so that the natural yellowish color has not had a chance to bleach out. This results in a heavier flour in texture as well as in color, making for a more compact and coarsely textured loaf of bread.

Whole Wheat—flour that comes right out of your wheat grinder (or right out of a bag after being put there after being ground). This is flour that includes the bran and the gluten (or protein). The results are a dark color, a coarse texture, and a harsh taste. Whole wheat flour is the healthiest of the flours, but it has an extremely short shelf life. Grind only as much flour as you think you'll need in a week or two. Store extra flour in the refrigerator to retard the spoilage.

When a recipe calls for flour, the implication is that the cook will be using some sort of white flour. With the exception of the heavier texture of unbleached flour, white flours produce results that are so similar as to be virtually interchangeable. Substituting wheat flour for the flour in a recipe will cause changes throughout the final product, however—not just in texture and appearance, but also in taste.

If you're acclimating your family to whole wheat flour, start small. Substitute just a half cup of flour, or even a quarter cup, for white flour in the recipe. If those results are satisfactory, gradually increase the proportions. Most cooks who are experienced with whole wheat cooking only substitute half the white flour called for in a recipe with whole wheat flour. Otherwise the texture and taste may vary too far from the original recipe to yield satisfactory results.

There are three other forms of wheat that are not flours, but are often used by siegers and non-siegers alike. If you store wheat, you can make and use these products. They include:

Bulghur—dried, cracked wheat that has been precooked. It has a texture that is similar to brown rice, and indeed, bulghur can be substituted for rice in many recipes. Bulghur is a staple of Middle Eastern recipes and is available in several textures in Middle Eastern groceries. If you store and use wheat, do some research on bulgur. The USU Extension Service web site alone has enough recipes to keep you experimenting for months.

Cracked Wheat—wheat that has been ground on its coarsest setting. Cracked wheat is used for cereals, and occasionally as an ingredient in whole grain breads.

Meal—wheat that has been ground on a coarse setting. A meal isn't as fine as a flour in that individual grains are distinguishable.

Troubleshooting Guide for Bread

Despite our aversion to a food storage plan that is exclusively comprised of siege food, bread is such an essential part of our diet that there are about a zillion recipes for bread throughout this book.

Whether you make sourdough or yeast bread, breadmaking is a hobby that can provide great satisfaction for you and your family. Like any new skill, breadmaking calls for a little trial and error. Your first loaf may be a great success, or it may resemble an anvil. Here is a table showing problems you may see in your bread, giving you possible causes so that you can correct each situation. With a little practice, you'll soon be able to produce blue-ribbon loaves of bread.

Bread Troubleshooting Guide

Problem	Possible Cause or Causes
Blisters or cracks in crust	too much liquid; oven too hot
Bread collapsed	oven not thoroughly preheated
Bread stales too quickly	insufficient first rising; too warm a dough; not enough salt or sugar; oven temperature too low; not enough moisture in dough; soft flour
Crumb is too dense	not enough leavening; weak sourdough starter; oven too hot; too much salt; insufficient proofing; over-kneading
Crust too dark	oven too hot; too much sugar; too much glazing or egg wash; long baking time (needs to be covered with foil)
Crust too pale	oven temperature too low; too little sugar used; loaf placed too low in oven
Crust too thick	insufficient baking, with too low an oven temperature; insufficient sugar
Large holes	too much leavening; failure to punch down; insufficient salt; insufficient mixing
Not enough rising	not enough yeast; stale or expired yeast; ingredients not at room temperature; drafty, cold, or dry rising environment

Problem	Possible Cause or Causes
Strong yeasty taste	bread not warm enough during rising; punched down too early
Too chewy or sticky	insufficient baking; oven temperature too low; poor leavening of sourdough bread
Too crumbly	not enough flour; too much liquid; insufficient kneading; low oven temperature; dough left too long at proofing stage
Too dry	too much flour; baking time too long
Too much rising	too much dough for size of pan; insufficient salt

A Corny Alternative

Technically speaking, cornmeal isn't one of the big siege foods. However, it shares a spotlight with rice and beans because it's also a good alternative to wheat. No, you can't make sandwich bread with it—but you can use cornmeal in ways that you might otherwise use flour.

Cornmeal is not a flour. It's too coarsely ground to be substituted for flour in any recipe. But even if you were to grind it so finely as to make a flour, corn flour isn't a wheat flour substitute because it doesn't form the gluten that is so essential to breadmaking. Although wheat flour and corn flour may look similar, the two just aren't destined to be interchangeable. However, cornmeal is similar to fortified wheat flour because it contains B vitamins and iron.

For your information, one pound of cornmeal equals about three cups. But that's a dry weight. Cornmeal expands during cooking, so that the three cups of dry cornmeal become four cups of cooked product.

Like whole wheat flour, cornmeal has a relatively short shelf life. You may be able to keep it on hand for a year without trouble, so its life is considerably longer than whole wheat flour. Nevertheless, cornmeal isn't something you can throw in your basement and forget. Nor is it something that can be successfully canned with the dry-pack method and then left to sit until you need it ten years up the road. However, if packed in an airtight container, cornmeal will keep for several years in the freezer.

Cornmeal has many uses. One of its most basic functions is as a hot cereal, similar to cream of wheat. This is referred to as cornmeal mush. Mush can be eaten in a bowl like cream of wheat, and can also be hardened and then sliced and fried so that it makes a dish that is served and eaten like French toast.

When you're cooking with cornmeal, you can eliminate the grainy texture by mixing the cornmeal with the liquid from the recipe, bringing it to a boil, and cooling before mixing with the other ingredients.

In case you don't know what to do with cornmeal, here are some recipes from the University of Missouri Extension Service. Visit their web site for useful information.

Spoonbread
(yield: six 2/3-cup servings)

3 cups milk
1 cup cornmeal
1½ teaspoons salt

2 tablespoons oil
3 eggs

Mix milk, cornmeal, salt, and fat or oil in a saucepan. Cook and stir over medium heat until thickened. Beat eggs in large bowl. Slowly pour and stir cornmeal mixture into eggs. Pour batter in a greased square cake pan. Bake at 400°F. for 35–40 minutes, until top is firm. Serve immediately.

Cooked Cornmeal Mush
(yield: six 1/2-cup servings)

1 cup cornmeal
1 cup cold water

1 teaspoon salt
3 cups boiling water

Mix cornmeal, cold water, and salt. Slowly stir cornmeal mixture into the boiling water in a saucepan. Cook and stir until thick. Lower heat. Cover and cook 15 minutes stirring as needed to keep from sticking.

Fried Cornmeal Mush

Put hot cornmeal mush in a loaf pan. Cool until firm. Remove mush from pan and cut into slices. Put slices of mush in heated greased fry pan and brown on both sides. Serve with butter and syrup or powdered sugar, as you would pancakes or French toast.

Cornmeal Gingerbread

1 cup flour
1 cup cornmeal
½ teaspoon salt
1 teaspoon baking soda
2 teaspoons ginger

½ cup butter
½ cup brown sugar
1 egg
½ cup molasses
¾ cup hot water

Mix flour, cornmeal, salt, baking soda, and ginger. Set aside. Mix butter, sugar, and egg. Beat well. Stir in molasses. Mix in half the flour mixture until smooth. Stir in half the hot water. Mix in rest of flour mixture until smooth. Stir in remaining hot water. Fill greased square cake pan half full. Bake at 350°F. about 45 minutes until gingerbread springs back when touched near center.

Mexican Meat Loaf

1 medium onion
¼ green pepper
1½ pounds ground beef
1 egg
½ cup cornmeal

2 cups drained canned tomatoes
1½ teaspoons salt
¼ teaspoon pepper
¼ teaspoon chili powder

Chop onion and green pepper. Mix all ingredients well. Shape into a loaf in a baking pan. Bake at 350°F. about 1 hour until browned. Serves 6.

Food Storage Cooking

None of the recipes in this appendix are fancy. Most of them are definitely not in the category of food you would serve if your boss was coming to dinner and you were trying to push for a promotion. The recipes here typically contain only a few ingredients, and they tend to be based around the foods that siegers would store as part of their siege food storage—or that you might store with your expanded home storage. Thus, using these recipes will not only rotate your siege food and canned goods, but they will introduce these types of foods into your diet. If you use recipes such as these on a regular basis, it should be easier to rotate your food storage supplies.

By the way, here's a note from your friendly authors. These recipes were given to us by people from all over the country. We specifically asked that nobody give us recipes that came from cookbooks or other copyrighted sources, and we can only trust that's what we were given. However, we were recently reminded that in this information age, people's creations have lives of their own. As this book was going to press in 1999, Clark found an Internet site that showed people how to build a year's supply of food storage for five dollars per week—only to find that the document was something he'd written in the late 1970s in order to promote food storage to a group of church friends who were long on enthusiasm, but short on cash. (By the way, our research for this book shows that you can still build a food supply for $5 per week, and that concept has been updated and presented in Chapter 2 as the Plan 5-5 program.) So even though Clark had almost forgotten his twenty-year-old document, it had been passed from hand to hand, and finally given a new life on the Internet—but without Clark's name on it to give him credit for authorship. These things happen. We've given credit to every recipe inventor whose name we know, but if we've inadvertently included a recipe or chart you invented, let us know so we can give you credit in future printings.

Our Daily Bread (Including Wheat Alternatives)

If you're unfamiliar with breadmaking techniques, see Appendix C for a troubleshooting guide that may provide assistance if your bread needs help.

Jalapeño Cheese Bread

2 boxes corn muffin mix
⅔ cup water
½ cup sugar

4 tablespoons minced jalapeño
2 eggs
1 cup shredded cheese

Mix all the ingredients, pour into a square pan, and bake at 400°F. for 20–25 minutes. If you'd rather have wagon wheel bread, omit the minced jalapeño and slice a fresh jalapeño into circles. Remove the seeds but leave the membranes intact to form "wagon wheels." Use a larger pan to make thinner cornbread.

Chapatis (African Flat Bread)
(yield: 1 dozen)

2 cups white or
   whole wheat flour
½ teaspoon salt

2 tablespoons cooking oil
½ to ⅓ cup water

Sift the flour and salt together, then mix in the oil. Add water a little at a time, stirring to form a soft dough. Cover and set aside for 10 minutes. Remove dough from bowl and knead thoroughly until it is smooth and elastic. Divide the dough into 12 equal pieces and form each into a ball. Roll the balls out as evenly as possible into thin circles about 7 inches across. Keep them covered to prevent drying. Heat a frying pan (cast iron is best). Cook the chapatis, one at a time, for a minute or so on each side. Do not grease the pan. If they puff up, just press them down gently with a spatula. Brown both sides. Stack them, brushing each lightly with butter.

Yeast Rolls

3¾ cups bread flour
⅓ cup sugar
1 teaspoon salt
1 package yeast

¾ cup milk
¼ cup butter
1 egg

Add all dry ingredients to bowl or bread machine pan. Heat milk and butter together until butter is melted, about 120°F. Start bread machine on dough setting. As it mixes, slowly add milk and butter mixture. Then add the egg. When the cycle has completed, remove dough from pan. Shape rolls and place them on a greased pan. Let rolls rise, covered with wax paper that has been sprayed with cooking spray to keep it from sticking to the rolls, for about an hour. Bake for 15–20 minutes at 400°F., or until rolls are nicely browned. Remove from oven and brush with butter. Remove rolls from pan and place on cooling rack to keep the bottoms from getting soggy. (To shape the rolls just put dough onto a lightly floured surface and shape into a rectangle and use a knife or pastry scraper to cut into the size you want. You can also roll into balls and place into greased muffin cups, three per cup, to have clover-leaf rolls.)

Ninety-Minute Bread

4 cups warm water
4 tablespoons yeast
4 teaspoon salt

½ cup sugar
4 tablespoons oil
7–8 cups white or wheat flour

Mix all ingredients except flour. Then begin slowly adding flour. Knead well by hand, adding flour until a soft smooth dough appears. Let rise until double, about one hour. Punch down and knead again. Form four loaves and place in four greased loaf pans. Let rise again until double (or one hour). Bake at 350°F. for 25–35 minutes. Turn out on racks, butter and cool.

Basic White Bread

from John Camelio and Joe Ruocco

1 quart warm water
1 package dry yeast
1 ounce salt

1 ounce sugar
3 pounds flour

Place water in electric mixer bowl or in a large mixing bowl if you aren't using an electric mixer. Add yeast, salt, and sugar. Mix one minute. Add half the flour. Mix well. Add half the remaining flour and mix. Keep adding flour until the dough has formed and does not stick to the sides of the bowl. (If you're kneading by hand, keep adding flour until the dough no longer sticks to your fingers. The dough should be soft and workable.) Remove from mixing bowl and knead for 5 minutes. Place in a large bowl for 1½ hours in a room that's about 80°F. If you don't have an 80°F. room, put the bowl next to an open pot of water that's kept boiling during the rising time. Turn dough out on breadboard and knead for five more minutes. Cut into 4 equal portions and place in bread pans (5x9x3-inch size). Let rise 15 minutes. Bake at 400°F. for 20–25 minutes, until done. Makes four loaves.

Variation: For chocolate bread, substitute 1 cup cocoa for 1 cup of the flour. Add a little extra sugar and a bag of chocolate chips to the dough, and proceed according to the recipe. (If you're using a recipe that calls for oil, you can add 4 melted squares of baker's chocolate and reduce the oil by half, rather than using powdered cocoa.) Don't add too much sugar; you don't want a sweet bread.

Irish Soda Bread
(yield: 2 loaves)

6 cups all-purpose flour
3 tablespoons cornstarch
2 teaspoons baking soda
2 teaspoons sugar

2 teaspoons baking powder
1 teaspoon salt
2½ cups buttermilk

Preheat oven to 375°F. Mix the dry ingredients in a large bowl. Add the buttermilk all at once and stir with a wooden spoon until a soft dough is formed. Dough will still be lumpy. Knead for a minute or two until everything solidifies and looks smooth.

Divide the dough into two portions and shape each into a fat round loaf, pressing the top down enough to just barely flatten it. Place the loaves on a large ungreased cookie sheet, preferably of the nonstick variety. Sprinkle some additional flour on each loaf and make a large "X" on top of each loaf with slashes from a sharp knife. Allow the loaves to sit for 10 minutes and then bake on the middle rack of the oven for 40 minutes, or until the loaves are golden brown and done to taste. Cool on racks.

Flour Tortillas
(yield: about 10)

2 cups unsifted flour
1 teaspoon salt

¼ cup shortening
½ cup lukewarm water

Combine the flour and the salt. Cut the shortening into the flour with a pastry blender or 2 knives until the particles are fine. Add the water gradually, stirring with a fork to make a stiff dough. Form into a ball and knead thoroughly on lightly floured board until smooth and flecked with bubbles. Grease dough surface and refrigerate for 2–24 hours before using. Let dough return to room temperature before rolling out. Divide dough into 8-11 balls. Roll as thin as possible on floured board. Drop onto very hot ungreased griddle or skillet. Cook about 20–30 seconds and turn over. Cook briefly and serve at once or store in an airtight container and refrigerate.

Italian Bread Bowls

2½ cups warm water
2 envelopes yeast
2 teaspoons salt

2 tablespoons cooking oil
7 cups flour
2 egg whites

Mix the water and yeast together in bowl, then let it stand for 5 minutes. Stir in the salt and the cooking oil. Add the flour gradually, beating with a mixer until soft dough forms. Turn dough out onto a floured surface. Knead it for 4–6 minutes, until smooth and elastic. Place dough in a lightly greased bowl, turning it to grease the top. Cover and let rise 35 minutes, or until doubled. Punch dough down, and divide into 8 equal portions. Shape each into a four-inch round loaf.

Make an egg mixture using the egg whites and 1 tablespoon of water. Brush the mixture over the loaves, then set aside. Bake loaves at 400°F. for 15 minutes. Brush with remaining egg mixture, and bake 10–15 more minutes or until golden brown.

After the loaves have cooled, cut a ½-inch thick slice from the top of each loaf, and then scoop out the centers, trying to maintain a ¾-inch thickness of bread for the sides and bottom of each bowl. When ready to eat, fill bread bowls with hot soup and serve immediately.

Oatmeal Biscuits

1 cup rolled oats
¾ cup flaked coconut
1 cup flour
1 cup sugar

½ cup butter
1 tablespoon corn syrup
1½ teaspoons soda
2 tablespoons boiling water

Mix oats, flour, sugar, and coconut. Melt corn syrup and butter together in a small saucepan. Mix soda with boiling water and add to corn syrup and butter mix. Add dry ingredients and mix thoroughly. Place globs (about 1 tablespoon each) of mix onto greased trays, allowing room for spreading while cooking. Cook for about 30 minutes at 300°F. Cool completely on racks.

Lemon-Poppy Muffins
(yield: 12-15 muffins)

2 cups unsifted flour
¼ teaspoon baking powder
¾ cup sugar
1 cup buttermilk
½ teaspoon baking soda
4 teaspoons poppy seeds

½ cup butter, softened
1 teaspoon vanilla
½ teaspoon salt
2 tablespoons grated
  lemon rind
2 eggs

Preheat oven to 400°F. Combine dry ingredients, including lemon rind. In a large mixer bowl, beat sugar and butter until fluffy; beat in eggs until smooth. Add buttermilk and vanilla; mix well. Stir in flour mixture until moistened. Fill paper cup-lined or greased muffin tin ¾ full. Bake 20 minutes, or until golden brown. Serve warm.

Basic Polenta

1 cup cornmeal, yellow or white   1 quart water
1 teaspoon salt

Bring about 2½ cups of the water to a boil in the top part of a double boiler over direct heat. Add the salt. Mix the cornmeal with the remaining water and add to the boiling water. Reduce the heat and cook, stirring constantly, until the mixture boils. Place the pan over boiling water and cook, covered, about 45 minutes, stirring occasionally.

Cheese Polenta

Follow the Basic Polenta recipe until cooked. Then make a depression in the center of the hot polenta and fill it with 3–4 tablespoons of butter and 3–4 ounces of shredded cheddar or Monterey jack. Spoon butter and cheese over each serving of polenta as well.

Grilled Onion Polenta

Follow the Basic Polenta recipe until cooked. Sauté some onions and add to the polenta mixture. Then pour the hot cooked polenta into a greased 9x9-inch pan. Spread it to make a layer about ½-inch thick. Turn the polenta out of the pan and cut it into squares, rectangles, or as desired. Place the pieces on a cookie sheet that has been lined with foil and broil until brown and well crisped on both sides. Brush with melted butter during broiling.

Mike's Multigrain Bread

1 cup uncooked cornmeal	6 cups water
1 cup uncooked cracked wheat	½ cup honey
1 cup uncooked regular oatmeal	2 cups whole wheat flour
2 tablespoons yeast	6–8 cups white flour

Heat 4 cups water to boiling. Pour over cornmeal, cracked wheat, and oatmeal in a large bowl. Add 2 cups warm water and honey. When mixture is cool enough to add yeast, do so. Add wheat flour and mix well. Slowly add white flour and knead well. Dough will be smooth but still somewhat sticky. Place small amount of oil in bowl to oil sides slightly. Let rise one hour or till doubled in size. Punch down and knead again. Place in four well-greased loaf pans and let rise again. Bake in 350°F. oven about 25–35 minutes. Cornmeal makes a crunchy crust. Center is a delicious nutty sponge texture.

Main Course Variation: Use dough to make a meat rollup. Spread onto large jelly roll pan, cut in two across short way so you have about two equal pieces. Spread some olive oil over the top, then sprinkle with Italian or other spices. Cook 1–2 pounds of ground meat with any combination of vegetables such as onions, carrots, peas, mushrooms. Add garlic. Spread this over the bread. Roll up each piece, seal, and bake. This is a versatile dish. Add eggs or cheese to the mix, or sprinkle with sesame seeds. Be creative!

Whole Wheat Bread

3 cups warm water
½ cup honey
¼ cup molasses
3 tablespoons yeast

5 cups unsifted whole wheat flour
¼ cup canola oil
butter

Combine water, honey, molasses, and yeast in a large bowl. Let rest for 10 minutes. Add flour and oil. Beat by hand at least 100 strokes, or 7 minutes with bread mixer on low. Put in oiled bowl, smooth side down; turn greased side up; cover, let rise in warm place (85°F.) until double in size, about one hour. Punch down to original size. Cover and let rise again until double in bulk. Punch down again. Divide into 3 loaves and place into buttered loaf pans. Let rise until dough reaches to top of pan; bake in 350°F oven about 50 minutes.

Granny's Banana Nut Bread

1 egg
⅔ cup mashed bananas
¼ cup shortening
3 tablespoons sour milk
2 cups flour

¾ cup sugar
½ teaspoon baking soda
½ teaspoon baking powder
¼ teaspoon salt
½ cup chopped nuts

Make sour milk by adding a tablespoon of vinegar to a cup of milk, letting it sit for 5–10 minutes. Mix egg, bananas, shortening, sour milk, and sugar, and set bowl aside. In another bowl, mix flour, baking soda, baking powder, and salt. Slowly stir in the dry ingredients to the banana mixture and mix well. Stir in the nuts. Pour batter into a greased 5x9-inch loaf pan. Bake at 350°F. for 1 hour. The bread is done when you can insert a knife or toothpick and it comes out clean. Place on a cooling rack and brush all sides of the bread with melted butter. Cool before slicing.

Baguettes
(yield: 2 loaves)

1 teaspoon sugar	2½ cups flour
1 tablespoon yeast	2 tablespoons wholemeal flour
¾ cup warm water	½ teaspoon salt

Add sugar and yeast to a little bit of the water. Set aside. Mix flours with salt in a large bowl. Add the yeast mixture and the remaining water to the flour bowl. Knead to a smooth dough. Place in a greased bowl and put in a warm spot to rise for 1½ hours, till doubled in bulk. Punch down; knead till smooth and satiny. Flour your hands and work surface, divide the dough in half, and make 2 long loaves, about 15 inches long. Let rise on a greased baking sheet. When loaves have risen again, make slits along the top with a sharp knife. Brush with water, place on top shelf of a 475°F. oven, and bake till golden (about 30 minutes), brushing the tops with salt water every five minutes.

Honey Granola Bread

2 cups milk	2 cups whole wheat flour
2 tablespoons butter	1 cup all-purpose flour
½ cup honey	½ cup toasted wheat germ
½ cup apricot jelly	2 teaspoons salt, scant
1 cup granola	2 tablespoons yeast

In small pan, stir together milk, butter, honey, and jelly. Heat over low heat until warm. In large bowl, mix granola, flours, wheat germ, salt, and yeast. Pour liquid into flour mixture, beat at medium speed for 3 or 4 minutes. Stir in about **3 additional cups of flour** to make a stiff dough. Knead on floured surface 8–10 minutes. Put in greased bowl. Turn once and cover. Let rise about an hour or so in oven that was preheated to about 125°F. and then turned off. Punch down. Divide in half. Form loaves, put in lightly greased loaf pans. Cover and let rise 1½ hours. Bake at 375°F. for 40 minutes.

Mrs. Boost's Mother-In-Law's Easy Yeast Bread

1 egg
1 cup milk
1 package yeast
vegetable oil

1 teaspoon salt
4 cups flour
⅓ cup sugar
⅓ cup shortening

Take the egg from the refrigerator and leave it in a bowl. The shell will sweat and then dry as the egg warms. When the shell is dry, the egg is ready to use. Heat the milk so it is warm, but less than 110°F. In a large bowl, pour about a teaspoon of oil. Use a paper towel to coat the inside of the bowl. Dissolve yeast in milk, adding about ½ teaspoon of sugar to feed the yeast. Add egg, salt, sugar, and shortening. Blend with a mixer. Continuing with the mixer, slowly add two cups of the flour. Then add the remaining two cups of flour to make a soft dough. Pour your dough into the large bowl you coated with oil. Cover with a towel and let rise till the dough has doubled in size. Flour a surface. Pour the dough out on the surface. Sprinkle more flour on top and then punch down the dough. Shape into rolls or make a loaf. Let the rolls/loaf rise again. Bake in a preheated 350°F. oven.

Hints: You may want to add about ¼ cup less flour on a dry day, or ¼ cup more flour for a humid day. If you're making rolls, an easy roll shape is to cut rounds with a biscuit cutter, coat the biscuit top with melted butter and fold it over, pinching it shut to make sure it stays that way.

Potato Bread
(yield: 2 loaves)

1 tablespoon yeast
½ cup lukewarm water
¼ teaspoon sugar
1 cup milk
⅔ cup sugar

1 teaspoon salt
2 eggs, lightly beaten
½ cup mashed potatoes
about 6 cups flour

Dissolve the yeast in water. Sprinkle with ¼ teaspoon sugar. In a saucepan combine the milk, ⅔ cup sugar, and salt. Heat to simmer, turn off heat, and let it stand until lukewarm. Beat the eggs into the mashed potatoes. Gradually add the cooled milk mixture. Add the dissolved yeast. Stir in enough flour to make a manageable dough. Turn onto a lightly floured board and knead until smooth, about ten minutes. Place in a clean greased bowl, cover, and let rise until doubled in bulk, about 1 hour. Knock dough down and shape into 2 loaves. Place in 2 greased 9x5x3-inch inch loaf pans. Cover with a damp cloth and let rise in a warm place until doubled in bulk. Bake 40 minutes or until done in a 375°F. oven.

Ninety-Minute Bread

4 cups warm water
4 tablespoons yeast
4 teaspoons salt

½ cup sugar
4 tablespoons oil
7–8 cups white or wheat flour

Mix all ingredients except flour. Then begin slowly adding flour. Knead well by hand, adding flour until a soft smooth dough appears. Let rise until double, about one hour. Punch down and knead again. Form four loaves and place in four greased loaf pans. Let rise again until double (or one hour). Bake at 350°F. for 25–35 minutes. Turn out on racks, butter and cool.

Lee's Best Oatmeal Bread
(yield: 4 1½-pound loaves)

3 cups quick oats	1 tablespoon salt
4 cups water	3 eggs
1 cup warm water	2 cups dry milk powder
½ cup molasses	5–7 cups flour
3 tablespoons yeast	

In a saucepan, heat oats in 4 cups water, stirring often until the oatmeal is thick. Pour into a large bowl and set aside to cool. In another bowl, combine 1 cup water with molasses. Add yeast and set aside until yeast is dissolved and bubbling profusely. Add salt, eggs, and dry milk powder to the oatmeal mixture. Continue cooling until oatmeal feels warm but not hot. Add yeast mixture. Then add at least 5 cups flour. Your dough will still be sticky. Knead until ingredients are thoroughly mixed. Place in an oiled bowl, cover, and let rise in a warm place about one hour. Punch down the dough and knead for a few minutes, then return it to the bowl for a second rising (anywhere from 30–60 minutes). Punch down again and divide it into 4 equal portions. Shape into loaves and place in greased bread pans. Let rise 20–40 minutes, then place in a preheated, 350°F. degree oven and bake no more than 25 minutes. Do not overbake! Soften the crusts after baking by spraying the tops with cooking spray or brushing them with melted butter. Put the loaves in bags when they are still slightly warm to ensure a moist bread.

Navajo Fry Bread
(yield: 6)

2 cups all purpose flour
½ cup dry milk powder
1 teaspoon baking powder
½ teaspoon salt

2 tablespoons shortening
¾ cup water
vegetable oil

Mix flour, dry milk, baking powder, and salt in a large bowl. Cut in shortening until mixture resembles coarse crumbs. Add water and stir until dough holds together. Turn out onto lightly floured board. Knead until smooth (2 or 3 minutes). Divide dough into 6 equal pieces. Work with one at a time, keep remaining covered with plastic wrap so dough does not dry out. Roll one piece of dough into a ball and then pat it out to make a 6–7-inch round. Cover with plastic wrap. Repeat to shape rest of dough. Line a tray with paper towels. In wide frying pan, heat ¾-inch of oil to 375°F. Add one dough round at a time. Cook, turning once, until puffy and golden brown (1½–2 minutes). Drain on paper towels.

Hint: If made ahead, let cool completely, then wrap airtight and refrigerate until next day. To reheat, place bread on baking sheets, uncovered, and cook at 375°F. for 3–5 minutes until heated through. Make Navajo tacos by filling with the standard taco fillings, or eat as is.

Homemade Onion Bread

1 medium onion
1 cube butter
2½ cups milk
2 tablespoons yeast
⅓ cup sugar

2 teaspoons salt
6–7 cups flour
milk for glaze
sesame seeds

Sauté onion in butter over low heat until onions are clear. Be sure not to burn the butter! Remove from heat. Add milk. When mixture has cooled to lukewarm, add yeast, sugar, and salt. Stir and set aside to rest. After yeast has had time to get frothy, pour mixture into large bowl. Add flour until dough is formed. Knead for 5 minutes on floured board or countertop. Cover and let rise in warm place until double in bulk (1–1½ hours). Punch down and separate into three loaves. Loaves can be baked on a cookie sheet or in a cake pan. Shape dough, place on or in pans and rise until double, about ½ hour. Glaze with milk and sprinkle sesame seeds on top. Make decorative slits on top with a sharp knife if you're in the mood to do so. Bake at 400°F. for 30 minutes. Let cool on a rack or serve warm.

Don't Know Beans—or Rice, Either

To make your beans more—well, digestible, refer to Appendix C.

Salada de Arroz (Rice Salad)

2 cups cooked white rice
4 teaspoons minced pimiento
¼ cup green bell pepper, minced

¼ cup minced onion
¼ cup Italian salad dressing
salt and pepper to taste

Mix all ingredients in a large salad bowl. Season to taste. Cover with plastic wrap and refrigerate for one hour. Serve cold.

Brazilian Pepper Rice
(yield: 6 servings)

1 tablespoon oil	1 or 2 jalapeño peppers, whole
½ cup diced onion	3½ cups hot water
1 clove garlic, minced	½ teaspoon salt
1½ cups long grain rice	

Sauté onion in the oil over medium heat until soft. Add garlic and rice and sauté for about 3 or 4 minutes, stirring constantly. Don't overcook the garlic! Add the jalapeño(s), hot water, and salt. Stir well, bring to a boil, cover, and reduce heat to low. Simmer until liquid has been absorbed, about 15 to 20 minutes. Remove peppers before serving.

Rice Pilaf

1 cup regular white or brown rice	1 cup celery, finely chopped
½ cup wild rice	1 teaspoon grated lemon peel
2 cans bouillon or broth	1 can mushrooms, any size
⅓ cup water, to rinse out cans and add to mixture	¼ teaspoon pepper, freshly ground
½ cup butter, sliced into several pieces	1 whole pimento, chopped
4 chopped green onions (bottoms and tops)	

Mix all ingredients together, except the pimento. Don't melt the butter; it will mix in as it bakes. Bake at 350°F. for one hour. Just before serving, garnish with the chopped pimento.

Baked Lentils with Cheese
(yield: 6 servings)

1½ cups dried lentils
1 medium onion
1 medium green pepper
2 carrots
1 cup celery
2 cloves garlic
2 8-ounce cans tomato sauce
2 cups water

1½ teaspoons salt
2 bay leaves
¼ teaspoon pepper
¼ teaspoon sage
¼ teaspoon thyme
¼ teaspoon marjoram
2 tablespoons fresh parsley
1½ cups shredded cheddar cheese

Wash and sort lentils. In a large bowl, chop onion and green pepper. Slice carrots & celery into bowl. Mash garlic and add to bowl. Set the vegetable bowl aside. Combine remaining ingredients except for cheese and parsley in a lightly greased 2½-quart casserole dish; cover and bake at 375°F. for 30 minutes. Add vegetables to casserole; cover and bake 30 minutes or until vegetables are tender. Chop parsley and stir into casserole. Sprinkle cheese on top. Bake, uncovered, 5 minutes.

Easy Feijoada

2 cups dry black beans
1 pound sausage
½ pound bacon
½ pound boneless pork
1 pound stew meat

bell pepper
onion
seasonings to taste
cooked rice

Pressure cook beans in 6–8 cups water for 40 minutes. Remove beans and liquid from pressure cooker. Sauté sausage, bacon, pork, and stew meat. Add bell pepper, onion, and the beans and juices. Pressure cook for 20 minutes. Season to taste and serve over rice. *Note:* You don't need a pressure cooker to make this recipe. Just cook the beans as usual. As for seasonings, be creative. The Brazilians use a whole assortment of seasonings, including small amounts of cinnamon. Throw in what you want, a little at a time, until you get a taste that knocks your socks off.

Ethiopian Bean Stew
(yield: 6 servings)

1 cup dried navy beans
1 pound beef stew meat
2 tablespoons oil
1 large onion
2 large potatoes
3 ribs celery

3 medium carrots
1 cup frozen corn
1 teaspoon curry powder
1½ teaspoons salt
1 box frozen peas

Add beans to 4 cups boiling water in large saucepan; boil for two minutes. Remove from heat; let stand, covered, for one hour. Chop onion; cube potatoes, slice celery and carrots; cube meat. (All slices and cubes should be about 1 inch thick.) Brown meat in hot oil; add onion and cook until brown. Add meat and onion mixture and all other ingredients except peas; add one cup boiling water. Simmer for 75 minutes; add peas; serve.

Soup, Glorious Soup

Yes, we know these recipes are heavy on the beans . . . but that's where the protein is. Besides, you should have tons of beans in your food storage anyway.

Easy Tortilla Soup

2 cans chicken broth
1 can Rotel (tomatoes and green chili)
1 can Mexi-corn

12 ounces pepper-jack cheese
tortilla chips

Heat all canned products together until boiling. Cut cheese into ½-inch cubes and arrange in bottom of serving bowls. Ladle soup over cheese and allow time for the cheese to melt. Crush tortilla chips into soup and serve quickly.

Baked Potato Soup

⅔ cup butter
⅔ cup flour
7 cups milk
4 large potatoes
4 green onions

12 bacon strips
1¼ cups shredded
   cheddar cheese
8 ounces sour cream
salt and pepper to taste

Bake potatoes and cool. Peel and chop. Fry the bacon strips until crisp. Cool and crumble. Chop green onions. Melt butter in a large soup pan. Stir in flour, heat and stir till smooth. Add the milk gradually, stirring constantly until thickened. Add potato and onions, bring to boil, stirring constantly. Reduce heat and simmer for 10 minutes and then add remaining ingredients. Stir until cheese is melted and serve immediately.

Hamburger Alphabet Soup
(yield: 5-quart crockpot of soup)

1 pound ground beef
1 onion, chopped
1 box frozen vegetables
1 can beef broth
1 envelope dry onion soup mix
1 8-ounce can tomato sauce
½ cup barley
½ teaspoon pepper
½ teaspoon dried oregano

½ teaspoon dried basil
½ teaspoon thyme
½ teaspoon paprika
1 bay leaf
1 teaspoon seasoned salt
1 tablespoon soy sauce
2 tablespoons dried parsley
water
1 7-ounce package alphabet
   pasta

Brown and drain ground beef. Put the beef and all ingredients except the pasta into the crockpot. Add water to within 1 inch from the top. Cook on high for 8 hours. Fifteen minutes before serving, add the pasta to the crockpot and continue cooking until pasta is done.

Mumsy's Pea Surprise Soup
(yield: 6–8 servings)

3 tablespoons olive oil
1½ cups diced onion
1½ cups diced carrot
1 cup diced celery
1½ teaspoons curry powder
freshly ground black pepper
1 pound green split peas

1 teaspoon salt
½ teaspoon dried thyme
2 quarts chicken stock
1 ham bone or hock
2 large sweet potatoes
2 cups ham

Heat olive oil in a large pot over medium heat. Add onion and cook, stirring often; add carrot and celery. Cook about five minutes, stirring often. Add curry powder and pepper and stir. Then add split peas, salt, thyme, ham bone, and chicken stock. Increase heat until soup comes to boil, then reduce to slow simmer. Cover and simmer about an hour. Peel and chop sweet potatoes. Add to soup mixture and cook about 30 minutes longer. Stir occasionally. When split peas are falling apart, soup is thick and sweet potatoes are tender, it is done. Chop the ham, remove the ham bone, add the ham, and cook a few minutes more, until the meat is heated through. (If you haven't figured it out, the surprise in this soup is the added sweet potato.) This soup freezes well.

Potato Pearl Soup

4 tablespoons butter
4½ cups milk
1½ tablespoons dried
   chopped onion
2½ cups chicken broth

1½ teaspoons salt
1⅓ cups potato pearls
½ teaspoon celery salt
⅛ teaspoon pepper

Heat butter, onion, salt, celery salt, pepper, and milk to scalding. Stir in potato pearls; continue cooking until smooth, stirring constantly. Slowly add chicken broth. (Soup should be consistency of heavy cream.) Garnish each serving with **paprika** and **parsley**.

Kentucky Soup Beans

½ bag pinto beans
1 onion
1 package onion soup mix
ham bone

salt & pepper
Tabasco sauce
¼ teaspoon hickory smoke flavor
bay leaf

Wash and sort beans. Cover with cold water and bring to boil. Boil 2 minutes; turn off heat and let sit for one hour. Drain water. Cover with water 3 inches above bean level. Bring to simmer and add remaining ingredients. Simmer till meat is falling off ham bone and beans are done, adding water as necessary. Remove bone, dice the meat, and add back to soup. Serve with cornbread.

Red Beans and Rice: Substitute a whole bag of red beans for ½ bag pinto beans. Serve over rice.

Grammie's Zucchini Soup

4 tablespoons butter
1 onion, chopped
large zucchini, chopped
garlic clove, crushed

¼ teaspoon dried basil
6 cups canned chicken broth
1 cup light cream
grated Parmesan cheese

Using a soup pot, sauté onions until golden in melted butter. Add garlic, seasonings, broth, and zucchini. Cook over medium heat until zucchini is almost soft. Then puree in the blender in batches. Return pureed mix to soup pot. To serve, stir in cream. Sprinkle Parmesan cheese atop each bowl and add a dollop of sour cream if you have any on hand. ***Note:*** Soup can be frozen before cream is added.

Senate Bean Soup

1 pound navy beans
3–4 quarts cold water
1 meaty ham bone
3 quarts hot water
1 cup mashed potatoes

1½ cups finely chopped onion
1¼ cups finely chopped celery
2 cloves garlic, minced
3 tablespoons minced parsley
salt and pepper to taste

Cover beans with cold water and let stand overnight. Drain beans and turn into large pan with close-fitting lid. Add ham bone and hot water. Cover and simmer for 2 hours. Stir in mashed potatoes and cook over low heat until beans are almost tender, about 30 minutes. Add onion, celery, garlic, and parsley and continue simmering for 1 hour or until beans are tender. Remove ham bone from soup, dice meat and return to soup. Add salt and pepper to taste. If soup is thicker than desired, add hot water.

Root Cellar Soup

1 meaty ham bone
8 cups water
8 whole black peppercorns
5 whole cloves
2 garlic cloves

2 large potatoes, peeled
    and thinly sliced
3 large carrots, thinly sliced
1 medium onion, thinly sliced
3½ cups coarsely
    chopped cabbage

In a large pot, combine ham bone, water, and spices. Bring to boil, reduce heat, cover, and simmer for 2½ hours. Remove ham bone. Remove meat from bone. Discard bone. Strain broth. Return broth and meat to pot. Add vegetables; cover and simmer until vegetables are tender.

Cabbage Bacon Soup

8 slices bacon

3 medium carrots

1 large onion

½ head cabbage

1 can chicken broth

1 can stewed tomatoes

2 teaspoons salt

½ teaspoon caraway seeds

⅛ teaspoon ground pepper

Chop onion. Fry bacon and onion in pot till onions are clear. (Don't burn the bacon!) Chop cabbage and dice the carrots; add them to the onion mixture and cook for about 20 minutes, stirring often. Add seasonings, put on lid and cover till cabbage is wilted and water is showing in pot. Add chicken broth and tomatoes. Simmer, covered, for about a half hour.

Nanny's Lentil Soup
(yield: 8 servings)

1 pound lentils

2 carrots

2 onions

2 stalks celery

3 cloves minced garlic

salt & pepper

1 16-ounce can crushed tomatoes

3 tablespoons grated
     Parmesan cheese

½ pound Italian sausage

Put lentils in a stockpot. Wash thoroughly. Cover with about 4 inches of water and bring to a boil. Cook for approximately half an hour, adding more water if needed. Chop vegetables and add with all remaining ingredients except tomatoes, cheese, and sausage. Remove sausage from casing. Brown meat in a frying pan and add to the lentils along with a spoon or two of the drippings. Cook for one hour. Add the tomatoes and cheese and cook for another half hour. Serve.

Soup From Cans

1 pound ground beef	1 can hominy
1 onion	1 can black-eyed peas
1 can minestrone soup	1 16-ounce can tomato juice
1 can green beans	

Brown ground beef and onion. Drain fat. Add minestrone soup, green beans, hominy, and black-eyed peas, all with juice included. Stir and add tomato juice. Simmer for 30 minutes and serve.

Entrées

Speedy Tomato Pasta

pasta of choice	2 garlic cloves
green onions	1 can Italian tomatoes
fresh mushrooms	Parmesan cheese (fresh is best)

Sauté onions, mushrooms, and garlic until the onions are clear and garlic is barely tender. Add tomatoes; heat. Add cooked pasta. Sprinkle with cheese.

Wheat Chili

Make your favorite recipe of chili, but instead of beans, cook wheat. Wheat is extremely filling, so you will not need to use same amount as beans. Once boiled to tender stage, continue to add spices, ground beef, etc. Don't serve heaping bowls of this chili, because a little goes a long way.

Tamale Pie

1 pound ground meat	1 can corn, drained
1 cup chopped green pepper	1 tablespoon sugar
1 chopped onion	1 teaspoon salt
1 clove minced garlic	1 dash pepper
16-ounce can tomatoes	2–3 teaspoons chili powder
6-ounce can tomato sauce	1½ cups grated sharp cheddar
1 can sliced, drained	3 cups cold milk
black olives	1 cup yellow cornmeal

Brown first four ingredients together. Drain fat and add tomatoes, tomato sauce, olives, corn, sugar, salt, chili powder, and pepper. Simmer 20 minutes until thick. Add cheese and stir until melted. Pour into 9x13-inch pan. Make cornmeal topping by heating milk in double boiler, adding **1 teaspoon salt**, and slowly stirring in cornmeal. Cook and stir until thick; add **1 tablespoon butter** and spread over top of meat mixture. Bake at 375°F. for 40 minutes.

Variation: Add ⅓ cup of cracked wheat for last 20 minutes simmering time. Add extra tomato sauce if the mixture is too thick.

Tuna/Salmon Loaf

canned tuna or salmon	1 egg, separated
¼ cup bread crumbs	basil, pepper for seasoning
1 tablespoon butter	1 grated onion

If you're using salmon, remove bones and skin. Next mash the fish well. Beat egg white till stiff. Set aside. Melt butter; mix into fish with remaining ingredients, including yolk from separated egg. Fold in egg white. Bake at 350°F. about 45 minutes. Top with **cream of mushroom soup** made into a sauce.

Night Before Tuna Casserole

1¾ cups shell macaroni, uncooked
2 cans tuna
3 hard boiled eggs
¼ pound grated cheddar

1 can cream of celery soup
1 can cream of mushroom soup
2 cups milk
1 chopped onion

Mix ingredients in a large bowl. Refrigerate overnight. Bake in greased casserole dish for 75 minutes at 350°F.

Easy Tuna Burgers

1 can tuna
2 hard-boiled eggs
2 slices Swiss cheese
3 tablespoons relish
¼ cup celery

⅓ cup mayonnaise
1 tablespoon Dijon mustard
¼ cup onion
additional Swiss cheese

Drain tuna. Chop ingredients and mix well. Place mix into buns, top with extra cheese, wrap in foil, and bake at 350°F. for 15–20 minutes.

Tuna Patties

Mix tuna with eggs and crackers just like you do with salmon and fry them till they're crispy. Serve as an entrée or on a bun.

No-Peek Stew

2 pounds stew meat
6 carrots
2 onions
6 stalks celery
1 potato per person, plus 1 extra
12 ounces V-8 juice

1 tablespoon sugar
2 tablespoons tapioca
2 teaspoons salt
pepper
dash Tabasco sauce

Trim stew meat. Slice carrots and celery. Chop onions. Dice potatoes. Mix together. Mix remaining ingredients in a bowl and pour over top. Place in a greased casserole dish. Cover tightly. Bake at 325°F. for four hours. DO NOT PEEK.

Tuna Tater Pie

2 cans tuna, drained
1 can mixed vegetables
1¼ cups mayonnaise
2 tablespoons lemon juice
1 teaspoon Worcestershire sauce

½ teaspoon mustard
1 medium onion, chopped
½ cup celery, chopped
2 cups mashed potatoes
1 deep dish pie crust

Mix the mashed potatoes with ½ cup of the mayonnaise, and set aside. Prebake pie crust at 350°F. until light brown, about 20 minutes. Mix together the other ingredients. Pour tuna mixture into prepared pie crust and bake 15–20 minutes. Remove from oven and top with potato mixture and, if desired, **shredded cheddar cheese**. Broil a few minutes until the top is brown.

Taco Casserole

Fritos
canned chili

chopped onion
grated cheddar

Crush the Fritos into small but distinct pieces. (They make less of a mess if you do it before you open the bag.) Layer in a casserole dish in this order: Fritos, chili, onion, cheddar. You should get three or four layers. Bake in 350°F. oven for about 45 minutes, until onions have had time to cook.

Tuna Noodles Romanoff

4 cups raw noodles
2 cans tuna
1½ cups sour cream
¾ cup milk
3-ounce can sliced mushrooms
1½ teaspoons salt

¼ teaspoon pepper
¼ cup dry bread crumbs
¼ cup grated Parmesan cheese
2 tablespoons melted butter
paprika

Cook noodles as directed; drain. Drain tuna and mushrooms; mix noodles, tuna, sour cream, milk, mushrooms, salt, and pepper in an ungreased 2-quart casserole dish. Mix bread crumbs, Parmesan cheese, and butter. Sprinkle on top, then sprinkle with paprika. Microwave, uncovered, on high for 6 minutes. Let stand, covered, for 4 minutes. Serves 4.

Chili from Cans

1 pound ground beef
2 cans Mexican style tomatoes
2 cans chili beans
1 can kidney beans

1 medium onion, chopped
3 cloves garlic, minced
chili powder
1 jalapeño, seeded and chopped

In a large pot, brown meat with onions and garlic. Add remaining ingredients, bring to boil and simmer all day. This is even better the second day.

Sage Chicken

1–2 chickens
cooking oil
2 cans cream of mushroom soup

rubbed sage
salt & pepper
rice or noodles

Cut chickens into pieces (with or without bones and skin). In a large pot that has a lid, brown chicken in cooking oil. Add soup and about ⅔ can water (you don't need exact measurements with this recipe!). Add about a tablespoon of rubbed sage, plus salt and pepper to taste. Stir well to break up the soup. Cook over medium heat until the chicken is done, stirring occasionally to keep from sticking. Serve over noodles or rice.

Just Desserts

Old-Fashioned Honey Caramels

2 cups honey
1 cup chopped nuts
dash of salt

1 can evaporated milk
3 tablespoons butter
1 teaspoon vanilla

Mix honey and milk and cook until it forms a firm ball (255°F.). Stir in butter, nuts, and salt. Pour onto a buttered dish. Cool and cut.

New Orleans Beignets
(pronounced ben-YAYS)

2 cups flour
1 teaspoon salt
1 tablespoon baking powder
1 teaspoon cinnamon
2 eggs

¼ cup sugar
¾ cup milk
½ teaspoon vanilla
oil for deep frying
confectioner's sugar

To make the dough, sift the flour, salt, baking powder, and cinnamon into a large mixing bowl. Cover it and set aside until later. In a separate bowl, beat together the eggs, sugar, milk, and vanilla. Mix this into the flour mixture to form a dough. Turn the dough onto a lightly floured surface and knead it until smooth and elastic. Roll the dough out into a circle ¼-inch thick. Slice dough diagonally into diamond shapes about 3 inches long.

Heat oil in a deep fryer to 375°F. Fry the beignets in the hot oil, a few at a time, turning once, until golden brown. Remove with a slotted spoon and drain well on paper towels. Before serving, sprinkle with confectioner's sugar. Serve warm with a cold glass of regular or chocolate milk.

Pineapple Nut Bread

2 eggs	2½ cups flour
½ cup melted butter	3 teaspoons baking powder
1 cup sugar	½ teaspoon baking soda
1 cup crushed pineapple with juice	¾ teaspoon salt
1 teaspoon vanilla	½ cup chopped nuts

Preheat oven to 350°F. Grease one 9x5x3-inch loaf pan. Beat the eggs slightly, then add the butter and sugar. Beat until smooth. Stir in the pineapple and vanilla.

In a separate bowl combine flour, baking powder, baking soda, salt, and nuts. Stir well and pour into the pineapple mixture. Mix well and stir until moist. Pour mixture into the greased loaf pan. Bake for about 1 hour. Test with a toothpick. After removing from oven, let stand for 10 minutes and then remove loaf from pan. Cool and serve or wrap.

Orange Crunch Muffins

1½ cups Grape Nuts cereal	2 tablespoons orange rind
¼ cup sugar	2 beaten eggs
3 tablespoons orange juice	½ cup honey
2 cups flour	1 cup milk
1 tablespoon baking powder	¼ cup melted butter
½ teaspoon salt	

Blend ½ cup of the cereal in a blender. Add the sugar and blend again. Add 2 tablespoons of the orange juice and set aside. Soak the remaining cereal in water and then squeeze dry. Mix the flour, baking powder, and salt. Add the soaked cereal and orange rind. Combine eggs, honey, remaining juice, milk, and butter. Add this to the flour mixture and mix until moistened. Fill muffin cups ⅔ full. Spoon remaining cereal mixture over muffins. Bake at 425°F. for 20 minutes. Makes one dozen.

Orange Blossom Muffins

2 cups flour
1 tablespoon plus 1
   teaspoon baking powder
¼ cup sugar
1 teaspoon salt

½ cup chopped pecans
½ cup orange juice
½ cup orange marmalade
2 tablespoons vegetable oil
1 beaten egg

Combine dry ingredients, except for the nuts, and make a well in the center. Add wet ingredients, stirring just until the dry ingredients are moistened. Fold in nuts. Spoon batter into greased muffin cups, filling ⅔ full. Bake at 400°F. for 15 minutes or until lightly browned. Makes one dozen.

Buttermilk Apple Muffins

¾ cup brown sugar
½ cup oil
1 beaten egg
1 teaspoon vanilla
1 cup white flour

½ cup whole wheat flour
½ teaspoon soda
¼ teaspoon salt
½ cup buttermilk*
1 cup apple, peeled and diced

*If you don't have buttermilk, add 1 tablespoon vinegar to regular milk and let sit for five minutes.

Beat together brown sugar, oil, egg, and vanilla. Mix dry ingredients and add them to the creamed mixture, alternately with buttermilk and apple. Spoon into paper-lined muffin tins. Sprinkle topping on muffins. Bake in a 325°F. oven for 30–35 minutes.

Topping:
   ¼ cup nuts
   ½ teaspoon cinnamon

¼ cup brown sugar

Texas Wheat Cake

1 cup butter

2 cups sugar

4 eggs

1 tablespoon lemon or orange extract

½ teaspoon vanilla

2½ cups wheat flour

1 teaspoon baking soda

½ teaspoon salt

¾ cup buttermilk*

*If you don't have buttermilk, make it by adding 1 tablespoon vinegar to sweet milk and let stand five minutes.

Cream butter, sugar, and eggs; add flavorings. Sift flour, soda, and salt and add alternately with milk to first mixture. Grease and flour tube pan or bundt pan and pour in mixture. Bake at 325°F. for 1 hour. Let cool five minutes and remove from pan. Pour on glaze while still hot. To make glaze, heat **1½ cups sugar** with **½ cup lemon** or **1 cup orange juice** until sugar is melted and glaze is formed. Pour over cake very slowly with a spoon, allowing it to soak in. Pierce the cake with a fork to make holes for the glaze. Serve cold.

Three-Minute Cobbler
(yield: 4 servings)

1 stick butter

1 cup flour

2 teaspoons baking powder

1 cup sugar

¾ cup milk

¼ teaspoon salt

1 medium can fruit

Melt butter in casserole dish. Add flour, sugar, baking powder, milk, and salt. Stir to remove as many lumps as you can. (Mixture will still be lumpy.) Drain fruit. Pour fruit on top of flour mixture. Do not stir! Bake at 350°F. until brown on top (about 50 minutes). Great with ice cream or whipped cream.

Honey Custard
(yield: 6 servings)

2 eggs
¼ cup honey
2 cups milk

⅛ teaspoon salt
1 teaspoon vanilla

Beat eggs slightly. Add milk, honey, vanilla, and salt. Pour into individual custard cups and set in a pan of water. Bake at 350°F. for 30 minutes. Allow to cool and chill in refrigerator.

Whole Wheat Apple Cake

4 cups apples, peeled and diced
2 eggs
1 cup oil
1 teaspoon vanilla
2 cups sugar

2 teaspoons soda
1 teaspoon salt
2 cups whole wheat flour
1 cup nuts
1 cup raisins

Place diced apples in bowl. Add eggs, oil, and vanilla. Mix thoroughly. Sift dry ingredients together, then add to wet mixture. Pour into greased 9x13-inch pan. Bake at 350°F. for 60 minutes or until cake shrinks from sides of pan. Cool and frost with cream cheese frosting.

Cream Cheese Frosting:
   2 cups powdered sugar
   ¼ cup butter

1 teaspoon vanilla
4 ounces cream cheese

Odds and Ends

Raisin Whole Wheat Cereal

Rinse 2 cups of **wheat** in water, but don't soak it. Cook slowly for 2 hours in 4 cups water. At the end of that time, cook 1 cup **raisins** in enough water to cover for 10–15 minutes. Add cooked wheat to raisins and cook 2–5 additional minutes, until thickened, stirring often. Add **cinnamon** or **nutmeg**, if you want. Serve hot with **milk**. The cereal should not need added sweetener. Also good to eat as is or with a little cream over it. This is a make-ahead recipe that should store up to a week in the refrigerator.

Homemade Grape-Nuts

3½ cups graham flour
1 cup brown sugar
2 cups buttermilk

1 teaspoon salt
1 teaspoon vanilla
1 teaspoon soda

Combine ingredients. Bake in a greased and floured cake pan at 350°F. until it tests done. Cool. When cold, crumble into small pieces. (You may want to use a chopper to get pieces that are similar to commercial Grape Nuts.) Return to oven and bake another hour, or until good and brown.

Breakfast Rice

3 cups cooked brown rice
2 cups milk
½ cup raisins
1 tablespoon butter
1 teaspoon ground cinnamon

⅛ teaspoon salt
brown sugar (optional)
fresh fruit (optional)
nuts (optional)

Combine all but the optional ingredients in a saucepan. Bring to a boil, stirring occasionally to prevent sticking. Reduce heat to medium-low; cover and simmer 8–10 minutes or until thickened. Serve with brown sugar, fresh fruit, and nuts.

Recipe Index

Subject Index

About the Authors

Clark and Kathy Kidd are the ideal people to write about food storage because they're the laziest two people in North America. They've experimented with every facet of food storage, allowing you to learn from their mistakes. Residents of Northern Virginia, the Kidds have written two previous books for Bookcraft—*A Convert's Guide to Mormon Life* and *A Parent's Survival Guide to the Internet*. Writing this book has rekindled their interest in food storage, and they're contemplating an exciting future in sourdough cookery, financed by the sale of their books to discriminating readers such as yourself.